John Quincy Adams

John Quincy Adams

A Public Life, a Private Life

PAUL C. NAGEL

Alfred A. Knopf   New York   1997

THIS IS A BORZOI BOOK
PUBLISHED BY ALFRED A. KNOPF, INC.

Copyright © 1997 by Paul C. Nagel

http://www.randomhouse.com/

Library of Congress Cataloging-in-Publication Data
Nagel, Paul C.
John Quincy Adams: a public life, a private life / by Paul C.
Nagel. — 1st ed.
p.   cm.
Includes bibliographical references and index.
ISBN 0-679-40444-9 (hc: alk. paper)
1.   Adams, John Quincy, 1767–1848
2.   Presidents—United States—
Biography.   I. Title.
E377.N34   1997
973.5ʹ5ʹ092—dc21
[B]   96-49640
CIP

Manufactured in the United States of America
First Edition

FRONTISPIECE: *This profile of John Quincy Adams, age 75, was made on March 8, 1843, in a Washington daguerreotype studio. Much intrigued by the new technique, he sat for three exposures (of which only this one is known to survive), and found it "incomprehensible" that each required only thirty seconds. Lost until recently, the daguerreotype appears here by courtesy of Mead Art Museum, Amherst College, to which it was given by William Macbeth Gallery in New York City.*

for

Joan Peterson Nagel,

my partner and pal—

And for her namesake, our granddaughter,

Margaret Joan Nagel

Contents

16 pages of illustrations will be found following page 178

Introduction

On January 12, 1779, an eleven-year-old New England boy named John Quincy Adams started a diary that continued, rarely interrupted, for almost seventy tumultuous years. It opened with nothing more than the announcement: "A Journal By Mc JQA." Today most scholars agree—although few have read more than segments of it—that Adams' enormous diary is the most valuable historical and personal journal kept by any prominent American.

Eventually, Adams became a diplomat, poet, orator, writer, scientist, silviculturist, Harvard professor, U.S. secretary of state, legislator at both state and federal levels, and president of the United States. After leaving the White House in 1829, he was a congressman until 1848, when he died in the federal Capitol in his eighty-first year. It was a life of unmatched public service, and yet also one of tormenting private struggle. Adams' first concern was to master his soul, seeking discipline, modesty, tolerance, calmness of spirit, and religious faith—all virtues in which he was woefully weak, as he was the first to acknowledge. And he was heartbroken that he could not be a Cicero or a Shakespeare rather than a politician.

Biographers and historians have written much about the public John Quincy Adams but little concerning his private side; thus his personality remains misunderstood. This book will try to illuminate the entire Adams, private as well as public. It is, to my knowledge, the first biography that draws upon Adams' massive manuscript diary. Earlier writers relied upon a published edition of the journal that was highly incomplete, omitting particularly many entries of a personal nature. But now Adams' entire diary and his surviving letters and other jottings are available on microfilm. The chapters ahead have been built upon these sources.

While this book must, of course, follow Adams as a superb diplomat (a role he tolerated) and as a besieged president (an office he disliked), it will feature him in less familiar settings. Here a different Adams emerges from the cold, aloof figure often pictured by historians, one of whom recently wrote, "In the long history of the republic, few men who have won high office have been as disagreeable as he." Such an opinion of John Quincy Adams does him and American history a disservice.

This biography will introduce the Adams whom four thousand citizens assembled in New York City in November 1840 to hear deliver his widely popular lecture on faith. When he is seen composing orations, hymns, and poetry—especially the charmingly erotic lines devoted to his wonderful wife, Louisa—the unknown Adams appears, a presence that banishes the "bitterness, austerity, and unfriendliness" ascribed to him by history.

This very different Adams was, in fact, one of his era's most brilliant dinner companions. He delighted in accompanying old friends on fishing expeditions, he enjoyed singing songs in French with his granddaughters, and Harvard students cheered his lectures.

Some writers, of course, have sensed that there must have been more to John Quincy Adams' personality than the familiarly dismal figure. One such was the distinguished scholar Samuel Flagg Bemis, who acknowledged with regret that he could not probe his subject's "inner life and character." After publishing two remarkable volumes about Adams' public life, Bemis said in 1956 that he was leaving the inner J. Q. Adams to be portrayed someday by others.

Thirty years later, no one had taken up Bemis' challenge, not even Leonard L. Richards, who, ably writing in 1986 about Adams' career in Congress, remarked that, "despite the thousands of words written by Adams and about him, no one has discovered the formula that will fully explain his life. He remains in many ways an enigma."

Even members of Adams' family admitted they were mystified by their kinsman's makeup. His son Charles Francis Adams once claimed that his father's feelings were "impenetrable," and that he hid himself behind an "iron mask." Long years later, the historian Brooks Adams conceded of his grandfather: "No one ever understood him," for he had "a nature so complex" as to be "an enigma to contemporaries." Adams himself advanced the mystery by often speaking of his "repulsive" nature.

I pondered that enigma when I wrote two earlier books about the Adams family. After finishing these, I was certain I had not captured the elusive John Quincy Adams. Determined to try again, in 1990 I returned to his diary and other manuscripts. Thanks to their frank and revealing nature, I came finally to feel that I was living with Adams, sharing his thoughts and his doings. The "iron mask" was removed, and the inner J. Q. Adams stepped forward.

I found the key to the mask when I learned to understand the effects of a recurring major depression that dogged Adams' life. And while he lived amid much personal travail, I came upon many occasions when his happy side emerged. He was never more cheerful than when he could escape politics and roam the Massachusetts seaside near his beloved home town of Quincy. Indeed, after completing this book I find myself not only admiring Adams for his many achievements but actually liking the man—despite his frequently exasperating behavior, now to be understood with sympathy.

Apparently many of his contemporaries shared this sentiment. When Adams died, in 1848, the public mourning exceeded anything previously seen in America. Forgotten was his failed presidency and his often cold demeanor. It was the memory of an extraordinary human being—one who in his last years had fought heroically for the right of petition and against a war to expand slavery—that drew a grateful people to salute his coffin in the Capitol and to stand by the railroad tracks as his bier was transported from Washington to Boston. In the nineteenth century, only the death of Abraham Lincoln would elicit a greater display of national sorrow.

I have tried to write a biography that embraces the private as well as the public side of the John Quincy Adams who could inspire such grief.

P. C. N.
Minneapolis, Minnesota
August 14, 1996

BOOK ONE

Facing Expectations
1767–1794

. . . in which a prodigy finds that life is uncooperative.

CHAPTER ONE

Youth

My head is much too fickle, my thoughts are running after birds eggs,
play, and trifles, till I get vexed with myself.

ON OCTOBER 25, 1764, in the parsonage at Weymouth, a coastal village in Massachusetts south of Boston, the local pastor solemnized the
marriage of his daughter. Standing in the parlor, Abigail Smith, second child of the Reverend William Smith and Elizabeth Quincy
Smith, took as husband John Adams, resident of nearby Braintree and
a rising lawyer in the colony of Massachusetts Bay.

The couple's first child, born on July 14, 1765, was named Abigail,
though the family always called her Nabby. Second in line was John
Quincy Adams, born July 11, 1767. Until his college years, he was
known as Johnny, and thereafter usually as John, despite occasional
confusion with his father. To avoid this, as a youngster Johnny began
signing himself as "JQA," a practice that he continued through life
and that his family often adopted.

After Johnny's birth, other siblings soon followed. Another sister,
Susanna, died in February 1770 after barely a year of life. Then
Charles arrived on May 29, 1770, and Thomas Boylston Adams was
born on September 15, 1772.

These Adams children had an ancestry remarkable even by New
England standards. Although Johnny's grandfather Adams, known
as Deacon John, had died before the boy was born, Grandmother
Susanna Boylston Adams, a doughty woman who outlived a second
husband, survived to be much admired by her grandson. As for his
mother's parents, William and Elizabeth Smith, Johnny Adams

recalled being so drawn to them that they became surrogate parents, and their parsonage in Weymouth his second home. William Smith was pastor in the village for forty-five years.

Johnny found Weymouth particularly appealing because his mother's younger sister, Elizabeth Smith, lived there before her marriage to the Reverend John Shaw in 1777 took her to the parsonage in Haverhill, Massachusetts. No one was ever dearer to Johnny than Elizabeth Smith Shaw, with her loving nature and her reverence for literature. Aunt Elizabeth must have been much like her mother, Johnny's grandmother Smith, who was renowned for her charm and who died in 1775 while nursing victims of a cholera epidemic.

Another favorite spot for Johnny was the home of his Aunt and Uncle Cranch. Mary Smith, Abigail Adams' older sister, had married Richard Cranch, a gentle fellow who made a meager living repairing watches and farming but preferred devoting time to sharing the contents of books with the youngsters of the family. All his life, Johnny would remain close to his Cranch kinfolk. Cousin Billy Cranch, two years younger than Johnny, became a distinguished jurist in the District of Columbia.

Among the ancestors of these Adamses and Smiths were many of the notable names in New England history, a record that brought the family much satisfaction. Later in life, JQA often was asked about his genealogy and usually responded eagerly by repeating how the clan's founder, Henry Adams, had reached Massachusetts Bay in 1632 accompanied by a wife, eight sons ranging in age from six to twenty-five years, and a daughter who apparently never married. John liked to describe how these Adams immigrants spread the family name throughout New England and beyond.

Where Henry Adams came from in England has remained uncertain. His descendants eventually compromised by agreeing that he had emigrated from the town of Braintree in Essex County, embarking at Ipswich with the party led by the Reverend Thomas Hooker, who soon went on to help found Connecticut. Henry Adams settled his brood in the new Braintree, a long walk from Boston along the south shore.

The dubious claim that the Adams line arose in thirteenth-century Wales through Lord ap Adam and his wife, Elizabeth de Gournal, made little impression on John Quincy Adams. Instead, he preferred to point out that until his father's day, the descendants of Henry Adams had followed ordinary careers, doing the same thing in life generation after generation. From Henry Adams' arrival until 1735, when his great-great-grandson John Adams was born, family members had toiled as farmers and brewers, taking their turn as selectmen in town management. When Johnny's father entered Harvard College, only one Adams cousin had been there before him.

Later in life, when JQA—being of a poetic bent—reflected upon his Adams ancestors, their stories reminded him of Thomas Gray's moving "Elegy Written in a Country Churchyard," which admonishes that "full many a flower is born to blush unseen." His Adams forebears, JQA said, were distinguished only for "industry, sobriety, and integrity." They had been men of "meek and quiet spirits" who lived "lives of humble labour," qualities that assuredly had skipped John Quincy Adams.

Adams often wondered why he was unlike his "meek and quiet" forebears. He found the answer by reaching back to three marriages he believed had infused his line with the vigorous new blood needed to make him a different sort of Adams. The first such transfusion came when his great-grandfather Joseph Adams wed Hannah Bass. To JQA's satisfaction, her grandparents had been John Alden and Priscilla Mullins of Plymouth Colony, whose romance ("Pray, speak for thyself, John!") became one of New England's endearing legends. JQA liked to repeat the tale that Alden had been the first *Mayflower* passenger to leap upon Plymouth Rock.

After the union of John and Priscilla Alden's granddaughter with an Adams, the next strengthening marital tie, according to JQA, was knit when his grandfather Deacon John Adams, a shoemaker and farmer, brought Susanna Boylston into the family. Susanna arrived from a line of distinguished medical men, her grandfather being Thomas Boylston, an eminent English surgeon who had immigrated to Massachusetts. Her uncle was the famed physician Zabdial Boylston, who introduced inoculation against smallpox into North America.

Susanna Boylston Adams gave her son John, Johnny Adams' father, the seal of the Boylston family, which he adopted with pride, affixing it when he signed the two treaties of peace with Great Britain, November 30, 1782, and September 3, 1783. John passed the seal to JQA, who solemnly bequeathed it to his descendants.

Invigorating though the Alden and Boylston ties seemed to be, JQA considered the marriage of his father to Abigail Smith the ultimate prize. He believed that she brought with her the blood of even more vigorous and able New Englanders. Abigail's father, the Reverend William Smith, was a Harvard graduate whose family had succeeded in business and shipping ever since the early days of the colony. The founder of the line in America, Thomas Smith, had judiciously married Susan Boylston, an earlier member of that family, thereby eventually making John Adams and Abigail Smith remotely related. These energetic Smiths spread down the Atlantic coast, so that JQA had a distant kinsman who served as an early governor of South Carolina.

But it was the Quincy family, from whom Abigail's mother sprang, that proved the connection in which JQA eventually took the greatest satisfaction. This renowned clan entered the Adams genealogy when Parson William Smith married Elizabeth Quincy in 1740. This union resulted in one of John Quincy Adams' proudest moments: when he inherited Mount Wollaston, the ancient Quincy estate on the seashore in Braintree.

The property was notorious even before Boston was founded, having been claimed around 1622 by Thomas Morton, adventurer and author, who called the place Merry Mount. It may have deserved its name, judging from rumors of the antics that went on there. Some of these reports were adapted by Nathaniel Hawthorne in one of his finest stories of Puritan life, "The Maypole of Merry Mount," published in 1837 in his *Twice-Told Tales*.

Eventually the magistrates of Boston intervened, hoping to bring sobriety to Merry Mount by granting about 400 acres of it in 1635 to Edmund Quincy, who had immigrated to Massachusetts Bay with the Reverend John Cotton in 1633. Quincy renamed the farm Mount Wollaston. One of his most famous descendants, Colonel John Quincy, was Abigail Smith Adams' grandfather, and it was after him that she named her first son.

The colonel had married judiciously, choosing as spouse Elizabeth Norton, whose antecedents were as notable as his own. He served the Braintree community and the colony nobly. An authentic New Englander, he was remembered in the family, according to John Adams, as being "remarkable for never praising any body. He did not often speak evil, but he seldom spoke well." In 1792, that part of Braintree known as the North Precinct, which included Mount Wollaston, became a separate town, named Quincy in honor of Colonel John Quincy.

Except for scars on the hillsides left by granite quarries, the town changed little during JQA's lifetime. As John Quincy Adams' grandson, the second Charles Francis Adams, remembered it in his *Autobiography*, Quincy was "quiet, steady-going, rural," with a "monotonous main thoroughfare and commonplace connecting streets, both thoroughfare and by-ways lined with wooden houses, wholly innocent of any attempts at architecture, and all painted white with window blinds of green." In the center were the meetinghouse and the town hall, as well as a tavern, fronted by huge elm trees, where stagecoaches stopped while winding their way on the coast road north to Boston or south to Plymouth.

Following the road toward Plymouth for almost a mile, one came to the farmhouse where Johnny Adams was born. Those who visit it today as part of the Adams National Historic Site see a typical New England dwelling whose modest dimensions literally kept the family close. Johnny and his brothers had to sleep together; meanwhile, their mother Abigail wished she had even a tiny closet with a window where she could find privacy. All available space had to serve as John Adams' law office. The house sat amid a working farm of over a hundred acres. In an adjacent home, where John Adams himself had been born, his mother still resided.

In November 1772, when Johnny was five, John Adams began moving his family back and forth between Braintree and Boston (usually in the area called Court Street), trying to keep pace with his prospering legal practice. Until the early stirrings of the now-imminent Revolution and the formation of the Continental Congress, Johnny's father was frequently absent, traveling the judicial circuit in search of business. Thereafter, he was mostly away in Philadelphia as a leader in the Continental Congress while Abigail and the children removed back to Braintree.

By then, it was apparent that Johnny was a vigorous boy. Already there were signs of the temperament that would make life difficult for him as well as for others. His mother worried about how impatient he could be, how determined to have his way, and how sensitive he was to criticism. He clamored to tackle tasks that boys older than he might hesitate to accept. In part, this was because Johnny considered himself the man of the house during his father's long absences. Among the responsibilities he claimed before he was ten was riding horseback the several miles between Braintree and Boston in order to carry and fetch the mail. News of this accomplishment brought cherished commendation from his father for undertaking "an office so useful to his Mamma and Pappa."

John Adams had not been in Philadelphia a year when the opening of the American Revolution brought events that indelibly marked his son's memory. By 1775, Abigail and her children and their neighbors were living in fear that British soldiers might raid the area. A desperately worried John urged Abigail to flee with their brood to the woods at the first sign of danger. Instead, on June 17, 1775, the anticipated violence between colonists and English troops took place on the other side of Boston, at Charlestown, from whence sounds of cannon fire reached south to Braintree.

Hearing the commotion, Johnny and his mother climbed the rise called Penn's Hill, across the road from their farm, and from that high spot they watched the Battle of Bunker Hill—an experience the boy never forgot. The recollection was particularly poignant because one of those who fell in the battle was Dr. Joseph Warren, the Adams family's physician. Not long before, when Johnny had broken a forefinger so badly that amputation was feared, Dr. Warren had saved the finger. Later, JQA often considered how brief his diary and letters might have been if his writing hand had been maimed.

The struggle for American independence encouraged Johnny's parents in their inclination to impose the pursuit of moral and intellectual excellence upon their children. From the contrasts in the ways his father and mother respectively exerted that pressure, Johnny began to view them differently, a difference he maintained throughout a long lifetime. But then, Abigail and John Adams were scarcely alike in temperament and outlook.

Since John Adams did his exhorting mostly while he was a participant in the Revolution, it was comparatively easy and sometimes even thrilling for Johnny to obey a male parent who was said to be a hero. This was the case even when John Adams showed how a Revolutionary leader could sometimes be unreasonable and short-tempered when playing the role of father.

From youth onward, JQA usually got on well with his father, surprising as this may seem to anyone who has heard only of the public John Adams, the side history depicts. He is reputed to have been thin-skinned, bad-tempered, and impatient, a person even a son might avoid. (These qualities attributed to John, by the way, were remarkably like those later commonly associated with the mature JQA.) The private John Adams, however, tended to be quite otherwise. By his fireside or out working his fields, Johnny's father, while strict with his children, usually was affable and relaxed.

This allowed JQA to have it both ways in his regard for John Adams. He admired his parent's public career and revered his lofty

principles, all of which made it comparatively easy to accept the father's stern decrees. Yet he could also embrace the warm-hearted, private John Adams as a kinsman and as a parent whom it was easy to
love and to obey.

Certainly, JQA always revered his remarkable mother, but his affection for Abigail Adams remained cool compared with that for his
father. Years of togetherness in Europe would give John and John
Quincy Adams the sort of male rapport that comes when father and
son must get on without a wife or mother. This was one of the disad-
vantages Abigail faced in seeking to make Johnny a respectful and affectionate son.

A person of high intelligence and sharp wit, Abigail made no effort
to hide her condescending attitude toward males. At least in part, that
attitude arose out of her mortification and dismay at the alarming fate
of her only brother. William Smith, Jr. abandoned a wife and children
to poverty while he lived among the fleshpots of Philadelphia, where
he ended his life as an alcoholic. This tragedy took place as Abigail was
rearing her own youngsters.

Convinced that her brother might have been saved had he received a severe upbringing, Abigail vowed that no child of hers would
come to maturity only casually disciplined. With John Adams so often
away from home, Abigail's deep-seated anxiety about being a successful parent took command as she saw that her reputation and that of
her children would rise or fall by her rigor in disciplining both herself
and them. In short, Abigail sensed a double responsibility to pull and
push Johnny and his siblings along the path of righteousness.

Her sternness helps explain why Johnny spent so much time in the
parsonage at Weymouth, where he was more comfortable with his
grandparents Smith and Aunt Elizabeth. While Abigail was undoubtedly affectionate with her children, her lifelong severity toward them
had a predictable result. This was surely the case with Johnny, who,
from youth onward, would put personal independence uppermost
among his goals while his mother continued to try aggressively to con-
strain him.

Not that she lacked help from her husband in guiding Johnny and
his sister and brothers toward virtue. She had their father's frequent
letters to call upon. Along with his siblings, Johnny would gather at
Abigail's side as she read aloud these paternal messages, which over-
flowed with admonition and concern. They were made to sound like
sacred scripture, handed down by a father who, the children were reminded repeatedly, was risking his life for a soaring ideal: liberty. After

all, as Abigail told them, were the British to catch their father as a participant in the Continental Congress, he would likely suffer as a traitor, a fate described vividly for the children.

Thus began Johnny's near-reverence for his father, whose views on righteous living can still be read on a granite stone honoring Henry Adams in the town burial ground. Upon it John Adams had inscribed his "veneration of the piety, humility, simplicity, prudence, patience, temperance, frugality, industry, and perseverance" that Henry Adams and other ancestors had demonstrated. It was an example John hoped he and his posterity would emulate.

The monument's pronouncement echoed the messages John sent home from Philadelphia. These letters from an admired parent did much to shape Johnny's evolving outlook. In one of them, John implored Abigail: "Above all cares of this life let our ardent anxiety be to improve the minds and manners of our children. Let us teach them not only to do virtuously, but to excel."

Despite his confidence in Abigail, John's anxiety about his eldest son soon led him to address messages directly to Johnny. These bore an overtone of warning—there were always reminders that the father waited to hear "a good account" of the son. This would be possible, John said, if Johnny fixed his "attention upon great and glorious objects" and tried to "weed out every meanness" in order to become "great and manly." The father asked his son to join him in being the sworn enemy of "injustice, ingratitude, cowardice, and falsehood."

Johnny was urged to make scholarship "the most ingenious and elegant entertainment of your life." Toward that end, John assigned a Latin sentence, challenging his son to be able "when I come home to give me the construction of the line, and the parsing of every word of it." And when Johnny was not studying Latin, he was to read history. There was no better way to discover righteous behavior than to scrutinize the past, where so much evil abounded: "Treachery, Perfidy, Cruelty, Hypocrisy, Avarice, etc. etc." If he learned this lesson, John predicted, Johnny was certain "to become a wise and great man."

Lest Johnny not catch on that he was being schooled for an eminent career, his father became explicit. In a letter of August 11, 1777, John urged his ten-year-old son to prepare for a role in the wars, congresses, and negotiations certain to recur as the nation developed. He must be studious as a youth in order to take a turn at public service— "the part which may be allotted you to act on the stage of life." The finest preparation, John announced, was to read Thucydides' *History of the Peloponnesian War,* and to do so in the original Greek, "the most perfect of all human languages," which Johnny was told he must master.

THE EFFECT of John and Abigail's style of parenting shines through Johnny's childhood letters. As an obedient lad, he wrote stilted epistles designed to please his seniors, messages that probably told more about Abigail and John Adams than about their son. Indeed, little in his early letters to his absent father was even in his own words, for Abigail usually dictated his boyish screeds.

The first of Johnny's surviving letters, dating from 1773, was sent to Betsy Cranch, a young cousin, saluting her as "Dear Cousing"; this was Abigail's style, for she often put a *g* after an *n,* for example rendering Ben Franklin's name as "Frankling." In a crude hand and with poor spelling, Johnny confessed to Betsy that too much of his time was spent in play, leaving "a great deal of room for me to grow better." In writing to his father in October 1774 in Philadelphia, Johnny conceded that it was a challenge and said he feared he would "make poor work of it." Nevertheless, he took pains to assure his father that he was seeking to "grow a better boy" so that his parent should never "be ashamed of me."

By June 1777, young Adams' style might have improved, but the abject tone had increased, perhaps because an anxious Abigail was coaching him as he wrote. He spoke of being ashamed of himself. Why? Because "My thoughts are running after birds eggs, play, and trifles." Lest his father be discouraged, Johnny explained that he hoped to grow better, thanks to "the perusal of history." John Adams could not help but be cheered when his son soon announced: "I am more satisfied with myself when I have applied part of my time to some useful employment than when I have idled it away about trifles and play."

Meanwhile, Abigail took care to assure her husband that Johnny was composing his own letters—mostly. She did review them, she acknowledged, but insisted she offered merely correction. Soon, however, there emerged what was probably a more accurate version of how mother and son had collaborated. In a letter to Abigail dated August 11, 1778, sent while he was with his father in Europe, Johnny apologized for writing to her so briefly and infrequently, explaining that he was now relying upon his own resources—"my Pappa being always a doing publick affaires or a writing to you cannot do it for me." Johnny then reminded his mother of how once he would "teaze" her to write his letters. Now, he asserted, "I am obliged to think myself."

Then, at age eleven, came a sudden necessity of doing for himself which prodded Johnny's talent. While he evidently was a youngster of superior abilities, these in themselves would hardly explain his eventual repute as a prodigy. He later acknowledged that his remarkable record before 1817 was due mainly to the good luck of having been caught up in John Adams' career when the father's role in world affairs was abruptly enlarged in 1778.

UNTIL LATE IN 1777, the folks in Braintree had assumed that John Adams was firmly fixed in Philadelphia, where the Continental Congress had recently named him to preside over the Board of War and Ordnance. This duty permitted him to be with his family only a bit of each year, and he often spent those times traveling around New England reviving his legal practice. This seemingly unending separation appeared to be the ultimate sacrifice the Revolution could ask of the closely knit Adamses—until an even greater one was suddenly required of them.

In December 1777, awaiting another brief visit by the father, the family received news that Congress had appointed him a commissioner, to join Benjamin Franklin and Arthur Lee in Paris to promote the American cause among the European powers. Word of this new assignment reached Braintree before John did, allowing Abigail to dream that she and perhaps her older children would accompany her spouse to France. But when John came home, he stressed mostly the danger, particularly to a female, of capture by the enemy on the high seas.

Crestfallen, Abigail gave up her plan, leaving the field to Johnny, who begged to accompany his father. The advantages of such an experience being obvious, Abigail and other family members backed the boy's cause. Despite her misgivings, Abigail decided it was important that her son be with his father; Johnny, she believed, had reached the age when he stood, as she put it, "most in need of the joint force of his [John's] example and precepts." Then there was the prediction of Johnny's tutor, cousin John Thaxter, that by going to Europe, young Adams would be "laying the foundations of a great man." These arguments were persuasive—the eldest son would go abroad with his father.

They embarked on February 13, 1778, sailing in the twenty-four-gun Continental frigate *Boston*. Their departure was without fanfare, lest the British navy be alerted that a fine catch would be crossing the Atlantic. Father and son were quietly rowed out to the *Boston* from near Uncle Norton Quincy's house at Mount Wollaston. The seas were high, but throughout, as a much-gratified John Adams noted, his son "behaves like a man."

The journey started calmly enough. Johnny was immediately captivated by a chance to learn the French language from a fellow passenger, Dr. Nicholas Noel, an obliging and well-educated surgeon in the French army. With this experience began JQA's fluency in French and also his enduring devotion to languages. His studiousness at sea persisted even after the ship sailed into peril brought by awesome storms and the vigilant British navy.

Though the *Boston* was like a mouse pursued by several cats, she somehow managed to elude capture, only to find that weather was the more relentless foe. A storm smashed the frigate for three days in late February with a severity that left the most seasoned sailor impressed and both Adamses seasick. The father's journal contains a narrative of what they endured. "To describe the ocean, the waves, the winds, the ship, her motions, rollings, wringings, and agonies—the sailors, their countenances, language, and behavior is impossible." Lightning struck three men on deck, killing one, while the wind carried away the *Boston*'s main topmast. John Adams called the scene a "universal wreck of everything in all parts of the ship, chests, casks, bottles, etc. No place or person was dry."

There was a cheering aspect to the upheaval, however. The proud parent could report that Johnny's deportment throughout the storm "gave me a satisfaction that I cannot express—fully sensible of our danger, he was constantly endeavoring to bear up under it with a manly courage and patience." The ship's captain, too, must have been favorably impressed with the boy, for he took time during calmer weather to teach young Adams about the compass, navigation, and how to work the sails. The respite was brief, for the *Boston* soon was helpless again before wind and swell. "How many dangers, distresses, and hairbreadth scapes have we seen?" John marveled.

A bit more than six weeks after leaving Massachusetts, the *Boston* reached the coast of France, and on April 1, 1778, Johnny and his father landed at Bordeaux. Arm in arm, the two walked about, gawking unabashedly at the sights. After shipboard fare, they could not speak too highly of the fine food served to them by a citizenry evidently pleased to be host to this emissary and his son.

What made the greatest impression upon Johnny was his introduction in Bordeaux to the theater and the concert hall. In fact, on their first night in the city, the pair went to the opera, where the dancing and music afforded them, as John recorded, "a very cheerful, sprightly amusement, having never seen anything of the kind before."

On April 4, they began the journey to Paris, reaching the city on the 8th, after pushing hard to cover a hundred miles a day. Once again, Johnny drew his parent's admiration: John recorded that "my little son has sustained this long journey . . . with the utmost firmness, as he did our fatiguing and dangerous voyage." Upon arriving in Paris, the visitors, accustomed to the comparative quiet of Boston, were astonished to see streets packed with carriages, most of them bearing liveried servants. They also discovered that it was difficult to find suitable living quarters for rent in a crowded city.

This brought John to accept Benjamin Franklin's invitation to reside in his commodious quarters in Passy, a suburb at the city's edge, near the Bois de Boulogne. The father and son, however, would remain here for less than a year. John quickly realized that the American commission was so internally divided and corrupt as to be impotent and ludicrous in the French government's eyes. Neither was the Continental Congress favorably impressed. In September 1778 it disbanded the commission and recalled Johnny's father, a summons by then much desired by the disgusted senior Adams.

Word of the recall did not arrive, however, before the son had had time in Paris for important intellectual and emotional development. To his great joy, at least according to an account by his father, Johnny was placed in a weekday boarding school soon after they had settled in Passy. The lad told his parent he found it inspiring to be off to classes where "rewards were given to the best scholars." The school was run by a M. Le Coeur. Franklin's grandson Benjamin "Benny" Bache was enrolled there, as were several other American boys. In addition to an emphasis upon Latin and French, the school provided training in fencing, dancing, drawing, and music, subjects some New Englanders might have considered frivolous at best.

In one of his first letters from Paris, Johnny described the school's schedule by informing his "Honoured Mother" that classes began at 6 a.m., then proceeded for two hours, followed by a sixty-minute break for "play" and breakfast. Studies then resumed until noon, when another interval allowed time for dinner and more recreation. Then it was back to class from 2 to 4:30, more play for a half hour, and final classes from 5 to 7:30, when the students supped. Afterward there were games until it was time to retire, at 9 p.m.

Although this scholarly rigor relented only on Sunday, Johnny claimed: "I like it very well." So did his father, who was clearly astonished at the progress his son made in his studies, and particularly in mastering the French language. The senior Adams confessed to being "mortified" that the lad "learned more French in a day than I could learn in a week with all my books." By August, he informed Abigail that her diligent son was "in high reputation here."

JOHNNY ADAMS HAD more than books on his mind, however. To folks at home, his letters seemed most at ease when they described the boundless cultural riches of Europe. Although he enjoyed the musical concerts, his favorite entertainment was the theater. His father also attended the theater, particularly performances of tragedies by Corneille, Racine, or Voltaire—and prodded his son to concentrate upon these.

Johnny conceded that such productions had their share of music and dancing, but he had another preference. For the best of "the language, the wit, the passions, the sentiments, the oratory, the poetry, the manners and morals," he contended that one must go to the French Comedy. This was the report the increasingly independent-minded Johnny sent off to his sister Nabby.

The two Adamses had arrived in Europe just as the theater was reclaiming prominence. Spurred by a revival of Shakespeare, whose work had a liberating influence, every major poet had begun writing plays. Neoclassicism gave way to Romanticism, and plays grew naturalistic and individualistic. Theaters had become larger; Drury Lane in London would soon seat thirty-six hundred. The names of prominent actors—Charles Kemble, Mrs. Sarah Siddons, Edmund Kean—would often appear in JQA's diary and letters. Caught up in the appeal of drama, he would be an enthusiastic patron of theater for the rest of his life—even in the United States, where productions during his time would be mostly poor European imports.

Recognizing how smitten his son was by Europe's cultural charms, John had to caution him against any excessive display of enthusiasm in his letters home about the rewards of life in Paris. The young man occasionally took pains to advise the folks around Braintree that he "would rather be amongst the rugged rocks of my own native town than in the gay city of Paris." Meanwhile, John himself assured his spouse that Johnny's "behaviour does honour to his Mamma."

Abigail, however, had not waited for the pair's first epistles before sending warnings about the worldly temptations that she pictured as luring young men such as her son into sinful ways. Consequently, the *Boston* had not been long at sea when Abigail sent Johnny a stern message: he must "never disgrace his mother," and he must "behave worthy of his father." In this way, she assured her son, he might acquire useful knowledge and virtue "such as to render you an ornament to society, an honour to your country, and a blessing to your parents."

She went on to speak ominously of the "inadvertency and heedlessness of youth," which led to her deepest concern. In an outburst that offers one of the most revealing glimpses of Abigail's chilling nature as a parent, she described the evil tugging at her young son and, doubtless recalling her brother's dissolute life, saw her own reputation as tied to Johnny's innocence. Abigail announced to her son: "For dear as you are to me, I had much rather you should have found your grave in the ocean you have crossed, or any untimely death crop you in your infant years, rather than see you an immoral profligate or a graceless child." The son was ordered to view vice of any sort as hideous. "You must keep a strict guard upon yourself, or the odious monster will soon lose its terror by becoming familiar to you."

Thanks no doubt to his father's guidance, Johnny tried in many ways by letter to reassure his mother. He was well aware of the "vice and folly" on all sides in Europe, he wrote, and "I hope I shall never be tempted by them." Likewise, John Adams did his share to calm Abigail's fears. "My little son gives me great pleasure," he reported, speaking of Johnny's "assiduity to his books and his discreet behaviour." With generosity and tact, John added that this was because "The lessons of his Mamma are a constant law to him."

There was a rising self-assurance in Johnny as he passed his eleventh birthday in July 1778. It was particularly evident when the boy took his father's side after the latter found himself a target in Abigail's letters. Having decided that the company of sophisticated Parisian women had made her husband indifferent toward her, she wrote letters sharply reproaching him. These accusations deeply troubled her son as he watched his father's patience give way to the point that he told his wife: "Let me alone, and have my own way." If Johnny himself wished for greater freedom, he could not rebel so openly. Instead, he began defending his father by insisting to Abigail that her complaints were unfounded.

In a remarkable epistle of February 20, 1779, he rebuked his mother for disregarding letters from her husband. "You complain as bad or worse than if he had not wrote at all," the indignant son said. "It really hurts him to receive such letters." The draft copy of this message contained a threat JQA chose not to include in the version he mailed, so Abigail never knew her son had at first intended to say that "if all your letters are like this, my Pappa will cease writing at all."

Fortunately, the marital furor could be put aside temporarily when John Adams' work as a commissioner was terminated by Congress. He and Johnny set out from Paris on March 8, 1779, hoping for a speedy journey to Massachusetts. Instead, for three months they lingered in such French ports as Nantes, Brest, and Saint-Nazaire as they vainly sought a ship to carry them to America. During this delay, they viewed what edifying sights the coastal towns offered, including a fascinating zoo. Father and son studied together the writings of Marcus Tullius Cicero, who became the historical figure JQA would most admire.

These weeks before sailing allowed John Adams more time to evaluate his son and to send another enthusiastic report to Abigail. He stressed how the boy "is respected wherever he goes for his vigour and vivacity both of mind and body, for his constant good humour, and for his rapid progress in French, as well as for his general knowledge, which for his age is uncommon." The father called Johnny "the comfort of my life" and advised Abigail that he "is much caressed wherever he goes"—which was not the exaggeration it might seem, as the voyage home demonstrated.

After finally departing, on June 17, 1779, in the French king's frigate, *La Sensible*, Johnny advanced his reputation by teaching English to two distinguished fellow passengers. These were the Chevalier Anne César de La Luzerne, France's new ambassador to the United States, and his secretary, François de Barbé-Marbois, who went on to an influential career in France and the United States. After three days, John Adams noted in his diary: "The Chevalier de la Luzerne and M. Marbois are in raptures with my son."

The two men and their young teacher seemed always at work. The ambassador read aloud from Sir William Blackstone's inaugural lecture as professor of English law at Oxford University, with "my son correcting the pronunciation of every word and syllable and letter," as John Adams recorded. "The Ambassador said he was astonished at my son's knowledge, that he was a master of his own language like a professor." According to Marbois, Johnny "shows us no mercy, and makes us no compliments." Nevertheless, the two French pupils said, "We must have Mr. John."

On August 2, 1779, the Adamses arrived at Braintree for what proved a stay of barely three months. In October, to John Adams' mingled astonishment, chagrin, and delight, word arrived from Philadelphia that the Continental Congress had unanimously decided to return him to Paris, where, as America's minister plenipotentiary, he was to seek treaties of peace and commerce with Great Britain.

John had narrowly escaped the censure Congress had laid upon his fellow commissioners. Suddenly finding himself a celebrated figure, the senior Adams prepared to return to Europe in November on the same French frigate that had recently brought him and his son home. This time, however, he intended that Johnny stay behind.

While the son did not wish to sail with his parent, neither did he intend to remain at home. Deeming schooling received in France inappropriate for a career in the rising Republic, the twelve-year-old had returned home resolved to prepare for entry to Harvard. Since John Adams espoused the importance of a Harvard education (and also was mindful of the sizable financial cost of taking a son to Europe), he endorsed Johnny's wish to study in America—until Abigail Adams intervened.

Even though she had feared that Paris would corrupt the lad and was thrilled by his safe return, Abigail believed that being accompanied by a son might have a wholesome effect on a husband she tended at times to mistrust. So she informed Johnny that he had more to gain than to lose from returning to Europe. Once Abigail had persuaded John of this, the son dutifully changed his mind—and promptly announced how he would mark this step: "Pappa enjoins it upon me to keep a journal, or a diary, of the events that happen to me, and of objects that I see, and of characters that I converse with from day to day."

The danger in this undertaking, he confessed, was that someday he would have to read "my childish nonsense." He could only hope that this future review would remind him "of the several steps by which I shall have advanced, in taste, judgment, and knowledge." In fact, before he would return to America, his diary would depend heavily upon borrowed material, with many entries copied from travel books or from *The Spectator* and the current newspapers. This youthful practice reflected less Johnny's interest in the subject than an effort to improve his penmanship, a project insisted upon by his father.

THE ADAMS PARTY set sail aboard the *Sensible* on November 13, 1779. Accompanying them was nine-year-old Charles Adams, Johnny's next-younger brother, who embarked in a state of inconsolable sobbing. Charles would find living in Europe more than his "sensitive" nature could endure, so that after eighteen months he was shipped back to Braintree. Also traveling with the Adamses were cousin John Thaxter, Johnny's tutor at one time, and Francis Dana, a lawyer and former delegate to the Continental Congress. Thaxter came along as John Adams' private secretary and Dana as secretary to the peace commission.

On December 8, Johnny and his companions made landfall in Europe, but not where they expected to be. The *Sensible* had encountered heavy seas during much of the voyage, developing a leak that required all on board to take turns manning the pumps. So dangerous did the situation become that the captain put in for repairs at the first available port, which was El Ferrol, at the very northwestern tip of Spain. From there, the Adams group had no choice but to travel overland to Paris on what proved to include "the worst three weeks that I ever passed in my life," as Johnny put it.

The journey began after a fortnight of gathering supplies and guides in El Ferrol and in the nearby town of La Coruña, a respite that allowed the opportunity for dining and attending the theater, and for John Adams to receive the respect of local officials. At one dinner, his son reported, more than fifty dishes were served, along with "twenty different sorts of wine." After the meal, the young diarist admitted that he and brother Charles got lost while trying to find their lodging.

It was the last happy time for many days. The Adams party set out for France on December 26. Struggling eastward over the rugged mountains along Spain's north coast, the caravan fought debilitating illness and foul weather while trying for more than a month to cover twelve miles daily. The terrain was treacherous, the food wretched, and the shelter—in the travelers' opinion—unfit even for animals.

Throughout the ordeal, Johnny managed a mostly cheerful style as he recorded the trip in his new journal. The journey began with some of the travelers astride mules and the rest, he wrote, in three battered carriages "made in the year one." The group appeared to be "so many

Don Quixote's and Sancho Pancha's," and he pictured the inns as offering "chambers in which anybody would think half a dozen hogs had lived there six months."

Most of the rooms, he said, were as muddy inside as out, a plight which the group did not escape until January 15, 1780, when civilization reappeared at the port town of Bilbao. Here Johnny and his companions lingered, meeting captains of two ships from Boston who were trading with the prosperous firm of Joseph Gardoqui and Sons. The Gardoqui family entertained the Americans in princely fashion, sending them off in much improved spirits to Bayonne and then Bordeaux, where they arrived on January 29, and where they once again relished the food and theater. Here Johnny put aside his diary, not to resume it for six months.

The Adams party reached the familiar scenes of Paris on February 9, where they settled in the Hôtel de Valois. Along with his brother Charles, Johnny immediately entered a pension academy in the suburb of Passy operated by the Pechigny family, a school to which many Americans in Paris sent their children. Gaining an education was of course intended as the primary benefit for Johnny from this second visit to Europe. Besides the essential subjects of Latin and Greek, he studied geography, mathematics, drawing, and writing. John Adams preferred that his son save dancing and fencing for a later time.

Both the pupil and his father seemed pleased with what the school offered. Johnny, in fact, found himself a bit overwhelmed by the range of subjects and sought his father's advice about which ones merited most attention. Should he put emphasis on Cicero, on fractions, on learning Greek—on geography, or writing, or drawing? "A young boy cannot apply himself to all those things and keep a remembrance of them all," he pointed out.

In reply, John Adams recommended concentrating on Greek and Latin. While he reminded his son that the most important of all topics was mathematics, the parent advised leaving this subject for their return to America. For now, let Johnny's full attention go to Virgil, Ovid, Horace, and Tully—and to improvement in penmanship, about which John was almost obsessive. "I will not overlook one such heedless piece of work," he growled after seeing a sloppily written letter by the son. Regretting his own poor script, the father said he was determined to spare Johnny a similar handicap.

Although the pupil complied obediently, he could not resist occasionally switching his attention to what would soon become one of his intellectual passions—the art of translation—as he took time to put the fables of La Fontaine into English. Then there was that other compelling diversion, attending the theater, which Johnny did whenever he could slip away from his books. One of these outings led to what he later at least half seriously called his first romance. "The first woman I ever loved was an actress," he admitted years afterward to Louisa Catherine Adams, his wife. "She belonged to a company of children who performed at the Bois de Boulogne near Passy."

While JQA assured Louisa that he had not met the young woman, whose age he guessed at fourteen, he admitted: "She remains upon my memory as the most lovely and delightful actress that I ever saw." Would that he could have told her "how much I adored her." He said he had left Passy carrying dreams of her that lasted long after he returned to America.

These visions persisted even though, as JQA took care to tell his wife, he had learned before leaving Europe of the legendary loose morals of actresses. He therefore gave thanks to "my stars and my stupidity" that he had not approached his beloved. The narrow escape did have a great benefit, he claimed. It gave him the "discretion" needed to pass safely through a lifetime of enjoying the theater.

Nothing about Johnny's morals seemed to worry his father in 1780. Instead, it was the expense of his son's education that troubled John. "My affections I fear got the better of my judgment" in his decision to bring Johnny again to Europe, he wrote. But for Abigail, back in Massachusetts, her son's virtue remained the prime concern. Once again, she extended her maternal reach across the Atlantic by letters that charged Johnny to be vigilant against temptation and sin, to recognize the importance of never wasting time, and to be resolute about attaining self-control by overcoming self-love. "If you could once feel how grateful to the heart of a parent the good conduct of a child is, you would never be the occasion of exciting any other sensation in the bosom of your ever affectionate mother."

Abigail was soon pushing Johnny to "let your ambition be engaged to become eminent." Besieged by these redundant admonitions, Johnny chose to reply only rarely. Instead, he became so caught up in his studies that his spare time went mostly to reports to his father on his scholarly progress, particularly after the Adamses moved to Holland in 1780. Convinced that the French foreign ministry was preventing him from seeking peace with Great Britain, John had decided to try his hand at persuading the Dutch government to recognize and support American independence. As a bonus, he was certain that opportunities for Johnny's education would be superior in Holland.

Consequently, on July 27, 1780, John, his two sons, and their cousin John Thaxter set out for the Low Countries. That day Johnny chose to revive his diary, continuing it while he saw Brussels, Rotterdam, Leyden, The Hague, and Amsterdam. The journal was mostly a narrative of sights seen, persons met, and long quotations from travel guides. Distracted only by lessons in the Dutch language, Johnny kept the diary until September 30, when he and his brother became students in the famous Latin school in Amsterdam—where Johnny soon found himself miserable.

The academy's imperious rector saw no merit in the bright and hardworking American boy who could not speak Dutch, and humiliated him by placing him with elementary students. Johnny endured it as long as he could before reporting his version of the situation to his father—as, also, did the rector, who was shocked by young Adams' rebellious attitude. Immediately, John Adams withdrew his sons from the school, fuming at the "littleness of soul" exhibited by the academy.

Soon afterward, fortunately, Johnny began one of his happiest intellectual experiences. Thanks to the suggestion of an Adams family acquaintance, Benjamin Waterhouse, who had come from Massachusetts to pursue a medical degree at the University of Leyden, Johnny and Charles were sent to study under Waterhouse's supervision, as well as that of John Thaxter.

Promptly, thirteen-year-old Johnny became an independent student within Leyden University, taking lessons privately and attending lectures in what was then one of the world's finest centers of learning. Thaxter also resumed his own studies while he, Waterhouse, and the Adams boys lived in the same house. The setting suited Johnny perfectly as he studied zealously, undertook regular walks, attended church services twice on Sunday, and sought the company of interesting adults. His zeal was soon rewarded. Early in January 1781, he was formally admitted as a scholar in the university.

If anyone took more satisfaction from this development than young Adams, it was his father, who now forgot his alarm at the cost of bringing his son to Europe and urged him to capture every intellectual benefit afforded by residence in Leyden. "You have now a prize in your hands, indeed," he told Johnny, so that if he did not improve rapidly, "you will be without excuse." But John also knew how to encourage, assuring his son that if he maintained his thirst for knowledge and his capacity for work, "you will do no dishonour to yourself nor to the University of Leyden."

Abigail Adams' response to her son's opportunity was different.

When she heard that Johnny and his father had transferred to Holland, Abigail laid on the boy a new challenge. He should seek to benefit from the "universal neatness and cleanliness" for which the Low Countries were famed. Let this influence "cure you of all your slovenly tricks."

The son ignored the letter, concentrating instead on describing for his father the joys of life at the University of Leyden, all of which delighted the senior Adams, who longed to be studying alongside his son. Imprisoned by the tedium of diplomacy in Amsterdam, the father advised Johnny to attend lectures in medicine, chemistry, and philosophy, and to send him full reports. In addition, the young student was directed to note every feature of the university that might be advantageously adopted at Harvard. It was an assignment that Johnny welcomed, and he did not disappoint his father.

Waterhouse and Thaxter kept John Adams informed about the remarkable diligence of his son. Indeed, during the spring of 1781, a cheerful Johnny was making such progress in Greek and Latin that his father feared he might be neglecting his own language. Consequently, John urged him to read the English poets, advising him that poetry was essential to happiness: "You will never be alone with a poet in your pocket." To this Johnny replied: "I have not read much of it, yet I always admired it very much."

Not that the student invariably complied with his parent's directions. To the dismay of his father, Johnny resisted following his order to read the philippics of the great Athenian orator Demosthenes. The senior Adams could not understand this aversion. "I absolutely insist upon it, that you begin upon Demosthenes."

This sort of rigorous supervision on his father's part may account, at least in part, for the son's hesitation about staying with his parent during the university's spring holiday in 1781. After reluctantly agreeing to visit, Johnny said he would remain in Amsterdam for only a fortnight, shrewdly explaining: "If I should stay any longer, it might do harm to my studies, of which I have just got into a steady course."

Barely had Johnny made this announcement when his devotion to scholarship faced more harm than might accompany any vacation with his father. That July he was uprooted from his student life in Leyden to accompany Francis Dana on a diplomatic mission to St. Petersburg, the capital of Russia. Valuable though the experience would prove in some ways, JQA always believed that the two-year interruption stunted his scholarly development. Years later, looking back over his youth in Europe, he complained that his education had been sadly informal, ill-organized, and disrupted. The result, he acknowledged, was that while he amassed a little information about many topics, he was never granted time enough to master one.

In 1781, Johnny could not appreciate that his future career would owe more to his ramblings across Europe than to any concentrated mound of knowledge he might have accumulated had he remained ensconced at the university.

CHAPTER TWO

Celebrity

Persons suppose I was obstinate, and dogmatical, and pedantic.

AFTER SERVING as John Adams' secretary, Francis Dana was qualified and available when the Continental Congress sought an emissary who might go to St. Petersburg for an indefinite stay, there to persuade the Russian empress, Catherine the Great, to recognize American independence. It was Congress' hope that by a formal treaty with the United States, Russia might use its leadership in the League of Armed Neutrality to bring the American Republic recognition by most of Europe's great powers. Unfortunately, the empress was not thus inclined, so that she and her ministers kept Dana at arm's length until Congress recalled him in 1783.

IN THE BEGINNING, it seemed a promising assignment, except that Dana spoke little French, the language used in Catherine's court. Since his young friend John Quincy Adams had become fluent in French, he was the logical choice to accompany Dana as interpreter and secretary. Though only fourteen, Johnny was mature for his age and accustomed to adult company and conversation.

Reluctantly putting his books aside in the summer of 1781, Johnny left the University of Leyden to begin what would become a great adventure lasting nearly two years. Viewing his son's opportunity with mixed feelings, John Adams consoled himself by predicting: "He will be satiated with travel in his childhood, and care nothing about it, I hope, in his ripe years." It was a futile hope and a poor prophecy.

After purchasing a sturdy carriage, Adams and Dana began their two-thousand-mile trek to St. Petersburg on July 7, 1781. The only notable excitement along the way was when the carriage overturned just before they entered Berlin on July 25. In Johnny's opinion, the Prussian capital was more impressive than Paris; it was, he reported in his diary, "the handsomest and most regular city I ever saw." On August 2, the pair set out once more, now often riding night and day. They passed through Poland, then stayed briefly in Riga before pressing on to St. Petersburg, where they arrived on August 27. Johnny found the city superior even to Berlin. Its beauty was for him the most gratifying aspect of his time in Russia.

Taking lodging in the center of town near the Imperial Winter Palace, Francis Dana found all too soon that his diplomatic overtures were unwelcome, which left him and Johnny ignored by official society. This was disappointing, but less so for Johnny than the discovery that there was no school or affordable tutoring available to him.

With little business to report and few persons willing to converse with the Americans, Johnny began to fill his diary, which he had resumed (after nearly a year's lapse) during the trip to Russia, with brief, dull reports on walks taken, persons seen, and severe weather endured. He was fascinated by the long winter season and asserted in 1782 that snow fell in July, tempting citizens once again to don their flannel-lined boots. According to an astonished young Adams, this footwear was invariably removed upon entering a building.

Although St. Petersburg was poorly policed, so that murders and robbery were commonplace, neither this threat nor foul weather kept Johnny idle. He haunted the booksellers, the start of a lifelong hobby, buying many volumes for shipment home. He began to study German, and became such a master of French that John Adams half seriously complained that his son wrote better letters in French than in English.

While Johnny corresponded regularly with his father, he continued to avoid writing to his mother, perhaps dreading more of Abigail's incessant demands that he be a good boy and dress neatly. He eventually explained—implausibly, it seems—to Abigail that he was too busy to write. When he did so, two months after arriving in Russia, the letter was mostly a copy of Voltaire's lengthy description of St. Petersburg. Abigail, however, was not alone now in worrying that life in the Russian capital threatened her son's morals. With her encouragement, John Adams wrote to warn Johnny of the temptations in a worldly place like St. Petersburg, where "innocence and a pure conscience" were sure to be in danger. But John seemed just as interested to learn what his son was reading; the answer was Cicero, Hume, Addison, Pope, Dryden, and Richardson's *Clarissa*.

It was not to escape temptations of the flesh, though, that Johnny left St. Petersburg. When it became apparent that, in order to continue his classical studies, he must "go on alone," his father agreed that Johnny should conclude his stay in Russia. If he returned to Holland, he would be allowed to resume his studies at the University of Leyden and also to act as his father's secretary, since John Thaxter was going back to America.

After fulfilling the elaborate legal requirements then imposed on persons departing St. Petersburg, including thrice publishing his intent to do so, Johnny set out for Stockholm on October 30, 1782. Traveling through Sweden was said to be the easiest winter route to western Europe, but the trip was hardly comfortable. He used boat and carriage to cross the Baltic Sea, island by island, and the Åland archipelago. Following the land route might have been easier, but it would have added seventeen hundred English miles to the journey.

Along the way, Johnny spent two days, November 8 through 10, in Helsinki, where he dined with the commander of Swedish forces in Finland (which had long been claimed by Sweden). Finally, at midnight on November 22, Johnny reached Stockholm. The taverns were all closed, so he had to sleep in his carriage, the only inhospitable experience during a stay in Sweden extending to mid-February.

During these months, and for years thereafter, JQA praised the Swedish citizenry, calling them "the kindest-hearted, friendliest, and most hospitable people in Europe." Regrettably, he left scant record of his time in Sweden, and nothing concerning his five weeks in Stockholm. His comments afterward indicated he had made numerous friends, prowled the bookshops, and chatted with many people about America and the prospect of Sweden's commerce with the new nation. Johnny recalled that all the Swedes he met claimed never to have doubted that the British colonies would gain independence.

These weeks in Stockholm may constitute one of the most important episodes in John Quincy Adams' life, for when he resumed his diary upon leaving the city, he seemed much more mature in what he recorded and how he expressed himself. Here he had been wholly independent, his parents and their reminders of duty and evil so far away as to seem in another world.

The personal and intellectual charm that Johnny displayed in his youth, which the strains of adulthood would so often smother or disguise, probably was never more manifest than during this period of freedom as he traveled in northern Europe. Many doors in Stockholm were opened to him because of a friendship he formed in a bookstore with Charles Bernard Wadstrom, a mechanical engineer who saw to it that the young American was widely welcomed. It must have been a reassuring experience for a boy of fifteen to talk on equal terms with leading citizens of Stockholm.

Not until thirty years later did JQA offer the most intriguing glimpse into his stay in Sweden. It took that long for him to acknowledge how struck he had been by the appearance and charm of the demure Swedish women, who were, he remembered, "as modest as they were amiable and beautiful." For him, Sweden would always be "the land of lovely dames." He admitted that he had never forgotten the "palpitations of heart" these women caused him—"and of which they never knew," he added.

Would that a Swedish female's diary had survived with a description of this American youth who had seen so much of the globe. Johnny had by now grown into his adult appearance. Most observers would speak of him as handsome, of medium height, and with a stocky, if not pudgy, frame. His countenance was quick to reflect his mood of the moment. In many ways, he was much the picture of his famous father—his hairline even began to recede at an early age.

Leaving Stockholm on January 1, 1783, Johnny traveled southwest toward Denmark, slowed by heavy snows and the insistence of new friends that he linger in one or another Swedish town or village. An attraction for him was the natives' habit of gathering after work, a custom that helped keep them warm and cheerful as they danced away what Johnny fetchingly called the "long white evenings." He also found that in Sweden, in contrast to other European countries, even "people of the lowest class" were polite.

He reached Sweden's second great city, Göteborg, early on January 25. Despite a night of travel and little sleep, the energetic young man was soon out exploring the town. The French consul arranged for Johnny to be properly introduced, particularly to a citizen whose brother had recently settled in Boston. The several diary entries of the time show that Johnny spent his days and nights conversing, dining, dancing, attending theater and concerts, and sightseeing. Too, the city was a port with many merchants, who soon sought out the well-informed—and well-connected—young American.

On February 11, Johnny reluctantly departed from Göteborg, but only after attending a masquerade ball—his costume is unrecorded—until 4 a.m., whereupon he "threw [himself] upon a bed and slept till about 7 o'clock." He then traveled the nearly impassable coastal roads to cross over into Denmark on February 15. Here Copenhagen offered another gracious welcome, so that Johnny was once more caught up in society. Again he lingered, claiming it was not the fun but the endless bad weather that detained him with the hospitable Danes. He offered the same explanation when he stayed with the cordial Germans in Hamburg for yet another month.

While winter conditions certainly would slow the progress of even the most eager traveler from St. Petersburg to Holland, perhaps there is a larger explanation as to why months rather than weeks were consumed before Johnny arrived at his father's residence. In Scandinavia and northern Germany he was hastening into manhood. It was a time of few worries and much freedom for young Adams, a state he would later recall with an envious sigh, remembering how the Swedes, Danes, and Germans had clustered about him. As a learned and linguistically skilled young man from the fabled land of America, Johnny had been the center of attention, and he remained in the role as long as he dared. Meanwhile, a frantic John Adams was asking everyone who had been in northern Europe if they had seen his wandering son, for Johnny made little effort to keep his father apprised of his whereabouts.

By NOW VERY MUCH a grown-up though still not yet sixteen, Johnny finally arrived in The Hague, the seat of government of the Dutch Republic, on April 21. His father was absent, working in Paris with John Jay and Benjamin Franklin to arrange a peace treaty with Great Britain. From Holland, Johnny began to write almost daily to his father, reporting that he now wished to concentrate on study.

In reply, John Adams offered his son the choice of resuming work at the University of Leyden or of being tutored by John himself in The Hague. Johnny elected the latter alternative, with the understanding that until John returned from Paris, the son should read under the supervision of Charles William Frederic Dumas, an agent representing America in Holland and a good friend of the Adamses. Dumas' broad learning more than qualified him for this task as he skillfully led young Adams to resume the bookish life—not an easy change after Johnny's recent months of pleasure.

Realizing that Dumas might have difficulty, John Adams sent the pupil directions for study, stressing that he should begin immediately with the New Testament in Greek, while recommending that he read sermons for relaxation. Then, overcome by impatience to see the son from whom he had been separated for two years, John Adams took time off from the negotiations in Paris to return to The Hague on July 22. There he found an offspring who was now verging on adulthood and who would no longer take easily to guidance.

Writing to Abigail about their child, who had just passed his sixteenth birthday, John reported, "He is grown a man in understanding and stature as well." Under paternal prodding, the son resumed writing in his diary, entries that now displayed something of the sophistication his father had detected in him at their reunion. Abigail, however, was made uneasy by her husband's accounts of the high praise for their son arising from so many quarters. She worried particularly that Johnny would be seduced by the appeal of European culture, an outcome she was convinced would render him unfit for success in America. Nor was her concern diminished by the infrequency of her son's letters to her.

Probably because of his father's urging, Johnny finally took time to write to "Honoured Mamma," saying that his long silence could be explained by his being "almost at the world's end." In reviewing his journey from St. Petersburg, he reiterated his praise for Sweden, "the country in Europe which pleases me the most." There was no mention of the attractive young ladies.

Soon after posting this letter, Johnny received one from Abigail that has failed to survive among the Adams papers—perhaps because it contained a particularly stinging rebuke to the son for not writing. Johnny countered by assuring Abigail on July 30 that his ordeal by travel had not chilled his affection for her. Instead, the journey had augmented "my reverence for the dearest and most honoured of mothers." He also let Abigail know that she had hurt him when she claimed to be "forgotten by my son." In defense, he spoke of the difficulty—and costliness—of mailing letters from Russia and from the routes to and fro. After this exchange, Johnny was careful for a time to send Abigail lengthy accounts of what he had seen and learned while traveling.

In her replies of late 1783 and early 1784, Abigail resumed the admonitions she had been writing six years earlier, aimed particularly at the vice and temptations she was convinced surrounded her son and urging that he always defer to his mother and father. Now a mature woman of thirty-nine, Abigail treated her eldest son in a way that vividly revealed her personality. Her badgering of him, a practice that would persist whether JQA was abroad or in the United States, made blatantly evident her need to dominate.

Nor was Johnny the only person to be affected by Abigail's attempt to rule. Her sisters, her other children, even John Adams, experienced the binding force of her determination, often with painful results. She was an aggressive person from her youth, and her domineering character—as well as its obverse trait of insecurity—never relaxed after the years when she directed her family in her spouse's absence. She continued also to be stung by the memory of her brother's scandalous failure in life, a disgrace Abigail seemed to feel peculiarly called to redeem.

Her daughter-in-law Louisa Johnson Adams said of Abigail that she would try to grasp even "the asperities of grosser nature" in order to mold them to her will. According to Louisa, Abigail sought to be "the guiding planet" around which family members performed according to "the impulse of her magnetic power."

Assuredly, Abigail Adams merits her place in America's pantheon, where she is featured as a courageous figure in the Revolution, a brilliant letter-writer, a keen analyst of public affairs, and one of the nation's most talented first ladies. But while the American feminist movement does well to claim her as its archetype, history should be mindful that her strengths caused her downfall in one respect. As the life of John Quincy Adams discloses, Abigail Adams was a calamity as a mother. She could not be restrained by love or judgment from seeking to instill in her children her own ambitions and apprehensions. In this, she would succeed to a fearful degree, despite the attempts by JQA and his siblings to escape her.

His mother's latest exhortations eventually reached Johnny in Paris, where he had returned with his father in August 1783. On September 3, John Adams and his fellow commissioners signed the final treaty of peace with Great Britain. John had brought his son to the city as his secretary, hoping they would soon be free to sail from France for America. Instead, their stay abroad was prolonged by more diplomatic assignments, including the need to secure further loans from the Dutch republic.

So displeased was John Adams at the new responsibilities keeping him in Europe that Johnny, observing his parent's chagrin, announced that he wished never to take part in politics if such unhappiness was the price. He could not, of course, entirely shun the talk of public matters. Thanks to his recent firsthand observations of conditions in northern and eastern Europe, young Adams brought valuable contributions to dinner conversation in Paris.

Nevertheless, he showed that his preferences lay elsewhere—in his studies, as well as in his almost nightly attendance at Parisian theaters and his frequently seized opportunities to view masterpieces of art. Rather than politicians, Johnny's diary recorded the men of letters he met, particularly those to whom he was introduced at the ascents of hydrogen-filled balloons—"flying globes," a fascinated Johnny called them—that were then the sensation of Paris.

Immediately after the Treaty of Paris was signed, a gloomy John Adams fell ill with a debilitating "fever," which led father and son to move from the incessant noise in the center of Paris to the suburban quiet of Auteuil on September 22. There John tried to throw off the sickness while his son continued to translate Caesar and Horace and to copy the work of English poets. The new location did nothing to hinder Johnny from frequent dining out and steadfast theatergoing.

After a month, John was so impatient with his slow improvement that he and Johnny decided a vacation in England, including a stay at Bath, might help. Using his now vast experience as a traveler, the son took charge of his invalid parent as the two departed for London on October 20. After much Channel sickness, they arrived at Dover, and Johnny began his evaluation of England by judging the size of sheep seen along the route to London.

In the city, Benjamin West and John Singleton Copley, two Americans who had become renowned painters in England, arranged for Johnny to see many of the finest art collections in royal, public, and private hands. He visited the great libraries and searched the bookshops, while each evening brought his supreme pleasure, the theater. He attended mostly at Covent Garden and Drury Lane, where he applauded Mrs. Sarah Siddons, who he happily reported was said to be "the first [best] tragic performer in Europe."

One evening, while enjoying Mrs. Siddons' appearance in David Garrick's *Isabella; or, the Fatal Marriage,* there was great excitement in the box next to Johnny's. "A young lady . . . was so much affected by it as to be near fainting and was carried out. I am told that every night Mrs. Siddons performs, this happens to some persons." Never having heard of such an effect in theaters on the Continent, Johnny at first wondered if it proved that "more sensibility" prevailed in England, or that plays here were better performed. He credited both reasons.

While young Adams frolicked, the time in England did little to improve his father's health, despite a brief stay at Bath. Although John

Adams was not yet fifty, he appeared emaciated and aged. Obliged to return to Holland, he feared he would not survive the trip in cold and snowy weather; indeed, had he traveled without his seemingly inexhaustible son, the elder Adams might not have lived to see The Hague again. Starting out on January 2, 1784, they quickly found the North Sea and some Dutch islands to be formidable barriers in the winter, so that it took ten days to cover the comparatively short distance. It was Johnny's turn now to exhort and encourage as he almost carried his father back to Holland.

Once settled in The Hague, where the distractions were fewer, Johnny resumed being a scholar while his father, on the Congress' behalf, sought another loan from the Dutch. Mainly, the son was busy translating Latin and French classics into English. Soon John's health had improved dramatically, allowing the Adamses to have a wonderful time together, particularly as they read Plutarch aloud over coffee and chocolate at breakfast. During these early months in 1784, Johnny was lost to his delicious revel in books, travel, theater, and the arts. It ended when word arrived that Abigail Adams was coming to join her husband and son, bringing daughter Nabby with her.

Johnny hastened to London in mid-May to await his mother and sister while his father remained at work. When the ladies failed to appear on schedule, Johnny lingered as long as possible—and to some advantage. He was allowed to listen to debates in the House of Commons, an experience that sparked his lifelong interest in rhetoric. After he had returned to The Hague in late June, Abigail and Nabby belatedly reached London—where Johnny was called back to welcome them.

Abigail did not recognize her son when he was shown into her room at the Hotel Adelphi. While her husband had reminded her that Johnny was "the greatest traveller of his age, and without partiality, I think as promising and manly a youth as is in the world," Abigail was nevertheless taken aback at seeing for herself that she had a European cosmopolite for an offspring. The change worried her.

Meanwhile, John had been ordered back to Paris, where he was to join Thomas Jefferson and Benjamin Franklin in negotiating treaties of amity and commerce with assorted European powers. While waiting for his father to arrive in London to escort the family to Paris, Johnny arranged for the trip, even buying a used coach. His experience would be familiar to anyone who has visited today's used-car lots. Finding one that had been driven only seventy miles, he proudly reported to his father, "It is second-hand, but as good as new." He also purchased Samuel Johnson's *Lives of the Poets* for family reading as they lurched toward Paris in the August heat.

They reached the city on August 13, stayed three days in a hotel, and then moved four miles into the country to set up housekeeping in Auteuil, the village where Johnny and his father had taken refuge during John's illness. Here they rented a house—"commodious" was how Abigail described it—where the Adamses stayed for nine months before John was reassigned to London as American minister to Great Britain. When that time came, the father would have to part with Johnny.

THOSE MONTHS IN AUTEUIL featured a lively family debate about Johnny's future. The topic dominated breakfast talk, replacing the reading aloud of Plutarch. The consensus was that the son had been abroad too long and must return promptly to the United States to establish himself there. Abigail Adams particularly urged that no more of Johnny's time be wasted abroad, an impatience growing from yet another fear: that she would have a son economically dependent upon his parents.

As for Johnny, his feelings in the matter appear to have been mixed, although in later years he insisted it was prudent for him to have come back to America when he did. Before he sailed, however, he admitted to his diary that after seven years abroad he felt discouraged at the prospect of swapping Europe's intellectual riches for America, the noble University of Leyden for a tiny college in the village of Cambridge, Massachusetts.

Once the family decided that Johnny should enroll at Harvard, John Adams opened negotiations with the Reverend Joseph Willard, president of the college. After describing his son's unrivaled experiences in Europe, the proud parent predicted that, given a few more months, Johnny could earn a degree at Leyden. That being the case, John announced that he would not consider entering his son at Harvard as a freshman. If the college would see fit to admit Johnny to the senior or junior class, John Adams announced, "I should choose to send him to you, rather than to Leyden."

This gambit succeeded up to a point. Acknowledging young Adams' record of study in Europe, Willard agreed to admit him to advanced standing, and added that he would not be charged tuition, a concession that elated the financially pressed Adamses. Johnny's precise class status must, however, await judgment by the faculty, a decision that left the family uneasy. John informed Willard that while Johnny was an excellent student, he would shine best in an admissions test if the examination "could be in French with which language he is more familiar than his own."

Meanwhile, now that Abigail Adams had seen something of what she deemed the appalling immorality displayed in Parisian theatrical productions—the same performances her son applauded almost nightly—she wondered if he would be safe even in proper Boston. She confessed to a "thousand fears" at the prospect of Johnny's attending Harvard, where she was convinced religious infidelity reigned. Rumors abounded of how Harvard faculty members treated Christianity irreverently. Solid faith, said Abigail, was indispensable if her son was to pass safely through young manhood without sinking to the level of other males whose "warm blood . . . riots in their veins."

Since Johnny's parents worried at being far away when he entered Harvard, they chose Dr. Cotton Tufts, a neighbor in Weymouth, who was also a cousin, a friend, and the family's business manager, to supervise their son. Tufts was instructed to keep a close watch on how the student spent the family's scarce dollars. John Adams prescribed that his son "must be as frugal as possible," and apparently the father had some grounds for concern. Johnny certainly had not hesitated to purchase an extensive library and wardrobe while abroad. He owned many coats and suits, all in his favorite blue, with four pairs of shoes to go with them, and he brought home sixty-five pairs of stockings.

These changes of attire were probably essential during the final months of Johnny's stay abroad. In his short time left in Paris, the seventeen-year-old sought to attend every theatrical production, to dine wherever he was invited or welcome, to search the Paris bookshops, and to view all the artistic and scientific creations available to him.

He also favored the edifying company of leading French intellectuals, particularly the abbés Chalut, Arnoux, and de Mably, and he visited with the artist Benjamin West and the Marquis de Lafayette. More often, he mingled almost as a peer with his famous compatriots Benjamin Franklin and Thomas Jefferson. Johnny said he "loved" the latter's company, calling Jefferson, who would succeed Franklin as America's minister to France, "a man of great judgment." It was an assessment the mature John Quincy Adams would drastically revise.

Amid the gratifications of these last weeks in Paris, Johnny found time to resume his diary. He opened the first volume with a quotation from Voltaire, "Indolence is sweet and its consequence is bitter," a sentiment he would repeat in a hundred variations over the years. He

also drew close to his sister Nabby. Nearly strangers at first, the two
quickly became inseparable as they walked and saw sights together.
Johnny found her to be dependent, yet admiring, intelligent, and even
a bit glamorous, for she had left America informally betrothed to Roy-
all Tyler, a young attorney and man of letters.

Abigail "Nabby" Adams was twenty, two years Johnny's senior. As
a female companion in the Auteuil household she offered her brother
an appealing contrast to their mother. Where Abigail could seem the
epitome of maternal severity, Nabby treated Johnny with adoration,
seeking to assure him of his wisdom and destined greatness. Always
submissive and imploring his help and guidance, Nabby evidently was
an antidote for the self-doubt and irritation that Abigail Adams' style
of mothering aroused in her son.

As Johnny prepared to sail for America while his parents and
Nabby would go to London, brother and sister pledged to exchange
long, journal-like letters, which would lead his mother later to complain bitterly that once again her son was not writing to her. He departed Paris on May 12, carrying his bed linen, trunks of clothing, and
letters consigned to his care by Jefferson, Lafayette, and others for
delivery in the United States. There were also two bottles of an
unspecified oil, which Jefferson sent to America in the hope that the
contents might prove advantageous for someone to import.

Young Adams also took with him stern reminders from his parents
that he must now put the seven carefree years abroad behind him and
discover how "I shall be able to get my own living in an honourable
manner." In his diary, Johnny pledged: "I shall depend upon no one."
He consoled himself with the thought that such independence would
remain beyond reach "if I loiter away my precious time in Europe,
and shun going home until I am forced to it." How much of this dutiful sentiment was Johnny's own inclination and how much perhaps a
view imposed by the senior Adamses is unknown. Certainly he put Europe behind him with reluctance.

Once Johnny reached the port of L'Orient, he had to wait until
May 21 for favorable winds. He spent the time at the theater, writing
to Nabby, or looking impatiently for her letters. From Grosvenor
Square, Nabby wrote to her brother, "If I ever take any important step
contrary to your judgment, it will be because you are not present to
give it." These were heartening sentiments for the youth, who passed
his eighteenth birthday at sea. Soon, however, Nabby evidently forgot
her pledge and married her father's secretary, Colonel William

Stephens Smith, a dashing American soldier who had recently been an aide to General George Washington. Smith would soon cause Nabby and eventually all the Adamses much sorrow.

On July 17, 1785, John Quincy Adams disembarked in New York City, then the national capital, where he stayed a month. His personal charm, talent for conversation, and experience as a person who had seen faraway lands stood him in good stead as his company was widely sought. Less experienced youths might have been dazzled by such a reception, but for Johnny there was nothing unusual in being pressed to reside in the home of Richard Henry Lee, the president of Congress. Under the Articles of Confederation, this office made Lee momentarily the nearest thing the new nation had to a chief executive. Young Adams carefully referred to him as "Mr. President," and was on hand to enjoy the grand dinners Lee gave thrice weekly for twenty-five male guests.

From these distinguished gatherings, as well as from friends who invited Johnny to tea, from members of Congress who greeted him, and even from strangers accosting him on the street, came requests for young Adams' opinions on issues of international importance.

To escape such topics, Johnny sought diversion among those young ladies of New York to whom he was introduced. Here he soon found one of the deplorable differences between Europe and America. While he was notably pleased by "the very fine shape" of one local damsel, he was generally disappointed with most of the women he met in New York. He considered them so "affected" that he wondered, "When shall I see a beauty without any conceit?" Did America's young women confuse affectation with grace? he asked. It annoyed Johnny especially when those few females who could speak a bit of French refused to do so with him. But then, to his dismay, he discovered that few Americans of either sex knew any tongue but English.

Hoping for better things, Johnny prepared in mid-August to travel north with a friend from France, Jacques Le Ray de Chaumont, son of Ben Franklin's landlord in Passy. Young Chaumont was touring the United States and, wanting to see the countryside, he proposed to travel by horseback. Agreeing to the plan, Johnny undertook to buy a horse from another acquaintance, Pieter Johan van Berckel, the Dutch ambassador. The diplomat asked fifty pounds for his horse while Johnny offered forty. After much haggling they settled on forty-five, and the journey began on August 13.

The young men had to stop almost immediately when Johnny's

bargain horse began to throw him or simply refused to budge. The animal behaved better en route back to New York when Adams returned to demand his money from van Berckel, who refused, claiming the horse had served him well. Stuck with his purchase, Johnny caught up with Chaumont, and the pair proceeded on a journey that had its comical moments as the travelers coaxed the balky steed to cooperate. "My horse stumbles considerably" was Johnny's understatement of his plight.

There was less humor in the heat, the thunderstorms, the frequent mistakes in routes, and the cramped conditions of the taverns where they took shelter. Johnny considered New York's roads "some of the worst I ever saw," though he later admitted that "I cannot recommend the roads of Massachusetts as a model."

Adams and Chaumont paused at towns along the way to deliver letters entrusted to them. The recipients were friendly and poured much tea for the struggling pair. It seemed to please Johnny that at several taverns he was recognized by virtue of his resemblance to his father, who had become a familiar figure along the route in the days of the Continental Congress. The longest stopover was in New Haven, where Ezra Stiles, president of Yale College, proudly displayed the institution's library, which Johnny told Nabby "is neither as large or as elegant as your Pappa's." Yale's president himself was the greatest curiosity for young Adams, who recalled Jefferson's opinion that Stiles was "an uncommon instance of the deepest learning without a spark of genius."

A more inspiring person was found in Hartford. There Johnny was delighted to find the poet and member of the Connecticut Wits John Trumbull, with whom he could discuss French writers. Gratefully, he accepted a copy of Trumbull's poem *M'Fingal,* a mock epic satirizing British stupidity and published in 1782; the gift prompted him to buy the work of another author, the Reverend Timothy Dwight, who would be Stiles' successor at Yale, and whose *The Conquest of Canaan* was just off the press, making him another leader of the Connecticut Wits, whose aim of celebrating the new nation's literary independence delighted young Adams. Johnny said it was appropriate that he should own the works, for "these are the two pieces in which Americans have endeavored most to soar as high as European bards."

Thus enlightened and with his horse a bit steadier, Adams parted from Chaumont, who proceeded on his western tour. Late at night on August 25, Johnny reached Boston, where he saluted relatives and delivered letters. From there, he proceeded to Cambridge and a visit with brother Charles, now a student at Harvard. Then it was on to Dorchester, where he paused to comfort the gout-stricken John Hancock. Finally, on August 27, he arrived in his hometown village of Braintree.

There he found himself deeply stirred by the reunion with kinfolk and friends. "No person who has not experienced it can conceive how much pleasure there is in returning to our country [meaning Massachusetts] after an absence of six years, especially when it was left at the time of life that I did." Writing to Nabby, Johnny described his meeting with Aunt Mary Cranch's family: "We sat and look'd at one another. . . . How much more expressive this silence than any thing we could have said."

It was Aunt Mary who caught something of the impression made by her nephew. She reported to Abigail Adams how Johnny's relatives were amazed at his "strength of mind" and "soundness of judgment," marvelous in one so young. The aunt also nodded approvingly at Johnny's modesty. "If his application is equal to his abilities, he cannot fail of making a great man."

So towering a figure did young Adams seem to some in Braintree that they tried tactfully to ask just why he had returned to America when he could have remained amid the wonders of Europe. Reporting this to Nabby, Johnny privately acknowledged that he might one day reappear in Europe if he ever became "at a loss about what to do" in the United States.

On August 31, he rode to Cambridge, peered at the few "curiosities" belonging to Harvard, admired the college's collection of portraits by John Singleton Copley, and noted that the library was "good without being magnificent." He then conferred with President Willard in what proved to be a sobering session. Less overwhelmed by young Adams than others had been, that worthy gentleman seemed disposed to dispel any notion that Harvard would be an easy conquest for this celebrated youth. After briefly testing him, Willard pronounced Johnny deficient in Greek and Latin and advised that he study privately during the approaching fall and winter.

The president recommended as tutor Johnny's uncle, the Reverend John Shaw of Haverhill, who was highly regarded for his prowess in preparing lads to enter Harvard. Thereafter, said Willard, Adams could present himself to be tested again for admission and, if successful, he might hope to join the junior class in April 1786 for the remaining three-month term.

This encounter was so humiliating that Johnny made only the

barest mention of it in his diary, leaving Aunt Mary to break the news to Abigail and John that their son was not without shortcomings. A few days after the meeting with Willard, Johnny hitched his horse to the Cranch family chaise and drove with Aunt Mary the considerable distance to Haverhill (pronounced "Hay-vrill") to meet with his uncle.

Compared with tiny Braintree, Haverhill was a bustling place with much river commerce. John Shaw was pastor of the town's Congregational parish. Elizabeth Smith Shaw, his wife, was younger sister to Abigail Adams and Mary Cranch. At first, Uncle John hesitated to tutor his nephew, as much intimidated by young Adams as he was by the unprecedented task of readying someone to enter Harvard's junior class. Eventually, however, he agreed. Johnny faced six months of living and studying with the Shaws.

Before settling into the parsonage, he had three weeks to spend in Braintree. He visited friends and neighbors, walked and went "gunning," read in his father's library, but mostly he moped around. After his chastening by Willard, Johnny's demeanor and outlook began to change as he put behind him the reassuring and comfortable life he had so recently enjoyed in Europe and New York.

Where once he had not worried about responsibility and expenses, seeking only to be an informed conversationalist, a diligent reader, and a critic of theater and concerts, now at Haverhill and Harvard Johnny recognized he must become an apprentice to ordinary life. In Scandinavia and France, his convivial personality was his ticket to success, thanks to a well-placed father. In America, this role fell away, leaving Johnny to create his own place.

No longer luxuriating in being a notable figure in his own right, young Adams now had to prove himself in an alien setting—a prospect that irked him. Here he was, formerly a student of the great professors in Leyden's university, now forced to accept tutoring from a simple village parson. Johnny wondered how many more humiliations he would face as the price of attaining success in America.

FEELING THIS BURDEN, he reappeared in Haverhill at the close of September to begin his studies with Uncle John. Determined to waste no time, he even considered putting aside his diary. Not only would the step save precious moments, he said, but the days ahead "will contain little that even I myself may desire to remember." On second thought, however, he decided to continue, hoping mainly to include more character study and interpretation than mere narrative.

This emphasis, he predicted, would help him toward more mature opinions.

The comely young women of Haverhill quickly became a prominent subject for his diary. Seeing them reminded Johnny that they could be no more than casually within reach until he was able to support a family. It was particularly frustrating to have an attractive woman named Nancy Hazen in the Shaw parsonage. She had been placed there as a boarder after her father died and her mother remarried. Nancy easily captivated the newly arrived Johnny. One day he adored her, the next he could scarcely abide her, all because she would veer from being calm and serious to acting the tease and coquette. Wrote JQA: "I never knew a young lady of whom I thought so differently at different times."

Recognizing that her nephew was in danger of what the young man himself called "a tender passion," his watchful aunt sent Nancy to live in another Haverhill household. Johnny saw her go with mixed feelings, conceding that it was best for her to depart. "When the blood is warm," he warned himself, imprudent choices were made. He must not give his heart exclusively to a woman for another ten years. And it was an experience he professed to anticipate with dread, claiming that to court a woman reduced a male "much below his natural dignity."

This seems a startling statement from a young man who obviously hungered after women. But then JQA would forever be fearful that female power—whether his mother's, his wife's, or eventually that of the feminist movement—would diminish or confine him. Save for the moments when he was painfully in love—and there would be some of these—he was to be, like most other men of his era, a believer in male superiority.

Miss Hazen's brief presence, along with the bustle of parsonage life and the town's social activity, soon forced Johnny to realize that if he were to study at the pace set by Uncle John, he must work late at night. He usually sat down with his books after the household retired and kept his candle burning past midnight, then slept until late morning.

The parsonage's nighttime quiet occasionally lost its soothing effect, depending on what Johnny was studying. In reading Horace and Virgil, he found himself concentrating on their contrasting views of women. Horace, Johnny discovered, overly exalted them, whereas Virgil was very "partial against the female sex." What most troubled the young man was the "gross indecency" in Horace's *Epodes,* a work Adams wished had been destroyed. He turned with relief, he said, to reading the New Testament in Greek.

From the start, the tempo of Johnny's studies did not please him. At the end of 1785, he began what became an annual New Year's Eve ritual, rebuking himself for wasting much time. He did take some comfort in being able to record that "at least I have not to reproach myself with vice." Aunt Elizabeth's report to her sister Abigail on Johnny's habits was less solemn: "Indeed, he searches out knowledge as if it was his meat and drink, and [he] considered it more precious than choice gold."

Elizabeth Shaw was devoted to Johnny, so it must have pained her that there was an aspect of his behavior she could not praise. He held opinions too strongly, she said, for he was always insisting that his views were correct, which meant he usually disagreed with almost everyone. Her nephew "had imbibed some curious notions, and was rather peculiar in some of his opinions and a little too decisive and tenacious of them."

Not even the sympathetic Aunt Elizabeth could fully appreciate how Johnny, once a young man-about-Paris, had to sustain his battered self-esteem after his comeuppance by President Willard at Harvard by ardently fighting for his ideas. The Shaws had been particularly disturbed one evening when, while talking with them, young Adams lost patience with his tutor. The topic of conversation was courtship, an unsettling concern very much on Johnny's mind. He sought to show how coldly realistic he was by contending that "self was the ultimate motive of all action." When Uncle John challenged this, the nephew stood his ground, and when his mentor chided him for being so opinionated, Johnny replied with considerable heat.

Later, in recording the episode for his diary, Johnny regretted not having shown proper reverence for his elder, even if the latter's views were "absurd and ridiculous." Adams said he must adhere to his ideas, although "it has made persons suppose I was obstinate, and dogmatical, and *pedantic*." In one respect, Aunt Elizabeth misread her nephew. Fretting that he seemed unable to relax, she wished he would realize that there was a time to sing and dance; what she didn't see was that, despite his new stuffiness, the young man had not quite lost the capacity to enjoy himself—even if it required that he be a social critic.

Of course Aunt Elizabeth usually did not accompany Johnny out on the town. What he encountered there filled many pages of the diary. He reported how Haverhill's social life involved the upper segment of the citizenry—largely the families of merchants, shippers, lawyers, landholders, and others who could claim notable lineage. These worthy folk, youthful or elderly, entered into almost nightly togetherness, with evenings usually devoted to drinking enormous quantities of tea, along with dancing, songfests, whist parties, and sleighing outings.

Generally, families with larger residences took turns as hosts of parties. Neighbors would gather in the parlor and sit in a circle where the conversation stayed with such safe topics as the weather and who in the town was ill. Typically, Johnny would join in these events and then be highly critical of them in his journal. "The way we have here of killing time in large companies appears to me most absurd and ridiculous," he growled. "All must be fixed down in chairs looking at one another like a puppet show, and talking some commonplace phrases." The conversation was sterile, he claimed, "because the children of ignorance and folly are so much more numerous than those of thought and science." It meant, therefore, that persons who might have offered a worthwhile comment were "by the tyrannical law of custom obliged to talk nonsense."

Not that young Adams was himself free of custom's grip. Though he admitted that he enjoyed the town dances, he was shocked at the open manner in which pregnant women participated. It startled him that such women were fully active in New England society until the time of their confinement—he had not found it so in Europe's best circles. In late February 1786, one Haverhill matron, whom Johnny delicately described as "in that situation," actually alarmed him by her antics on the dance floor. "I feared she would, while she was *throwing* herself about, be taken with a different kind of *throes*."

On the other hand, Johnny applauded the freedom with which youths mingled in New England. Young ladies and gentlemen of Haverhill were often together without the presence of elders. Couples huddled during the long sleighing outings, although, as JQA recalled with amusement years later, these excursions were necessarily chaste, since the participants had to be heavily clad against the cold.

While Johnny was in Haverhill, the town's Baptists undertook to ban dancing on the ground that it had "a dark purpose." Johnny was indignant and rushed to defend the innocence of the practice. Where but at dances could he best view the behavior of the ladies? The Baptist assault was turned back, but not Johnny's interest in the ladies. He grudgingly conceded that even in Haverhill, with its scant choice of attractive young women, he could not help being drawn to the opposite sex. He went so far as to report in his diary that several times he had withdrawn from "a passion which I could not indulge, and which would have made me miserable had I not overcome it."

To avoid these frustrations, he tried concentrating on women's shortcomings. A diary entry of January 13, 1786, complained: "Most of our damsels are like portraits in crayons, which at a distance look well, but if you approach near them, are vile daubings." He was grateful, he said, for the few exceptions, since they kept him from having to decide whether "to hate, despise, or pity" all women.

Once, for reasons unknown, Johnny read some of his observations about women to his cousin Betsy Cranch. She later reported in her own journal: "He is monstrously severe with the follies of mankind, upon our sex particularly, but tis only our follies he condemns." When Johnny shared his opinion of women with Nabby, his usually admiring sister challenged his views: "A gentleman who is severe against the ladies is also upon every principle impolitic. His character is soon established for a morose, severe, ill-natured fellow, and upon my word I think it is the most convincing proof that he can give that he feels their power's importance and superiority."

It was a discerning letter, for it went to the center of Johnny's apprehension about women. But if he ever responded to Nabby's words, his reply has vanished. Soon afterward, however, he had little time to evaluate the ladies. Word reached the Shaw parsonage on February 16 that if Johnny hoped to join the junior class at Harvard, he must do so in mid-March, when a series of lectures would begin a month earlier than scheduled. Not disguising his eagerness, Adams redoubled his efforts. On March 14, after a round of farewell visits in Haverhill, he hastened toward Cambridge on roads muddied by the spring thaw. His examination for admission was set for the next day.

AT MID-MORNING, Johnny appeared before a committee consisting of Harvard's entire faculty: President Willard, three professors, four tutors, and the librarian. They first questioned him concerning the Latin of Horace, followed by the Greek of Homer. Next was logic, and then inquiries about Locke's writings—"very few of which I was able to answer." Finally, the faculty turned to geography and mathematics, after which Willard led the candidate into another room and asked him to convert a statement from English into Latin. It was an edifying paragraph but too familiar: it warned of giving an air of importance to contemptible amusements.

When Johnny had finished the translation, the president took it into seclusion with the faculty. After fifteen minutes, he emerged to announce, "You are admitted, Adams," and gave him the necessary papers to carry to the registrar. The rest of the day Johnny spent getting settled, during which he watched members of the sophomore class erupt into a drunken spree, breaking windows in the rooms occupied by tutors. "After this sublime maneuver," Johnny recorded, "[they] stagger'd to their chambers. Such are the great achievements of many of the sons of Harvard."

Taking stock of these new classmates, Johnny decided that when he was first tested for admission, he had been at least as prepared as any other student. What Harvard had failed to recognize, he assured himself, was that his reading had been different from that done by most entrants.

News of his son's admission was greeted with joy by John Adams, who wrote from London to express delight that Johnny was now a student in "our dear Alma Mater." Reminding the youth that Harvard was a breeding ground for statesmen, the father besought him to breathe deeply the "atmosphere of science and literature" and to "take care to do nothing now which you will in any future period have reason to recollect with shame or pain."

As for Abigail, even though Cambridge was not an evil Paris or London but was set in semi-rural Massachusetts, she wrote to remind Johnny that "chastity, modesty, decency, and conjugal faith are the pillars of society." If these were sapped, "the whole fabrick falls sooner or later." Abigail did not attempt to disguise her continuing dismay that Johnny was still writing regularly to sister Nabby and "not a line for Mamma!"

Mother Adams would not have been pleased had she known that, during the fifteen months he spent at Harvard, Johnny's diary would tolerantly describe many student revels. Although he was hardly a roisterer, young Adams clearly enjoyed nearly every other extracurricular aspect of college existence. What annoyed him about Harvard was the faculty, whom he tried to shrug off as deplorable impedimenta to serious study. The haughty airs of these instructors were for him the institution's greatest vexation and "hard for me to submit to."

Even so, Johnny admitted that being obliged to defer to such inferior minds might be beneficial, for the experience could "mortify my vanity." Nothing was more likely to teach "humility," he said, "than to see myself subjected to the commands of a person that I must despise." Nevertheless, he always recalled his residence at Harvard as one of his life's happiest intervals, a time when he could grow intellectually.

Subjects favored by Johnny were mathematics and science, especially astronomy, and he considered algebra to be "as entertaining as it is useful." In addition to lectures, each day's routine included reading, writing, daydreaming, talking to compatible classmates, and even playing the flute. After purchasing that instrument, Johnny studied music and joined Harvard's Handel Sodality, a group of players who, Adams acknowledged, had trouble staying in tune.

Like other students, of course, Johnny had certain weaknesses. For instance, a tendency to sleep late occasionally prevented his hearing the bell for prayers, so that he was fined for absences from these solemn moments. He was known to miss lectures and recitations, sometimes because fine weather drew him and his friends into long walks. On one occasion, he skipped two lectures and went fishing. He was also seen out late, as when, after a dancing party with Cambridge girls, he got to his room at 4 a.m. and slept until early afternoon. The bookish side of the young scholar obliged him to concede one drawback to dancing: "when the feet are so much engaged, the head in general is vacant."

Johnny was fortunate in his first roommate, Henry Ware, with whom he shared quarters in Hollis Hall that afforded a handsome glimpse of Boston in the distance. A recent graduate now reading theology, Ware possessed the sort of vigorous, independent mind that Johnny admired. With views already steering toward Unitarianism, Ware would be elected Harvard's Hollis Professor of Divinity in 1805 amid controversy. After Ware's departure, Johnny moved into inferior quarters in the hall with his brother Charles, by then a sophomore, while brother Thomas, now a freshman, lived nearby.

From London came parental orders that Johnny be watchful over his younger brothers. Because the trio ran with different crowds, they managed to get on quite well. They were together mostly only when they went for holidays to Braintree, where they stayed with Aunt and Uncle Cranch, sharing one room. Still in the habit of studying late, Johnny preferred to sleep well into the morning. Charles and Thomas would not permit the luxury and created a great racket as they pulled the bedclothes off the protesting Johnny. Aunt Mary tried to be amused by the noise the Harvard scholars made.

The three brought enormous appetites from Cambridge, so that, with much apology, Mary was obliged to ask Abigail for ten shillings per week for their board. Since Harvard was liberal in scheduling vacation time, the boys frequently had the opportunity to be in Braintree. Johnny, however, soon went down less often than his brothers. He was so fond of the reading and fun that came with remaining in Cambridge that he became bored with holidays spent in rustic Braintree, which afforded "a dull life, and convinces me how grossly the whole herd of novel and romantic writers err in trumping up a country life." A rural setting so enervated the mental powers, Johnny felt, that he feared those caught in it would be brought near the level of animals.

Part of Cambridge's appeal was that, after many years spent abroad in the presence of renowned elders, at Harvard Johnny had the company of individuals his age and with interests and aspirations much like his. The other students made Adams feel welcome, recognizing his ability by electing him to Phi Beta Kappa. His room became a gathering place where friends could talk and drink tea, and he soon was reading essays before the A.B. Club, a society devoted to literary study.

Aunt Mary could not disguise her pleased surprise when, after a visit to Cambridge, she wrote to Abigail of finding Johnny a charming and popular fellow. And indeed, much of his appealing style in Europe seemed now to have revived. His diary was filled with such entries as "the tea club were at my chamber. . . . We had a supper and spent the evening in Freeman's chamber." He even dropped his guard ever so slightly against the wiles of women.

Johnny's favorite companion was James Bridge, a student from Maine. The two hit it off personally and intellectually, Johnny acknowledging that "with no one have I contracted since I entered the university so great a degree of intimacy." The pair often talked until after midnight, for Bridge was enthusiastic about planning a career as a lawyer, which gave Adams some assurance about what seemed to be his own professional fate. The two hoped eventually to establish a practice together. When Bridge chose not to go home during Harvard's Christmas vacation in 1786–87, Adams decided to do the same. His most enjoyable weeks at Harvard ensued.

The holiday began on December 13 and extended for nearly two months—twice the usual time, because of a crisis caused by weather. Firewood had become scarce and costly as a result of heavy snows that kept timber cutters from getting into the forests. Although Johnny was awarded the care of college buildings during this interval, the burden was light because the halls were shut. Therefore, he and Bridge boarded in the home of Professor Edward Wigglesworth, whose daughter Peggy was one of Johnny's favorites in Cambridge.

While his avowed purpose in staying away from Braintree over Christmas was to study, Johnny reported plenty of time for visiting. He turned up frequently at the parsonage of the Reverend Timothy Hilliard, where he could observe that the pastor's "daughter look'd prettier than she ever did before." Then there was the Cambridge residence of his companion in the St. Petersburg adventure, Francis Dana, now a judge and infirm as a result of a stroke. One of the pleasures of teas and dining at Dana's home was a chance for Johnny to talk with Almy Ellery, "who has a larger share of sense than commonly falls to an individual of her sex." Miss Ellery intrigued Johnny during one rainy Sunday evening by calling him "vapourish," a seventeenth-century word for a fanciful or "frothy" mood.

This routine of reading and visiting so delighted him that he complained: "Our time flies extremely fast. One half of the vacation has already eloped, and I shall soon, with a mixture of pleasure and pain, see my fellow students assembled, and be called again to attend to the public exercises." For a change, he had no need to berate himself for accomplishing little during a holiday. Instead, he was pleased particularly by reading Montesquieu's *The Spirit of Laws* and Thomas Sheridan's *A Course of Lectures on Elocution*.

When the relentless snowfalls finally abated, allowing students to struggle back, Bridge and Adams resumed participation in one of their supreme collegiate delights: reading essays before the A.B. Club. It was from here that Johnny drew the most profit for his future career. His presentations obliged him to think and write carefully about moral, social, and political issues.

He did the same in talks before meetings of Phi Beta Kappa. Among his topics: "Nothing is so difficult, but it may be overcome by industry." Others included the origin of ideas, the benefit of Christianity to temporality, and that inevitable subject of interest, women. In one lecture, he invited his colleagues in Phi Beta Kappa to consider "Whether love or fortune ought to be the chief inducement to marriage." Adams argued on behalf of fortune, claiming that the best basis for marriage was mutual esteem and enduring reason. He dismissed passion because it was soon "satiated by enjoyment." If mere physical desire bound a marital union, he warned that soon "discord introduces herself into the family, and the astonished couple find themselves chain'd to eternal strife." He called for all marriages to be based "upon reason."

Three months later, Adams again had the attention of Phi Beta Kappa when he argued that since a woman was useful only when married, single females should be permitted to make overtures to men whom they found attractive. In short, a woman should be able to initiate courtship without demeaning her reputation for chastity.

These views may not have been in earnest, but they helped make

Johnny what Aunt Mary Cranch called "quite a gallant among the ladies." Many Cambridge, Boston, and Braintree belles now began to appear in his collegiate diary, along with his speculations concerning each. For instance, to honor the silent, beautiful Hannah Miller of Braintree, Johnny composed this ditty:

> *Her face is as white as the snow,*
> *And her bosom is doubtless as cold.*

Of Catherine Jones, whom he came to know at gatherings in Judge Dana's home, Johnny observed: "Her shape is not inelegant, but her limbs are rather large. She is susceptible of the tender sentiments, but the passion rather than the lover is the object of her affection." He was fond of noting how, when young ladies and gentlemen sat together in parlors, the conversation invariably shifted from scattered topics to "love," a subject he claimed was always brought up by the females.

He admitted to being intrigued by the mysterious process that led some females into marriage and others not, as well as by the visible effect that matrimony had upon the demeanor of those who did marry. Why, he wondered, did "some girls, without either fortune, beauty, or any amiable qualities have a talent in engaging a man's affections" while others, "with every qualification," become old maids?

These studies of the opposite sex gave way with the approach of Johnny's graduation ceremonies, and with them the close of his brief sojourn in college. Harvard's commencement exercises, always a major social and political event for Boston, occurred in 1787 between July 16 and 20. Rather than relish thoughts of these great days, as most students did, Johnny professed to shrink from the moment.

Unlike most American males about to graduate from college, Johnny did not see himself as standing on the threshold of life. Already he had completed one career—admittedly a brief one—as an international traveler, an achievement that had made him a celebrity. Now, seeing that he must begin competing for his bread, Johnny complained that he was starting a second life at a disadvantage. While his friends might seem satisfied with the workaday world, Adams saw it as a dismal place compared with the pleasures of his intellectual life in Europe and at Harvard. In these he had been a success, but now he must grub for sustenance. "The hurry of affairs" repelled him, Johnny said.

What heightened young Adams' misgivings was that neither he

nor his parents could foresee for him any calling except the law. Here he would have to be in the shadow of his father's notable success as an attorney. Just as distressing for Johnny was the knowledge that John and Abigail Adams fancied he would become a leader in public service like his father. This was particularly intimidating for Johnny because of the unsettled state of national affairs.

AT THE TIME of Harvard's 1787 commencement, the Congress of the United States, operating under the severe restrictions contained in the Articles of Confederation (the national constitution until 1788), seemed unable to cope with the young republic's growth. This was especially apparent in interstate and foreign commerce. The national economy had become sorely depressed. The previous autumn, farmers in western Massachusetts had sought relief from their debts by openly rebelling.

This so-called Shays' Rebellion was put down in February 1787, but not before it and the uneasiness prevailing in other states had led in May to the calling of a constitutional convention in Philadelphia, whose purpose was to create a more effective federal government. The shadow of Shays' Rebellion and the uncertainties being discussed in Philadelphia were unsettling as Johnny entered the commencement season.

HE MADE TWO public presentations during that time. The first was a spirited defense of the legal profession when he spoke at Harvard's spring exhibition of student achievement on April 10. He proposed that lawyers not be blamed for the recent Shays episode. According to young Adams, the profession was not to be judged "by the short lived frenzy of an inconsiderate multitude" displaying "the errors, the infirmities, and the vices of mankind."

Suggestive as this oration was, it was less helpful to Johnny's career than the speech he gave during the graduation exercise on July 18. His topic was especially relevant to the hazardous times: "Upon the importance and necessity of public faith to the well-being of a community." President Willard had given it to him some weeks before when parts for the ceremonies were awarded.

Commencement Day began at 11 a.m. with a series of declamations, which lasted until 3 p.m. Preceding Adams' appearance were several "forensic disputations," some in Latin, some in English; a poem in English; and a salutatory oration in Latin. The subjects were imposing, including "Whether thought be the essence of the soul?" and "Whether any man be so depraved as to have left all sense of virtue?"

Then Johnny spoke, and with a result that satisfied even him. After the conventional professions of inadequacy and fright, he proceeded cogently to explain why, in the current national crisis, citizens must see to the restoration of America's financial probity if the Union was to be respected at home and abroad. His closing statement caught the tone of the oration: "May national honour and integrity distinguish the American commonwealths till the last trump shall announce the dissolution of the world, and the whole frame of nature shall be consumed in one universal conflagration."

After this stirring performance, Johnny acknowledged that he was "complimented and flattered on every side." His aunts Elizabeth and Mary sent enthusiastic reports to John and Abigail about their son's triumph. Elizabeth assured them: "Upon my word, I know not a likelier youth." Henry Knox, the secretary of war, told a friend that young Adams had distinguished himself by a "manly" oration. Another admirer in the audience was Jeremy Belknap, clergyman and historian, who asked permission to publish the address in a Philadelphia periodical, *Columbian Magazine;* it appeared in the September issue.

Once the student orators had finished, dinner was served, after which the governor, faculty, scholars, and audience moved, at 5 p.m., to the conferring of degrees. John Quincy Adams graduated second out of a class of fifty-one. Afterward, students and their families welcomed guests to social gatherings that went on until 9 p.m., a custom Johnny's relatives followed, thanks to the hard work of Aunt Mary Cranch.

She had rented two of the largest rooms in Cambridge, hoping these would contain the crowd, but it was still a squeeze. One hundred guests, including the governor and lieutenant governor, sat down to Aunt Mary's food, featuring roast chicken, a rump of beef, a leg of pork, and tongue. After dinner, wine and cake were served to four hundred more persons who dropped by at intervals.

Eventually, the celebration ended and quiet settled on Harvard and on Cambridge itself. Johnny admitted his relief that it was all over. "One such day every year would ruin me," he said. Even though his oration and the other events had pleased him, he concluded that public commencements did more harm than good, serving mostly as "a gratification of vanity."

Now the graduate faced what he dreaded, the world of affairs, prefaced by "three long years" of legal study, after which he foresaw his prospects as barely improved. And all the while he knew his parents would be clamoring for him to become independent and prominent. Despite this discouraging prospect, he saw no choice but to "plod along mechanically . . . before I really get into the world." Could he possibly have the patience? he wondered. "I sicken at the very idea."

No LONGER JOHNNY but now John, Adams began the life of a Harvard graduate by quoting from the Book of Ecclesiastes: "Vanity! Vanity! all is vanity and vexation of spirit." Little that he experienced during the next seven years brought him a more optimistic outlook.

CHAPTER THREE

Misery

*God of Heavens! if these are the only terms on which life can be granted
to me, oh take me from this world before I curse the day of my birth.*

THE SUMMER HAD TURNED downright chilly as John Quincy
Adams rode away from Harvard on July 20, 1787, college behind him.
Claiming to be "pretty much fatigued," he welcomed a holiday with
Aunt and Uncle Cranch in Braintree. That vacation, however, could
hardly be relaxing for a person who kept thinking of how he must now
be pitted against the world.

It might have cheered young Adams had he known that Harvard's
president, Joseph Willard, was sending congratulations to John and
Abigail Adams upon their son's collegiate attainments. "His attention
to his studies, proficiency in literature, strict conformity to the rules of
the University, and purity of morals have gained him the high esteem
of the governors of this society, and indeed of all his acquaintances."
Then Willard added words that seemed to endorse the parents' hope:
"I think he bids fair to become a distinguished character."

In Braintree, however, such a prospect seemed remote as a gloomy
son prepared for legal study, the route his parents insisted he follow. So
eager were they for their oldest son to be self-supporting that John
Adams had considered returning from England to train his son. The
family decided, however, that JQA would become sufficiently well prepared under the guidance of Theophilus Parsons, one of New England's ablest attorneys and a future chief justice of the Supreme Court
of Massachusetts.

A member of Harvard's class of 1769, Parsons was renowned as a law teacher. Usually, several young men were gathered around him as they underwent the three years of reading and discussion prescribed for admission to the bar. Each student paid the mentor an honorarium. Parsons practiced and taught law in Newburyport, a town situated at the mouth of the Merrimack River, about forty miles northeast of Boston and fourteen miles from Haverhill. After accepting Adams as a student, Parsons invited him to arrive in Newburyport no later than mid-September.

Adams did not wait until the last moment to visit the town, which he had never seen. Unfortunately, his trip in early August revealed little about the community that he could find desirable. It was a small seaport with a population of around five thousand. By comparison, Boston numbered eighteen thousand persons. Nor were his spirits boosted when he learned that there might be as many as six students crowded around Theophilus Parsons' table in a small office.

After arranging to rent a room in the quiet Newburyport home of a widow lady, Adams hurried to Haverhill for a visit with Aunt and Uncle Shaw. Here nothing much relieved his glum mood. Even a usually prized invitation to dine at Judge Nathaniel Sargeant's home was disappointing. The occasion was marred when the judge's daughter arrived with her six-week-old baby—which the impatient Adams reported had to be "handed about from one to another, and very shrewd discoveries were made of its resemblance to all the family by turns."

Grumbling about having to see an evening lost to "a misshaped, bawling, slobbering infant," Adams returned to Braintree, where he spent a few more days of vacation. He managed to use some of the time for reading his friend Thomas Jefferson's recently published *Notes on the State of Virginia* and praised it for displaying "learning without ostentation." Nothing much else was accomplished, however, since Adams found himself so drowsy that he often napped away the afternoons, waking with a start from strange dreams that, unfortunately, he failed to record. "I cannot imagine where my imagination ransack'd the ideas which prevailed . . . in my mind. This part of the action of the human soul is yet to be accounted for."

While John might keep the contents of his dreams from his journal, he could not hide his despair from the eye of his astute Aunt Mary. She was astonished that her nephew, who had roamed all over the world, should be downcast at the prospect of going to Newburyport. Describing to Abigail what happened when he departed, Mary said the young man had blurted out that Newburyport was a place "where he cared for nobody and nobody cared for him." According to Aunt Mary: "Dear youth, he found it necessary to draw the back of his hand across his eyes when he said it." This tearful gesture said more than many words could about John's shaken state as he faced an inelegant, workaday world.

On his way to Newburyport, he could not resist stopping once more at Harvard, where his unhappiness grew worse. "An involuntary sigh arose in my breast," he acknowledged, as he looked again at all he must miss, especially "the pleasures of conviviality." Adams remained in Cambridge for a few days, persuading himself that he must be present for a Phi Beta Kappa society meeting, which included orations, a fine dinner, and election of some new members—activities he particularly relished.

Finally, he could tarry no longer, so after pausing in Boston to observe what actually went on in courts of law, John arose at 3 a.m. on September 7 and boarded the stage for a twelve-hour ride to Newburyport, where he presented himself promptly at Parsons' office. He was slightly encouraged when he met some of those who would be studying law with him. All were known to him from his Harvard days: Horatio Townsend, Thomas W. Thompson, Moses Little, William Amory, and Samuel Putnam. Having them nearby would enliven Adams' stay in Newburyport, although for the first few nights he found himself going to bed early from boredom.

Much as he enjoyed being a scholar, standing at the threshold of legal training hardly inspired Adams. He faced three years of reading and reflection about the law in a cramped office overflowing with Theophilus Parsons' clients and friends. Thoughtful study was often nearly impossible. And yet Parsons urged his apprentices to read for twelve hours daily. When Adams complained about time lost as a result of noisy visitors in the office, Parsons insisted that he disregard all distractions when reading—"a direction with which I believe I shall never be able to comply," Adams wrote. When he sought quiet by remaining in the office after it closed for the day, he was often driven out by the cold, the thrifty Parsons having decreed that there be no fire in his chambers after he himself had departed.

Slowly, John drudged through tomes penned by such deities of Anglo-American law as Sir Edward Coke and Sir William Blackstone. He found Coke's writing in his *Reports* and *Institutes* to be "heaped up in such an incoherent mass that I have derived very little benefit from it." While he had high praise for Blackstone's *Commentaries on the Laws of*

England, Adams took more value and pleasure from other reading assignments, particularly David Hume's *History of England* and Edward Gibbon's *History of the Decline and Fall of the Roman Empire.* On his own, he explored Jean-Jacques Rousseau's *Confessions,* which immediately struck him as "the most extraordinary book I ever read in my life."

Mostly, he and his colleagues worked independently, for even the persistent Adams found it difficult to gain the attention of a very busy mentor. Parsons was frequently away for weeks at a time, traveling the judicial circuit or involved in the debate over ratifying the proposed federal constitution, so he left his scholars to read along lines he had advised. There were sessions when Parsons talked to his flock, a cud of tobacco in his mouth, but for Adams there seemed never enough opportunity for inquiry. It worried him that he had "a thousand questions" remaining to put to Parsons, predicting there would be "the de--l" to pay "if I have not some stock of law."

Consequently, his first year of legal study left him dissatisfied with his progress. Mainly, this was because he found it difficult to concentrate. He wished he could read "one book at a time, but I never can. If a book does not interest me exceedingly, it is a task to me to go through it." What did this weakness imply? he wondered. "Indolence, indolence, I fear, will be my ruin." For a time he blamed an irregular schedule and made fresh resolves "to be periodical" in his habits. "If this will not do, I can only submit to my fate."

When he finally got around to writing to his mother, John admitted he now often wished he had chosen another career, but he announced, "I am determined not to despond." Fortunately, he had the lively company of his fellow students to divert him. Having enjoyed the revels at Harvard, it was natural that Adams joined in the good times around Newburyport and Haverhill. He justified this by saying: "Dissipation is so fashionable here that it is necessary to enter into it a little in order not to appear too singular."

He proved a success as one of the regular fellows, so that his diary contains many descriptions of "frolicks." The first of these took place at dinner one Saturday evening soon after he reached Newburyport. When he and his friends began to sing, "the bottle went round with an unusual rapidity, until a round dozen had disappeared." After getting to bed early in the morning, John awoke with a "very disagreeable head-ache." Although he stoutly insisted he had not been intoxicated, he was unable to attend church and could not muster the strength to read or write. On Monday, he was still suffering.

For a time thereafter, Adams sought greater self-control. When he went to Haverhill to help celebrate the marriage of his cousin and friend John Thaxter, many bottles again were passed along the table, but this time JQA got away a bit sooner in order to take a walk and breathe in the fresh air. He also emerged in better shape after he attended his first dance in Newburyport. While seven young men "got rather over the bay," Adams claimed he was not one of them—even if "the clock struck four just before we went to bed."

A few weeks later, he again fell from grace. After he joined twelve other men and fifteen women in dancing until 5 a.m., Adams was "incapable of doing anything" the next day. That evening, when he and his chums assembled to play violins and flutes, they soon gave up to exhaustion. He admitted he was in bed by 9 p.m.

A social existence of such demanding proportions was prompted by a club John and his Newburyport friends formed. The group met often, usually by turn in the rooms of the members. Conversation frequently was the rule; at other times the fiddlers and flutists took over. Once the talk or the music had worn out, club members became as active as weather conditions and the state of their endurance permitted, as when, just before midnight on a May evening, the group—Adams with flute in hand—"sallied forth upon a scheme of serenading. We paraded around the town till almost four in the morning." Only a steady rain forced them off the streets, and the citizens could get some rest. The next morning brought a now familiar wail from young Adams: "Unfit for almost every thing."

If the club helped make life in Newburyport bearable for him, so did the presence of a few remarkably attractive women. Sarah Wigglesworth owned "a shape admirably proportioned." Even more memorable was his unnamed partner at whist one evening: "Soon after we sat down she complained that her gloves pinched her arm excessively; and with some difficulty pulling one of them off, she exhibited an arm, the beautiful contour and snowy whiteness of which might fire the imagination of a sensual voluptuary." Alas for Adams, "I unfortunately did not think of admiring [it] till it was too late."

He did more than study women from a distance, though. He seemed to make good progress in overcoming the standoffishness he had earlier felt toward American females. Now he sought their company at dances, church services, and dinners, as well as at sleighing parties, which often took a group into the countryside, where they would dance at a tavern until early morning. One such excursion briefly proved promising when Adams found himself enjoying the companionship of a Miss Fletcher, "who had what is called a very genteel figure." It was disappointing when he found she was already in love. Next was Miss Elizabeth Coates, who he assured his diary was *not* in love and who was "quite sociable." She could make "agreeable" conversation, certainly a valued attribute in John's judgment. He also appreciated her other virtues: she was "an only daughter and her father has money." Once again, however, the young lady proved to be engaged.

When the young people in Adams' circle were not sleighing or dancing, apparently they played what he called "kissing games." Participation did not always go well for him. An occasion in January 1788 left him scolding: "Tis a profanation of one of the most endearing demonstrations of love. A kiss unless warm'd by sentiment and enlivened by affection may just as well be given to the air." He claimed to be much relieved the next evening when he and a group of male friends gathered to sing "good, jovial, expressive songs such as we sang at College." One such gathering, he said, "gives me more real satisfaction than fifty pass'd in a company of girls."

While he seemed to be finding women ever more physically appealing, nothing in Adams' Newburyport experience altered his opinion that they were far inferior to males. He expressed severe assessments, sometimes earnestly, occasionally sardonically, and at other moments poetically. Because he was suffering doubts about himself and his future, Adams may have felt strengthened by demeaning the character and behavior of women. "It requires a much longer acquaintance to form a just opinion of a man than of a woman. The distinguishing traits [of males] are deeper and much more numerous."

This comforting condescension kept John working on what became his first serious poetic effort. Finished in 1790 and entitled "A Vision," it was a satirical portrait of nine young women. When it was ultimately published in 1839, about fifty years later, an elderly John Quincy Adams called it his best poem—but then he would say this about other poems as well. Something of this one's flavor can be caught in lines describing Rebecca Cazneau, who, like many Newburyport women, could rouse JQA's sarcasm:

> *Around her face no wanton Cupids play,*
> *Her tawny skin defies the God of Day.*
> *Loud was her laugh, undaunted was her look,*
> *And folly seem'd to dictate what she spoke.*

These excursions into verse were an outlet for Adams' growing frustration with himself and his mission in Newburyport. The more time he gave to legal tomes, the more he seemed to realize that for him such a direction led to misery and that in his heart he aspired to a literary career. He made the point clearly in his diary: "Such a superiority do the pursuits of literature possess above every other occupation that even he who attains but a mediocrity in them merits the preeminence above those that excel the most in the common and vulgar professions."

Adams craved to be one of those "who can invent, who can create." He wished to escape "commonplace thoughts." This was not an immature or temporary ambition. From Newburyport days to the time he died, JQA ached to give posterity a noble literary creation. Even while reading law he did not fail for lack of trying. "I have begun I suppose a hundred times to write poetry. I have tried every measure and every kind of strophe."

THWARTED IN THESE YEARNINGS, Adams decided after a year of legal study to have a holiday in the summer of 1788, hoping "the change may be for the better." When he heard that his parents had returned to America in early June, he set out to spend five weeks in Braintree. During this time, his journal was drab, recording little more than daily domestic events—notably "gunning" outings, endless visits with kinfolk, and helping to unpack the many books John Adams had brought with him from Europe. Even his twenty-first birthday seemed no reason to celebrate as he became increasingly depressed. Listening to his parents express concerns about him kept JQA painfully aware that he was still "in a state of dependence."

Back in Newburyport, his melancholy persisted, although it did not prevent his acceptance of an invitation from Harvard's chapter of Phi Beta Kappa to deliver its anniversary oration in September. His agreement to speak was encouraged by James Bridge, his favorite companion in their Harvard class, who had arrived in Newburyport to study with Theophilus Parsons. After Adams and Bridge arranged to room together, the latter accompanied John to Cambridge for the oration.

Without his best friend at his side, Adams might have been unable to deliver the address, so disabling now was his depression. Somehow he managed to read his thirty-minute remarks before an unusually large attendance, including Governor John Hancock.

The oration featured two yearnings—to be a literary giant and a great statesman—that would leave Adams no peace throughout his life. While his words may have sounded unrealistic and immature, they were heartfelt as he praised people who sought to produce intellectual achievements of eternal greatness as well as those who aspired to be world leaders. He called a career devoted to letters and science "the most honourable avenue to the temple of Fame." Then Adams blessed his own hopes: "To you therefore who are conscious of possessing the divine spark of transcendent genius, suffer me to express my ardent desire that you may cherish the generous flame."

His talk concluded, Adams lost his struggle against melancholy and sank into full-fledged clinical depression, a condition that recurred occasionally throughout his life. Without the benefit of medication or psychiatric therapy, unavailable in his day, the impact of this affliction upon his personality and career was profound.

Quite possibly, this depressive illness was the familiar sort that grew from perfectionist expectations. At intervals, JQA's diary would be filled with self-reproach for falling short—far short—of the social, intellectual, and political goals he had set for himself. Today, psychiatrists call the condition "self-critical depression." Ultimately, depression is mediated by the brain, where chemicals such as an amine called serotonin evidently have much to do with maintaining an individual's self-esteem in the face of life's tribulations. In persons such as Adams, who think they are failing, or in those who actually are failing, serotonin levels may drop, and depression becomes likely.

Nowadays, medications can artificially boost the level of serotonin. If, however, a depressed state lasts a long time, it apparently alters the brain chemistry, leaving the victim more vulnerable to a recurrence. With each episode the weakness grows, and eventually depressions may arise spontaneously, with no precipitant at all. Ultimately, this would be the case with John Quincy Adams. In someone with such fearfully high expectations of himself, self-esteem was all too easily eroded, a sense of failure all too easily aroused. After the Phi Beta Kappa oration, he left Harvard showing the depressive symptoms that would become so commonplace in late-twentieth-century American society: hopelessness, anxiety, a sense of worthlessness, self-reproach, sleeplessness.

With Adams, as with most victims, this condition did not begin suddenly. He had first experienced symptoms a year earlier, when he noted: "I felt a depression of spirits to which I have hitherto been entirely a stranger." It was a mood much different from any he had known before, he said, explaining that it was far worse than merely being "low spirited." Wondering what might happen if he could not shake his melancholy, he seized an extreme conclusion, predicting that he would become "an object of charity, or at least of pity." By the autumn of 1788, the gravity of Adams' state was heard in his cry: "God of Heavens! . . . take me from this world before I curse the day of my birth."

Understanding that he needed help in this crisis, he turned in mid-September to his gentle, sympathetic Aunt Elizabeth Shaw in Haverhill. When he arrived, Elizabeth saw at once that she must first relieve his sleep deprivation. Her remedy was a "mug of valerian tea" (made from a root often employed in those days as a nerve sedative) and then bed. Thereafter, her healing potions were mainly much rest and sleep, along with doses of "bark," the name given at the time to quinine derived from the cinchona tree.

John was a very good patient. His aunt acclaimed him "the best man to take his medicine that I ever saw. He hardly makes a wry mouth." Indeed, "he thinks he is half-cured because he has got somebody to care for him." As for the cause of her nephew's malady, Elizabeth had an astute diagnosis: his condition stemmed from an obsessive need to succeed. "He is so avaricious in courting the best gifts that I fear such intense application will injure his health more than he is aware of." Not until John had been able to sleep for three consecutive nights was Elizabeth cautiously encouraged.

Recognizing the serious nature of her patient's condition, Elizabeth sent word to Abigail Adams that John was "unwell." He had arrived in Haverhill "to experience a little of my maternal love," Elizabeth pointedly remarked. Since she knew that the young man's serious symptoms had appeared after a visit to his mother, Elizabeth asked: "What did you do to him?" Could Abigail have told him "some *woeful story*"? Elizabeth was well aware of the strain between her nephew and her sister. Indeed, when her own son Billy Shaw left home, Elizabeth begged him not to throw her letters away, "as your cousin John used to his mother's."

Perhaps encouraged to do so by Aunt Elizabeth, John wrote a brief note to Abigail from Haverhill. He reported that "my nerves have been disordered" and that he was being soothed by his aunt. He then cited lines from Shakespeare that evidently had much meaning for him at the time, for he also copied them elsewhere. The quotation (from *Henry IV, Part II,* Act III) needed no comment from a young man who yearned to escape what he feared was a hopeless life.

> *O gentle sleep,*
> *Nature's soft nurse, how have I frighted thee*
> *That thou no more wilt weigh mine eyelids down*
> *And steep my senses in forgetfulness?*

Over his aunt's protests, John returned to Newburyport on October 1. He quickly discovered that Elizabeth had been correct—he was still ill: "I cannot possibly attend at all to study." No alternative remained but to go to Braintree for relief. Learning of this intent, Elizabeth sent a letter ahead to Abigail, warning that she had been sparing the Adamses the truth: John was much sicker and with more alarming symptoms than she had earlier intimated. Saying that she remained "very uneasy" about her nephew, Elizabeth urged that the patient's diet and exercise be carefully supervised, and that "study most certainly be laid aside for the present."

And so, with only a trip to Haverhill at Christmas, John recuperated in Braintree from early October 1788 until the end of March 1789. During much of that time, Abigail Adams vanished from the scene, perhaps unwilling to watch her eldest son sit incapacitated while her hopes dwindled that he would glorify her name. Instead, she chose to visit daughter Nabby and her growing family, now living in New York. Upon hearing this, Elizabeth Shaw was indignant, confiding to sister Mary Cranch: "I should not have thought his mother would have left him." How the son interpreted his parent's absence is unknown, for after a brief entry on October 14, 1788, John's journal remained largely silent for five years.

Only the daily lines of six to ten words in an almanac which he kept instead of a diary, along with a scattering of letters, suggest what was happening while his health mended. There are indications that even during the most acute phases of his illness, Adams tried to keep active—reading, riding, shooting fowl, visiting relatives, and even observing court sessions in Boston. All the while, he strove against sleeplessness and gloom, reaching moments when he felt somewhat encouraged, only to relapse for a time.

With the arrival of spring in 1789, Adams decided he was strong enough to make another try at his legal studies. Returning to Newburyport in April, he reopened his books in Theophilus Parsons' office and sought the fellowship of friends, male and female. Long walks and playing the flute began to have their former appeal, but the most effective treatment for his lingering melancholy began when he found himself in love with a beautiful teenager named Mary Frazier.

THE ROMANCE, begun two months after Adams reappeared in town, was the first of his life's two great passions. Whereas much is known concerning the second, which led to his marriage in England in 1797, the love affair in Newburyport remains a shadowy story. One reason is Adams' disregard of his diary at the time. Another explanation is that he seemed deliberately close-mouthed about the romance, so much so that he was very slow to report it to family members and kept even his best friend and roommate, James Bridge, in the dark.

Adams' reticence may have sprung partly from embarrassment. After graduating from Harvard, he had spoken often about love and marriage as being far in the future for him. Furthermore, he had gained notoriety in Newburyport for his openly condescending attitude toward females. Now, aged twenty-two and reputed to be a scorner of women, he may have so surprised himself by his sudden reversal of form that he shrank from astonishing or amusing his friends by notifying them that he had fallen in love.

The Mary Frazier who captivated him was sometimes called Maria or Polly. Her parents, Mr. and Mrs. Moses Frazier, were leading citizens with a family of two attractive daughters, and their residence in Newburyport was often visited by Adams and his chums. When the romance began, Mary, the younger of the girls, was not yet sixteen, a birthday she would celebrate on March 9, 1790. Her blond attractions made her, according to New England lore, one of the region's loveliest women.

In wooing Mary, John had to cope with the cautious rituals of romance practiced in the late eighteenth century, particularly in a small town like Newburyport. Courtships somehow had to be conducted mostly in public. Young ladies and gentlemen ordinarily arranged to meet in homes as part of groups. Love may have had an easier time during sleigh rides, or on walks to "the grove" in warm weather, or at the dances and "assemblies" that crowded the social calendar. But even in such settings, it was rarely a simple matter for a couple to talk privately.

In August 1789, Mary and John discovered they had moved beyond a casual relationship. Possibly the magic moment was during a stroll on the 24th, for a year later on this date Adams cryptically reminded himself that it was an important anniversary. If so, the pair soon ran out of time to be together, at least for the moment. In early September, Adams traveled to New York City for a long-planned reunion with his parents and to observe the new federal government in which his father was now vice president.

No sooner had he appeared in New York than John displayed an impatience to return to Massachusetts. This mystified his mother, who at this point knew nothing of Mary Frazier. After he hurried back to Newburyport on October 14, there was no time to resume the courtship, for he had arrived just ahead of President George Washington, who was then on a tour of New England. As son of the vice president, John was called upon to help the community prepare for the president's visit and to be present at ceremonies held in his honor. When he returned to New York City, Washington assured Abigail that her son was more interested in law books than in young ladies.

After the president's tour had ended, John's almanac once again recorded visits to Mary's home. A few proved "somewhat dull and silly" or "tolerable" or "somewhat tedious" or "disappointed" or "female caprice." Given the frustrations caused by the presence of family members and friends who may not have known what was on the couple's minds, these adjectives could have been understatements. More often, however, Adams reported successful encounters; indeed, there were occasions when he used one word to describe himself: "happy." Visits in the Frazier household frequently were pictured as a "clever evening" or simply "good." The couple often walked "very agreeably" and had "a good time." Adams sometimes reported being "much diverted." No wonder, then, that by spring 1790, the Adams-Frazier romance evidently had deepened to the point where John found himself alternately joyful and anxious.

Finally, his situation made him disclose to cousin Billy Cranch the perils and temptations of his attraction to Mary. Writing on April 7, Adams admitted being torn between a desire to "flee to safety" and a yearning to stay. He spoke of the battle "between *my sentiments* and *my opinions*," and predicted that his emotions were about to gain the upper hand. It was not uncertainty about Mary Frazier that caused his ambivalence. It was his painful awareness of being unable to support a wife.

This discouragement dominated a letter (now lost) to Nabby in which John shared his predicament. In her reply, his sister announced that she would be "very sorry" if her brother's attachment to "so amiable and deserving an object should meet eventually with any effacement from mercenary views or be repulsed by too wise maxims of prudence." From what she had heard of Mary Frazier, Nabby said, "you may worship without idolatry." Upon the heels of Nabby's view came another encouraging opinion, this from brother Charles, who himself sounded smitten (or cynical) when he described JQA's beloved thus: "There has nothing so like perfection in human shape appeared since the world began."

For John Quincy Adams the beau, such sentiment was no exaggeration. He had enlarged upon it in his poem "A Vision," whose lines were severe with all women but Mary. Here he took pains to conceal Mary's identity by calling her "Clara." The result was an eloquent description of his beloved:

> *Come, and before the lovely Clara's shrine,*
> *The mingled tribute of your praises join;*
> *My Clara's charms no vulgar poets claim,*
>
> . . .
>
> *The partial gods presiding at her birth*
> *Gave Clara beauty and yet gave her worth;*
> *Kind nature form'd of purest white her skin,*
> *An emblem of her innocence within;*
> *And called on cheerful Health her aid to lend,*
> *The roses' colours in her cheeks to blend,*
> *While Venus added, to complete the fair,*
> *The eyes blue languish and the golden hair;*
> *But far superior charms exalt her mind,*
> *Adorned by nature, and by art refined,*
> *Hers are the lasting beauties of the heart,*
> *The charm which virtue only can impart.*

After this tribute, who could blame Adams for closing with these lines:

> *On thee thy ardent lover's fate depends,*
> *From thee the evil or the boon descends;*
> *Thy choice alone can make my anxious breast*
> *Supremely wretched, or supremely blest.*

"A Vision" was the most serious and sustained of several literary efforts by Adams during his Newburyport stay. It was probably finished in the spring of 1790, when he had to leave to begin practicing law in Boston—a move he dreaded, but one insisted on by his parents, who still paid his bills. Although he had once scorned Newburyport, romance now made the place enticing. There could be no delicious walks with Mary in "the grove" if he lived in the shadow of Boston's State House.

Writing to his father about locating a law office, John cautiously introduced Newburyport as a possibility. Careful not to mention Mary Frazier, for he continued to keep the courtship a secret from Abigail and John Adams, their son spoke vaguely of his "agreeable circle of acquaintances" there, a fact that "would render the station peculiarly pleasing so far as respects the intercourse of society." As for Boston, "I cannot say I am pleased with the manners of the town," nor did he wish to think about "the opportunities and temptations to dissipation" that lay in wait there.

These broad hints did not stir his parents. From Philadelphia, now the federal capital, Vice President and Mrs. Adams kept pressing their son to establish his law practice in Boston. The obedient son therefore arrived in the city and formally began business on August 9, 1790, having been sworn to the office of attorney on July 15. He took this important step while admitting that once again he was "not in good spirits." The distractions of reading and long walks brought no comfort. Billy Cranch, to whom young Adams turned for advice about his symptoms, was hardly reassuring when he replied that depression was "a disorder or disease to which a man may necessarily be subjected as to the stone or the gout."

Billy had remained one of the few persons with whom Adams shared the secret of his love. Only after he was settled in Boston did John finally tell James Bridge the story. In a moving letter, Adams informed Bridge, then practicing law in Maine, that while "it is known to very few," he was in love with Mary Frazier. Indeed, said Adams, "all my hopes of future happiness in this life center in the possession of that girl." In contrast to Adams' rather cavalier description of the goal of his love, James Bridge was graciousness itself in wishing John and Mary "the richest of all earthly harvests, sincere domestic felicity." Bridge, however, had to add: "I have scarce ever been more surprised."

Three months later, in November, John's ardent yearning was crushed. The Adams-Frazier romance ended. It was Abigail Adams who saw to this, along with some assistance from Mary's kinfolk. Once John's mother had figured out whom he loved, soon after he had unpacked in Boston, she started issuing orders. Although Abigail never mentioned Mary by name, she told her son: "Common fame reports that you are attached to a young lady. I am sorry that such a report should prevail." After voicing her regret, Abigail began a series of stern letters that, John admitted, "added not a little to the weight of anxiety which before hung heavy upon my mind."

Relentlessly, Abigail reiterated her decree: "Never form connections until you see a prospect of supporting a family. Never take a woman from an eligible situation and place her below it. . . . As you never wish to owe a fortune to a wife, never let her owe poverty to you." Furthermore, she went on, "a too early marriage will involve you in troubles that may render you and yours unhappiness the remainder of your life."

Reminding her son that he had recently told her he had no plan to marry at present, Abigail asserted it was "cruel" to encourage a young lady. According to Abigail, a gentleman and lady must utter nary a hint of their affection for each other "when his situation will not permit him to speak [of marriage]." Yet such an arrangement was exactly what John sought with Mary Frazier.

His love spurred him to disobey his mother—he asked Mary to agree to an informal pledge of betrothal. They would privately acknowledge their love to each other and plan to marry as soon as John's legal business would permit. Mary's reply was not what he expected. While she was certain of loving John, she faced her own pressures from family members, who instructed her to insist upon a formal engagement with this son of the vice president of the United States.

According to JQA's almanac, the couple's discussions of a betrothal entered a "critical period" after Mary arrived on October 11 for a stay in the Boston suburb of Medford, where Frazier relatives sheltered Mary while she and John held agonizing meetings. Their talks concluded on November 2, after what Adams tersely called "Final conversation with M.F." On this date, Mary told him that they must either make a public commitment to each other or end their relationship. What she requested was no less than a full and formal engagement, the sort of bond that in those days was usually broken only by death.

When John could not agree without further disobedience to Abigail, the couple parted, vowing not to marry until they found partners with qualities they had discovered in each other. It was a cruel experience. Adams was compelled to bid farewell to his beautiful beloved, helpless to do otherwise because he was still wholly dependent on his parents. He had made the best offer he could, and he forever felt that he might have kept her if not for the intrusion of relatives.

John waited a week before coldly reporting the news to Abigail Adams: "I conjure you, my dear Mamma, not to suffer your anxiety on my account to add to any other evils with which you are afflicted." She should now forget "the report of my attachment." The broken-hearted son could not resist adding a word in his own defense. While his mother might "censure" him for having indulged "a weakness," he was confident that she would "excuse" him if only she had known the young lady.

With no reply from his mother, John wrote again on December 14, using bravado to hide the wound left by the loss: "I am perfectly free, and you may rest assured I shall remain so. I believe I may add I was never in less danger from any entanglement which can give you pain than at present." In telling Billy Cranch that the affair had ended, John boasted: "I am proof against every thing." Eventually, Abigail wrote to say she was content and would forget the subject.

From Elizabeth Shaw, however, came characteristic support and sympathy. His aunt wrote in answer to a letter in which John evidently had told her candidly how bitter he was at surrendering Mary Frazier. Indeed, he spoke of fearing that he would never be able to love again. Elizabeth replied that she could appreciate the emotional price he was paying at parting (the aunt had once herself suffered a broken romance). "I could have sat by your side and counted out tear for tear," she said. Even so, Elizabeth assured him that a heart such as his would certainly "gravitate toward one he finds in unison with his own." He would soon be restored by finding a woman "who excelleth them all in real worth, as in beauty . . . one who looks like Nature in the world's first bloom."

Her letter was carefully preserved by Adams as his "troubles of the heart, deep and distressing," were left slowly to be worn away. Nearly a half century would pass before his papers mentioned Mary Frazier again. In a long diary entry of November 18, 1838, written when he was seventy-one years old, JQA recalled the romance. He was stirred to do so after visiting the fashionable Mount Auburn Cemetery, recently established on the outskirts of Boston. While looking at graves, he spotted the burial site of Maria Osborne Sargent (Mrs. Charles P. Curtis). Curious, he drew closer and found that Maria had been the daughter of Mary Frazier.

In 1802, Mary had given her hand in marriage to Daniel Sargent, an early friend of Adams'. In a short time, she was dead of consumption at age thirty, soon after giving birth to her daughter. Upon seeing his once beloved Mary named on the gravestone as mother of the deceased, John said, "a mingled emotion of tenderness, of melancholy, and yet of gratitude to Heaven affected me to tears."

Returning from the cemetery and opening his diary, Adams shared for the first time the details of how he had loved Mary, who was, he acknowledged, "to me the most beautiful and most beloved of her sex." She had given him, he said, "the assurance of her affection and the pledge of her faith." Then came the most painful part of his reverie: "Dearly! how dearly did the sacrifice of her cost me, voluntary as it was," after she "insist[ed] upon a positive engagement or a separation." The old man then recalled how "four years of exquisite wretchedness followed . . . nor was the wound in my bosom healed till the Atlantic Ocean flowed between us."

As far as JQA was concerned, these 1838 recollections marked his private interment of the Mary Frazier story. Six years later, however, her memory was resurrected when, in January 1844, he received by mail a tattered copy of "Clara," the portrait he had drawn of Mary in his poem "A Vision." It was sent to him by Thomas Curtis of Rye, New Hampshire, who was possibly related to the late Maria Sargent Curtis.

Noticing at once that the copy was in Mary's handwriting, an obviously stirred Adams went so far as to tell Curtis that the lines had arisen from "a genuine but not a fortunate passion. The heart, which, when they were written, responded to mine, was shortly afterwards estranged from me by the intervention of a colder bosom." Never mentioning Mary by name, Adams spoke of "the unrivalled beauty of Clara" and said that seeing the lines ("I have written nothing since in a loftier strain") had "awakened in my breast emotions more fitted to slumber till the last trump of the Archangel."

John Quincy Adams died four years after this exchange with Thomas Curtis. But the story of his love for Mary Frazier did not depart with him. Instead, a version became public when, in 1864, James Morss published a memoir in the *Newburyport Herald*. It featured a conversation that Morss reported having with ex-President Adams when the latter was seventy, which would have been about the time he visited the Mount Auburn Cemetery. Morss wrote of how JQA had extolled Mary Frazier's intellectual endowments and perfect purity of life and heart, and of how he'd called her the most beautiful woman in Europe and America. Morss said Adams had conceded that it had been right that the attachment had been severed, given his poor prospects at the time.

FOR THE REST OF HIS LIFE, JQA frequently recalled how bleak his future had seemed that summer in 1790 when he opened his law office. At the time, he sorely doubted his capacity to be an attorney. Instead of finishing the three years of legal study imposed upon fledgling attorneys, he had completed hardly one before he moved to Boston. Extended periods of illness, along with holidays, had taken him away from Newburyport for months at a stretch. In Boston, he was surrounded by tormenting reminders of his dependence upon others. His office was in a house his father owned in Court Street. He had no library of his own but had to rely upon John Adams' fine collection of law books. He was without regular income save for the nine pounds his father sent him each month. Finally, to reside in Boston, JQA had to impose upon charitable distant relatives, Dr. and Mrs. Thomas Welsh.

He began to write complaining letters to his parents and to call his many years abroad mostly a waste of time. The experience had served mainly to create "peculiar circumstances in my education which have retarded my advancement." It chagrined Adams to think of those successful men his age who had been able to start the race of life ahead of him. For instance, Billy Cranch seemed to be making great progress in his Braintree law practice. Adams told him: "Your situation must for some time at least be vastly more eligible than mine." What were people talking about, he wondered, when they persisted in telling him about his great advantages?

When Adams lost his first case in court, his humiliation seemed complete. He was defeated by Harrison Gray ("Harry") Otis, who, though not a great deal older than Adams, was already well launched on his successful career. "You may judge of the figure I made," JQA told Abigail, forgetting momentarily that she was indeed concerned about the appearance her son presented to Boston. She had been indignant when she learned from relatives that he had arrived in the city with "not a pair of stockings or drawers fit to put on." His shirts were so disgraceful that they had to be cleaned by soaking in buttermilk. Such reports brought Abigail's sarcastic comment that the one advantage of her son's recent love affair was that it might have inspired him to become attentive to his person.

Finally, by the end of 1790, John and Abigail Adams awoke to the realization that a thwarted romance and an unpromising professional future were pushing their eldest son back into depression. Both parents now tried to be patient. John Adams undertook to show confidence in his son by offering him the management of the family properties in Braintree. For the moment, JQA politely declined the opportunity, saying the responsibility would disrupt his studies. Abigail sought to cheer him by claiming that only some "calamity" would keep him "in the shallows."

As it turned out, however, the Adamses' most helpful strategy was to invite their son to Philadelphia early in 1791, tempting him with descriptions of the city's literary and scientific activity. His interest stirred, JQA remained in the capital for several weeks, which became a turning point in his life. The seat of national government gave him the reassuring experience of moving once again as an insider among important people. He dined with George and Martha Washington and, on February 22, helped celebrate the president's birthday. Meanwhile, he listened to debates in Congress and hearings before the Supreme Court. He dutifully followed Abigail as she introduced him around town.

Not that the visit brought complete restoration. When her son left Philadelphia in early March, Abigail was still worried. "He appears to have lost much of his sprightliness and vivacity," she reported to Nabby. "He wishes sometimes that he had been bred a farmer, a merchant, or anything by which he could earn his bread, but we all preach patience to him."

Certainly, it was a calmer and more thoughtful young Adams who returned to Boston. His visit to the capital had helped make him less impatient with the world's realities and particularly those of politics. But he still resented the thought of a career as an attorney. His almanac jottings make clear how bored he was with his legal practice. He yearned openly for a life given to reading, writing, and the theater. Yet how thus to make a living? "All day at court. Dull. Anxious. Heavy," he wrote. "The present a deadly calm, and the future a chilling mist." About his still occasional melancholy he wondered: "Why am I thus treated by fortune?" and "When will the vulture leave my bosom?" That moment was at hand, as it turned out.

BEFORE HIS TRIP, JQA had used the words "imbecility" and "ridiculous" in speaking of the workings of government. There was a discouraging truth, he said, in knowing "that even in this free country, the course of public events depends upon the private interests and passions of individuals." Now, after Philadelphia, he seemed mindful of his father's encouragement that he enter public service, a destiny the family had nurtured since his boyhood. John Adams was also pleased that his son had agreed to take charge of the family's business affairs through power of attorney.

Somewhat reassured, young Adams began showing a new competitive spirit after reopening his law office. Although clients remained discouragingly few, he now used his spare time for larger participation in Boston's goings-on. He grew fonder of the town. Its wooden houses and streets paved with pebbles sat upon a peninsula with three "mountains," the most famous being Beacon Hill.

Adams climbed that hill soon after his Philadelphia visit, joining several others to observe an eclipse of the sun. To his regret, he made a dreadful and unscientific mistake by failing to take with him a piece of smoked glass for direct viewing. The result was predictable: "Hurt my eyes much," he reported, and he went on to suffer through the summer. As late as the end of August 1791, he recorded: "Almost blind." His vision never quite recovered, and his eyes remained a concern for the rest of his life.

Eye distress did not prevent Adams from beginning a strenuous social life. He especially enjoyed meetings of the Crackbrain Club, which, along with dances, parties, and long walks, helped him as he "brushed up my spirits as well as I could." After his experience with Mary Frazier, he fell back on his old haughtiness toward the opposite sex. Now he seemed to enjoy emphasizing that strong feelings were wholly unsuitable in women and that "there is something in the very nature of mental abilities which seems to be unbecoming to a female." He claimed to be bored by any occasion where young women were present: "Dull, more than dull!"

But these "insipid" events involved only the socially acceptable young ladies. There were other Boston women whom Adams found more attractive—ones unlikely to challenge his memories of the well-born Mary Frazier. His almanac vaguely discloses how he began looking for females who would be unwelcome in the city's respectable homes. As he put it in 1791, he did not feel drawn to women who were cautious and correct, conceding that "my taste is naturally depraved." No longer did the female qualities of "prudence and discretion" charm him. "I revere them as virtues; I should be sorry to find them strangers to the object of my affections. Yet freely must I confess it, never can they rouse those affections, never can they deeply interest me."

As a result, Adams' evening strolls frequently were with women who could not be described as prudent and discreet. He met them on the Mall, a walking area near what today is the Tremont Street side of Boston Common. How he and these women passed the time is somewhat cloudy—but not very. His almanac has only the briefest record: "Evening at my office. Foolish adventure afterwards. Discretion prevailed." There were other outcomes, however, recorded simply as "I was imprudent," "Silly again," "made a lamentable mistake again," and "I must be the sport of chance."

On December 29, 1793, he confessed to being a "victim of folly," leading him the next day to pledge: "Determined on a course of more discretion." There were many such resolves as long as he saw himself "on the bridge between wisdom and folly." For a time, he felt so drawn to the ladies of the Mall that he could explain the weakness only as "a fatality against which I find it in vain to resist." These encounters rarely gratified him, however, and left him speaking of "painful occurrences and mortifying reflections."

WHILE ONE MIGHT readily guess why John Quincy Adams said little about his experiences with lower-class women, it is difficult to understand why he was similarly reticent about a triumph in his Boston years. The story of this success began with the publication of a series he called "Letters of Publicola." These essays appeared during 1791 in Boston's *Columbian Centinel,* whose editor, Ben Russell, favored the politics of John Adams. The first letter was printed on June 8, and the eleventh and last appeared seven weeks later, July 27, 1791. All were signed "Publicola" (a classical Latin term meaning "friend of the people"). During this time, he reported in his almanac only that he was writing.

JQA became a leading newspaper controversialist because of his target in "Publicola." He chose to reply to the radical Thomas Paine, whose *The Rights of Man* had just appeared. In it, Paine had summoned the British people to follow the example of the French Revolution in overthrowing the established order and in writing a constitution. As "Publicola," JQA defended the same conservative viewpoint that John Adams had espoused in 1790 when he published his own series called "Discourses on Davila." Like his father, the son warned that passion, not reason, was the source of individual and group political behavior.

What particularly inspired JQA to take up his pen was the attitude of Thomas Jefferson, his once-admired companion in Paris and now secretary of state. Jefferson had publicly endorsed *The Rights of Man* and implied that the earthy views of John Adams broke faith with the rationalist principles of the American Revolution. When JQA's father visited Boston and Braintree in the spring of 1791, the son reviewed the Paine-Jefferson issue with him before beginning his first essay.

The conservatism that filled "Publicola" grew from beliefs JQA had held since his student days at Harvard, when he spoke scornfully of demagoguery—the doctrine of "popular infallibility." Now, in 1791, he used that viewpoint to defend British and American arrangements for balancing governing powers. Near the end of the "Publicola" series, he summed up: "Let us remain immovably fixed at the banners of our constitutional freedom, and not desert the impregnable fortress of our liberties for the unsubstantial fabric of visionary politicians."

Naturally, many readers assumed that John Adams was "Publicola." One of the first to guess that Adams' son was the author was James Madison, Jefferson's close associate, who observed that the essays had a style more graceful than John Adams'. In some quarters, JQA's writing was compared favorably with that of Edmund Burke. In the United States, "Publicola" hastened the opening of party warfare. Factions called Federalists and Republicans began dividing over the issues raised by Thomas Paine and John Quincy Adams.

With "Publicola," Adams became so successful as a newspaper essayist that his anonymous Boston writings between 1791 and 1794 were republished elsewhere in the United States, as well as in England, Scotland, Ireland, and France. He had little to say, however, about this sudden and astounding development, perhaps because he was himself becoming involved in Boston politics.

He first worked as a member of a committee charged with improving the Boston police system. After he and his colleagues reported to a town meeting in early 1792, Adams was not surprised when their report was rejected, amid disorder, by a vote of 701 to 587. He soon had better luck when citizens of the north parish of Braintree asked him to draft an enactment transforming the parish into a new town, to be named Quincy after his great-grandfather Colonel John Quincy.

The next cause young Adams took up was theatrical productions in Boston, for his favorite form of entertainment had been banned by the Massachusetts legislature even though an overwhelming vote by a Boston town meeting had welcomed theaters. He led the opposition to any such restriction, even if these early Boston productions were, as their defender put it, "miserable stuff."

Since Boston's citizens had spoken in support of the stage, it seemed not to occur to Adams that conniving to put on what the legislature called illicit dramatic productions might be part of the anarchy he feared was rising in America. After foes of theater broke up a performance, Adams once again took up his pen, this time as "Menander," defending stage performances in three essays that appeared between December 19 and 22, 1792, in the *Columbian Centinel.*

In these, he sought to shame the culprits who had disrupted the performance, and he assailed those local officials who supported the theater ban. At one point, however, "Menander" allowed Adams' outrage to overcome his sound judgment. When he proclaimed "no obedience is due to an unconstitutional act of the legislature," he had stepped into the kind of political quicksand that a few decades later would entrap the American South.

At this point, fortunately, his attention was drawn to a cause of global importance. He turned to address the most controversial issue of the day: whether the United States should remain neutral in the war that had begun between France and England. As it happened, neutrality was challenged by American politicians friendly to France who also opposed the powerful federal government that George Washington, John Adams, and Alexander Hamilton, among others, were seeking to create.

JQA entered the combat in mid-1793, soon after France's minister to the United States, Edmond Genêt, openly condemned President Washington's recent proclamation of neutrality. To young Adams' dismay, the impudent Frenchman told the American people that their chief executive had exceeded his powers, and that American ships were thus free to privateer in France's behalf. Despite much loud praise for Genêt, mostly from the Jeffersonians, President Washington promptly instructed France to recall its envoy.

Genêt's talk had stirred up so much clamor against the administration that the president was delighted when he received the forthright and intelligent support of an essayist in Boston, who did not remain anonymous for long. Washington and the public quickly learned that it was John Quincy Adams whose writings against the French envoy were being widely circulated. Adams wrote three groups of essays. The first, under the name "Marcellus," was published in April and May 1793, the second, by "Columbus," in November and December of that year, both in the faithful *Columbian Centinel;* the third group, the "Barneveld" essays, appeared in Boston's *Chronicle,* beginning in December and closing in mid-January 1794.

In these essays, which were based on his substantial knowledge of

international law, Adams argued convincingly that if American priva-
teers raided English ships, these acts "to the eye of reason and justice,
can appear in no other light than that of highway robbery." On the
"political villainy" of Edmond Genêt, JQA was equally severe, charging the French minister with trying to arm one part of America against
the other. "If he cannot corrupt the sacred fountains of legislation, he
hopes at least to poison some of the streams which flow from it."

By vigorously defending the power of the chief executive and opposing Genêt's idea of state supremacy, Adams moved onto much
higher ground than the road he had taken when he urged friends of
drama to disobey laws opposing public theaters. In condemning
Genêt, he became a pioneer in arguing that the federal Constitution,
at least by implication, gave the central government important powers.

His role in the tumult of 1793 made Adams a favorite of his conservative neighbors in Boston. They began to give him what he craved,
respect and honor, by inviting him to deliver that year's Fourth of July
oration before the citizenry. Instead of the frequently pugnacious tone
of his essays, he chose for his speech on the Fourth a theme that was
moderate and unlikely to offend; he predicted that the love of freedom
in America would eventually inspire the oppressed peoples of Europe.

His experience as an orator and essayist led a newly vigorous and
even happy JQA to take seriously the encouragement and praise of his
friends. He foresaw that perhaps he could achieve literary success if he
spent his free time at his writing desk. Also cheering was his discovery
that there were actually young ladies of good repute in Boston whose
company he enjoyed and with whom he began to stroll. Miss Sally
Gray was particularly favored.

Calling upon his courage, Adams decided it was demeaning to
keep himself "between hope and fear." Instead, he announced that he
must confront the "unpleasant dilemmas" before him. His patience at
the thought of a career in the law now worn thin, Adams believed the
time had come when he, not his parents, must shape his future.

This bravado was, in part, rebellion against an April 1794 letter
from his father, which reemphasized an old theme: John Quincy
Adams must seek to be a great man. "You come into life with advantages which will disgrace you if your success is mediocre," John Adams
warned his son, adding that "if you do not rise to the head not only of
your profession, but of your country, it will be owing to your own *Laziness, Slovenliness,* and *Obstinacy.*"

Against this succinct summary of the towering expectations his
parents had always imposed, Adams chose at last to stand fast. In the

pleasant spring of 1794, he replied to his father that he was putting aside any plans for a political career, admitting that each day he had "less ambition than the former." This acknowledgment led to even greater heresy against family doctrine. "I see very few things in this life beyond the wants of nature that I desire," JQA announced, adding that "whether it be philosophy or insensibility, I find myself contented with my state as it is."

With this assertion, Adams seemed finally to have arrived at a juncture in life he had long ardently hoped for: to start doing for himself as he, not his parents, deemed best. Had circumstances not quickly overwhelmed him, his career might well have turned out very differently from the one history records. Unfortunately for John's resolve to make his own way, fate played into his father's hands.

Just as the son was proclaiming his declaration of personal independence, John Adams was excitedly dispatching news from Philadelphia certain to demolish JQA's aspirations to a quiet, bookish life: President Washington had submitted the name of John Quincy Adams to the Senate for confirmation as America's minister resident in the Netherlands. The nomination, the vice president joyfully stressed, meant the end of his son's struggles as a fledgling attorney and the opening of a career in public service.

Quite naturally, the father expected such glorious tidings to be gratefully received by his fortunate son. Instead, the report left JQA in torment. "My heart unfit for examination," he fumed, as he watched his newly emerged independence and contentment fall to pieces.

BOOK TWO

Discouraging Choices

1794–1805

. . . in which a pleasing career is snatched away.

CHAPTER FOUR

Hesitations

*I have found here exactly what I wanted, and feel myself once
more to be my own man.*

INSTEAD OF REJOICING over his appointment as American minister
to Holland, with its annual salary of $4,500, John Quincy Adams was,
true to form, dismayed. "I wish I could have been consulted before it
was irrevocably made," he grumbled. "I rather wish it had not been
made at all." He was also suspicious that his father had had a hand in
this astonishing development. Since personal independence was his
goal, he knew no better place to reach it than in Boston, where he had
chums and where Harvard was nearby. "The thought of leaving all my
friends [is] very painful."

Fearing that his son might hesitate, John Adams remained in
Philadelphia only until the nomination was unanimously confirmed by
the Senate before he hurried home to dispel any misgivings on the new
diplomat's part. Reaching Quincy in early June of 1794, the father emphasized to everyone that he had "never uttered a word" to seek a
public post for JQA. While this was less than accurate, John Adams
was honor-bound to make the claim. He and Secretary of State Edmund Randolph had in fact discussed such an appointment, Randolph sternly insisting that no one must know they had done so. And,
indeed, after JQA's name was promptly sent to the Senate, John
Adams was so eager to see his son enter the diplomatic service that he
probably was relieved at being obliged to keep the full story to himself.

There were, of course, other reasons that made the appointee hesitate. Not yet twenty-seven, he doubted that he was mature enough for

so important a place—besides The Hague, there were then United States embassies in only four other capitals: London, Paris, Lisbon, and Madrid. Furthermore, John winced at what he anticipated as the tedium entailed in the duties of this new post. The routine, he feared, would allow little time for reading and writing.

Nor was his inner turmoil eased by his father's admonition that the appointment would "require all your prudence and all your other virtues as well as all your talents." John Adams kept stressing the "serious trust" reposed in the new minister and even mentioned the topic most certain to annoy his son—the latter's habitual casualness, if not slovenliness, in appearance. How John dressed would now be important, said the parent. It was apparent to JQA that his father was far more pleased by the appointment than he was.

Adams became so physically and emotionally upset at the thought of entering the diplomatic corps that a fortnight passed before he could bring himself to prepare for a briefing in Philadelphia by Secretary of State Randolph. His father worked to soothe his misgivings, until finally the son decided to believe his parent's protestations of innocence in arranging the appointment.

On June 30, young Adams departed for Philadelphia, and thereby ended the only extended period in his life during which he would hold no public office. Arriving in the capital on July 9, he promptly went into conference at the State Department and then began reading the department's confidential records as background for his assignment. This task proved to be a happy chore, since, at least in JQA's view, the documents put his father's career in an admirable light.

When he was not studying the young nation's diplomatic history, Adams was called to confer with such worthies as George Washington and Alexander Hamilton and to dine with other members of the administration. On his twenty-seventh birthday, he was handed the papers containing his commission. After recording this important moment, he filled the remainder of the day's diary entry (he had discarded his almanac and was once again an avid journal-keeper) with vivid descriptions of how he had spent his time. He reported joining Washington in a meeting with Chickasaw Indians. He had dined with Secretary of War Henry Knox, after which he attended the theater and concluded the evening by chatting with Joseph Fauchet, Genêt's successor as French minister.

Such opportunities in Philadelphia were so appealing that JQA lingered for several days after finishing his official tasks. The time allowed him to coax his youngest brother, Thomas Boylston Adams, who lived in the city, into accompanying him to Holland as his private secretary. The choice delighted their parents, for Tom had been struggling to begin his own legal practice. Like his brother, Tom was not at first enthusiastic about going, for he, too, would be leaving many friends and a promising entry into journalism. But JQA was persuasive, and Tom was consoled by his brother's assurances that they would remain abroad no more than three years.

Back in Boston on August 19, John packed his trunks and endured a round of farewell parties with his friends—all the time being "very anxious to get away." Not that that proved easy to do, for no ship was ready to leave for Adams' first destination, London, where he was to deliver official messages. A long month later, John, Tom, and a servant named Tilly sailed aboard the *Alfred*, a vessel JQA ominously claimed had all the substance of an eggshell, being "old, crazy, and leaky."

Two of John's closest friends—Nathan Frazier, Mary's cousin, and Daniel Sargent, who would eventually wed her—accompanied the *Alfred* to the Boston lighthouse. The sight of these friends being rowed back to Boston in a pilot's boat, John said, brought him pain as poignant as any he had ever felt. "It was like severing the last string from the heart. I looked back at their boat as long as it could be seen, and when it had got out of sight, I did not, but I could have, turned my eye and wept."

The voyage began with Adams trying to forget the warnings of skeptics in Boston that the *Alfred* could not possibly survive the crossing. Actually, the ship seemed to sail under a lucky star, and he was amazed by what he considered its near-miraculous success. The flimsy boat escaped by a mere hundred leagues a violent storm that wrecked much stronger vessels. It also missed "one of the most tremendous tempests known," which had struck the English coast a few days before the *Alfred* arrived.

Not that the voyage was easy. John and Tom suffered much from seasickness. The surging seas often made it impossible to play card games. When JQA questioned the captain as to the vessel's whereabouts, he received only mystifying replies, leaving him convinced that "there is as much quackery in navigation as in law or physics." Consequently, with the *Alfred* leaking "like a water spout," the party was vastly relieved to see the cliffs of Dover. The next day, October 15, they docked at Deal, twenty-two miles from Canterbury, an occasion Adams called "one of those instants of real and perfect satisfaction which occur seldom in the course of human life."

On the following evening, the brothers' chaise rolled into London after an eighty-mile ride from the coast. It had been a blissful journey as Adams marveled at the English countryside. He wrote that he and Tom might easily have "gazed ourselves insensibly to stupefaction" at the "infinite variety of delightful prospects." Being on land had not, however, brought an end to danger.

The brothers were traveling behind a carriage hauling their baggage, and, entranced by the landscape, John neglected to keep his eye on the trunk containing the confidential State Department dispatches he had been entrusted to deliver. Just as they reached London Bridge, in semidarkness, a noise startled John, making him peer forward to the luggage. With "sensations of the severest distress," he saw that the container of precious government documents was missing.

As a stunned JQA watched, Tom Adams had their driver stop while he leaped out to look around. He found the trunk beneath their carriage—it had fallen from the baggage rack moments before. The brothers concluded that while they were distracted by the scenery, some "dexterous felon" had cut the straps holding the trunk and was then waiting for the oblivious Americans to pass on before picking up the prize.

So horrified was JQA by this close call that all the anxiety bottled within him came bubbling out. Had the trunk and its highly secret contents been stolen, he said, it would have been better if he and the *Alfred* had gone down at sea. He recalled how the dispatches had been solemnly put into his hands by Washington himself, and that his stop in England had been arranged solely to assure safe delivery of the papers to John Jay, chief justice of the U.S. Supreme Court, whom Washington had sent to London to negotiate a treaty with the British.

If the papers had been stolen, Adams was certain they would have reached the English Foreign Office, immediately jeopardizing Jay's mission. "[W]ith what a face," he wondered, could he have told Jay that the papers were lost? And how could he have notified officials at home? Even worse to contemplate, Adams admitted, was his certain disgrace once the story of such carelessness, "with a thousand alterations and aggravations," had circulated "from one end of the United States to the other." His blunder, he was convinced, would have opened "a field for the aspersions of malice! What a fund for the suspicions of jealousy! What an opening for the insinuations of envy! And what a groundwork for the fabric of slander!"

This nearly hysterical reaction came from a young man who customarily demanded of himself a perfect performance of duty, but who now saw how utterly he had nearly failed in a vital assignment. The realization made an anxious and insecure Adams fill pages of his diary with disclosures of his acute sense of responsibility—and his expectation that any misstep on his part might make him ludicrous. It was no exaggeration, he claimed, to say that the miracle of foiling the theft had rescued "my peace, and the welfare of my country." With the dispatches back in his hands, an impatient Adams hastened to deliver them immediately to Jay, bursting in late at night upon the chief justice, who was sick in bed.

The remaining days in London brought much pleasure, notably when Adams attended London's thriving theaters. He took care to rise with the audience whenever "God Save the King" was played—"I am always averse to an appearance of singularity." He was particularly thrilled when his favorite actress, Mrs. Sarah Siddons, played Queen Katharine in Shakespeare and Fletcher's *Henry VIII* in Drury Lane.

London's greatest satisfaction, however, was the heady experience that came when Adams was called to share in talks between Jay and Thomas Pinckney, United States minister to England, as the two older statesmen reviewed, article by article, the treaty Jay was concluding with the British government. These discussions, which frequently adjourned for dining and theater, greatly heartened young Adams. Only weeks before, he had complained of being an obscure attorney, and now here he was, discussing with no less than the chief justice of the United States the hazards of negotiating with imperious Great Britain.

The issues were emotion-laden: U.S. trade with the British West Indies, the status of British troops and posts in the American Northwest, war reparations claimed by U.S. shippers, and compensation to owners for slaves abducted by the British during the Revolution. And, as JQA knew from writing his political essays, the most delicate issue of all was America's demand that, as a neutral in the Anglo-French war, its rights on the high seas must be respected. Jay's negotiations brought only very partial healing to these and other sore spots between the two nations, so that the treaty bearing his name met with violent criticism when its text reached Philadelphia in March 1795. It was nonetheless ratified the following June.

Adams, however, had thought well of Jay's treaty as soon as the latter shared a draft with him in London. And when Jay invited his opinion, Adams said he believed that, imperfect though the document might be, it was preferable to war. In highly perceptive letters to his father, he emphasized the same point: it was vital that America steer clear of Europe's controversies. These messages reached the eye of

President Washington, whose venerated *Farewell Address* of 1796 would contain passages on the merits of neutrality that were strikingly similar to ones found in JQA's letters. Members of Washington's cabinet soon heard him predict that young Adams would quickly rise to the head of America's diplomatic corps.

JQA's letters to family and friends, particularly those to his father, were discerning and thoughtful, and often became invaluable descriptions and interpretations of a tumultuous era in Europe. They were also the means by which he nurtured the intellectual activity he found most appealing: using his pen. He wrote informal letters as readily as official reports, although his messages to those close to him often sounded as if sent by a newspaper correspondent. In fact, it rarely displeased him when excerpts from his letters appeared in American newsprint.

Amid his correspondence, Adams managed to keep up with London's social whirl. Fortunately he could now work later, having found, to his astonishment, that the city's best households had dinner at 5 p.m., whereas Bostonians preferred 2 p.m. for the first meal of the day after a mid-morning breakfast. Rising from the table, most guests repaired to the theater, and afterward conversed or played cards until 2 a.m., the fashionable hour of retirement in London.

With his brother invited elsewhere on the evening of October 23, 1794, Tom Adams found himself going alone to dine at the home of Joshua Johnson, the American consul in London, where Chief Justice Jay was another guest. Also present at the table were the hosts' three eldest daughters. If the Johnsons hoped that one of their young ladies might captivate a bachelor Adams, they were not disappointed. According to Tom's diary entry, he was "particularly pleased with the middle sister." This was Louisa Catherine—a woman near twenty who would in time become Mrs. John Quincy Adams.

Although JQA had skipped the occasion at the Johnsons, it was not because he was totally distracted by business. "There is something so fascinating in the women I meet with in this country, that it is well for me I am obliged immediately to leave it." On October 28, with brother Tom in tow, he left England to take up his post as U.S. minister to the Netherlands. To get away, he had to borrow money from John Jay—the funds he had expected from the State Department had failed to arrive in time.

Along with the loan of money came Jay's discouraging report that the Dutch were about to be overrun by victorious French troops. Early in 1793, Revolutionary France had declared war against Holland and also Great Britain and Spain. A French triumph in the Low Countries could mean that Adams might soon have to flee his post and return to America. And, indeed, the French did seize Holland, but their doing so simply allowed him to use his fluency in French to get on as well with the occupying officers and troops as he did with the Dutch citizens.

MAINLY, MINISTER ADAMS' obligation in the Netherlands on behalf of the State Department was to understand events in Europe. For a diplomat-observer, The Hague was a splendid listening post, but Adams was not satisfied. He sought further international gossip and insights by corresponding with his colleagues stationed at the other American embassies: James Monroe in Paris, William Short in Madrid, David Humphreys in Lisbon, and Thomas Pinckney back in London. Only Monroe, despite his partiality for the French Revolutionary movement, had talent approaching Adams' for a diplomat's calling.

While in Holland, JQA undertook another memorable assignment with his pen. On March 1, 1795, he began the diary of his adult years. Until then, his journal had been kept intermittently, sometimes by lengthy, thoughtful entries, occasionally by brief jottings. For the next fifty years, with rare exception, he would make daily entries of a substantial, often voluminous, character. He did so, he said, in order to have a record to which he might refer, as indeed he often did. The resource would serve him well—as it has historians.

ADAMS' DIARY DESERVES a comment at this point. It is rightly acclaimed the most discerning and useful personal journal kept by an American. As a record of important events and conversations during his lifetime, its value is indisputable. The diary is also an unmatched report on the less weighty aspects of life in the youthful United States and in Napoleonic Europe. Issues of statecraft and politics are discussed alongside more modest topics, such as achievements by authors of Adams' time, perils of travel, eccentricities of medical practice—a full listing would go on and on. Adams omitted only sexual matters from his journal, although he sometimes hinted even at these.

There are, however, a few occasions when the diary becomes vague or even silent about an important event—as when Adams was seeking to be elected president by the House of Representatives in

1825. Inevitably, these omissions tempt us to wonder whether there were other episodes in his life whose import JQA blocked from view—his own, perhaps, as much as ours. But such moments, if any, must have been rare. When Adams wrote in his journal, he was communing with his soul. He did not play games in his diary, so that historians and biographers need not let suspicions about Adams' intent hinder them from enjoying and making use of one individual's remarkable candor with himself and history.

How helpful for a biographer are the innumerable entries in which JQA evaluated himself? The answer comes with remembering that, severe as Adams usually was when assessing the character and behavior of others, he placed even larger demands upon himself. He rarely offered excuses for his personal weakness or failure, and in fact often exaggerated these shortcomings. His frequent confrontations with himself (many of which are in those parts of the diary yet unpublished and available only on microfilm) must not be seen as self-indulgence. They represent the soul-searching of a brilliant human being with his share of flaws, a man inordinately vexed by his own blunders and inadequacies.

In resolutely facing his failings in the solitude of his journal, Adams believed that elaborate statements of confession and fresh resolve were essential if he was ever to improve. These entries should be taken at face value. They were not an effort to mislead biographers, for Adams claimed he wrote only for his own use, and perhaps those of his descendants. And what if he did have an eye cocked toward history? By joining so many descriptions of his inward state with innumerable astute reports on his larger life, Adams created a diary that deserves to rank near, if not next to, that of Samuel Pepys.

KEEPING UP WITH THIS DIARY in The Hague, along with his correspondence and reports, soon left Adams grumbling mildly that he did little else. As soon as the brothers arrived, John began spending at least six hours a day at his writing table, while Tom was busy making copies of dispatches and letters. After dining at 4 p.m., the two usually went their separate ways for recreation. John walked whenever possible, often with fellow diplomats, after which he returned home to resume writing before retiring at midnight, to rise before dawn, usually. Whatever time remained from this schedule he gave to reading or purchasing books.

JQA seemed to enjoy the routine, although he sometimes spoke of tedium, especially if the city was quiet, which was usually when his fellow diplomats were on summer holiday. Among these associates, his favorite was Baron de Bielfeld, the minister from Prussia. After several months of relaxed talk with Bielfeld, Adams said, "I find him still agreeable and entertaining." Some chats were more valuable than others, as when Adams reported after one exchange: "Our conversation was political, literary, and critical, without sliding, as it often does, into the bottomless pit of metaphysics."

Much was learned from dining with the French representative, François-Joseph Noel, and with Baron de Schubart, the minister from Denmark. Occasionally, Adams was amused by the simplemindedness shown by other colleagues, some of whom he found held sentiments that "might be expected in the creed of an old woman of the last century. The mystical union of souls, the impossibility of a second love, a state of pre-existence, a tutelary angel, etc. etc."

These years in the Netherlands were ideal for the improvement of Adams' emotional health. "My mind [is] very easy," he reported to his friend James Gardner back in Boston. "I have found here exactly what I wanted [i.e., needed], and feel myself to be once more my own man again." He was now financially independent. He had much time for writing and reading. There were interesting colleagues in the diplomatic corps with whom to walk and talk. Above all, he could assure himself that his life had become significant. If there were occasionally dull and frustrating days in The Hague, it was mostly because Adams was not charmed by the Dutch females. He found these "nymphs" to be as unappealing as he remembered from his student days at Leyden.

His satisfaction did not, however, keep him from hungering for public and private news from America. He sorrowed at word that Uncle John Shaw had died suddenly, leaving Aunt Elizabeth a comparatively young widow. In a loving letter, he promised to send his aunt $40 annually to help her son Billy meet expenses at Harvard. Meanwhile, he had left his slender savings to be invested by his brother Charles, a decision that proved to be only the first of many financial missteps.

And then there was the lottery ticket that Adams, "owing to some inattention," had carried away from Boston instead of leaving it with cousin Thomas Welsh to look after. He mailed it back to Welsh, fearing that "the ticket will not improve in its good fortune by two passages across the Atlantic." When he learned that he had won a small sum in the lottery, Adams instructed his cousin to use the amount to purchase tickets for him in the next drawing.

News of his winnings, however, like all mail from the United States, seemed irritatingly slow to reach The Hague, the war making ocean transport uncertain. During the first year of his absence from Boston, he received scant word from friends at home. He complained to the Sargent brothers that he needed "a *female* correspondent" who could send him "all the idle tattle." These letters to Boston pals show a cheerful and outgoing side of JQA that is rarely remembered. In such epistles, he appears at ease, candid, and at times even boyish.

HOWEVER NEWLY INDEPENDENT and relaxed Minister Adams might feel, he still had to answer to the State Department back in Philadelphia. From Secretary Randolph he received orders on October 14, 1795, to be in London by the 25th to exchange formal ratifications of the Jay treaty. Thomas Pinckney, who ordinarily would have presided, happened then to be in Spain on business.

Muttering that this summons away from his comfortable routine in Holland was "unpleasant and unpromising," Adams set out on October 21, but contrary winds kept him and Tilly, his valet, prisoners in a dreary Dutch port, "Helvoet Sluys" (JQA's spelling for Hellevoetshuis), until November 9. There was nothing for Adams to do in the harbor for entertainment but write and read the few books he had brought along; these soon ran out, leaving him "anxiously looking, twenty times an hour, to all the vanes and weathercocks within sight," always finding them "inflexibly fixed in the same direction." When sailing at last seemed feasible, the captain discovered other reasons to delay. "Is it impossible to deal with a trading man without being deceived or imposed on?" Adams wondered.

After sending word back to Tom Adams, whom he had left in charge of ministerial affairs, that he was trying to be mindful how "the only remedy against moral as well as physical evil must be patience," JQA settled in for a long delay before he reached London. The interval was by no means a total waste, however, for he completed long letters to each of his parents, epistles in which he opened his heart. The first, sent to his father on October 31, spoke of his contentment with what he was doing in The Hague, and emphasized how much he shrank from returning one day to Boston and reopening his law office. What pleased him about diplomatic work was how it suited "my talents, and leaves me leisure to pursue any course of studies."

The more he wrote, the more emphatic the letter became. "Indeed, sir," John stressed, life in Holland provided "a situation in itself much preferable to that of eternal expectation in a lawyer's office for business, which when it comes, is scarcely sufficient to give bread, and procures one more curses than thanks." Pledging that he would accept any honorable employment before that of an attorney, JQA bluntly told his father, "I shall not be willing to go through it again," adding that "my feelings on this subject become daily more strongly confirmed." He then pained his parent further by asserting that he wished to have no more public posts. Nor did he fear public neglect, saying he knew all about obscurity—"I suffered it for three long years at my entrance into the world." The memory of his exile in Newburyport and Boston still rankled.

In closing the letter, John asked that it be shown only to Abigail Adams, to whom he began an epistle a week later, still "cooped up . . . in a paltry little European seaport." Writing to his mother made him remember how he had lost Mary Frazier. He reminded Abigail of how he had sacrificed "an ardent affection" to "the shrine of worldly prudence." The more he spoke of his doomed romance, the more eloquent he became, until he proclaimed that his love had been torn from his bosom "by voluntary violence."

While he assured his mother that being in The Hague had brought him inner peace, it was at the cost of blunted sensations. He described his condition as suffering "a widowed heart," one that was "rather exempt from pain than conscious of pleasure." John told Abigail that if he ever found another lover, it would be romance kindled by spontaneity and not "from the will." The son was correct in suspecting that Abigail had in mind such an arranged union for him, so he warned her that in novels such marriages required "a pistol or a bowl [i.e., strong drink]." He told her that he would have to be "five and forty" before he would consider a "marriage of convenience."

These letters to John and Abigail Adams have a special value because they disclose JQA's outlook, particularly on romance, when he arrived in London on November 11, 1795, more than a fortnight after the deadline for exchanging ratification of Jay's Treaty. He found his task had been completed by William A. Deas, the legation secretary. Officials in the British Foreign Office, however, were pleased to see Adams. Implementing the treaty would now involve delicate issues that the king's ministers preferred to discuss with almost anyone but Deas, who could not disguise his hostility toward the British.

Since Pinckney continued to be detained in Spain, the situation meant an indefinite stay in London while Adams awaited instructions from the State Department concerning the questions raised by the treaty. Doubting his own ability to cope with the crafty British states-men, JQA allowed his dormant fear of failure and public ridicule to awaken and once again handicap him. Convinced that he was out of his depth, he soon began to behave suspiciously toward anyone who approached him about matters of diplomacy.

He tried to escape official conversation by emphasizing that he did not carry the rank of minister plenipotentiary and should not be treated as such. All of this amused the more relaxed British spokesmen, such as William Lord Grenville, who were quite willing to accord Adams full standing. John was not persuaded. "Surrounded by man-traps and spring guns, I cannot take a step without risk of error." To his father, he put his difficulty in the best light: "I have been accus-tomed all my life to plain dealing and candor, and am not sufficiently versed in the art of political swindling to be prepared for negotiating with an European Head of State."

The exacting standards he now was trying to meet revived the harsh self-judgment Adams had imposed in Newburyport and Boston. Repeatedly, he rebuked himself in his diary for being vain and talking too much. "The more sensible I am of my fault, the readier I am to re-peat it—Totally dissatisfied with myself." On another day, he wrote: "Stupid blunder. Never can be satisfied with myself." And on a differ-ent occasion: "Dissatisfied again. I can never please myself but in soli-tude. At least I find it so in England."

And so, withdrawing as much as he could from London's public affairs, Adams distracted himself by reading Homer, claiming it was superior to "lounging in the streets." He was grateful for his attach-ment to "poetical beauty" and that he could still recognize "with de-light the flashes of original genius." And then, of course, the theater continued to serve as an honorable refuge, for "Shakespeare's attrac-tions are irresistible." Mrs. Siddons' performance as Cordelia in *King Lear* profoundly moved him.

DURING HIS ENFORCED STAY, Adams might easily have remained sheltered by his books and in crowded theaters, except that now he found himself drawn irresistibly to a London household, the residence of Joshua Johnson. The American consul's hospitable home soon be-came John's refuge from political posturing, while Johnson's daughters soothed the young man's heart with their music and fed his vanity with their admiration.

Only a few hours after arriving in London, Adams had called at

the Johnson house, mainly to drop off papers related to consular matters and to arrange for his own mail to be delivered here, entrusted to
Johnson's care. He stayed for dinner and then, as he put it, "Mr. Johnson's daughters entertained us with good music." These were the three
eldest, charmingly attired in similar dresses, who played harp and
piano, and sang the melodies of Handel and other favorite composers.
Adams was made to feel very welcome and at ease.

Eventually, he became a regular guest of the Johnsons as he
awaited orders from the State Department, and he came to call their
residence more his home in London than his own quarters at
Osborne's Hotel. The Johnsons lived in grand style, as implied by
JQA's genial complaint that their butler, one of eleven servants, was
much too generous in pouring the finest Madeira. This was merely one
of many outward signs that ample wealth supplied the expansive hospitality that the Johnsons offered to noteworthy Americans who passed
through London. Not only did Joshua appear to have a highly profitable trading business in addition to his consular income, but he spoke
of owning a vast estate in Georgia.

Born in 1742, Joshua Johnson belonged to a distinguished family
in Maryland, where his brother Thomas had been the first Revolutionary governor before serving as an associate justice of the United
States Supreme Court from 1791 to 1793. Joshua Johnson came to England in 1771 to represent colonial tobacco and commodities enterprises.

When the American Revolution began, he removed with his family and business to Nantes in France until the end of the war. The
Johnsons then returned to London, where their household soon was
particularly admired for putting music foremost as entertainment. At
home, Joshua's wife, Catherine Nuth, reigned like a queen—perhaps
by necessity, since Johnson was subject to extremes in mood, veering
from elation to depression. Their family included, in addition to the
three talented daughters, four more girls and a boy. Another daughter
had died in France.

By Christmas, Adams' journal was recording daily visits to the
Johnson residence. An early feature was his description of a splendid
ball given to honor the eldest daughter, Nancy, on her birthday. Two
days later, JQA noted that he was still "quite stiff in my limbs" from
having danced until 3 a.m., mostly with Louisa, the second daughter.
For Louisa's twenty-first birthday, the family gave another ball, on
January 27, 1796, and this time, Adams did not get to bed until 5 a.m.

Usually, however, evenings were spent more casually at the Johnsons'—dining, listening to music, playing whist, or taking long walks in Hyde Park with Mrs. Johnson and her daughters. As the weeks passed, Adams' rising favorite among these young ladies was Louisa, although he kept his preference to himself, leaving the family to assume that he was courting Nancy, for she was the eldest.

The Johnsons had reason to be confused; after spending an evening with them, Adams often returned to his hotel in some distress as he chided himself for missteps in his efforts to woo Louisa with others almost always within earshot. After one such frustrating occasion, he admitted "how much wiser I should be to stay at home." Finally, on February 2, he had his chance to disclose to Louisa that it was she whom he most admired. When he seized a moment at the Drury Lane theater to speak privately to her, Louisa's response "gave some satisfaction."

Louisa later recalled how she had been thunderstruck when Adams explained himself, so certain was she that his intentions were toward Nancy. This belief had allowed her, Louisa remembered, to be much more relaxed and natural with him than if she had suspected his designs. Unknown to Louisa, her straightforward manner appealed to Adams, who was well known back in Massachusetts for complaining about the silly, artificial ways of young women.

And yet Louisa's many talents would make for a difficult romance with John. Part of him would be drawn to her intelligence, beauty, and musical skill. She also spoke French, his favorite language, like a native, thanks to her early schooling in Nantes. Another side of Adams, however, would recoil from Louisa's independent and unrepressed nature. She was not then, nor would she ever be, a woman cowed by males, while he never could be comfortable when facing a strong female personality. Such encounters apparently roused irritating memories of the domineering manner of his mother, Abigail Adams.

Consequently, Adams approached Louisa much more cautiously than he had Mary Frazier. Once he made his interest known to Miss Johnson, he remained very guarded with her and everyone else about his intentions as this strange courtship proceeded into the spring. Its progress was erratic. Misunderstandings arose because he was trying to keep quiet about his preference and because Louisa's vigorous manner alarmed him. As a result, the suitor often appeared to be indifferent, which left Louisa doubtful and angry and both of them "sullen."

The bumbling Adams admitted to himself that the situation was embarrassing as he kept putting off declaring his selection of Louisa to her parents. Perhaps he was somewhat mortified that he could be in love again so quickly, particularly after his stern prediction to his mother that any new romance was far in the future. He was also taken aback at how romance affected him. With Louisa on his mind, he found he could no longer concentrate on reading and writing. To an Adams, this was a high price to pay, leaving him to marvel at his plight: "Wherefore must this be so pleasing?"

The winter and early spring of 1796 passed with Adams saying nothing about his feelings for Louisa to her parents, and little to Louisa herself. With still no instructions to return to The Hague, Adams' appearances at the Johnson residence continued daily, save for two interruptions. One of them entailed welcoming several members of Boston's Crackbrain Club and showing them around London and vicinity. The more important distraction, however, came when he consented to Mrs. John Singleton Copley's suggestion that his portrait be painted by her famed artist husband as her gift to Abigail Adams.

Posing for Copley began on February 11, and after many sittings the portrait was finished on April 4. The flattering result has been acclaimed one of the finest paintings of an American figure (see illustration in insert). Even the subject himself was impressed. "He has made a good picture of it," Adams conceded as he dashed away from the final sitting to keep another daily appointment "with the ladies."

Little else detained him from courtship, although he continued as tight-lipped about his romance in diary entries as he was often voluble about international matters. Back in Philadelphia and Quincy, in order to keep track of JQA's personal affairs, the Adams family had to rely on rumors. Tom, on duty in Holland, chided John for his silence, saying that he was about to give him up for dead. When John did finally write to Tom, he tried to tantalize by mentioning a charming girl he had discovered. With his mother, the swain was even more coy. When he eventually apologized to Abigail for a long silence, John hinted: "Perhaps I may tell you the reason of this at a future day; or perhaps you may guess at it without being told."

Once again, Abigail surmised that her son was in love. Suspecting that he had fallen into the hands of the Johnson family, whose household glitter she scornfully remembered from her own days in London, Mother Adams took the offensive without mentioning names. Instead, she admonished John to be on guard against what she called the fleeting appeal of feminine beauty. The choice of a mate must be guided by more than physical attraction, for he could be sure that "time will trim the lustre of the eye, and wither the bloom of the face." He must aim for the "more lasting union of friendship." The prudent step, Abigail advised, was for John to wait and find a wife in America.

JQA obviously preferred to keep his new love beyond his mother's reach. Remembering the disastrous aftermath of her learning about Mary Frazier, he wanted Abigail to remain in the dark until there was no turning back—if, indeed, he chose to marry or even to become formally betrothed. His wavering on these issues—he called it his "awkward" plight—might have continued even after he left London except that, abruptly, he was compelled to speak. Unfortunately, he was obliged to declare himself first to Mrs. Johnson rather than to Louisa.

On the morning of April 13, when everyone knew his sojourn in London must soon end, he received a message from Catherine Johnson asking to see him. Despite a badly infected finger, he hastened to the residence, where, in reply to pointed questions, he revealed a wish to marry Louisa. After giving Mrs. Johnson what he termed "a full explanation of my views and intentions," Adams reported that Louisa's mother "declared herself satisfied."

Louisa's response, however, was quite different. She was distinctly displeased that her mother had heard Adams' announcement before she had. Throughout his life, JQA considered his social manners inept, but this error was monumental—especially for a gentleman in the business of diplomacy. After Louisa learned from her mother about Adams' wish to marry her, she displayed such a chilling face to her suitor that he asked for an explanation. Not wishing to appear taken for granted, Louisa replied that she needed time to consider his offer. She promised to give him an answer soon.

On April 18, the couple came to a partial understanding, at least. Adams reported that he was explicit with Louisa about his feelings and hopes and apologized for having been less than forthright with her. Louisa then accepted his proposal, after which he spoke to Joshua Johnson, who gave his blessing. But there was a hitch. Father and daughter objected to one vital point in John's proposition. He discovered that becoming engaged had been the easy part; the difficulty was naming a date for the wedding, a matter that caused him once more to become evasive as he sought to postpone the event.

An exasperated Louisa could not get him to talk about why he insisted on deferring their wedding because there was little JQA felt he could say that anyone, especially Louisa, might appreciate. Put baldly, as much as he may have loved Louisa, he did not wish at that moment to be burdened with her. In his heart, in fact, he may have hoped to remain a bachelor indefinitely. The situation, therefore, required that he devise an elaborate rationalization for a long engagement.

He built it upon what he claimed was the need to compensate for so many months of dissipated living in London. He said he must escape the idleness into which life around the Johnsons had sunk him. Amends must be made for this distressing behavior, he believed, and doing so should be in solitary and disciplined circumstances. He urgently needed to prove to himself that London had not turned him into an idle fop—which was the fate his parents warned could come to him if he dallied at places like the Johnson residence. Furthermore, he became convinced that his salary as minister to Holland would not support a wife who was accustomed to luxury. And who knew how much longer he would remain at The Hague?

Until State Department orders arrived on April 26, Adams heaped shame upon himself for time wasted during his six months in London: "What a mere slave to circumstance!—nothing of the better sort of clay about me." Whenever the question of a marriage date came up, he remained adamant but vague. No ceremony at present was the "one point . . . to which I *must* adhere," he vowed. "The right and the reason of the thing are . . . indisputably with me, and I shall accordingly persist."

He kept to himself how much he may have been affected by a rising suspicion that his prospective father-in-law might not, after all, be proprietor of a vast Southern acreage, and that there would be no generous dowry accompanying a Johnson daughter to the altar.

As it happened, Adams was correct. The Johnsons faced financial ruin. Unwise investments, expenses beyond income, and large debts would soon send Joshua Johnson and family sailing for America in fiscal disgrace. With them would go Adams' anticipation of retiring to a Georgia plantation and pursuing his literary ambitions in ease a plan that had once seemed such a certainty as to evoke his impetuous prediction to his parents and to Tom that he would soon settle in the South. This hope was crushed when, perhaps a fortnight after Mrs. Johnson had called upon Adams for an explanation, he watched Louisa's usually ebullient mother grow "very low in spirits" while Mr. Johnson was overcome by melancholy. These observations strengthened Adams in his refusal to make any plans for marriage. He must return alone to The Hague.

Once the papers allowing him to depart England arrived, Adams immediately arranged to take the first available boat to Rotterdam. Seeing that her betrothed was indeed serious about abandoning her,

Louisa accused him of being "unaccountable," which led him to charge her with being the same. When they tried to talk, "the usual asperities arose." Fortunately, the prospect of an imminent parting soon stirred the lovers to put aside their distress and enjoy what Adams called evenings "of satisfaction." Then, on May 27, his London stay closed with a visit at the Johnsons he characterized as one "of delight and of regret"; after a final conversation with them, he "took my leave of all the family with sensations unusually painful."

His vessel was to depart Gravesend for Rotterdam at noon on May 28, a time JQA had agreed to, even though he knew the permission he needed from London officials to embark would not be issued until the precise moment his ship was to sail. Although Adams sought an exception to this bureaucratic rule, no clerk would budge until noon. At the stroke of twelve and clutching the necessary order, he jumped into a carriage to make the twenty-five-mile ride to Gravesend. He was too late. The vessel had departed minutes before, after waiting since noon. Determined not to be left behind, he next chartered a small boat, paid an outrageous price, and was alongside his ship by 6 p.m. Three days later, exhausted, he was reunited with Tom Adams, whom he kept awake "chatting upon various subjects til after one in the morning."

The next day, rested, an eager Minister Adams slipped into the harness of a studious schedule that he had been obliged to abandon in London. This was "the life on the whole infinitely better suited to my taste." His "solitude" in The Hague again brought him much satisfaction, as did the lightness of his diplomat's duties.

He arose at 5 a.m., read instructively until 9, breakfasted, and then, after a glance at the papers, toiled until noon at his latest literary enthusiasm: making translations from classical literature. He was charmed especially by Tacitus, the Roman historian and politician, whom he called "this incomparable author," as well as by another Roman, Lucretius, the poet of cosmology. In the presence of such superb literature, his aspirations to be a writer took on new vigor, although he cautioned himself that "the time for original composition has not yet come; I know not if it ever will."

Following a morning of study, he would dress for the day and resume where he had left off the previous afternoon in writing letters, many of great length, particularly those concerning European affairs that he sent to John Adams. He did this until 3 p.m., after which he walked a bit, dined, and conversed until 5. Then it was back to books until he took an hour's stroll at 9, often with Baron de Bielfeld, the Prussian minister, who soon became his partner in studying Italian.

Before retiring at 11 p.m., he usually enjoyed a "light supper" accompanied by a cigar.

Over and over, Adams announced that the wholesome contrast of this routine with the "bustle" of London gave him complete satisfaction. He prized its mostly solitary nature: "I am not formed to shine in company, nor to be delighted with it." His goal, he said, was to "become perfectly studious." Toward that end, no taskmaster could have been more severe. On his twenty-ninth birthday, he apologetically confessed in his diary that he sometimes stayed in bed rather than rise at 5 a.m.; after being a slugabed, it was necessary the next morning "to atone" by beginning work at 4. When it struck him that he might be "undertaking too much," Adams reminded himself that he must endure a season of penance for having surrendered to "the irresistible dissipation of London."

He armed himself with a new motto: "Endeavoring at self-examination, self-correction, and self-government," qualities he particularly needed once Abigail had guessed correctly that Louisa Johnson was her son's betrothed. Immediately, the bitterly disappointed mother began to reproach John by emphasizing that the young woman doubtless "inherits the taste for elegance which her mamma is conspicuous for." Never deigning to name Louisa, Abigail spoke of her as a "*half-blood*" (a reference to Louisa's Anglo-American parentage) and surmised that she probably "plays music delightfully" (a broad hint that Louisa was trained to be an ornament and not the spouse schooled in practical matters needed by an American male).

In opposing the match, Abigail enlisted the services of JQA's father, and John Adams obediently chimed in by warning his son of the danger brought to a man by a wife "of fine parts and accomplishments, educated to drawing, dancing, and music, however domestic and retired from the world she may have been in her father's house." This sort of mate would soon impoverish a husband. The best advice the vice president could offer was: "I give you a hint and you must take it"—the son would have to keep a close watch on his purse.

The marriage must be postponed, JQA's mother ordered, and he should allow his betrothed to return to America with her family. According to Abigail, the "tender and inexperienced" Louisa would thereby escape further exposure to the costly temptations of European life. Visualizing the girl as a pathetic creature helpless before Europe's depraved ways, Abigail predicted that should Louisa remain abroad as John's wife, she would acquire "such inclinations and habits as to endanger her youth and inexperience [and] unfit her for the discharge of those domestic duties which cement the union of hearts and give it its sweetest pleasures."

While this time Abigail's encouragement that he defer marriage could have been welcomed by JQA, his mother's scornful views instead made him spring to Louisa's defense. To Abigail, he stressed Louisa's strength of character and insisted that she would be a wife who had "goodness of heart and gentleness of disposition, as well as spirit and discretion." If he had made a poor choice, "I shall be the principal sufferer," he reminded Abigail in a blunt letter of August 16. And what, he asked, if he had waited until his selection of a spouse met all the "requisites" laid down by his mother? "I would certainly be doomed to perpetual celibacy." Only words from the Adams matriarch could thus rouse the suitor who had been so hesitant in London.

Receiving her son's letter, a considerably startled Abigail realized that her strategy had backfired. Trying to apologize, she explained to him that she had written out of genuine concern. "My fear arose from the youth and inexperience of the lady." Seeing her cause was lost, she surrendered and asked John to tell Louisa that "I consider her already as my daughter."

Then, suddenly, a delay in the marriage became even more essential—at least JQA thought so—when he learned that President Washington was reassigning him; he was now to be minister to Portugal. The change was a promotion, and while it might mean he would not be reentering private life for several more years, it could also extend his sojourn in the bliss of a bachelor's routine. He foresaw in Lisbon a long stretch of uninterrupted time to enjoy his books, the pleasures of cosmopolitan male colleagues, and the delight of spending his salary on enlarging his library—rather than on supporting a wife.

Going to Lisbon also had the advantage of excusing Adams from returning to the States to practice law. This escape became doubly welcome as disturbing reports of American politics reached Holland. He now had good reason to fear that his reappearance in Massachusetts would propel him, if only as an essayist, into the vicious partisan warfare that had broken out between his father's Federalists and the Jeffersonians over issues ranging from foreign policy to the nature of the Union. Were he at home, he believed his parents would press him to seek "a career of fame" or "a career of ambition," either of which would oblige him to submit to "the revolutions of *popular opinion*."

The danger called for another courageous letter to his father in which he announced that "the first and most strenuous of my endeavors will be to preserve my independence entire." While speaking of

preferring "silent obscurity," he moved closer to candor when he acknowledged that his aim was eventually to "adopt a mode of life which
will allow me leisure for my private pursuits and literary studies."

In replying, John Adams sent the reassurance his son wanted:
parental influence had had nothing to do with the appointment to Portugal. Washington himself had urged that Minister Adams be retained
in diplomatic service regardless of whether the young man's father became president and had called JQA the most valuable of America's officials abroad, a tribute John's parents wasted no time in reporting to
The Hague.

Consequently, the benefit of remaining abroad now took command of JQA's mind, particularly after Tom agreed to stay with him
as secretary. John also seemed newly impressed by the cultural advantages of Lisbon over Boston. He knew he would deplore the absence of
sophisticated Europeans were he to reenter a law office or a legislative
hall in the United States. Nor would he have at home anything resem-
bling the caliber of European theater. Even in Holland he had enjoyed
performances far superior to anything he predicted he would see in
America.

And then there were Europe's bookshops, which he said he would
sorely miss in Boston—a thought that reminded him of the comparatively meager collection at Harvard. Moved to be generous, John sent
President Willard choice volumes from among his most cherished purchases "as a small token of gratitude and veneration to the Library of
the University."

The news about Portugal had a very different effect in the Johnson
household. Louisa notified John that surely now they need not put off
their wedding, and that she would gladly accompany him to Lisbon.
She proposed to come to The Hague and be married there. At this, he
sharply rebuked her for what he claimed was an undignified and improper suggestion. He also spoke of "childish weakness," which in turn
made Louisa indignant. She replied that she was not concerned about
how her conduct might appear to him, for "I am perfectly satisfied
with its appearance to the world." If she had lost any dignity, it was by
accepting his insulting letters. Where she had been open about wishing
to join him, Louisa charged he had in turn humiliated her.

These words were the start of a bitter exchange that seared each of
them until nearly the moment of their wedding. Louisa said to John,
"Alas, how you have changed," and he responded that he hoped he
would never have to show her how stern he could be if necessary.
Louisa retorted that he had once told her she was perfect. John

undiplomatically attributed such a statement "to the blindness of an irrational love." He still loved her, John admitted to Louisa, but his affection had been refined by a return of the sound judgment that he claimed had abandoned him in London. The restoration of his reason was beneficial, he assured her, for he now would be a better man for her.

He told her she must forget Portugal and accompany her parents to America and await him there. "Let us, my lovely friend, rather submit with cheerfulness to the laws of necessity than resort to unbecoming remedies for relief." Louisa had already heard much talk from John about the merit of fortitude, and she replied that she had not realized how much she would need that quality. Even at this point, she never retreated before her increasingly perplexing beau. "There is not anything on earth can afford me equal happiness [than] to accompany [you] to whatever part of the globe the fates may destine you."

When word of John Adams' election as president reached London early in 1797, Louisa was quick to send the information to JQA, who seemed genuinely dismayed. His father's victory left him stewing in the knowledge that he would be holding a federal office while his father was president of the United States. Believing that many persons would claim he was receiving preferment, he momentarily wished he could disappear from public service, taking his books with him.

To this talk, Louisa astutely responded that from his earliest days, he had been placed in "flattering positions," and that he ought to recognize how he had "insensibly acquired a taste for them." Going to the heart of his dilemma, she advised him that "however free you may fancy yourself from ambition, you would feel infinite mortification when you reflected that by resigning these [public posts,] you gave up the many advantages resulting from them."

Louisa warned Adams to beware of his penchant for withdrawing from the boredom of life into his books. "I think it is a pity that you, so calculated to adorn society, should encourage a disposition improper for the station in which you are placed." And, cleverly, she reproached his "excessive fondness for books" by pointing out that although she continued to play the harp, it had not "usurped the primary place in my heart that he held, while "your *books*" had taken her place in his.

When she gently suggested that JQA's absorption in reading made him irritable, he was indignant. "I believe that my temper never was and never will be hurt by my devotion to study." He advised Louisa to learn that "any attempt by those whom I love to cross the current of my character or control my sentiments or manners" would anger him.

(This was a response the imperious Abigail Adams had by now encountered several times.) Only in one respect was a wife welcome to reprove him, he told Louisa: whenever she might find him wasting time. It would be to her advantage, he emphasized, to encourage his study, for "I shall love you the more in proportion to my degree of application."

Eventually, both John and Louisa realized that their battle by letter was becoming dangerous. He conceded that he had occasionally written to her in acrimony, and he asked her forgiveness. Louisa replied that, "much as I avow myself offended and hurt at your late conduct, I would not relinquish the smallest particle of my affection if I could." When she said she wanted to earn both his love and his esteem, he was delighted and praised her for displaying "a kind of spirit that I admire, a resolution that I most cordially approve, and which I am sure you will carry into effect."

Although peace was declared, the couple's epistolary altercation had revealed the temperamental differences that would plague their marriage through fifty years. Adams was stiff; dominant, especially toward females; and rarely could take teasing. Louisa was clever, occasionally lighthearted, and impatient with male pretentiousness. Discerning as she was, however, she could not yet realize how truly painful it was for JQA to be torn between two prospects: the excitement of public service and the soothing seclusion of literary endeavor. Nor could she see that both led him away from marrying at present.

THE JOHNSONS LINGERED in London through the spring of 1797, keeping alive the issue that Adams had hoped to evade: would the advantages of continuing in diplomacy be diminished by his marriage? He was keenly conscious that a wife, particularly a spirited one like Louisa, would hamper his prized personal independence. And then there were worries over the cost of maintaining a wife in Lisbon and over Louisa's safety if Portugal became a battleground as the war between France and England continued.

No doubt Adams did love Louisa—events after their marriage proved that—and had the physical desires usually accompanying betrothal to a beautiful young woman. That part of him would welcome marriage, but another part wished Louisa was in faraway America. This conflict only grew more difficult, with the result that his letters became even more bewildering to Louisa. Reading messages that were sometimes loving, other times harsh, gloomy, and chillingly severe, she could be pardoned for suspecting that he wished he were not engaged, especially when he seemed to paint himself in disagreeable hues just for her benefit.

Adams had to remain at The Hague until July before he could depart for his new assignment in Portugal. In the months before William Vans Murray, his successor in Holland, arrived, the vexing issue of when he and Louisa should be married grew more divisive. As her family continued to press for an immediate wedding, Adams kept finding new reasons to postpone the event, most involving vague uncertainties about his departure from Holland as well as the possibility that Napoleon Bonaparte would occupy Portugal and make American representation there untenable. These were reasons enough, he insisted to the Johnsons, for Louisa and her family to sail for America at once.

At this point, Joshua Johnson's worsening financial plight obliged him to reveal to JQA details of his bankrupt state. In reply, Adams hastened to stress his own poverty, implying that anyone who thought a son of the new president of the United States was wealthy was sadly mistaken. JQA began to insist with new vigor that not until he returned to the States could the wedding take place. Joshua's impoverishment had the effect of making Lisbon much more desirable. A penniless father-in-law meant that if Adams went back to private life, he must dust off his law books to support a family.

Not surprisingly, the embattled engagement came close to ending as a mystified Louisa kept talking of a wedding. After assailing her with more dire warnings of the hardship that marriage to him would mean, an astonishingly tactless and insensitive John finally took courage and put the question to his betrothed: did she want to remain engaged to him? "Choose, Louisa, choose for yourself, and be assured that [my] heart will ratify your choice."

Louisa's reply was a marvel of self-control. First, she turned aside his request that she reconsider marrying him. In a decision very different from Mary Frazier's, Louisa said that she had pledged her love to him and thus he ought to know she was immovable. Then she admitted her amazement at how easily her statements offended him. "Whenever I write you, I feel a sort of fear lest I should inadvertently repeat them." She had no intention of interrupting his studies. "My whole life shall be devoted to render you happy." Could he not remember "that there lives not a being who loves you as well as your faithful Louisa C. Johnson"?

To prove her devotion, Louisa then surrendered her hope of a prompt marriage. On May 19, 1797, she told Adams that, much as she yearned to be with him in Lisbon, "if it is attended by any inconvenience to you, I am the last person on earth to desire it. Your letters all tend to convince me that this is the case, and I have relinquished the pleasing hope of our meeting."

She spoke a bit too soon. Neither she nor her betrothed had anticipated the shrewd intervention of her father. Joshua Johnson had noted carefully a concession JQA made in mid-April that if an American vessel could be found to take Louisa and him to Portugal, then it might—just might—be possible for them to be married and remain together. This statement was mostly a hollow gesture, for Adams knew no such vessel was likely to turn up, given the danger then prevailing for neutral commerce. If it was a bluff, Johnson called it.

On May 26, as Adams packed in preparation for boarding a Danish ship that was to carry him directly to Lisbon, he received a startling announcement. In what must have been an astonishing feat given his desperate financial state, Louisa's father had arranged that one of his last trading schooners would convey his daughter and her husband to Lisbon. Ironically, it was named the *Mary*, a coincidence the humorless John did not seem to notice. The boat would be specially prepared for the comfort of the bride and groom, and berths would be provided for Tom and for the two servants attending Mr. and Mrs. Adams.

Suddenly, Adams found he had no honorable choice but grudgingly to consider Johnson's arrangement. Rather than display gratitude, he actually scolded Louisa's father, saying he had not intended for a ship to be used so extravagantly. If another voyage could be assigned to the *Mary*, Adams urged that it be done. Once again, he spoke vaguely of "uncertainties" that might yet prevent his coming to London en route to Lisbon.

Meanwhile, Louisa wrote of her delight in what her father had accomplished. "Our difficulties ended!" she announced, to which he coldly replied by urging her to reflect carefully on whether she should accompany him to Lisbon. "I wish you may never have reason to consider as the commencement of difficulties what you now regard as their termination." He warned her that marriage might disappoint her. "You put too much gilding upon your prospects," he said darkly. "You have promised yourself too much." Louisa, of course, was not to be dissuaded.

In mid-June, when he could delay no longer, he capitulated, but with little grace. He reminded Louisa that it was she who insisted upon going with him to Lisbon. Then, the long season of hesitation over, America's new minister to Portugal set out on June 30, reluctantly planning a stopover in London so that he could be married.

In his mood at the moment, it evidently gave JQA little satisfaction that his service as American minister to Holland had been deemed a great success on both sides of the Atlantic.

CHAPTER FIVE

Berlin

*There are certainly more volumes published here in one year
than there are of volumes worth reading in the world.*

THE ADAMS BROTHERS left The Hague on June 29, 1797, but they
did not get far. Once again, unfavorable winds at the Channel imposed a long wait. John apparently bore the delay with astonishing fortitude, mainly because this time he was in Maasluis, near the
attractions of Rotterdam, where friends, books, and a billiard table
were available. These pleasures were interrupted when "some very unpleasant intelligence" caught up with him: a report that President John
Adams was planning to name his son the United States' first representative to the court of the king of Prussia. Consequently, Berlin, not Lisbon, apparently would be JQA's next residence.

Angered and disappointed by this rumor, which meant he would
owe his office to his father, John arrived in London on July 12, so
dismayed that he put off appearing at the Johnson home until the next
day. For Louisa, the possibility of Berlin instead of Lisbon was much
less disquieting than her discovery that her fiancé had waited nearly
twenty-four hours before coming to call. Nor could she accompany
Adams and her father when they went to secure authorization for the
nuptials—in those days fathers handled this matter for daughters.
Johnson then proudly displayed his vessel, the *Mary*, which he had
converted into a honeymoon bower.

Only a day later, Adams learned for certain that the *Mary* would
not be needed. Rufus King, the new United States minister to England, brought verification to JQA's quarters at Osborne's Hotel that

the president had indeed appointed him minister plenipotentiary to the Prussian court. Among the documents King handed over were orders from the State Department that Adams must wait in London for commissions and instructions.

There was also a letter from President Adams regretting any inconvenience caused by the new assignment, but insisting that even if his son was already in Lisbon, he must pack up again and head for Berlin, where the president believed his son's sharp eye would have a better view of Europe's upheaval. After a tour of duty in Prussia, JQA was told, he could expect a move to Sweden. Both Prussia and Sweden were nations with which America wished to renegotiate important treaties.

In the face of these unsettling changes, Louisa's father displayed more of his characteristic generosity. When Adams lamented that there would be no acceptable accommodations in London where he and Louisa could await orders to proceed to Berlin, Joshua urged the pair to share the Johnson home after the wedding.

This hospitable gesture was little comfort as Adams viewed the destruction of his plans for Portugal. Amid the bustling preparations for his marriage, he took time to write indignantly to his parents. It was bad enough, he complained, that most of his possessions, including his precious library, were on their way to Lisbon. Much more annoying was that he must fill a post awarded by his parent. He bluntly told President Adams that he had seriously hesitated about accepting the appointment. Could his father not see "the degraded and humiliating aspect" in which the position put a son?

It gave "a colour of reason to those who would represent me as a creature of favour." Even worse, JQA fumed, in Berlin he would be seen as unqualified, holding the post merely because of kinship. What particularly angered him was that, months earlier, he had taken pains to warn his father as well as his mother that never would he accept an appointment from President Adams. But his hands were now tied. He acknowledged that it would be harmful for him to refuse the post after being confirmed by the Senate. In the privacy of his journal, however, young Adams conceded that he must have money to support the wife he was about to acquire, and that remaining in the diplomatic corps was for now his only assured means of income.

The solemnization of matrimony took place on July 26 in the Johnsons' Anglican parish church, which bore the intimidating name of "All Hallows Berkyngechirche by the Tower of London." Custom had simplified this to "All Hallows Barking." One of the oldest surviving London structures, dating back to 675, the building had a Saxon cross and doorway, and the crypt held the remains of Romans. The rector who blessed the union was the Reverend John Hewlett; Tom Adams served as one of the witnesses. The marriage agreement pledged a £500 dowry. (It was never paid.)

The bride was twenty-two; the groom had just passed his thirtieth birthday. They made an attractive pair. Louisa was dark-haired and petite, with an eager, vivacious quality that enhanced her considerable feminine beauty. John, too, was slight in stature, five feet seven inches tall. His receding hairline and tendency to stoutness—characteristic of Adams males—did not detract from his handsome, well-chiseled features. Louisa's delicate appearance would be little changed by fifty years of marriage. John, however, would become bald and bulky, eventually weighing about 180 pounds.

WHAT WAS IN JQA'S HEART that morning at All Hallows Barking church? His journal is very quiet about his mood as the moment arrived that he had sought so strenuously to postpone or prevent. He was worried about the responsibility of a spouse; he was greatly disappointed that Joshua Johnson was not the man of limitless wealth he had once seemed; and he was outraged that he must now fill a place on the public payroll supplied by his father. The groom's attitude toward the bride in the face of these concerns was veiled, just then.

Soon, however, JQA's diary and his letters began to proclaim his delight in Louisa. He was fortunate in marriage, he asserted, and he would repeat and enlarge upon this sentiment throughout the half-century of his wedded life. He seemed at last to recognize that in marrying Louisa, he had the great good fortune to be linked with a spouse whom any male would yearn to have.

Of course, as the years passed, it would have been uncharacteristic had he not mentioned difficulties in their union. These arose mostly from differences in temperament, for when it came to defending a position contrary to her husband's, Louisa shared Abigail's courage—and beyond, since JQA would prove much more difficult to get along with than his father ever was.

While the amount of Louisa's writing in memoirs and letters remains far less than John's, there is enough to give a vivid display of her nature and her understanding of her husband and their marriage. This evidence discloses her as an intelligent, passionate, discerning, deeply religious, and musically talented person. She was also sensitive, so much so that she became subject to emotionally based physical disorders, although she would suffer no more than ordinary melancholy, rather than her husband's chronic depression. When family crises would occur, often incapacitating John, it would be Louisa who proved the family's source of strength and comfort.

From some vantage points, Louisa would appear much like Abigail Adams. Both were gifted letter writers. They were astute critics of literature. They were shrewd judges of political behavior. But there were also significant differences, which may well have saved the day for Louisa as a wife. She was a compassionate, gentle person, rather shy except when she sang or performed on the harp or piano. She assuredly did not share Abigail's aggressiveness, or her need to dominate males, particularly sons.

Perhaps the crucial contrast between the two women would amount to this: where Abigail could often be terrifying, Louisa was always lovable. John would have been justified in coming away from the wedding wondering whether his mother would ever accept the wife he had selected—or any wife of his choice rather than of hers.

THE JOHNSON-ADAMS MARRIAGE ceremony only began the nuptial events, as JQA discovered when the wedding party set out to visit a family friend's country seat. Afterward, the Johnsons presided at a lengthy dinner. "The day was long and closed at about 11," Adams reported in his journal. He and Louisa then settled down with the Johnsons on Coopers Row to await State Department instructions. These did not arrive for three months, a honeymoon period that, in Adams' opinion, proved less than idyllic.

Late July and August 1797 were very hot by English standards, but this did not deter the Johnsons and their friends from a monthlong marriage jubilee. Dinners, concerts, dances, and parties consumed nearly every moment, leaving the new husband grumbling, except when there were outings to the theater. On August 25, the celebration closed as the Johnsons gave a grand ball that lasted until 4 a.m., after which the family was utterly exhausted, none more so than the groom. "I am even scarcely capable of thinking," he recorded on the twenty-sixth.

He candidly deplored his tendency to linger in the marital bed until 9 a.m. After breakfast, he did slip away occasionally for a walk to the Adelphi Building, where Tom was staying. There he could read and write letters, among them rather stiff announcements of his marriage that he dispatched to family and friends.

To John and Abigail Adams JQA reported that he had the honor to present another worthy daughter, and he predicted that "she, who has in an amiable and respectable family, adorned the characters of a daughter and sister, will prove an equal ornament to that of a wife." Of Louisa he said to Daniel Sargent: "She is fit for the praise of any tongue—but mine." Then, perhaps seeking a bit of revenge, knowing that his parents wished to have Tom return home, he told them he must have his brother in Berlin, if only to provide agreeable companionship in a remote city where Americans were rarely seen.

It was Tom who sent the most relaxed and comforting report on the marriage. He told his mother how much he delighted in his new sister-in-law, whose "softness of temper" he admired. He asserted that Louisa "seems to love as she ought" and was worthy in every way of his brother. As for the Johnson family, Tom praised their kindness; if he knew that financial woes had overtaken them, he gave no sign, instead assuring Abigail: "I feel proud of an alliance with such worthy people."

Unfortunately, Joshua could no longer evade his creditors and was compelled to carry out his plan of escaping with his family to the United States. Shortly before the Johnsons departed in early September, Louisa and John removed to a furnished apartment in Osborne's Hotel. There the clan gathered for a farewell supper, after which "we had a distressing scene," John reported, "while the whole family took leave of Louisa." At 4 a.m. on September 9, Joshua Johnson led his wife and daughters out of London to Margate and a ship bound for America.

Immediately, Louisa and John were hounded by bill collectors who had discovered that Joshua had left town. Joining the uproar were the family's former servants, who had not been paid. When Adams was told the full extent of Johnson's fall from wealth, he realized that Louisa and her family had indeed become penniless. The situation contrasted sharply with what he had anticipated when he asked for Louisa's hand, leaving him now little more than the consolation of having gone through with the marriage. "I have done my duty—rigorous, inflexible duty." To have been "less faithful," he said, would have been unthinkable.

En route to America, Joshua Johnson wrote to his son-in-law boasting anew of grand prospects in the States. In his reply, Adams could not resist a bit of sarcasm. If Joshua was truthful, then surely, John pointed out, there was no basis for worry or, for that matter, for such a disgraceful flight from Europe. Why then delay in paying his debts? he asked Johnson.

In truth, no wealth awaited Louisa's father in the United States, and only his appointment as postmaster in the District of Columbia by President Adams saved the family from destitution.

Knowledge of her dear papa's disgrace turned Louisa for a time into a gloomy spouse who often had "blue" spells. Even so, the couple spent their last weeks in London agreeably enough. They dined with friends, walked in Hyde Park and Kensington Gardens, appeared regularly at church services, and attended the theater virtually every night. Most memorable was the Covent Garden performance on October 6 of Shakespeare's *Much Ado About Nothing,* for which the great Mrs. Abington—who was "old, very old, and grows fat"—came out of retirement to play Beatrice, which JQA conceded she did "very well."

Adams also haunted the bookshops and, during the few evenings they were free, read aloud to Louisa. On September 22, instructions for his mission to Prussia at last arrived. The couple promptly began final preparations for Berlin, which seemed rather like the end of the world, especially after they learned that they would need their own carriage to travel from Hamburg to their destination.

On October 18, the Adams party, consisting of John, Louisa, Thomas, and servants Epps and Whitcomb, set off for Hamburg. They arrived in Gravesend to learn that the captain of their vessel had been unable to wait and had sailed. Having paid the group's fare in advance, a sum he was loath to lose, John commandeered a skiff to pursue the ship, determined to gamble on the chance that they would find where it had put up for the night.

Fortunately, the evening was calm, making the chase less of an ordeal. Their quarry was eventually overtaken while riding at anchor, and Mr. and Mrs. Adams were welcomed aboard at 10 p.m. At once, Louisa became seasick. The voyage across the North Sea to the mouth of the Elbe River soon proved so rough that even Adams felt ill, although he was comforted that Louisa bore the experience "remarkably well."

What made him complain most was that of his countless books, he had only brought a novel with him, *Ferdinand Count Fathom,* which he considered one of Tobias Smollett's less successful efforts. When the ship began moving up the Elbe, he groused even more because the banks were not as lovely as those along rivers in England and France.

His spirits brightened considerably, however, on October 26 at Hamburg, where port officials amused him by inquiring whether he and his party were immigrants.

The Adamses found several acquaintances in Hamburg who made them comfortable during the ten-day respite John had arranged for his party before starting for Berlin. He saw to it that their carriage was removed from the ship so that he could take Louisa on rides through the countryside. He also was careful to purchase more books, including a volume of German maps, which became useful when travel resumed on November 2. Many of the German roads were sandy trails—"bogs of mud," JQA called them. The inns along the way were little better, obliging them to sleep German fashion, between two feather comforters—"I like not the custom," he said.

In trying to find something praiseworthy about the villages and towns they saw, Adams nodded approvingly over indications that Germans were fond of music and reading. He had much time to take in the sights, for the going was slow, usually at twenty miles a day. Even so, such a pace required riding from 6 a.m. to as late as 10 p.m., often passing through woods where tree branches loudly scraped the carriage.

On November 7, they entered the gates of Berlin, where they were momentarily barred by "a dapper lieutenant" who did not know "who the United States of America were" until he accepted the reassuring explanation of a soldier. It was not the only nuisance John encountered in the city. His baggage was either in Lisbon or in Hamburg, perpetual rains kept him from walking, and he was so tired from travel that he could scarcely read without nodding off. For a time he had to "grope" his way. "In a strange country, not understanding the language, and having no friend to consult, I find imposition of every kind recurring at every moment."

In six weeks, however, his outlook had improved remarkably, so that he could assure his diary: "Find myself much more at my ease." Even the shopping went better, he reported, while he and Louisa enjoyed daily walks together as they began an extended honeymoon. Official business made very few claims upon Adams' time, so that most of his attention could go to Louisa and to his literary interests.

Not that there were no professional difficulties in Berlin. The king of Prussia, Frederick William II, died a few days after JQA's arrival, an event that at first threatened months of inaction before freshly issued papers might arrive from America properly presenting the minister to the new king. Fortunately, Frederick William III, who now began a reign of more than forty years, possessed a no-nonsense outlook and consented to receive Adams' original commission. On December 5, he was formally welcomed by the king and the dowager queen, after which he ran the gauntlet of greetings from minor royalty.

Soon, he was on cordial terms with the king, the three ministers who handled foreign affairs, and other Prussian dignitaries, including Prince Henry, brother to the late Frederick the Great. Henry enjoyed talking about the inevitable rise of American power—and the decline of Europe's—in a fashion that gratified the American minister.

It also pleased John that diplomatic manners in Berlin were more open than such customs in London. It made one of his objectives easy: that of renewing the United States' treaty with Prussia, which was at the point of expiring after ten years. The agreement reflected the two nations' wish neither to challenge British sea power nor to hamper England in its struggle against France.

While official life went well in Berlin, Adams' personal affairs were another story. Louisa had become pregnant before they set out for Prussia. A week after arriving in Berlin, signs warned of an approaching miscarriage, and John became frantic with worry. Although there was a competent English physician in Berlin to attend Louisa, it was John who, day after day, sat with his wife as she went through "the most excruciating pain." He often reported "a dreadful night again," until on November 19 he had to record these words on the miscarriage: "we were relieved." He tried not "to murmur at the ways of Providence."

Louisa's ordeal had occurred in the hotel—"tavern," the couple called it—where the Adamses stayed after arriving in the city. To comfort his wife, John began a search for an apartment more convenient and comfortable where she could feel at home. He found one near the Brandenburg Gate, with a landlord who played an overpowering game of chess. Eventually, they would move again, this time to the corner of Frederic and Behren streets.

Once settled, Louisa rapidly recovered her strength. The weather improved, making companionable walking a pleasure, as it did their search for the necessities to furnish their apartment. Much did they rejoice when, shortly before Christmas, their baggage began arriving. Amid this brightened life, John discovered that he was more than ever in love with Louisa. She had fought so tenaciously against miscarrying and had maintained such a courageous disposition in travel and in personal tribulation that, stern though he was in expectations of himself and others, he began to admire his wife.

To Abigail Adams, he said of Louisa: "It will, I am very sure, give you pleasure when I assure you that I find her every day more deserving of all my affection." To sister Nabby, he reported that we "find our mutual affection increasing, rather than suffering any abatement." By the spring of 1798, he wrote again about Louisa to his mother, "I will not indulge myself in the panegyrics which my inclination dictates," as he pretended he did not wish Abigail to detect "that the lover had not yet subsided into the husband."

Unfortunately, it soon was evident that Louisa's first miscarriage had only begun a series. The effect upon both her and her husband was devastating. "The anticipation of evils that we cannot prevent is itself a great misfortune," John observed in July 1798, when Louisa again lay desperately ill. Yet when the miscarriage occurred, he said, "I feel it with no less poignancy than if it had been unexpected." Once more, the ordeal moved him to praise "the loveliness of temper and excellence of character of my wife."

Louisa had indeed blossomed. Attractive, a fine dancer, an intelligent conversationalist in both French and English, and the daughter-in-law of the president of the United States, Mrs. John Quincy Adams became a favorite at court and in diplomatic society. This left her husband with mixed feelings. He was proud of Louisa's success, but doubtful as he was about women having any place in public affairs, he worried that his wife might speak out of turn, embarrassing him and the United States.

Consequently, and much to her disgust, John rarely talked with Louisa about official business or about events in Europe's turmoil. Since she had many female friends with whom she often passed the time, he could easily be off to male gatherings or to the Casino, Berlin's library-club where gentlemen could read the latest newspapers and periodicals.

Both John and Louisa enjoyed royal society, though they saw so much of it that sheer weariness occasionally made them devise excuses for missing an event. In their letters home, to be sure, they carefully stressed their democratic preference for humbler styles. Yet they indeed played their part in Berlin society. One evening, they gave a dinner for forty guests, after which they went to a ball, where they danced till about four in the morning. The Prussians, often out on the town from 6 p.m. to 6 a.m., seemed inexhaustible to the Americans.

When JQA found it prudent to talk shop at a ball, Louisa could depend on her brother-in-law Tom to dance with her until, after a year, Tom decided for the sake of his own independence to depart for the United States. Although the redoubtable Abigail took it upon herself to arrange for Thomas Welsh, a second cousin, to replace Tom as JQA's secretary, John and Louisa mourned Tom's loss. "He has ever been a faithful friend and kind companion," mourned JQA. "It is with a heavy heart that I part with him."

SOMEHOW, THE MINISTER MANAGED amid his social doings to find the many hours needed to report European developments to the State Department and to his father. His dispatches became even more eloquent and farsighted concerning the continuing peril posed by France. The Directory—established under the Constitution of 1795, the latest of Revolutionary France's attempts to be an imperialist republic—was eager to see the United States and England at war. In a badly divided America, where Federalist New England had an hysterical fear of France and where areas dominated by the Jeffersonians sympathized with France, President Adams sought to steer for the goal urged by his son in Berlin: neutrality toward Europe.

JQA was convinced that France would eventually reach accord with the United States on neutral rights. When William Vans Murray, his successor at The Hague and President Adams' special envoy to France, negotiated such a treaty with Paris, he did so with JQA's guidance from afar. Signed on September 30, 1800, the pact somewhat reassured John, although he warned of the return of absolutism to France—which indeed came to pass when Napoleon Bonaparte was named consul for life in 1802.

From his observations in Europe, JQA regularly predicted to those at home that all nations must be prepared to see the French submit to a military government, and he expressed his fear that France might by turns be "anarchical and despotic," all the while carrying "the democratical forms . . . and considering itself the champion for the liberties of the human race." In retirement at Mount Vernon, George Washington read and admired Adams' essay-letters interpreting the European scene.

There were, of course, goings-on in Berlin best not described for American eyes—as on the morning in April 1799 when the Adamses breakfasted with the Prussian queen mother. There they were introduced to a Madame de Harberg, who Her Majesty explained was separated from her husband and was recently arrived in the city in order to meet her lover, a gentleman named Graves, also a guest at breakfast. John was mildly taken aback when the queen mother told him of her delight at seeing the couple "so well together" and of her hope that the liaison "would last."

Adams usually accepted Berlin's "life of dissipation" as "in some measure indispensable here." Nevertheless, with Louisa in good health, he made fresh resolves that being an author must become his life's goal. More and more, he seemed certain that, in his case, literary accomplishment must be the only sure proof of personal independence. The conviction left him uncomfortable when news arrived that he had been elected to the American Academy of Arts and Sciences. He was convinced that his father had made the tribute possible, although it was actually Jeremy Belknap, historian and editor, who had led the campaign to make Adams a member.

Why, JQA wondered, did his parents still seem not to understand that he wanted "no advantage, no notice, no distinction but such as my own qualities should require from impartial judges"?

Toward that end, he became all the more earnest in concentrating on literature, particularly after he discovered the German poets and philosophers. As his enthusiasm for them grew, so did his impatience at his slow progress in learning German. In March 1799, he employed Samuel Henri Catel as a tutor. A pupil of B. H. W. von Kleist, the Romantic poet and dramatist, Catel was himself soon to be a great teacher, as his success with John Quincy Adams would demonstrate. Within six months, Adams' skill had greatly improved, but he still fumed at delays in translation. "I have long suffered under the curse of bad dictionaries," he wrote.

Nevertheless, there was satisfaction in knowing he was mastering the best German writers of the day. Even before he hired Catel, John was reading Gotthold Lessing's dramatic poem *Nathan der Weise,* and had been amused by Friedrich von Schiller's unfinished novel *Die Geisterseher,* with its supernatural emphasis, which reminded him that many Berliners believed in ghosts. He witnessed this at firsthand one evening when his host, Baron Alvensleben, told the guests of being visited in his bedchamber by the spirits of three beautiful women—bringing the near-speechless Adams to comment: "A minister of state!" He soon learned, however, that all members of the royal family firmly believed in ghosts, apparitions, and all the "farago" of witchcraft. Surely, he marveled, these individuals could not be the successors of Frederick the Great.

In the spring of 1799, JQA decided that he would try to be a translator of German authors. He began cautiously—"I have again commenced upon [one] of those plans which I so frequently begin and never finish." In this case, however, there were to be gratifying results, due in large part to some inspiring travel the following summer.

AFTER LOUISA HAD YET another miscarriage, the couple agreed they would benefit from a vacation away from Berlin, where summer was considered unhealthy. The trip would be their first visit to other parts of Germany (an association formed in 1785 and called the League of German Princes) since the journey to Berlin. Departing on July 17, they took with them Epps and Whitcomb and a hired driver for their carriage. Changes of horses and drivers would be arranged as they went along.

The first six weeks of the outing were spent in Bohemia, where they were showered with kindness by friends from Berlin, or friends of these friends, who were summering in the region. Local princesses called upon Louisa while John went about with assorted barons and dined with the Elector of Saxony. Louisa began taking the baths at Toplitz, which proved so beneficial that she soon was able to keep up with her husband for long walks and horseback riding.

Suddenly, for a change, it was he who was ill. During much of August he suffered from fever and chills, sometimes not venturing out from the five-room apartment they had rented, along with servants' quarters. In this crisis, Louisa was strength itself, he wrote, as she "nursed me with all the tenderness and affection which women only can display, and which she possesses in a degree so eminent even among her own sex."

Sickness led John to acts of foolish defiance, the sort of behavior that became his lifelong response to being ill. He acted as if he believed there was no malady he could not shrug off, so that he repudiated all the advice doctors—and Louisa—gave him in Toplitz. Rather than rest and sip lemonade, he insisted on trying to walk about town. The penalty came at night, when he soaked his bed with perspiration, his pulse beating as though it would burst through his chest. He demanded many emetics and purgatives, believing he could not overdo such drastic remedies.

Although he made recovery very difficult, Adams somehow survived, and by the end of August he and Louisa were again seeing the countryside around Toplitz in the daytime and attending opera in the evening. Their most enjoyable experience was a long walk to the Schlossberg castle, which had lain in ruins since the early seventeenth century. Louisa's stamina so elated John—"a great proof of how much her health has improved"—that they celebrated by drinking beer at a tavern near the castle.

At 5 a.m. on September 10, the Adamses set out for Dresden in Saxony. Their carriage was loaded onto a boat that floated down the Elbe River, navigated by three rowers. They arrived in Dresden at 10 p.m., and thus began one of the most rewarding experiences of JQA's life. The ensuing month's stay opened to him the array of superb art, architecture, music, and books that placed Dresden among the finest of Europe's cultural treasuries, particularly of Flemish and Italian paintings. He was forced to confess "how little I knew" about many of the world's masterpieces.

Reluctantly, the couple returned to Berlin, arriving on October 12. Reporting to Tom in Philadelphia about the trip, John mainly emphasized the powerful literary impulse being felt throughout the German states. In a glowing description, he announced: "There are certainly more volumes published here in one year than there are of volumes worth reading in the world." The thought made John impatient to begin his own major creative effort.

With the encouragement of Catel, Adams was soon translating Christoph Martin Wieland's *Oberon,* a poetical treatment of the legendary king of elves or fairies. John had begun reading it during the holiday in Saxony, and though he admired all of Wieland's romances and tales, he proclaimed *Oberon,* with its twelve parts and seventy-three hundred lines, as among the best of German writing.

From November 1799 until he finished a first draft in May 1800, John gave his writing time almost entirely to *Oberon.* What little respite he took from work in German sources went to translating Juvenal's satires of Roman vices, some of which he found too bawdy to read aloud to Louisa. *Oberon,* however, was a near-obsession, leaving Adams frustrated at interruptions, although he never seemed to resent the evenings when he and Louisa could read aloud together from works of Pope and Spenser, particularly *The Faerie Queene.*

Although there was a saddening distraction in January 1800 while Louisa experienced a fourth miscarriage, John managed otherwise to keep *Oberon* uppermost. "I could scarcely snatch from it here and there an hour for any other purpose whatsoever." It had become, he admitted, his sole amusement, leaving him little time for any other thought. When the translation was finished at the end of May, revision began. This continued sporadically until early in 1801, when Adams learned that William Sotheby had recently published a translation of *Oberon* that Wieland himself admired. By then preparing to return to the

States, John put the finishing touches on his manuscript and laid it aside, where it languished for well over a century.

In 1940, Adams' version was published in the United States in a handsome volume amid such acclaim as might have convinced even John that his time had not been wasted. The editor, A. B. Faust, said Adams' translation was "of unusual scholarly and literary merit, remarkable for its fidelity to the original and [for] its genuine artistry. It takes rank with the few outstanding translations done by American scholars." Faust put Adams in the company of Longfellow and Bayard Taylor as translators.

Faust was one of many specialists who had come to admire Adams' scholarship in German literature, as well as his campaign to place German titles in American libraries. In 1899, Frederick H. Wilkens, a noted bibliographer, called Adams "the father of German studies in America." The repute arose from more than JQA's devotion to *Oberon*. He undertook several other projects, including a verse translation of Christian F. Gellert's fables, and an English version (published in Philadelphia in 1800) of Friedrich von Gentz' *The Origin and Principles of the American Revolution Compared with the Origin of the French Revolution.*

NONE OF THESE LITERARY ENTERPRISES, however, proved to be as significant or as gratifying to Adams as another creative venture, one that grew from a second extended summertime trip. He and Louisa decided in 1800 to set out for Silesia, where he wished to write essays featuring the observations of a traveler, a genre very popular at the time.

Silesia was then a part of Europe rarely reached by travelers, and certainly not by Americans. Adams especially wished to ascend the mountains at Silesia's border with Bohemia. Also, since the province produced fine glassware and linens, the minister thought he should investigate whether these commodities might be shipped directly to the United States, rather than via England. The literary aspect of the journey took the form of letters John sent to Tom Adams, who had himself expressed an interest in learning about remote Silesia.

Tom received more information than he anticipated, for John put aside his diary and let detailed letters to Tom serve as a record of both the trip and his days. Ultimately, there were forty-three of these journal-like epistles, of which the first was dated July 20, 1800. This letter and twenty-eight to follow featured scenes and events of the travel. Then came fourteen that detailed historical and other information. The last letter was finished well after John and Louisa had returned to Berlin. No wonder Tom said of his brother: "He is the most exhaustless writer that I ever knew."

It was indeed an astonishing physical feat, for before they were dispatched to Tom, the Silesia reports first had to be copied faithfully by John into his letter-book, which was his companion on every outing. Years before, his father had impressed upon him the importance of making a copy of every significant letter sent—good advice, but what an assignment in those days before electronic scanners and computers.

The Adamses arrived in Silesia on July 23, using their own carriage and accompanied by servants. Five days later, they were in Bunzlau, where they first glimpsed the Silesian mountains, a view that captivated them. They found vistas from the summits were invariably glorious—and frustrating for Adams the writer, who complained: "I must always use the same words to express things of which the eye alone is competent to perceive and enjoy the difference." He told Tom that "you will thank me for not entering into details which could only be tedious to you."

Even so, it was a skillful Adams who portrayed landscapes, towns, and Silesian citizens. Of the latter he wrote in some dismay: "These mountaineers have been represented to us . . . as the most perfect models of patriarchical virtue, happiness, and simplicity," but the ones they had observed "tended to give us ideas of them directly in reverse of these." He described a typical Silesian as sleeping on hay, surrounded by cattle and mounds of manure.

With so much "filthiness," Adams worried that even the dairies were unclean. As for the people, he considered them "as dirty as any other peasants in the most wretched hovels of Europe." The children were "loaded with vermin like the land of Egypt at the last of its plagues." While John called the manners of the populace "coarse," "disgusting," and "insulting," he managed to sound more amused than disappointed when he closed his description of Silesian peasantry: "Such is the condition of these venerable and blissful beings, whom we had extolled as the genuine children of nature—the true sample of mankind in the golden age."

There were, of course, more sophisticated parts of Silesia, including the environs of Bunzlau, where the Adamses met two "mechanical geniuses." One had made a moving stage with puppets representing the phases of the Passion of Jesus Christ. To his astonishment, John found himself deeply moved. No sermon he had heard or read on the subject "touched my heart with one half the force of this puppet show." He was also much stirred by the writings of Silesian authors, about whom he wrote in letters completed after he and Louisa ended their holiday.

These final letters became a series of essays treating the history, economy, politics, and literature of the province. The last of them, dated March 17, 1801, contained sketches of Silesia's greatest authors, chiefly Christian Garve, Christian von Wolff, and Martin Opitz, whom Adams called the father of German poetry. "Such men as these are the highest ornament and glory of the country which gave them birth," he asserted, having carefully omitted any political leader in his listing of national treasures—only men of letters were named, as befitted John's own aspiration.

Meanwhile, his travel writings were attracting attention in the United States. Tom Adams had been a skillful press agent, for on January 3, 1801, John's initial letter of the Silesian series was the leading essay in the first issue of *Port Folio,* a mostly literary periodical published weekly by Joseph Dennie in Philadelphia. Dennie, who wrote under the pseudonym Oliver Oldschool, went on to publish the Silesian letters in forty-four installments, concluding in November 1801. The editor then called for more contributions from John, so that nearly half the contributions to the weekly's first volume were written by JQA, including a translation of Juvenal's thirteenth satire.

Publication in *Port Folio* was by no means the end of the Silesian letters' career. An enterprising but anonymous person took them to London, where, in 1804, they were published as *Letters on Silesia* by "His Excellency John Quincy Adams." The British edition had 387 pages of such admirable print and paper that it remains as handsome today as when it was new. The following year, it was translated into German and published at Breslau. In 1807, a French copy came out in Paris.

None of these editions appeared with JQA's knowledge; his response when he found out about them was chagrin that his first book was not of finer literary quality. "If I should ever appear voluntarily before the public as a candidate for the reputation of *an author,*" he admitted to Louisa, "it should be with pretensions of rather more elevation." Eventually, he hoped to offer "something of more value to the world." For now he wished merely to "excite a taste for poetry among my countrymen."

Louisa, of course, accompanied her husband as he traveled and wrote about Silesia. She had been present even when he had turned to the study of local glass, pottery, and linen works and to visiting cannon foundries and yarn spinners. To relieve him, she led the daily search for clean, comfortable inns, appetizing food, and any theaters in the neighborhood.

Finally, on September 7, 1800, the Adamses parted from Silesia and three days later began a return visit in Dresden. This year they had to settle for an apartment three flights up, but once again, the city offered much to encourage John's thoughts about a creative career free of politics as he joined Louisa in revisiting some of the delights of the previous summer. After Dresden came a stop at Leipzig, where they went to the University Church to hear a performance of Haydn's *The Creation*. Although he acknowledged that the oratorio was "much celebrated" and that the music was fine, John could not shake off some disappointment. Speaking as a budding poet, he complained: "It would have been better if the airs had been rhymed."

On September 28, Louisa began to experience the now all-too-familiar signs of miscarriage. John tried to comfort her by reading aloud from Chaucer's *Canterbury Tales*, meantime reminding himself that "We have a dismal month ahead of us." When doctors gave encouragement as they sought to halt Louisa's bleeding, John could say only "'Tis to no purpose." This time, however, Louisa recovered safely and insisted that she was able to travel, which enabled them to be back in Berlin on October 25.

Immediately, the demands of the city's already humming social season kept JQA from his writing table. To repay many obligations, the Adamses held a large dinner party on November 6, an event Louisa's pregnancy easily withstood, although afterward John himself fell ill and had to be treated with leeches. He watched the vigorous Louisa with amazement, hardly daring to hope that she might at last carry a child to full term. When the Adamses attended the splendid Christmas Day dinner given by their new friends Lord Carysfort, ambassador from Great Britain, and his wife, Louisa danced until after midnight.

By Easter 1801, Louisa was still robust as she neared the end of her pregnancy. The couple often walked under Berlin's famed linden trees and even called at the Charlottenburg palace. As this went on, her physical and emotional condition remained far superior to that of her apprehensive spouse. With the birth approaching, John suffered from another of his many severe colds while Louisa kept up her walks and outings without him.

The strain was enough to prod Adams into a search for religious understanding, a campaign he would pursue into old age. Until his thirtieth birthday, he had shown no special enthusiasm for spiritual faith and worship. Except for attending Anglican services in London during the weeks following his marriage, he had rarely entered a European church on Sunday morning. Now, however, his Berlin journal began recording his Bible reading, particularly after a deeply affecting event on New Year's Eve 1800 put John, as he acknowledged, "in communion with my own soul."

At the height of a party, a handsome young army officer, a favorite with the diplomatic corps, fell dead as Adams looked on. Calling the event "an awful admonition," he began earnestly to consider "the vanity and frailty of earthly enjoyments." He turned for guidance to the sermons of John Tillotson, archbishop of Canterbury from 1691 to 1694. Tillotson's popular homilies, often reprinted in ten volumes, would be read by John for the rest of his life.

The tone and content of the archbishop's preaching appealed to JQA, as it had to John Adams. Tillotson was a latitudinarian Anglican, perhaps even an Arminian moralist, who taught peaceableness among Christians (although he was stoutly anti-Papist). His was a highly practical theology, emphasizing the need for humanity to live kindly together, and his homilies were beautifully presented in a brief, understated fashion that stirred John. He preferred preachers to speak of the fruits of religion rather than to linger over dogma.

Tillotson's sermons were temporarily put aside on April 12, 1801, when John recorded in his diary: "I have this day to offer my humble and devout thanks to almighty God for the birth of a son at half-past three o' clock afternoon." The christening ceremony, held on May 4 at the English embassy, saw the baby baptized George Washington Adams; Lord and Lady Carysfort stood as godparents, and the legation chaplain officiated. The name given the baby was considered a sacred trust, leading little George's father to say, "I implore the favour of almighty God that he may live and never prove unworthy of it."

Louisa had not reported her pregnancy to family members in America, fearing to disappoint them with another sad termination. It fell to the new father to notify the Adamses and Johnsons. Although Louisa's delivery had been difficult and her recovery would be slow, he assured everyone that she was "fat and rosy as her boy." To John Adams, he wrote, "Heaven be blessed for this favour beyond my hopes."

The esteem in which the Adamses were held by the Prussian

monarchy was immediately evident. To assure perfect quiet for Mrs. Adams' recuperation, the king ordered all traffic prohibited in the street where she lived. The young queen, herself several times a mother, sent a servant daily to inquire how Louisa was recovering. Although she made steady improvement in the ensuing weeks, JQA remained "in a crucifying state of suspense. My own health suffers from it in proportion." As a welcome tonic, he began arising at 6 a.m. to walk three miles to a "proper spot," where he swam in the Spree River.

THROUGHOUT LOUISA'S PREGNANCY, John's worries had been enlarged by messages from America. According to these, nothing seemed to be going well at home. In seeking peace with France, John Adams had deeply divided his Federalist party, leaving the president much abused by both Jeffersonian and Federalist factions. While JQA supported his father's courageous action, the reports of such partisan warfare disgusted him. In commending his father for averting war with France, he said that the elder Adams was "the man not of any party, but of the whole nation."

Political tales from America reminded John that if he returned to Massachusetts, he would face an existence much less appealing than his life in Europe. Consequently, he informed his father that he had changed his mind about wishing to be recalled. He acknowledged that he was pleased to be abroad and particularly in Berlin, where on every side he found encouragement for literary projects. In Boston, he would face "the dry and drudging study of legal questions," a profession he predicted would not sustain him financially. The other alternative, a career in American politics, was even more disagreeable, especially considering the sickening rancor that now dominated the scene.

In faraway Berlin, Adams found it soothing to concentrate on his elegant letters to the State Department, in which he continued to interpret the rise in France of Napoleon Bonaparte, "the Corsican ruffian" who was "beyond all doubts a hero in the common acceptance of the word, and I suppose in other respects as good a man as the rest of his class." In the face of Napoleon's success at home and abroad, the minister continually counseled American officials that neutrality was much preferable to war with England. This policy, he said, was the best hope of carrying the United States "through all the inconveniences, embarrassments, and vexations" that surely lay ahead.

On April 26, 1801, came the dreaded announcement from Secretary of State John Marshall that, as one of his last acts in office, President John Adams had recalled his son. Division in the ranks of the Federalist party—caused mainly by his administration's pursuit of peace—had thwarted John Adams' bid for reelection in 1800. Feeling much bruised, he refused to give his successor, Thomas Jefferson, the choice about continuing JQA's service in Berlin. This pleased Abigail Adams, who had been urging her son's recall. She wanted him at home, where "his light will shine before men."

JQA would have preferred to risk the favor of Jefferson. At least there was a chance the new president would have kept him at his post, thus assuring him and Louisa of more delightful concerts, gallery visits, and evenings at the theater. It was therefore a despondent Adams who rode to Potsdam on May 5 to deliver his letter of recall to King Frederick, who informed the American minister that he "was well satisfied with my conduct." Then John saw the queen, who appeared even more chagrined to learn that the Adamses must soon be leaving. "In less than half an hour, all was over," he reported.

He then turned to the only half-pleasing task he associated with departing: cataloging and packing the books he had purchased in Berlin. To distract himself further, he read Schiller's history of the Thirty Years War and more sermons by Tillotson, particularly one on rules for faith, which, said Adams, was "a great question." He also began discussing literary topics in letters to his father, now retired in Quincy.

These subjects could not, however, prevent JQA's expressions of misgiving at returning to a republic that had shown the poor judgment to refuse to reelect his father. The son wrote with no illusions about the nation in which he must prepare to live, announcing that clearly a democracy would be no more free of "bad passions and bad practices" than any other government in history. His father's example of "patriotism sacrificed to intrigue and envy" was solemn proof of this. To his mother, whom he suspected of harboring political aspirations for him, he sent a warning: "I will sooner turn scavenger and earn my living by cleaning away the filth of the streets than plunge into this bottomless filth of faction."

But what might he do in the United States? He recognized that the so-called Jeffersonian revolution of 1800 threatened his chances of living independently as a man of letters. In a democratic society, he wondered whether anyone, least of all a person past age thirty, might expect to prosper as an intellectual. He looked with envy at those with his aspirations who lived in Europe, where a literary class basked in public respect.

Nevertheless, to Jefferson's United States he must go, so in early June the Adamses had George inoculated against smallpox, then gave a farewell dinner for many of their friends and associates. On June 17, the couple and their baby began the ride through dust and sand toward Hamburg and a boat bound for America. When they arrived in Hamburg at sunset on June 21, they found that Captain Wells of the *America* seemed in no hurry to set out for Philadelphia.

It was July 12 when the wind finally allowed the *America* to move slowly down the Elbe River and enter the North Sea. On August 31, after an uneventful voyage, the ship's lookout spied land birds, and on September 3, in oppressive heat, the *America* entered the Delaware River. The next day, JQA and his party disembarked at Philadelphia, where Tom Adams greeted them with the welcome news that their father had proclaimed politics no career for son John. The elder Adams had announced, "If I were to go over my life again, I would be a shoemaker rather than an American statesman," and he urged that JQA hasten home to ponder the future.

As independent-spirited as when he left for Europe seven years before, John seemed in no hurry to oblige his parents by dropping everything and rushing to Quincy. Nor did he accompany Louisa to Washington for a reunion with her parents. Despite her uneasiness about traveling without her spouse, he refused to go with her, preferring to linger until September 13 with his literary friends in Philadelphia.

These must have been wearying days, for when he arrived for a five-day stopover in New York City at sister Nabby Smith's residence, he slept around the clock. Then he undertook what proved a futile attempt at retrieving some of his savings that had been imprudently loaned to Nabby's husband, Colonel William Smith, by John's brother Charles, who had died from alcoholism the previous December. John had better luck playing chess with Nabby, which suited him, since he much preferred his sister's company to that of the colonel, who could talk of little but "grouse shooting and gaming."

REACHING THE ADAMS MANSION in Quincy on the evening of September 21, JQA began one of the most difficult periods of his life. No longer a salaried diplomat, he had to seek a means of sustaining his family. For several weeks, he and his parents, along with Uncle Richard and Aunt Mary Cranch, Cousin Cotton Tufts, and other members of the closely knit clan, debated what John ought to do with his life. His dismaying prospects appeared to cause his kinfolk even more despair than he himself felt. Abigail, now age 57, grieved most over the discouraging fate that had befallen her son, a young prodigy no longer.

Here he was, Abigail complained, obliged to start life over when he had a mind "so richly stored for the employments of the highest pride, and a capacity which has been cultivated and improved . . . beyond any other native American." Now, however, even she rejected a political career for her son. Dismayed at her husband's defeat by what the Adamses claimed were sordid Jeffersonian tactics, Abigail believed that the only honorable place for JQA under the new administration was "a private station." Consequently, she insisted that John now resume the practice of law.

This time the son agreed with his mother—at any rate, for the moment he saw no other choice. Having made this decision, he set out to purchase a home in Boston. He found a familiar one, the former Hanover Square residence of his now bankrupt cousin Dr. Thomas Welsh, where in earlier days John had often stayed.

After paying $6,000 for it, John sent the news to Louisa in Washington. He assured her the place was much less than she deserved or desired, "but it goes to the utmost bounds of my powers, and you have so long submitted to inconveniences with me that I hope you will cheerfully continue to put up with others." He invested the balance of his reserves in realty, bonds, and the stock of banks and a bridge company. Astonishingly, six years of government employment had netted him substantial savings, despite the losses caused by the imprudence of brother Charles.

With business matters behind him, Adams readily found time for visits and dinners with the chums of his bachelor youth, all of whom seemed to have prospered in his absence. He told Louisa that they had three to seven children apiece. There were other signs as well that he had been left far behind while his generation moved ahead. His legal business hardly promised a means of catching up, but as he told Tom, he must be a lawyer, if only to keep "peace" in the family "and for the want of better employment."

On October 14, JQA departed for Washington, having changed his mind about Louisa's making her way without him to Boston. Earlier, he had insisted on it, claiming it was too costly in time and money for him to come and fetch her, but once Louisa reached Washington she began sending indignant letters saying that she and George needed him and, more gently, that all she required for complete happiness was to have John beside her. Stirred by her plea, John decided to comply. A fortnight of separation had taught him how much he also desired his wife's company. He was counting the days, he told her, until he was in "the arms of my best beloved."

In this frame of mind, Adams arrived in Washington on October 21, once again exhausted from endless bouncing in a stagecoach as his driver perilously raced another coach to reach the capital first. Finding his wife and child in good health, John went promptly to bed in the residence of Walter Hellen, the wealthy husband of Louisa's older sister, Nancy.

Restored by sleep, John began a busy two weeks in Washington during which he visited with President Jefferson and other officials, including those who might expedite payment of Adams' claims for personal expenses while serving abroad. He found dining at the president's house a chilling affair, and Jefferson disposed to tell stories about Europe that John knew to be full of exaggeration. There was a much more cordial reception for him and Louisa when they visited the widowed Martha Washington at Mount Vernon for two days.

With winter weather approaching, Adams ordered an early start toward Boston on November 3. They took with them Louisa's father, who intended going as far as Fredericktown (now Frederick), Maryland, in order to visit his brother, former governor Thomas Johnson. Barely had the party set off when the frail Joshua Johnson suffered such a severe attack of his prostate disorder that Louisa begged to remain in Maryland with him for a time. Another reason for delay was that George came down with a sudden case of dysentery, hardly a welcome disorder for child or adult riding over a rutted road in a near-springless stagecoach.

On November 11 the family resumed their journey. In Philadelphia, where they stopped to visit Tom, Louisa was examined by Dr. Benjamin Rush, who sensed immediately that the young woman dreaded her impending first meeting with Abigail Adams. The physician found Louisa "under great apprehensions and still more depressed in her spirits than really ill." Reassured, John next took his family to New York City for a short stay with Nabby Smith, who gave Louisa a warm welcome.

On November 24, the day before Thanksgiving, John presented his wife to his parents and all the other relatives who had gathered to behold this creature brought from Europe to enter the family. John Adams immediately offered Louisa an affectionate greeting. From Abigail came just the opposite: a cool reception for this frail and fancy daughter-in-law. Unfortunately, Louisa's apprehension, exhaustion, and racking cough created a first impression that seemed to confirm Abigail's foreboding. Her condition brought Louisa no mercy, however, as she was compelled by Abigail to make a series of unnerving visits to all family and friends in the area.

Seeing the strain between his wife and his mother, John demanded more speed from the workers who were readying the house he had purchased in Boston. Meanwhile, he tried to comfort his unhappy spouse by taking long walks with her and by reading to her. The remaining hours went to putting his papers and affairs in order, "to be ready for any event that may happen." He even tried to cultivate the habit of rising early, and to toughen himself by more exercise, including ice-skating.

On December 21, John took Louisa, George, and their two servants to the residence in Hanover Square and became once again a citizen of Boston. Guests called in the afternoon, but in the evening he and Louisa had the pleasure of a quiet game of backgammon. The hullabaloo of the overcrowded mansion in Quincy was now at a distance, although not so great as to allow John to ignore his parents' insistence that he spend weekends with them.

For a short time, Boston seemed to restore John and Louisa's good spirits and health. The writings of John Locke were usually John's choice for reading aloud in the evenings. On Sundays, they attended the Congregational church where the Reverend William Emerson was pastor—his son Ralph Waldo Emerson would be born in 1803. The couple's social appearances offered one uncomfortable moment when Louisa was introduced to Mary Frazier, soon to marry JQA's close friend Daniel Sargent. Louisa also had to hear the Boston gossip about the affection that had once bound Mary and John.

Meanwhile, JQA had to face a tightening domestic budget. He released their servants and undertook himself to do the family's marketing. Louisa handled the household chores, often helped by one or more of her sisters, who were now regular visitors. Even so, by the early months of 1802, cash for paying bills was so scarce that John narrowly averted having to dip into principal and sell his stock in the Bank of North America. This brush with "penury" dampened his enthusiasm for life in Boston as he remembered the comfortable stipend he had enjoyed as minister to Prussia. Income from his legal practice was disappointing, and he forced himself to spend much of each day attending the courts in the hope of enlarging his business.

The best measure of his dissatisfaction with his new life—the dreary law practice, the pressure from his parents, and the lack of time for reading and writing—was his brief flirtation with a plan to live on the American frontier. The inspiration to do so came when he learned that the money Charles Adams had loaned on his behalf to the Smith brothers was invested in a piece of land somewhere between Skaneateles Lake and the village of Sherburne in central New York. John proposed to take ownership of the property.

"I have thoughts of making a settlement there and removing with my family to that part of the country," he confided to his brother Tom. Gullibly quoting the Smiths' exaggerations in calling his property "the most promising spot on the continent for enterprize and industry," he invited Tom, still a bachelor, to come along: "What say you to joining me in the plan and going with me?" They could promise themselves the status they most craved, "independence," as well as "sport."

"Why should we," asked John, "wither away our best days and sneak through life, pinch'd by penury . . . for a few luxurious indulgences in a large town?" Urging Tom to respond at once, John claimed that his residence in Boston was only "temporary," explaining that "some sacrifice I have consented to make, but my stock of patience is not large and will not last long." By this he meant his pledge to give the legal profession a try.

Tom Adams did not need to be asked twice. Upon receiving John's solicitation, he replied that he would be ready at short notice to join in "rustic independence." If John was prepared to sacrifice "'luxurious indulgences' and consent to penetrate the wilds of a new, unsettled country in quest of honest though homely independence," then, said Tom, "I should feel a pride in emulating such an example, indeed." After reiterating that "I am your man for a new country and manual labor," Tom suggested that they keep the plan to themselves.

What Tom feared was Abigail Adams' discovery of John's determination. The concern was justified when, in early February 1802, she did learn of the plan. Although no record survives of how she did so or what she said to John, Abigail's scornful rebuke to Tom was the death knell of his westward migration. She predicted that if Tom followed any such wild idea, he would soon lose his polish and fall to the crude level of those around him. Besides, she said, life away from the city "would soon render you discontented and unhappy."

No one can say how influential Abigail was in squelching JQA's

dream of becoming his own man in the West. Her campaign received
a powerful boost, however, when he discovered that the Smith brothers had indeed overstated the merit of any property acquired with his
money. Having shown John's willingness to consider almost anything
to escape his musty law practice, the idea of heading west was quietly
put aside.

Later in the spring of 1802, he seemed to grow more content with
Boston life, thanks in part to evenings spent genially with friends. He
had returned to find the Crackbrain Club grown into an association of
mature men whose interests now inclined toward natural philosophy.
With their former leader back in town, the companions soon orga-
nized themselves into the Natural Philosophy Club and began buying
scientific books and equipment, all to JQA's delight. At a club meeting
devoted to electricity, he "took several shocks and a succession of
sparks while standing on the insulation stool." The experiment must
have required considerable courage; earlier in the meeting members
"broke two of our Leyden jars by charging them too highly." According to Adams, the shock treatment relieved his muscular distress.

Though he continued to find the practice of law stultifying, his
boredom was now relieved by club members and friends dropping by
the office in State Street to talk politics. From these sessions came pressure on John to take part in "political controversy," so that in the early
months of 1802 he began telling his diary that he was less averse to entering politics.

But if he should do so, he asserted, it must be on his own terms.
For him this meant being a civil servant without being contaminated
by partisanship. He told Tom Adams that there was no party in America wherein an honest man could enlist "without blushing." Claiming
to be motivated by principle rather than ambition for office, JQA fell
victim to the tempting hope that he could serve the Republic while
standing apart from factions. "I would fain be the man of my whole
country."

CHAPTER SIX

Capitulation

*The interest with which my mind seizes hold of the public business is greater
than suits my comfort or can answer any sort of public utility.*

THE CLOSEST JQA CAME to explaining his abrupt embrace of politics was in a letter to Tom Adams: "A man may as well be as busy
about nothing for the public as for himself." In this understated way,
he announced the most important decision he would make about his
career. He may have said so little concerning this switch to politics because he himself did not entirely fathom why he had pushed law and
literature aside.

Had he been capable of the concerted effort required, he most
likely would have become a successful lawyer. His father had once
been among Massachusetts' ablest attorneys, and his two brothers
were each well begun in their legal practices before alcoholism over-
took them. In John's case, a blend of temperament and circumstance
made the story turn out differently.

A hunger for creative attainment, a nature intolerant of tedium,
and a tendency to be inefficient were hardly qualities disposing him to
enslave himself in the routine of a law office—which he knew, from his
father's experience, would be a harsh taskmaster. This was especially
so since in Boston the legal field was crowded, and being abroad for so
long had left him far behind other attorneys of his age.

Beyond detaining him professionally, JQA's years in Europe, and
particularly those spent in The Hague and Berlin, had had a much
more profound effect upon him: they had spoiled him for the routine

of ordinary men. Ironically, it was the fate Abigail Adams had feared for her son. The life of a diplomat had shown him how he might meet his family's expenses through public service while having leisure to pursue his literary interests. Compared with his existence in the Netherlands and Prussia, a lawyer's uninspiring grind repelled John, who remembered that it had been his success as an essayist, not as a lawyer, that had opened to him a life of comparative self-indulgence in the Foreign Service.

Another key factor turning him away from the practice of law was a nagging doubt about himself. He knew that while he might occasionally exhibit disciplined vigor, the display was misleading. Instead, as he had begun to recognize while in Europe, his life was to be a perpetual struggle against indolence. His diary abounded with shamefaced admissions of wasting time or of reading to no purpose. What he needed, Adams now declared, was the diligence imposed by a regular schedule, such as one that would come with a seat in the legislature.

Since the literary and scientific career he dreamed of demanded initiative and discipline, it was more than a facile rationalization when he claimed that being in public office would help make him a better-organized person. If he became a legislator, his duties, he felt, would require him to carry through on matters placed before him. He thought the beneficiary would be his literary pursuits.

There was yet another reason for JQA's abrupt entry into politics: he acknowledged that his ambitions were drawn even to that field. While he was more open about yearning for acclaim as a writer, poet, or scientist, there were moments when he hungered to be a statesman on the order of a philosopher-king. As a leader who moved above party, he visualized being a blessing to humanity while adding luster to the family name. He seems actually to have been naïve enough to believe he could be independent as an officeholder.

And so, although he had once announced in Prussia that he would rather clean filth from the streets of Boston than be a politician, he chose to run for office. Furthermore, he did so against his family's advice. Because John Adams had been ousted from the presidency, the Adamses believed that all family members should stand aside and let the Republic suffer the consequences of having elected Jefferson president. Consequently, in early 1802 JQA's relatives were contending he was meant for a higher calling than politics.

John countered this advice by saying he would be a statesman, not a politician. Of course, he recognized that the independence he cherishcd could be threatened in an elective position. Running for a public post implied subservience to friends and faction. His best defense, he believed, was to insist that the electorate must request his services. Thereafter, whenever he sought office, he invariably pretended that he was awaiting the people's summons. Should anyone charge him with being a party man or with actively seeking votes, he became indignant.

JQA's CAREER IN POLITICS began on April 5, 1802, with his election as a state senator from Suffolk County, which encompassed the city of Boston. His ticket, with its three other Federalists, won by a vote of 2,345 to the opposition's 1,498. Conceding that Tom Adams would be "a little bit surprised" at this event, John asked his brother to believe he had agreed to run because "it was extremely doubtful and generally doubted" that an Adams could be elected. "I did not choose either to shrink, or even to have the appearance of shrinking from the trial."

Assuring himself that he would be "an independent member," he took the oath of office on May 26. His diary entries thereafter became livelier and more lengthy, applying the same careful attention to events and personalities in Massachusetts politics that they had earlier given to international intrigues in Berlin, London, and The Hágue.

These entries were made with few illusions, however, for Adams emphasized that he was well aware of the dubious company he must keep in politics. As he scornfully asserted, ordinary lawmakers, state and national, had one guiding principle, which was to "be satisfied to provide for the occasions of the day, and leave future times to take care of themselves."

A realist, if not a cynic, Adams sat in the upper house during the session of May and June 1802, and again when the Senate reassembled in January 1803. "It was the novitiate of my legislative labors," he recalled. "I was not able either to effect much good, or to prevent much evil. I attempted some reforms, and aspired to check some abuses, I regret to say with little success."

He was so inexperienced that he did not appreciate "the danger of opposing and of exposing corruption." By this, he referred to his attempts to strengthen the independence of the Massachusetts judiciary, to improve the system of representation, and to defeat a plan to create a bank that made financial payoffs to members of the legislature. As Adams watched his protests swept aside, he marveled at how "the mammon of unrighteousness [is] too strongly befriended."

While he may have fallen short in the way he wished to serve the public interest, his entrance into politics enhanced his private life. The need to be reasonably punctual in the Senate led to early rising, prodding him to be out at 6 a.m. for an hour's walk along the Common and then around Beacon Hill to the Charles River and back. Next came reading and writing until breakfast. After 10 a.m., he was off to the State House. At 2 p.m. he, like most Bostonians, went home to dine. Afterward, he addressed other business or gave attention to son George. The evenings went to scientific experiments or to reading aloud with Louisa and one or more of her visiting relatives, usually a sister or her mother, who had been widowed on April 21, 1802. Dependent upon his post office sinecure and the aid of sons-in-law, the once high-flying Joshua Johnson may have succumbed as much to brooding over his disgrace as to uremia.

The Adamses' pleasant routine was rudely broken in July when JQA suddenly lost his appointment as a commissioner of bankruptcy, which had put him on the federal payroll. He had been appointed to the post by his friend Judge John Davis, but this good luck was soon undone when federal legislation placed bankruptcy posts at the president's discretion. Jefferson had acted swiftly to replace incumbents with his supporters, later claiming that he had not known John Quincy Adams was one of those turned out of office.

Having lost the income brought by bankruptcy work, Adams found himself listening to suggestions that he run for the federal Congress in the autumn election of 1802. After making certain that Cousin Josiah Quincy, who had a longer record of service as a moderate Federalist, did not wish to run, Adams agreed to be the candidate on the Federalist ticket for the congressional district which included Boston, Charlestown, Medford, Hingham, Chelsea, Hull, and Malden.

Tom Adams' response to this decision probably reflected the family's dismay as John moved deeper into the thicket of politics. Upon hearing that his brother was in the race, an incredulous Tom wrote from Philadelphia to say he could not imagine what John's motives could be. Surely he was not seeking to be popular? Tom hoped the story was a Boston ruse, and that John would announce he had no intention of seeking a seat in Congress.

John did indeed make the race against the Jeffersonian incumbent, Dr. William Eustis, and narrowly lost by 59 votes out of 3,739 cast. While there was modest consolation in carrying Boston (1,496 votes to Eustis' 1,430), the only other town Adams won was Medford. His advisers ascribed his loss to the rain on Election Day, which they said discouraged the Federalist faithful. The candidate, however, drew a more profound message from his defeat. If climate must be the excuse, he said, it was merely "one of a thousand proofs how large a portion of federalism is a mere fair-weather principle, too weak to overcome a shower of rain. It shows the degree of dependence that can be placed upon such friends."

A cheered Tom Adams congratulated John on being spared from joining those who were, in the younger brother's opinion, "profligate and abandoned." Giving thanks for John's "non-election," Tom said, "I most ardently pray that the voice of the people may never prove more detrimental to your welfare than it has on this occasion." Replying that he was surprised at "the warmth" of Tom's views, John claimed he never really wished to win the congressional contest and expressed relief at being spared "a heavy burden and a thankless task."

Two months later, in reviewing the year 1802 for his journal, JQA reported that he had been able "to preserve my health, my principles, and my Independence." Indeed, he said, "seldom at the close of a year has it been in my power to look back with less of self-reproach." The only charge against himself was the reappearance of "that indolence which creeps so insensibly upon my strongest resolutions and which I have never subdued." He was thinking mainly of his delays in sending contributions promised for publication in *Port Folio*.

To excuse his tardiness as an author, he explained that he had been obliged to prepare and deliver two important orations during the year. On May 28, John and Abigail Adams had proudly listened in King's Chapel as their son presented the annual address to the Massachusetts Charitable Fire Society, an organization formed to benefit victims of disaster. His message was that Bostonians should overcome their inveterate fondness for wooden houses. By this plea, JQA believed he was helping to convert the city from "stubble into brick, clapboards and shingles into granite walls."

The second oration was before the Pilgrim Society in Plymouth on December 22. Here John had contended that Europeans had the right to take the American wilderness from "the aboriginal Indians," although, of course, on "just and reasonable terms." He did not explain the nature of these terms.

Both orations had been well received, which helped make 1802 one of JQA's happiest years—and busiest, for he was now representing the state senate on Harvard's Board of Overseers and had been elected to membership in the Massachusetts Historical Society. Also, he had joined in establishing a company to plan and build a bridge across the Neponset River, a project that meant a generous investment in money and time. There was a similar cost when he and his colleagues in the Natural Philosophy Club set up a chemical laboratory, which they hoped was a safer venture than continuing electrical experiments. An enthusiastic Adams had tried to stay awake over Lavoisier's *Elementary Treatise on Chemistry*. Less demanding and more fun were the numerous swimming and fishing excursions he made during the year.

Meanwhile, Louisa had entered into an active life of her own, so that Adams sometimes found her absent when he returned home from his outings. They kept to their practice of walking and reading together, and Louisa began to find herself somewhat more comfortable during trips to Quincy. The couple even considered spending future summers there, living in one of the smaller houses owned by the Adams family in the area around Penn's Hill. Now a second child was eagerly anticipated, for Louisa had become pregnant in the late autumn of 1802.

THE NEW YEAR would prove an unsettling one. It began cheerfully as John and Louisa devoted many of their winter evenings to reading Shakespeare's plays and sonnets. Sometimes they trooped out to a ball or assembly, where they often danced or played whist until 1 a.m. When Louisa's advancing pregnancy kept her at home from a social event, she persuaded her husband to escort a visiting Johnson sister in her place. Occasionally, the Adamses themselves entertained. On January 7, they were hosts to forty guests for dinner and a ball that lasted past midnight.

Such festive times were customary when the General Assembly convened, as it did in January. This session, however, suddenly found the members doing more than the usual business of creating towns, banks, insurance companies, roads, and charitable societies. The solons received announcements from both of Massachusetts' United States senators, Jonathan Mason and Benjamin Foster, that they did not wish to continue in office. The news set the assembly to wrangling over successors—in those days state legislatures elected members of the U.S. Senate.

By the end of January, JQA was being prominently mentioned for one of the seats. Clearly, he hoped for success. A place in the Senate would assure him a dependable source of income for six years. Also, he believed that the Senate's schedule would leave him time for the reading and writing he still aspired to do. Nevertheless, he chose not to disclose to his diary what role, if any, he played in launching his candidacy, nor how he allowed himself to be caught up in a partisan fight that, at the very least, gave a hollow tone to his preachments about responding only to an unsought call of the people.

Two factions battled to claim the Senate seats. One, a Federalist group called the Essex Junto, led by John Adams' enemy Timothy Pickering, could be expected to oppose the former president's son. The other faction, bound perhaps more by hostility toward the Pickering crowd than by love of John Adams, considered John Quincy Adams its best candidate.

The lure of a Senate seat apparently was compelling enough that JQA put aside his claim of operating above partisanship and allowed his supporters to enter into an understanding with the Essex Junto. As a result, his rise in politics emerged from a backroom "caucus" by party regulars which produced an agreement that when the lower house began voting for senator, backers of Timothy Pickering should have two ballots in which to try to put him across. If they failed, then supporters of Adams could expect many Essexmen to come to their side on the next ballot.

The lower house reached its decision on February 3 while JQA remained dutifully at his seat in the upper house. It fell to Harrison Gray Otis, a Pickering supporter, to bring him the results of the fourth ballot, which gave JQA a winning majority. With 86 votes required for victory, the first ballot had seen Pickering take 67, with 10 votes for Adams. In the second round Adams had only 6 to Pickering's 79. But the latter had failed to gain a majority, so that his supporters were free to join those few who had stood by Adams. On the third ballot Adams had 56 votes while Pickering dropped to 33. The fourth try brought Adams 86 votes to Pickering's 6. The tally, of course, also gave JQA a majority over the Jeffersonian faction's candidate.

On February 8, on its first ballot, the Massachusetts Senate gave Adams a winning margin of 19 votes to 7 for his Jeffersonian opponent. John Quincy Adams had now been elected a United States senator. "Of course I did not vote at all," he assured his diary. The legislature then turned to fill the second U.S. Senate vacancy. At this point, John fulfilled a pledge that further disclosed his eagerness to go to Washington: he had assured his colleagues that if he was chosen, he would gladly vote for Pickering (whom he and his father profoundly detested) or "for any other man upon whom the federalists would agree." The legislature promptly settled on Pickering to join Adams in representing

Massachusetts in the U.S. Senate. More unlikely colleagues could not be imagined.

THE ENSUING MONTHS before he went to Washington found JQA particularly busy as a Harvard overseer representing the legislature and as a participant in Boston's intellectual life—he now served as corresponding secretary of the American Academy of Arts and Sciences. None of this, however, kept him from the now familiar self-rebukes about his "indolence." Even more severe was a diary entry written on July 11: "I enter this day upon my thirty-seventh year with sorrow to think how long I have lived, and to how little purpose."

To anyone who reads the diary today, these complaints can soon become tiresome, but they appear to be sincere, given Adams' obsessiveness about the disciplined use of time and his general proneness to deploring his perceived failures. Ordinary mortals, however, would have been exhausted by what he accomplished on most days of that summer. He sought to rise at 6 a.m. for bathing in the bay at the foot of the Common or at the wharf behind the almshouse. Thereafter, he gave many hours to scholarly work before turning to family life. What apparently vexed him was that he was so disorganized in his reading and writing.

When word arrived from Washington that Congress would convene on October 15, Adams' studies set off in a new direction. He decided that he must master American history, believing this essential for any member of the United States Senate. The project soon faltered, however, as he managed to read little more than William Robertson's treatment of colonial America. Wearying of this fare, he resumed a project begun in Berlin, the translation of Juvenal's seventh Satire. Adams did not tarry here either, but went on to the comedies of Plautus, the early Roman dramatist. It was just this sort of bouncing from project to project that John so deplored about himself.

A different cause for Adams' discomfort was the beginning that summer of what would be a lifetime plague of hemorrhoids. This meant that for some weeks he found it much more comfortable to stand while reading or writing—"for the sake of health," as he delicately put it. The disorder was not eased by his worry over Louisa as the time for giving birth approached, although once again she seemed much stronger than he. Even as late as the end of June, she insisted that they continue their daily walks together.

On July 2, there being no sign that the baby was about to appear,

Adams left Louisa with her sister Carolina and three maids while he hiked down to Quincy, despite the dust from an exceptionally dry summer. His Fourth of July holiday was interrupted, however, when word came from Boston that Louisa's labor might be starting; he returned to town to find that he had become the father of a second son at 3 a.m. The delivery had been comparatively easy, the baby weighing just over six pounds. "For this new blessing," he wrote, "I desire to offer my humblest gratitude to the throne of Heaven."

On July 17, the Reverend William Emerson baptized the baby, christening him with the name John. After the sacrament, the father returned home and read two sermons by Bishop Tillotson. His prayerful thanks that Louisa and little John enjoyed good health were especially fervent because the Adamses' latest concern was an illness suffered by Abigail. The cause was a prolonged infection from damage done, ironically, by a "blister" Abigail had applied to herself—a favorite remedy of hers for removing inner poisons. (After a "tumour" was removed, Abigail lived for another fifteen years.)

Along with other relatives, JQA spent much of August in Quincy, believing he was keeping a deathbed vigil. Awaiting Abigail's fate, he and his father talked of many matters, ranging from the contents of John Adams' will to the cultivation of fruit trees. For the son, however, the most useful experience was walking with his parent over the latter's extensive landholdings. Much of this acreage had become the younger Adams' property when he rescued his parents from financial ruin after the collapse of the London banking house of Bird, Savage, and Bird some months earlier.

In that crash, John Adams had lost about 3,500 pounds sterling— a nest egg resulting from maturing Dutch bonds—leaving him land-poor and deeply in debt. Checks drawn on his account in London had been returned as worthless and were heavily penalized.

Because he had encouraged John and Abigail to do business with the London bank, JQA immediately saw it as his duty to relieve them. "The error of judgment was mine, and therefore I shall not refuse to share in the suffering." In April and May 1803, he sought to raise money to cover his parents' obligations, beginning by trying to sell back to the previous owner the house in Hanover Square where he and Louisa were living. When that failed, he sold a dwelling in Franklin Place at auction and unloaded some insurance-company stock and other equities. In this way, together with money from loans pressed upon him by friends in Boston and in London, JQA came up with the $13,000 needed to cover the family's debts.

In exchange, John and Abigail turned over 275 acres to their son, although they retained title to the land for life. It was this acreage that JQA's father showed him as they awaited Abigail's recovery. The son was greatly moved and announced that he would "make my future abode at Quincy in the old paternal mansion." For now, he intended to occupy the small farmhouse where he had been born, which was part of the property coming to him.

Returning to Boston after his mother began responding to treatment, JQA found a buyer for the residence in Hanover Square, a sale that allowed Louisa and John barely three weeks in September to remove their books, china, furniture, and papers to Quincy. Amid the ensuing hubbub, which included several farewell dinners for the senator-elect, Adams somehow found the hours to organize his treasured papers, diaries, and letter-books accumulated during seven years abroad. With satisfaction, he announced that they were now "perfectly well sorted—and they are the only papers I have in that situation. I never spent any time more profitably." The documents were placed in a huge trunk and installed in an outbuilding behind John Adams' "mansion."

The last cart was loaded and sent off to Quincy on September 26, followed by Louisa, her sons, a sister, and the servants. JQA remained in Boston one more night to close the house and sign documents for its sale. Three days later, he and his family set out for Washington.

IT REQUIRED TWENTY DAYS of extraordinary frustration and hardship to complete the trip. In part this was because Adams had chosen the water route to New York City, only to have foul weather create endless delays in New London, Connecticut. When the packet's captain bowed to Adams' prodding and ventured into Long Island Sound, seasickness brought the family universal misery. And when little George recovered slightly, he tested his father's self-control by throwing overboard first the keys to his parents' trunks, and then his shoes.

When the Adamses finally reached Newark, they found it so crowded with refugees from a yellow fever epidemic in New York City that they were reduced to camping in one room in a tavern, the only space available. When Louisa fell ill, bringing John to fear that she and the rest of them were coming down with yellow fever, they were rescued by Nabby Smith, who took them to larger quarters she had located in her own flight from the plague. Finally, Tom Adams, who was

still in Philadelphia, arranged for a carriage to haul the woeful travelers and their mountain of trunks the rest of the way to Washington.

Entering the federal capital at dusk on October 20, JQA suffered
the greatest disappointment of the trip. Everyone in the streets, it
seemed, was talking about how, only moments before, the Senate
of the United States had ratified President Jefferson's purchase of
Louisiana from France. In part because none of his Federalist colleagues had joined the majority, Adams regretted that he had arrived
a day too late to be recorded as voting for the treaty. He was one of the
few New England Federalists who foresaw that by acquiring the vast
western region, America was assured of becoming a world power.
Overnight, the purchase had doubled the area of the United States.

Disgusted by his tardiness, Adams was only partially mollified by
the warm welcome he and his brood received when they reached what
was to be their home in Washington: the sizeable residence of Walter
Hellen, his prosperous brother-in-law. Hellen, a speculator in tobacco,
was a generous man who sheltered the widowed Catherine Johnson
and her younger children, as he now took in the Adams family.

Hellen's place—near Georgetown, and just under a three-mile
walk to the Capitol—remained home for JQA while he was a senator.
It was a happy choice, for he promptly found a quiet corner upstairs
where he could read and write away from the family noise. Since
Hellen would never discuss compensation for his hospitality, Adams
was left to estimate a fair price for room and board and then to insist
that his brother-in-law accept payment—usually about a hundred dollars for each congressional session.

The Adamses' status in politics, as well as their place in the prominent Hellen-Johnson family, immediately drew them into Washington
society. Although the city had a population of less than four thousand,
of whom perhaps seven hundred were slaves, white residents enjoyed
dinners, balls, whist parties, and horse racing. The last was a great favorite in autumn and spring; even the business of the United States
ceased when government agencies shut their doors in the afternoons so
that officials could rush out to the track.

For a time, Adams willingly partook of these diversions, including
dining at the President's House, as the White House was first called.
He and James Madison, the secretary of state, customarily played
chess at parties. He also sought to be a good family man. When Louisa
became enthusiastic about horseback riding, he joined her in outings,
and he resumed his Boston practice of reading aloud to the ladies in

the evening. Nor did he ignore his sons, George and John. And of course he made ambitious plans for writing essays.

All in all, JQA would make a comfortable life in Washington. Ordinarily, he gave the early hours of each day to reading and writing until breakfast was served, between 9 and 10 a.m. He then enjoyed a forty-five-minute walk to the Capitol, where he usually found the Senate already in session—he would rarely be a prompt member. The Senate met from noon until 2 or 3 p.m.; this less than rigorous workday became even shorter when committees met. Afterward, Adams usually went home to dinner, which customarily was served at 4 p.m., then resumed his reading and writing. As time went on, except for an evening stroll, he tended increasingly to avoid social excursions. The Hellen household supped lightly at around 10 p.m., which allowed John and Louisa to retire by 11.

Accustomed to attending church in Boston and Quincy, Adams had a limited choice in Washington: two nondenominational services were available each Sunday, one in the Capitol and the other in the Treasury Building. No Protestant churches had yet been established in the District of Columbia (itself barely three years old), nor had the demand for separating church and state grown to the point that anyone seemed alarmed at worship going on under a government roof. Adams noted that President Jefferson sometimes attended services in one or the other public building.

It was not meditations upon literature or theology, however, that were to dominate JQA's thinking in Washington. Somewhat to his surprise, he found congressional affairs so fascinating that he abandoned most of his scholarly plans. In town barely ten days, he admitted in his diary: "The interest with which my mind seizes hold of the public business is greater than suits my comfort or can answer any sort of public utility." Not that this diminished his determination to behave independently, although he foresaw that his new colleagues and the public might not accept him upon his terms.

Resolved to be his own man, Adams went out of his way to demonstrate how individualistic he planned to be. From his first moments in the Senate, he behaved in a manner that sometimes amused his colleagues, frequently baffled them, and occasionally angered a number, particularly the few New England Federalists still in Congress. A few days after arriving in Washington, Senator Adams put on a small but graphic display. He called at the Post Office Department and told the clerk he wished to deposit "a specimen of my signature as required by law, for the purpose of franking my letters." The astonished clerk assured him that such a step was unnecessary, for "the law was almost universally neglected." All the more reason, JQA insisted, that he should leave his signature.

This was one of various ways in which he showed his scorn for his colleagues, whom he saw as mostly blind to the difference between disinterested behavior and hypocritical self-service. He believed that so long as he himself recognized this important distinction, he could function in the company of his egocentric cohorts. Further comfort came from the conviction that his approach to public service followed the example of his father, who also had set out to serve the Union's well-being selflessly. Both Adamses vehemently professed not to care what an independent devotion to principle might cost them personally.

JQA was not, however, so otherworldly as to ignore the informal benefits of his office. Now that he was on the scene in Washington with a vote to cast on issues important to the Jefferson administration, he succeeded in persuading the federal government to pay his remaining claims for expenses incurred in Prussia and on the trip home. Secretary of State James Madison and Secretary of the Treasury Albert Gallatin had been reluctant to accept his accounts, but their intransigence yielded graciously once Adams took his seat in the Senate and showed he would support steps to incorporate Louisiana into the United States. The State and Treasury departments did more than stop quibbling; instead of paying the $61.30 he claimed, the Treasury insisted it owed him $118.38.

Supporting Jefferson's Louisiana measures did not mean that Adams had formally joined the Republicans. He preferred to believe it was his sternly impartial study of each issue that brought him to vote on the Jeffersonian side. Actually, this was no mere self-serving defense. Most of the questions facing his first session in Congress addressed national growth, an issue to which he was as committed on principle as Timothy Pickering, his colleague from Massachusetts, was opposed.

Pickering and other Federalists from the Northeast—fearing that their area would soon be outvoted in national debate by spokesmen from the South and West, particularly if those regions continued to expand—scoffed at Adams' contention that legislative action promising to benefit the entire nation would ultimately help Massachusetts and other New England states.

Perhaps the most significant contribution of continental scope made by JQA came soon after he arrived in the Senate. In November, he found himself leading a select committee assigned to recommend action by the Senate on a treaty with England known as the Convention of May 1803, which sought to fix the northwest boundary between the United States and Canada, an issue left unresolved at the close of the Revolution.

JQA was dismayed to find that the proposed convention abandoned the boundary that followed westward from near the Great Lakes along approximately the 49th parallel, which was the line endorsed by John Adams and other Founders. The new boundary, negotiated by Rufus King, would move the line southward about 150 miles to begin at the headwaters of the Mississippi River. JQA foresaw only dangerous consequences if this huge strip of land extending west to the Pacific Ocean was turned over to the British, along with the access it afforded to the Mississippi. When he urged that the Senate repudiate this part of the convention, his colleagues agreed, against the wishes of the Jefferson administration.

Afterward, Great Britain refused to proceed further in the dispute, leaving the boundary issue unsettled for another fifteen years. Later, in 1818, as secretary of state, John Quincy Adams guided fresh negotiations with England that finally confirmed the 49th parallel as the boundary line west from the Lake of the Woods. It would be one of his greatest diplomatic triumphs. In 1803, however, his defense of the 49th-parallel line succeeded in annoying not only the British but also the Jeffersonian faction, while heightening the suspicions of his New England brethren.

Adams' independence was also generally considered obnoxious when he pushed for a constitutional amendment to answer those critics, mostly from the Northeast, who claimed that the Louisiana Purchase had no justification in fundamental federal law. By proposing an amendment, he intended to put an honest face on the acquisition, as well as to sanction all future purchases of realty by the federal government. While almost no one, including President Jefferson, agreed with him on the need for the amendment, some Republicans were willing to concede that the strong-minded Senator Adams had good intentions.

His laudable motives on another issue notwithstanding, few senators supported Adams a few weeks later when he sought a voice for the citizens of the Louisiana area in creating their government. Over his protests, the administration, understandably in a hurry, prodded Congress to impose a constitution and a tax system on Louisiana. The Senate ignored Adams' reminders about the sacred principle of no taxation without representation. Such a position was a further sign of his willingness to stand alone—although he joined often enough in supporting other Jeffersonian legislation.

It did not seem to trouble Adams that most New England senators invariably voted on any side against his. The reason, he said, was because they "hate me more than they have any principle." He considered Timothy Pickering to be the prime example of how partisanship corrupted an individual. Claiming that Pickering would rely upon the expedient rather than support "the right," Adams shrugged off his colleague as a person who "cannot possibly think like me."

There were moments, however, when JQA did entertain a doubt or two about his own rectitude. "Pride and self-conceit and presumption lie so deep in my natural character," he acknowledged. He wished he could find someone to support him as he strove for quietness and humility, feeling himself "a feather" as the "whirlwind" of politics swirled around him.

But to whom could he turn? No one, it seemed. Louisa was not eligible, because he wanted her to remain above politics. Nor could his Adams relatives give support, for neither his parents nor his brother Tom were pleased to see him in national politics. From Tom came the apt warning: "You lay the publick cause too seriously to heart and give too much dominance to the crosses and vexations which are strewn along your path by the wayward nature of the times."

Tom could not recognize the degree to which his brother lived in fear of contamination by the widespread partisanship. According to JQA: "The country is so totally given up to the spirit of party, that not to follow blindfold the one [party] or the other is an inexpiable offense." Any chance that he might be seen as acting for party reasons caused him agony, as, for example, when he voted with the Federalists on March 12, 1804, against convicting John Pickering, judge of the New Hampshire district court and no close kin to Timothy Pickering, on impeachment charges brought by the Jeffersonians. Immediately afterward, Adams wrote in his journal: "Before Heaven, I have not suffered a party thought to intermingle with my judgment in the case."

ON MARCH 27, Congress adjourned and Adams found himself short of money. Mainly, he had been relying on his senatorial salary to pay expenses. There was little income from legal services, even though he had been admitted to plead before the United States Supreme Court and had represented a few clients—at the time custom allowed senators to do so. The revenue he had once expected from investments and realty had been greatly reduced when these assets were surrendered to rescue his parents from the wreckage of their London banker.

This fiscal embarrassment brought JQA to a domestic decision in the spring of 1804. He announced to a thunderstruck Louisa that he could no longer afford to support her and their sons in two residences; she would have to remain in one spot year-round, either in Quincy or in Washington. Her response to the ultimatum brought Adams his turn to be taken aback. An angry Louisa replied that she would remain in Washington and live with her family; her husband could return alone to his Massachusetts constituency between sessions of Congress.

This arrangement was not what Adams had expected or desired, nor did it please Louisa. Both of them, however, were too proud and hurt to suggest that they reconsider. Instead of loving farewells, an unprecedented frostiness prevailed between them when John set out for New England on April 2. After arriving in Quincy, he immediately began a painful exchange of letters with Louisa, telling her that he felt "like a fish out of water without you and my children."

His bruised ego could not rest, however, pushing him to reproach his spouse for having preferred separation from him to parting from her Johnson kinfolk. Louisa dismissed this contention, pointing out that it was he who had forced a choice between her remaining behind in Washington for the summers of the balance of his term or "living alone at Quincy during five dreary winters." As for his implying that she was fonder of her relatives, she retorted: "I didn't think that my affection for you admitted of doubt."

Soon, however, Louisa melted, saying that she would prove her love for him by agreeing to live in Quincy, for without his affection and esteem "I must be wretched every where." Stirring words such as these, along with his loneliness, brought Adams quickly to change his mind about the cost of keeping his family together. After a face-saving lament that he was now obliged to spend principal to meet expenses, he assured Louisa that she could hereafter join him both in Quincy and in Washington. "The whole of the arrangement, however, shall be altogether as you chuse." He asked her to kiss the boys a thousand times—and he sent twice that number for her. Louisa responded by saying how much she missed his "tenderness," and that with him she enjoyed "almost perfect happiness." This exchange was the first in a series of ever more passionate letters between the couple.

By the end of May, his thoughts now downright erotic, Adams was stirred at the sight of some of Boston's finest ladies clad in the comparatively scant attire that was becoming fashionable. This led him to assure Louisa that "a very little clothing, you know, upon a lady will answer all my purposes." He reminded his spouse that when a lady "goes to bed at night, [she] should have something to do besides opening the sheets."

For Louisa's eyes he copied a poem by John Donne. The lines were from "To his Mistris Going to Bed," as contained in Donne's 1669 edition. What John sent to Louisa included such imagery as:

> *Your gown going off, such beautious state reveals,*

and:

> *Off with that wyerie Coronet and shew*
> *The haiery Diademe which on you doth grow.*

This revelation of his beloved, as the poet put it, sets "our flesh upright," after which the lines pleaded:

> *Licence my roaving hands, and let them go,*
> *Before, behind, between, above, below.*

and then:

> *Full nakedness! All joyes are due to thee,*
> *As souls unbodied, bodies uncloth'd must be,*
> *To taste whole joyes.*

The closing lines made the lonely husband's point more than vividly:

> *To teach thee, I am naked first; why then*
> *What needst thou have more covering than a man.*

Louisa was greatly pleased and perhaps titillated to receive the poem. Putting aside any remaining reserve, she began assuring John that she yearned to clasp him to her, clearly happy that her often stern senator-spouse had been beguiled by Donne's rapturous lines.

After this exchange, Louisa and John's letters managed to return to commonplace discussion over such questions as whether money should be spent to enlarge their simple Quincy residence—he apologizing for asking her to accept such rude quarters, and Louisa replying that she would dwell happily anywhere with him. They wrote each other often about their two sons, particularly three-year-old George, who was becoming ungovernable. He drove the Hellens' ducks and chickens into a wild state and could not be left untended.

Stuck in Quincy, JQA tried to subdue his eagerness to be with Louisa by enlarging an orchard, hunting, swimming regularly, fishing, and walking great distances. Having rented out his own house, he lived with his parents, where one of the summer's delights was to have at hand his father's superb library. He gave much of each day to reading and writing, even to the point of worrying that "I shall get involved in studies more than will be suitable for my health."

When he was not comparing translations of Homer's *Iliad* with the original, he was drawing up a chronological index of the laws and treaties of the United States. He did relax after sunset; he and his father usually talked until bedtime, often about politics, conversations that inspired Senator Adams in October 1804 to publish a five-part series of newspaper essays called "Serious Reflections, Addressed to the Citizens of Massachusetts." These articles mainly encouraged voters to adopt a national outlook on the eve of that year's presidential election. He besought his constituents to believe that what strengthened the Union also furthered the interest of Massachusetts, claiming that this was valid even if it entailed some of the Jefferson administration's program.

AND SO PASSED the quiet summer of 1804—until there was a startling interruption. On September 28, the day after word arrived that Harvard's president, Joseph Willard, had died, Cousin Josiah Quincy appeared at the Adams mansion to speak for a group wishing to see JQA become the next president of the university, as Harvard College was increasingly called. Just how and why this offer came about is unclear. Possibly he seemed to various people a plausible candidate for those who were opposed to another clergyman as president. He was scholarly, certainly, as well as being the bearer of a prominent New England name. On the other hand, perhaps bringing him to Harvard was viewed by some Federalists as removing an obnoxious member of the Senate.

For the moment, JQA chose to believe his kinsman was joking—although he knew Josiah was influential in Harvard matters. But because he was intrigued by what he had heard, John and his father decided to attend President Willard's funeral on September 29. During a long delay in Cambridge before the burial service began, JQA

learned from friends that the university was deeply divided on two issues: who would succeed President Willard, and who would be the
next Hollis Professor of Divinity? John said that these questions filled
the academic community with the sort of intrigue that pervaded the
Vatican when a pope was to be chosen.

Four days later and back in the quiet of Quincy, JQA learned how
serious his cousin had been. In his second visit, Josiah Quincy "opened
to me more fully" why Senator Adams was the person to lead the university at this juncture. The next day, October 4, two of John's
esteemed friends, Judge John Davis and the Reverend John T. Kirkland, arrived to pick up where Josiah Quincy had left off in urging that
Adams allow his name to be proposed as Harvard's president.

Unfortunately, JQA's diary and letters do not relate these arguments or explain why he declined to be a candidate. He may have
sensed that his brusque and impatient nature would not be helpful
qualities in the delicate situation confronting Harvard. More likely, he
believed that his chances of election were slight. For whatever reasons,
his supporters went away empty-handed, and Samuel Webber, professor of mathematics, was chosen president, a compromise figure who
was neither liked nor disliked.

IN THE MIDST of this unexpected development, Adams had begun
packing his trunks for the return to Washington, but before he could
depart, Massachusetts was struck by a memorable hurricane—he
called it "the most violent storm I ever witnessed upon the land."
Around his father's house he counted a hundred trees uprooted or
shattered. By October 11, the storm was exhausted, and JQA set out
toward the loving welcome promised in Louisa's latest letters. The trip
by stagecoach had to pass through the wreckage deposited along the
eastern seaboard by the hurricane.

It seemed to take forever, but on October 29, John finally reached
the Hellen household in Georgetown. "I had the happiness to find my
wife and children and all the family well." There followed many walks
with his sons and much time spent with Louisa. Briefly, Adams' spirits
thrived amid the reconciliation he and Louisa had achieved during the
summer. Now the couple often enjoyed a new pastime: using their
shared fluency to translate French songs into English.

There were, of course, the inevitable social outings for JQA to contend with, including his frequent dinners at the executive mansion
(which the public would soon call the White House). He was chagrined

to observe that Jefferson was more than ever in the habit of telling "prodigies," or exaggerations—he hesitated to label them falsehoods—a practice Adams had observed when he visited Washington in 1801. These ranged from the president's claim that for six weeks while he was in France, the thermometer remained below zero—which John knew to be patently untrue—to Jefferson's insistence that he had mastered the Spanish tongue during a voyage to Europe. "He knows better," Adams fumed, "but he wants to excite wonder."

After such encounters, riding horseback with Louisa was especially welcome, not least because it provided private companionship away from the crowded Hellen home. Louisa insisted that her husband had returned sallow and lethargic, so she prescribed long excursions into the woodsy wilderness around the District of Columbia. This seemed an ideal remedy until the day when Louisa's saddle turned and she was thrown from her horse. Unhurt, she calmly brushed herself off while John nearly collapsed from alarm. Soon thereafter, he himself was twice unseated by an unruly horse en route to the Senate chamber.

These upheavals were a sign of what was to come in the new session of Congress. It began as a disgusted Adams watched colleagues put off any business until the racing season was finished. His impatience overcame him on November 12 when, once again, the Senate voted to go into executive session so that the official journal would imply to the unsuspecting public that matters of state had been under consideration when in fact members actually were off to the racetrack. This time Adams decided to vote against this daily subterfuge, the only senator to do so. He attributed his nay vote to his "natural abhorrence of tricks to give appearance contrary to the real truth of things."

Thus goaded, he put aside a vow he took when the session began: not to tax excessively the patience of the Senate. He began deliberately to make a nuisance of himself by offering what most senators considered unnecessary amendments, which sought to correct grammar in legislation. This included the language in a bill containing forty-three new Articles of War, a measure that originated in a committee led by Senator Andrew Jackson of Tennessee, who, John said, believed the bill had "the last polish of perfection."

Senator Adams charged privately that Jackson's product contained "the most barbarous English that ever crept through the bars of legislation." It was "grossly and outrageously defective and blundering," and he refused to allow this "mockery of legislative deliberation" to proceed unchallenged. He demanded the reading of the lengthy bill, despite the rage of Jackson, who taunted Adams for offering "so many amendments of *who* and *such* and *as*." JQA saw "no alternative but to encounter this tempest."

Glum at heart over what he considered the deteriorating state of affairs in the Senate, Adams certainly did not spare himself. Acknowledging that while many fellow solons might have little of substance to say, he believed that most members easily surpassed him in speaking quickly and cleverly. He blamed his shortcoming upon a "slowness of comprehension, an incapacity to grasp the whole compass of a subject . . . an incapacity to form ideas properly precise and definite with the rapidity necessary to give them uninterrupted utterance."

Nor was he any happier with his endeavors outside the Senate, convinced that he was wasting his time on intellectual pursuits that would never be profitable. After more breast-beating about lacking discipline in the "search for knowledge," he conceded he was now so close to "the borders of discouragement" that he was tempted to abandon his studies. But he soon drew back, saying that to put his books away would be "impossible, for the habit has so long been fixed in me as to have become a passion." Indeed, he acknowledged, "once severed from my books," he would find nothing in life of interest. "I must therefore continue to plod."

It was no surprise when, after such thoughts, Adams began another bout with melancholia, leaving him, he said, in a state "which requires ministering to a mind diseas'd." Fortunately, the ordeal was briefer than usual, for his attention was soon absorbed by action in the House of Representatives. The Jeffersonian majority had brought impeachment charges against a member of the federal Supreme Court, Justice Samuel Chase, who was said to be so outspoken in his condemnation of the administration as to color his statements from the bench.

Chase's impeachment meant that he would be tried before the Senate. Were the judge to be convicted, Adams believed the result would be to destroy the Constitution's design of checks and balances. The importance of separating executive, legislative, and judicial arms of government had been Adams family dogma ever since John Adams had been among the first to promulgate the doctrine.

Chase's trial began on February 13 and dominated Senate business until March 1. JQA expected the worst. "As much as I depend upon the dispensation of Providence, just so little is my confidence in the wisdom and virtue of men." The senators sat in judgment daily, beginning at 10 a.m., pausing at 3 p.m. "for a cold collation," and then continuing until 7 p.m. With this demanding schedule, Adams found he had time only for events in the Capitol, so that he actually made an effort to arrive punctually at his seat. He did not wish to miss a word as the lawyers for each side presented their cases.

At night, he returned to the Hellen residence "much fatigued and exhausted" from taking detailed notes for his diary. He reminded himself that because each senator was literally a judge in the proceedings, he must be disinterested and discreet. He refrained even from sending bulletins about the deliberations to his father.

Finally, the senators were called upon to vote on whether Chase was guilty on eight articles of impeachment. The galleries were so crowded on that first day of March that Vice President Aaron Burr ordered the sergeants at arms to face the spectators and "commit to prison the first person who should make the smallest noise or disturbance." The roll call seemed to take an eternity, but finally Adams heard to his great joy that Samuel Chase had been acquitted on all charges.

Thus was defeated what JQA called a "party prosecution." The vote "has exhibited the Senate of the United States fulfilling the most important purpose of its institution by putting a check upon the impetuous violence of the House of Representatives." The defection of six Jefferson senators had, for the moment, arrested "the career of political frenzy." Such a happy result restored Adams to cheerfulness.

He was often on his feet during the two days remaining in the Senate session, usually presenting objections or offering amendments to last-minute business. Finally, his impatient colleagues voted to make him a member of the committee that worked outside the Senate chamber to review and perfect copies of legislation for the president's signature. This was an assignment they thought would speed up Senate proceedings by taking Adams away. Although he managed to wriggle out of the honor, JQA did so not to avoid work, he claimed, but because he knew that those who voted for him sought "to get rid of a troublesome member." "I did not wish to gratify them," he wrote as Congress adjourned.

AFTER TRYING AND FAILING to hear Thomas Jefferson's nearly inaudible reading of his second inaugural address on March 4, 1805, John and Louisa started for Massachusetts. They did not reach Quincy quickly, for both sons came down with chicken pox. When the boys proved too sick to travel, the Adamses decided to stay for a time in Philadelphia. The stopover had an unnerving beginning when their luggage disappeared after being piled on a wheelbarrow to be delivered to their lodgings by a hired man. JQA spent the better part of a day chasing around the city before he located the baggage.

The visit quickly improved once he was surrounded by literary friends, a pleasure rarely possible in Washington. At the office of Joseph Dennie, editor of *Port Folio*, Adams read the latest English journals. Dennie located reviews of John's recently published volume on his Silesian travels, among them a rather harsh criticism in the *Edinburgh Review*. The commentary left Adams remarkably unruffled as he took the occasion to announce that he would reform his use of time in the summer ahead. This pledge led to agreement with Dennie that Adams should complete more translations of Juvenal's *Satires* for publication.

The Adamses were weary and cranky when they finally arrived in Quincy a month after departing Washington. The trip had seemed particularly tiring, and now John had to oversee settling into the small house in the Penn's Hill neighborhood where his family would live for the summer. Although the work was hampered by a storm of snow and rain, by April 25, Senator and Mrs. Adams, their two sons, Louisa's sister Eliza, and two servants were able to move into the structure, which had barely four rooms below and three above stairs.

For the first time, John recognized how cramped this modest dwelling was. While he was resigned to making the house his summer residence until the end of his term as senator, he vowed thereafter "to remove again into Boston." In the meantime, he urged himself to be stoical—with scant success, for his mood soon sank into melancholia. Once again, he heaped reproaches upon himself for what he called unmethodical and frivolous reading and study. Now, peering intently at himself in the quiet of Quincy, he claimed to see only mediocrity and failure ahead, even though he insisted he was eager to put politics behind him as soon as his Senate term expired.

But what then? His dormant legal practice would surely yield neither "profit nor honour." More than ever, he seemed convinced that, "from both natural and adventitious circumstances in my composition, the bar is not my element." All that was left to justify his existence, it seemed to him, was a career in scholarship and writing.

But rather than deriving inspiration and hope from this vision of his future, John found himself, to his dismay, unable to begin the intellectual work he had planned for the summer. He had no excuses now. His father's library and quiet study were available as a refuge from noise in the Penn's Hill house. Yet he found he could concentrate upon nothing, a plight convincing him anew that he lacked the self-discipline and imagination for a career as an intellectual.

He spoke of his "mental imbecility" and grew even gloomier as he observed how Tom Adams was pushing ahead in life. Tom had given up his career in Philadelphia, returned to Massachusetts, found a wife, and now had a seat in the state legislature. Not even the sermons of Bishop Tillotson soothed John into the sleep he desperately needed. His prospects were "blasted," he announced.

Hearing of her son's latest decline, an impatient Abigail Adams took him to nearby Weymouth to be examined by their cousin, Dr. Cotton Tufts. The amiable physician discovered a "slow, nervous, and irregular fever" and prescribed medicine, exercise, "and a total relaxation from study." Obediently, JQA took up gardening—but his usual excess of seriousness and the naturally meager immediate results from the soil soon made him newly despondent. Always fond of fishing parties, he agreed to join one, only to find that even here fate seemed against him as storms kept the anglers ashore.

When the weather cleared on Sunday, June 23, there was no corresponding lifting of John's spirits. Then, three days later, came news that promptly pulled him out of his despair.

BOOK THREE

Cautious Hopes

1805–1817

. . . in which achievement beckons from several directions.

CHAPTER SEVEN

Professor

Perhaps I have too much indulged the suggestions of my own judgment,
and paid too little deference to that of other men.

ON JUNE 26, 1805, Cousin Josiah Quincy again appeared at the Adams mansion with news from Harvard: Senator John Quincy Adams had been elected by the University Corporation to the new professorial chair of rhetoric and oratory. The possibility of such an appointment had been the topic of gossip during the past three years, but John had thought little of it, and said even less. Now the prospect did more to restore his mental health than any amount of Cousin Tufts' medication. The appointment brought him what his depressed state required: a demand from outside himself for intellectual exertion. What was more, he felt, a professorial chair meant that his efforts could benefit mankind.

So welcome was the appointment that JQA apparently chose not to notice the irony accompanying it. Where once he had deplored owing his extraordinary beginning in life to a famous father, now he stopped praising personal independence and accepted a faculty chair endowed through the generosity of another kinsman. The Boylston Professor of Rhetoric and Oratory had been created by a gift to Harvard from Nicholas Boylston, a first cousin of Susanna Boylston Adams, JQA's grandmother.

Upon his death in 1771, Nicholas Boylston left Harvard 1,500 English pounds to found a professorship in rhetoric and oratory. After putting the money out to interest, the school forgot the benefaction until 1801, when legal action brought it to mind. Boylston's nephew,

Ward Nicholas Boylston, a close friend of JQA's, filed suit against the university to recover the neglected endowment, which by then amounted to $23,200. Faced with litigation, Harvard suddenly discovered that it wanted very much to add a professor of rhetoric to the faculty. Boylston agreed to withdraw his suit, but only if John Quincy Adams became the first occupant of the chair.

After receiving news of the appointment, John was as vigorous and cheerful through the remainder of the summer as he had been incapacitated during the earlier months. He now had two enterprises to occupy him. The first was to complete negotiations with the university concerning his duties. The second was to begin preparing lectures. Announcing that he was much recovered, a spirited JQA gave himself over to both projects. Thereafter, his journal entries frequently used the soul-satisfying words: "Industriously employed."

Harvard found itself in awkward circumstances. If it was to retain the Boylston endowment, it must add to the faculty a person whose qualifications for the post were obscure, to put it politely. Nor was the institution pleased when Professor-designate Adams insisted upon a series of modifications to the rules for the chair. Knowing that he and Ward Boylston had the university in a tight corner, John asked for preferential treatment. This led to months of gentlemanly dispute with the president of the university over how far the senator could stray beyond the rules to which professors customarily conformed.

Several points were at issue in JQA's demands. He would not reside in Cambridge. He would teach only part of each school year. He would not make the declaration of religious conformity required of all faculty members. Furthermore, he insisted that he, not the university, would select the instructor who would substitute for him should he ever be absent on public business. Finally, he emphasized that he must continue as a United States senator.

There was no explanation of why Adams did not resign the seat in Washington, as he had often talked of doing. He could have managed without the salary, and the time thus released might have gone to the writing he clamored to do. Perhaps it was because, despite his exclamations to the contrary, he was enjoying politics. Or, quite possibly, he was reluctant to give away his best excuse for putting off the demanding literary toil he talked so much about desiring.

Whatever the reasons, Adams proved surprisingly aggressive about these "suggestions" made to Harvard, although he was careful to assure the overseers that he was "highly sensible" of the vast honor coming with the chair. To win his demands, he lobbied influential friends who were members of the overseers and the corporation. Particularly he sought support from Judge John Davis, who sympathized, and from cousin Ward Boylston. On the especially delicate matter of his refusal to make a public assertion of religious conformity, Adams said that he objected as a matter of principle and believed in "reserving my confession of faith for my Maker." After much discussion, his terms were accepted by the overseers on November 7, 1805.

Long before that triumph, however, the appointee had begun preparing his lectures, working mostly in John Adams' library, which contained numerous works about oratory and rhetoric by such favorites as Cicero and Aristotle. As another step to ready himself, he pledged to write critiques of the sermons he heard each Sunday. Unfortunately, few clergymen pleased him by what they said or how they delivered their homilies. The New England pronunciation now began to offend Adams' ear, made fastidious by life abroad. He particularly deplored a tendency among preachers to debase their sounding of *e* and *o*. Two examples he cited were "good-noss" and "pormitted."

He also listened closely during Harvard's commencement exercises on August 28 from the seat he was coaxed into accepting on the platform with the faculty and dignitaries. The student orators showed Adams much that needed improving. They wandered far from their subjects, digressions that the critic laid at the door of poor training in logic given at Harvard. Even worse was the students' forgetfulness. JQA blamed this on Harvard's indifference to memorization, a power that, according to the professor-designate, the ancients had cherished. In short, graduation exercises showed clearly that he had his work cut out for him.

Thus his vacation from Senate duties in 1805 closed gloriously after beginning miserably. This time, winter brought a complaint that, under the circumstances, rang rather hollow: by returning to the Senate, he must abandon "the studies which have so agreeably occupied me since the beginning of July." There was no mention of resigning, a subject usually brought up when he had to return to the capital.

Senator Adams did have the grace, however, to admit that the beguilement of Washington politics would likely encourage him "to fly from the most urgent object of study to anything else." His weakness before distraction he called the most pernicious of enemies, for "it prevents me from acquiring a profound knowledge of anything." A professor must do better, he said, and with this resolve he regretfully departed for Washington on November 11.

Nor was Louisa happy at leaving, since her husband had decreed that her sons should stay in New England rather than spend another winter in what Abigail Adams called a boarding-house environment. Four-year-old George was to study with Aunt and Uncle Cranch at $2.50 per week, while John, age two, was to live with Grandmother Adams.

BOTH SENATOR AND MRS. ADAMS were in low spirits as they began the journey southward. Once they arrived in Philadelphia, however, they cheered up. After "much agreeable literary conversation," John had an intriguing talk with his good friend Dr. Benjamin Rush, a confidant of both President Jefferson and Secretary of State Madison. According to Rush, these dignitaries had asked that he approach Adams about accepting appointment to a diplomatic post.

John's reply was characteristic: he assured Rush that while he sought no office, he would not refuse one just because it had been offered by Jefferson. But with salary from the Harvard professorship now forthcoming, he wanted Rush—and the president—to know that "I possessed the means of maintaining my family without feeling the necessity of any public station." After he had conveyed this proud message, the Adamses boarded a boat to Baltimore that was so crowded, John found himself sleeping on a bench.

He was not treated much better on reaching Baltimore in the early hours of November 29. He and Louisa had to sit up until 8 a.m., when they were assigned an unmade bed left by tavern guests who had departed early. By the time the Adamses appeared at the Hellen household in Georgetown, they were exhausted. For some weeks thereafter, whether from the fatigue of travel or from the frictions of reentering Washington's partisan atmosphere, JQA's emotional and physical health was poor.

Try though he might, he could not shake off the foul mood. The sight of a visiting Indian tribe outraged him as he watched them "making a hideous howling and a disgusting appearance." During a Capitol religious service, a preacher performed so poorly "that Holiness itself could not command attention to his discourse." Even Adams' reading, "with which I [once] could be sure never to have a wearisome moment," now seemed to drain his energy.

Nor were his spirits improved when Mother Abigail's letters began once again to chide his carelessness in appearance, a topic Abigail admitted she had brought up so often during the previous summer "that I was fearful you would get callous to my admonitions." Would he not please her by purchasing a new coat? she asked. "I do not wish a Senator to dress like a beau, but I want him to conform so far to the fashion as not to acquire the character of singularity." And surely, Abigail hoped, her son would not choose to "give occasion to the world to ask what kind of mother he had?"

But JQA's thoughts were far from a new coat. His grouchy mood came mostly from watching "the jealousy and acrimony of party" dominate Congress, beginning with a quarrel over approving in secret an appropriation of $2 million. President Jefferson wished that amount at hand to acquire West Florida by paying for Napoleon's help. Although the hushed-up bill eventually passed, Adams would have nothing to do with it, contending that the United States already owned the area.

Presently, however, the Senate took up topics where his interest made him happier. One was the need to clarify rules governing the behavior of representatives of foreign governments. Another was the increasing danger that the war between France and England posed to America's rights as a neutral. There was also a diverting debate over an accord with Tripoli, whose pirates in the Mediterranean were a nuisance to American shipping. Adams voted to ratify this treaty, although his New England colleagues opposed it. "Everything on earth but a sense of duty dictated silence to me on this subject," he said. "I have acted upon inflexible principle and am to take the consequence."

He might thus occasionally applaud his own motives, but on the whole it was no easier in this session than the last for him to be satisfied with himself as a senator. On April 1, after a debate over an insignificant relief bill that he had opposed, he growled: "I was as I always am, *miserably defective.*" Partly, this was due to his rising embarrassment as rumors went around Washington that Jefferson intended to name him minister to Great Britain.

The more Adams' votes tended to support the Republican administration, the more gossip flourished about his reward. By standing with those who should be his enemies, for JQA was still listed as a Federalist, he wondered whether he was being corrupted, despite his effort to be disinterested and selfless. "The gratification of my own vanity or ambition by a display of influence would be a despicable motive of which I am utterly unconscious." His only aspiration, he repeatedly insisted, was a desire to be "a mighty agent in the service of my country." He warned himself never to confuse personal ambition with the dictates of patriotism.

There was one Senate duty in which John could be safely impartial. He thoroughly enjoyed serving on the committee for the congressional library, especially because it allowed him to select many of the new books. After the session adjourned in April, he took $494 of the library appropriation to spend on behalf of Congress in Boston's bookstores. Here, at least, he found public duty and personal pleasure in perfect harmony. Two other committeemen were to shop in New York City and Philadelphia.

His book-buying assignment helped John overcome a very displeasing feature of his return to Massachusetts. With Louisa well along in another pregnancy, they had reluctantly agreed that she should not attempt the journey but, rather, remain behind in the comforting presence of her mother and sisters.

After the couple spent a few days together, much of the time at fishing, a sport they now both enjoyed, John left Washington for a stopover in New York City with Nabby, whose marital problems grew worse as a result of the escapades of Colonel Smith. The trip from New York to Quincy took only forty-nine hours, the shortest travel time in JQA's experience. New turnpikes helped account for the speed, which he welcomed, for he was impatient to begin preparation of his inaugural lecture as Boylston Professor. His induction into the academic chair was just five weeks ahead.

ONCE BACK IN NEW ENGLAND, the prospect of taking part in academic life so pleased him that he wrote to Louisa of his eagerness to leave the Senate, assuring her that he would immediately resign his seat if she were with him. He said he no longer dreaded reestablishing his legal practice, knowing that he would need income from it to replace his senatorial pay and to supplement his professorial salary. Later that summer, he did open an office in Boston's Court Street and agreed to tutor a law student.

He arranged to have his room and board in the Cambridge home of Dr. Benjamin Waterhouse, an old friend and fellow faculty member. The new professor's first duty was to appear at the installation of Samuel Webber as president of Harvard. None of the speeches Adams heard that day satisfied him, and he pledged to be even more careful in composing his own inaugural address.

He kept so busy with his writing, along with visits among old friends, that the time for his June 12 installation arrived before he was ready. The day before, he had suddenly realized that he ought to appear wearing an academic gown; after vainly searching Boston for an available seamstress, he gave up and borrowed a robe.

The great day was sultry as Adams, heavy academic attire over his arm and his parents in tow, appeared for dinner at President Webber's house, where they were joined by Cousin Ward Boylston. As the group finished the meal a violent storm broke, causing the ceremony, scheduled for 3:30 p.m., to be delayed for nearly two hours. Finally, Webber offered the opening prayer before an audience reduced to a patient few. Anthems were sung, statements made in Latin, and regulations governing the Boylston chair read, including notice that the incumbent's first tenure would be a term of seven years. To these regulations Adams subscribed by signature; then he presented the document to Governor Caleb Strong, seated on the platform.

Thereupon Webber solemnly declared John Quincy Adams to be the Boylston Professor, and John at last began his inaugural lecture. The storm had not relieved the heat, and the speaker, enveloped in his woolen gown, suffered mightily but managed to finish his remarks, in which he established what would be the foundation of his course: the classical rhetorical tradition as exemplified in Cicero and Quintilian. After singing another hymn, the audience and officials gathered for a reception and to praise John. In reporting the occasion, the *Columbian Centinel* said that Professor Adams had shown "the hand of a master" in his address. *The Repertory* called the oration "elegant, classical, and energetic."

There were, however, complaints from some members of the faculty, who wished their new colleague had followed custom by delivering his opening lecture in Latin. On this academic issue, as well as so many others, the independent-spirited Adams had his own ideas. Since his remarks were intended to sketch the nature, history, and practice of oratory, he insisted they ought to be understood by the entire audience, so he spoke in English.

Barely into his academic work, he attempted to secure additional preferential treatment by asking to be allowed to complete in one day his entire weekly teaching responsibility, which amounted to one lecture and an afternoon of judging student declamations. The regulations called for faculty members to be present a minimum of two days, and Harvard's president insisted that Professor Adams comply. But John rallied his friends on the board and ultimately defeated Webber.

JQA had also successfully argued that sophomores be allowed to join the upper classes in attending his lectures. This caused a delay of two weeks before the course on oratory and rhetoric could finally have its first meeting on July 11, the instructor's thirty-ninth birthday. Professor Adams eyed his students with considerable misgiving. "None of them appear to have any idea of the first elements of public speaking," he complained. With such poorly prepared pupils to redeem, he called his pedagogical task an "undertaking of magnitude and importance." To succeed, he would need "power from above."

His first lecture went better than he had anticipated, although he regretted that no townsmen had been present (in those days, the public considered itself invited into Harvard's lecture rooms). At the end of two months, the students appeared to be enjoying Adams' lectures, but in the professor's judgment, he was faltering. "My own present ideas are so crude and indigested," he said, calling his tenth lecture the most unsatisfying writing he had ever done.

There were other problems. JQA found that great care was needed to check the faulty arithmetic of Ebenezer Storer, Harvard's treasurer. For his first period of service, June 12 to 30, Adams was due $72.46 but received only $23.20. This error was modest compared with Storer's next blunder, when he paid John $171.20 instead of $348 for the period June 30 to September 30. Only after presenting a detailed accounting did Adams finally receive full remuneration from Harvard.

As it turned out, worries over his class presentations and the treasurer's mistakes were trivial concerns for JQA that summer, compared with a more personal woe. Since leaving Washington, he had exchanged frequent and loving letters with the pregnant Louisa, who reported that her health was good as she passed along political gossip. But her optimism proved groundless. On June 30, Adams learned that after twenty hours of labor she had been delivered of a stillborn son. Louisa, however, recovered quickly and soon wrote animatedly of setting out for Boston to be with her husband and boys.

Adams was much shaken by Louisa's experience. On the day he learned the infant's fate, he managed to carry out his tasks before going to his room to weep and "to reason myself into resignation to the will of Heaven." He spoke admiringly of Louisa's message, with "its tenderness, its resignation, and its fortitude." He, however, "had given up my heart to hope and joy in the hope of a third [child]. It is gone."

The next day, he began planning for Louisa's arrival. After failing to locate a residence he could rent in Cambridge, he reluctantly decided to assemble his family once again in the cramped farmhouse in

Quincy. Louisa appeared on August 11, and the cottage soon was bulging with Professor and Mrs. Adams, two boys, two servants, and Louisa's sister Carolina.

Despite the crowded quarters, John tried to arise each day at 6 a.m. and read six chapters of the Bible—three of them in Greek. Then he spaded in his garden until breakfast, which was followed by stints of lecture writing. These did not prevent him from instructing son George in French and from going to his father's house for a daily chat of at least an hour.

From Quincy, JQA faced a nearly eight-mile walk into Boston (he timed himself at three hours, three minutes), where he would hitch a ride to Cambridge. Being away from the farmhouse had its advantages. His happiness at seeing Louisa soon had calmed enough for him to confide in his diary how much he missed the quiet of his room at Waterhouse's home. "Nothing can be more fatal to study," he grumbled, "than petty avocations continually recurring. My lectures are already losing two thirds of their value." By insignificant tasks he meant working with his young trees, walking with his sons, and evenings spent reading to the ladies.

Nevertheless, none of these causes for complaint made Adams eager to return to Washington as the time approached, especially after Louisa decided that she did not wish to be separated from her sons for the winter and rented a Boston apartment. The prospect of a painful leave-taking in mid-November kept John from fixing his mind on much of anything, including the Sunday sermons. "I could not help it," he apologized to his diary after sitting distracted through a worship service. He rambled with son George across the Adams family's hilly farmlands along the shore in Quincy, hoping to make the lad familiar "with the scenes upon which my own earliest recollection dwells. I feel an attachment to these places more powerful than to any other spot upon earth."

After leaving Louisa and his family, JQA was comforted by two events that occurred en route to Washington. When the stagecoach stopped at New Haven, he was introduced to a geographer named Elliott, who announced that he had recently purchased a copy of John's book about travel in Silesia. He had read it carefully and pleasurably, Elliott said, and he proceeded to recite at length from its contents.

Heartened by this encounter, John later paused in the town of Princeton, where he was told that its College of New Jersey had recently conferred upon him the honorary degree of Doctor of Laws. At that time, such recognition was often made without ceremony. After expressing gratitude to college officials for this "personal notice," Adams continued toward Washington, arriving on November 27 to settle into his comfortable room in the Hellen household.

ONCE AGAIN, he was annoyed as the Senate loitered for a month after opening the session. This winter, however, senatorial indolence was a windfall for Professor Adams, who put the time to use in writing the next series of lectures he would deliver when he returned to Harvard. During the past summer and autumn, he had given eleven lectures, and he foresaw preparing at least that many more in Washington—after starting each day by reading four chapters of the Bible, followed by passages from Homer and particularly from Marcus Fabius Quintilian, the Roman rhetorician and teacher of the first century A.D.

There were less noble claims on Adams, of course. Being very much part of the Hellen-Johnson family, he often escorted Mrs. Johnson and her spinster daughters to parties, balls, and other occasions where most of tiny Washington's acceptable society felt obliged to appear. After one such event, John recorded: "I played again at cards, an amusement which has become to my taste a toil, but to which at these parties I am driven from a want of light conversation." He wished "that I had been [a] man of elegant and accomplished manners."

He wrote often to Louisa and, being a chronic worrier, lived in ceaseless apprehension that the next letter from her would bring alarming news about the family's health. He left no doubt that he was very lonely for his wife—especially at night during one of Washington's harshest winters in memory. To Louisa's quip that while she often found him exasperating (she called him "my testy friend"), she could not live without him, John replied: "I will not say I can neither live with you nor without you; but in this cold weather I should be very glad to live with you."

By early February 1807, Louisa was so much on his mind that John began composing poems to send her, some again with an erotic flavor. An inspiration for one came to him, he admitted, after attending a ball where one of the guests, a young lady, was "rather more than usually undressed." He asked Louisa whether women actually understood "the effects which their exhibitions have a tendency to produce upon sensation."

The poem inspired by this experience contemplated how women had forgotten their mother Eve, whose fate should have taught that nakedness was shameful and that dress implied innocence. Now, according to Adams' jocular lines, women stood with arms, neck, and breasts "displa'd to all" and used only "a bare spider's web" to conceal the rest. To the vast amusement of his spouse, he closed the poem with a plea that a certain lady—clearly Louisa—

> *Fling the* last *fig leaf to the wind,*
> *And snatch me to thy arms!*

Louisa replied that her husband "must be in great spirits" to have written some of the "sauciest lines I ever perused." Would he wish that she have them published? she teased.

Around the 12th of February, which was Louisa's thirty-second birthday, John devoted nearly a week's spare time to composing a long poem which he dedicated to her as "Friend of my bosom." It sought to show how he spent each day, closing with a picture of himself alone at night as he would "gaze at the fire with vacant stare" or "the chamber pace like one distracted," all the while thinking of "the partner of my soul" until he finally "to my lonely couch return."

The poem, "A Winter's Day," closed with these lines:

> *Louisa! thus remote from thee,*
> *Still something to each joy is wanting,*
> *While thy* affection *can to me*
> *Make the most dreary scene enchanting.*

Such loving lines made Louisa eager to have her husband back with her. She wrote that her thoughts were constantly upon him and that her dreams were full of their being together. Mornings were mournful, she lamented, when she awoke to find him absent. She would not be content until "I have the happiness of clasping you once more to the heart of your tenderly affectionate wife."

Poetry eventually had to give ground to politics when the Senate finally shook off its lethargy. Several issues kept Adams' attention, including the status of persons accused of conspiring with Aaron Burr to pull much of the Mississippi Valley region out of the Union. There were interesting debates over bridge construction and the abolition of the slave trade. Also, he was intrigued by a proposal to build a national road from New England to Louisiana; in this, as in most issues, Senator Adams voted on the side of national development.

While he feared that these topics unduly excited him, the passive

outlook of many of his colleagues appalled him. They seemed to trans-
act such important business with unrivaled "indifference and carelessness," which unnerved John when he sought to keep the Senate's
attention while speaking. Fortunately, there were those redeeming
moments when his performance "would not shame a good speaker."
His suspicions about a bill to give federal land to the Chesapeake and
Ohio Canal Company brought him twice to his feet. On his second
appearance, "there was some degree of weariness manifested when I
began, but much attention was given as I advanced, and the effect was
manifest when I closed." Afterward, a colleague privately congratulated John for having "broken them up." And, indeed, almost single-
handedly, he got the issue postponed until the next year.

CONSEQUENTLY, WHEN THE SESSION ENDED, Adams left for New
England not quite as disgusted with himself as in the past. He was up
at 3 a.m. on March 5 to be ready for the stagecoach, which in those
days picked up passengers at their residences. Once on his way, he
stopped in New York City, where he found that Nabby's husband
had vanished, literally abandoning his family. At her brother's insistence, Nabby gathered her things and accompanied him to New England. Her bad luck came along, for just as they crossed into
Massachusetts, their trunks were thrown off the coach and the contents scattered. Clothing and books had to be retrieved from the mud.

In a bedraggled state, JQA arrived in Boston to find that he had to
search for Louisa. She had been unhappy in the apartment where she
and the children had spent the winter, so when a house John owned on
Nassau Street fell vacant, she immediately moved into it. Consequently, his first chore was not the literary work he anticipated. Instead, he found himself hauling furniture from Quincy into town since
he and Louisa intended to remain in Boston for the summer. This was
only the start of a round of domestic drudgery that made him often
lose "the due command of my patience or of my temper." Nor did toil-
ing at his lectures improve his outlook. "The difficulties of my subject
grow upon me instead of diminishing," he complained.

The professor was heartened a bit by the teaching schedule Harvard's authorities had finally approved. Each Friday he would lecture
at 10 a.m. and then hear student declamations at 2 p.m. Accordingly,
on March 27, he was ready to deliver his twelfth address, one of those
he had prepared in Washington. Getting an early start, he walked
from Boston "up" to Cambridge, where he found to his dismay that

the college functioned at a pace slower than his. He had wished to consult the library, but it was still closed. His only refuge until it was time for his lecture was Dr. Waterhouse's residence.

When the hour arrived for afternoon declamations, only four of his ten students appeared. Inquiring about such poor attendance, Adams learned that the young scholars were "out of humour" over harsh punishment imposed in a case of student misbehavior. Giving up, Professor Adams started for the city on foot, only to be overtaken by heavy rain. Reluctantly, he climbed onto the stagecoach headed for Boston, where he found his home in an uproar because the male servant had vanished.

The servant's disappearance left a rain-soaked JQA facing so many domestic chores that, once again, he could not settle down with his books. And there were more annoyances. The hullabaloo resumed soon after the family retired, when the lost employee returned noisily drunk, stumbling in through an unlocked cellar door with a commotion that roused children and adults. All in all, the day had not been an encouraging start for Professor Adams' second season with the Harvard faculty.

Matters were slow to improve. By the next Friday a heavy snow had fallen and melted, obliging JQA to walk to Cambridge "half-leg deep in mud and in the face of a violent gale." When he arrived at Harvard, he could not find the freshman who was assigned to ring the bell for the lecture. When the lad turned up, it was too late for the class, leaving Adams trying to keep calm while he waited for declamation time. Once again, few of the young orators appeared as the university continued much disordered by student rebellion. It affected even a meeting of the Harvard Corporation, which became so heated that the governor of the commonwealth collapsed in an epileptic seizure.

Amid such distractions, Adams tried to concentrate on class preparation. "These lectures are indeed precisely the labour of Sisyphus," he grumbled. It took a fortnight of close application to prepare for the performance of half an hour. By late June, however, work was moving more rapidly, and he was satisfied with his progress. He was also encouraged by finding his lecture chamber now nearly filled by class members and many "friends" from around town. The quality of student declamations also took a turn for the better.

But, just as these academic tasks began to please Adams, a violent public controversy arose over an event that he and most citizens could not disregard. On June 22, the U.S. frigate *Chesapeake* had been fired on by the British frigate *Leopard* near Norfolk, Virginia. American lives were lost as the English sought four of the *Chesapeake*'s seamen, who were said to have deserted British ships. The incident caused a fierce debate to erupt between Federalists and Republicans over a long-festering issue: defense of the United States' rights as a neutral.

JQA considered the *Chesapeake*'s fate an "occurrence of very gloomy complexion." He anticipated that most of his Federalist associates were so fearful of alienating Great Britain—the main source for New England's immensely lucrative overseas trade—that they would submit even to this latest indignity rather than retaliate. Consequently, when Boston's Republicans called a mass meeting at the State House on July 10 to protest the *Chesapeake* affair, Senator Adams was present and was asked to serve as moderator. He declined, but consented to be on the resolutions committee. This outraged his Federalist associates, one of whom told John that "I should *have my head taken off* for apostasy."

The crisis so estranged Adams from his nominal Federalist affiliation that a complete break proved unavoidable. Indeed, within ten days, tempers were so heated that he got into a public shouting match with Harry Otis. Other critics rebuked John in personal encounters and in the Federalist newspapers, and when President Jefferson called Congress to assemble on October 16 to consider action against Great Britain, Adams found himself angrily accosted by persons he once counted as friends. "I had this day a debate somewhat warm with Mr. John Lowell at the Suffolk Insurance Office" was a typical diary entry.

While his Federalist adversaries fumed over having a senator likely to be sympathetic to Jefferson's determination to defend the nation, JQA tried to ignore them in the quiet of Boston's recently established Athenaeum—destined to become one of America's great libraries, thanks to the efforts of John's cousin Billy Shaw. Adams found escape also in meetings of the Natural Philosophy Club, where his stand against England's policy toward neutrals would not be flung in his face.

Also, Boston's tensions could be left behind when JQA went on weekends to Quincy for talks with his father and to choose books to carry back with him to town. When not sorting through his library, he took long walks, inspected his real estate, and on Sundays attended the old church of his youth.

If he stayed over until Monday, his father usually hitched up his chaise and took him part of the way to Boston. It must have been a stirring sight: an ex-president of the United States traveling like any local farmer and accompanied by a United States senator. Left with a walk of an hour and a half, JQA usually went home first to see how Louisa was faring.

Nearing the end of another pregnancy, she had been remarkably well. On August 17, she and John took their customary stroll through the Boston Common. At two the next morning, she sent for her doctor and nurse, and by 8:30 the baby was born. A month later, young Charles Francis Adams was taken to First Church for baptism, named, as John noted "in remembrance of my deceased brother" and "as a token of honour to my old friend and patron, Judge [Francis] Dana."

Immediately after the christening, the Adamses began preparing for Washington. Only Louisa and the baby would accompany JQA; young John would remain with his grandparents in Quincy, and George would attend an academy in Atkinson, New Hampshire, operated by Aunt Elizabeth Shaw and her second husband, the Reverend Stephen Peabody.

ON OCTOBER 6, Professor Adams delivered his last lecture of the Harvard term. After paying a farewell call on Governor Sullivan, a Jeffersonian, during which the two speculated about war with Great Britain, JQA set out with his wife and son for Washington in blustery weather that delayed their arrival at the Hellen residence until October 24. The journey allowed John to reflect on his four years as a member of the Senate, service that he concluded had been largely a failure.

He reviewed how little business he initiated had succeeded in the face of "an opposition of great obstinacy." But when one of his failed projects was taken up by another senator, Adams recalled, it was usually approved "without the least resistance." Some colleagues, he claimed, took pleasure in thwarting him. Nor, in his opinion, had his assignment to committees improved. He was still a subordinate who carried "the merely laborious duties."

Adams was not clear about the reasons for what he deemed his poor showing in the Senate, but he implied—no doubt correctly—that his lordly manner, his arch-seriousness of purpose, and his constant jumping into debate combined to make him an annoyance to his colleagues and resulted in his being treated as such. In any event, he decided to reform, resolving that in the session about to begin, he would "restrain rather than indulge the propensities to debate."

Toward that end, he planned to spend more time companionably with Dr. Samuel L. Mitchell, one of the few colleagues whom Adams admired. The New York senator was a man who preferred conversation made up "of chemistry, of geography, and of natural philosophy"—in short, who "knows a little of everything" (that is, someone very much like John himself). Being with Mitchell at the president's table was a special treat, since Jefferson shared Adams' high regard for the erudite senator.

The Senate opened on October 26 in what John impatiently called "a continued state of nihility," so annoying him that he faltered in his resolve to be better behaved on the floor. From mid-November until final adjournment in April 1808, he was as active in debate as usual. Mostly, this was because he found the important issues to be irresistible. They derived mostly from foreign affairs as the war between England and France became ever more a threat to America's maritime prosperity.

Some months earlier, Napoleon had issued decrees from Berlin and Milan aimed at isolating the British Empire from the world's trade, to which the English responded by stopping more American merchant ships, confiscating their cargoes, and retaining some of their sailors for impressment into the navy. The *Chesapeake* episode had been only the most dramatic result of Britain's policy. Now, with Congress assembled, the Jefferson leadership met these outrages by a proposal that drew Adams into the center of Republican politics and widened the breach between him and the Federalists.

In December 1807, Jefferson asked the Senate to enact an embargo that would prohibit export from American ports by any vessel, U.S. or foreign. Adams was named with four Republican senators to form a committee to consider the drastic measure. The committee supported it unanimously. John believed that the United States must defend its rights as a neutral nation and that the proposed embargo was a better means of doing so than going to war.

He knew that American products were considered essential by England and France, and that an embargo would cut them off from importing these goods. While foreign ships might bring commodities into ports in the United States, these vessels would have to leave empty, which no shipowner could afford. Thus, the embargo promised to end imports as well as exports, thereby playing havoc with American merchant ships, most of which sailed out of New England. These vessels were now forbidden to leave port, to the dismay of Adams' numerous and influential mercantile constituents. He could only urge them to believe that "private interest must not be put in opposition to public good."

He might as well have spoken to the wind. The embargo proved to be a disaster, rather than the basis for negotiation Adams had anticipated. Massachusetts' powerful merchant community led a national protest against the policy, while at the same time shippers and traders devised ways to evade the law. Meanwhile, as JQA's support for the embargo brought cries of outrage from other Federalists, he went a step further by proposing a bill to exclude British commerce from American ports until the English made amends for their high-handed tactics on the seas.

Adams' performance seemed clear proof—not that much was needed—to all but his greatest admirers that he was a traitor to the Federalist party. He behaved as if he wanted to anger or taunt his critics, whose outrage was intensified by his next action: a committee report he wrote to recommend that Senator John Smith of Ohio be denied his seat as punishment for allegedly conspiring with Aaron Burr to lead the lower Mississippi Valley out of the Union.

Burr's purported scheme had many sympathizers in New England, so that in his native region, JQA's leadership against the plot seemed more evidence that he had sold himself to the Jeffersonians, who had loudly condemned Burr. No one seemed surprised when the Republican leadership began awarding Senator Adams more significant committee assignments, which led his critics to denounce him even more warmly. "It is indeed a fiery ordeal that I must go through," he observed. "God speed me through it."

Senator James Bayard, Federalist from Delaware, used his gifted tongue to lead the Adams critics in casting what John called "insidious and false imputations" upon him. These insinuations mostly hinted at appointments, in the cabinet or abroad, that John was said to expect from the next Republican administration in exchange for his support. Another rumor held that Adams would be nominated as the Republican ticket's vice-presidential candidate, leading John to deplore this "talk about me for offices to which I have neither pretension, expectation, nor wish."

But, given his nature, what else was he likely to say? It therefore remains impossible to be certain whether he nurtured secret hopes for an appointment from a grateful Jeffersonian administration. If he did, which seems likely, he disguised them by continuing to claim emphatically that his backing of administration measures was because that side had America's interests at heart. What choice had an independent man, he asked, but to stand wherever righteousness abounded?

Actually, gossip about a deal between Senator Adams and President Jefferson might have subsided had not John himself revived it by a move that led even those closest to him to suspect his motives: he chose to attend the Republican congressional caucus on January 23, 1808. This was a gathering called to consider James Madison as the party's nominee for president. Adams' presence seemed the ultimate sign of collaboration and suggested to many observers that he was announcing his availability for service to the next administration. It was a plausible reaction, for as a professed independent devoted only to national duty, John surely was under no obligation to appear at such a party conclave. He could much more easily have remained at home that evening, reading and writing in his study.

Instead, he was very much present when ninety caucus participants overwhelmingly nominated Madison. The group then balloted for vice president. One vote was cast for Adams. Given earlier rumors that the Republicans would choose him for vice president as a gesture of national unity, even the single vote he received gave his critics new ammunition. He reported the event to his diary without comment. One newspaper gleefully printed as fact that John Quincy Adams had voted for himself in his own handwriting.

John was scarcely forthcoming about this delicate moment in his career. Not even in his diary did he disclose his wishes as he, along with everyone else, continued to hear stories of good things in store for him from the Jeffersonians. He also began to receive flattering attention from such administration leaders as Senator William Branch Giles of Virginia, who told Adams that "he believed I considered every public measure as I should a proposition in Euclid, abstracted from any party considerations."

A pleased Adams warned himself that such conversations were designed to lead him to divulge what personal expectation he might have in exchange for aiding Republican party strategy. To all such overtures, he cannily replied by repeating that he supported Jefferson's administration because it sought the welfare of the nation.

Despite this lofty talk, JQA was certainly aware that if his Republican stance caused him to be defeated for reelection, a grateful Madison would likely reward him at the very least with an ambassadorial post. A new place in the diplomatic corps would bring an honorable release from the partisan antics he claimed to detest. He would return to a career where there was even more time for reading and writing than the Harvard chair allowed, and where conversation moved in edifying realms.

While Adams confided in no one about what his altruism might gain him, his family and friends begged him to be candid with them as the gossip increased. One who approached him was Josiah Quincy, now a member of the House of Representatives. He "inquired into the motives for my late conduct," John noted, adding that his cousin warned against having principles "too pure for those with whom I was acting." He should not expect the Republicans to show him gratitude. To this Adams replied that "I did not want their thanks." He then tried to change the subject by pointing out to Quincy the danger to the Union posed by New England's opposition to the Republican administration. Claiming that most Federalists were prepared to dissolve the Union and become subservient to Great Britain, John assured his cousin "that to resist this I was ready, if necessary, to sacrifice every thing I have in life, and even life itself."

Unsettled by this conversation, Adams decided that he ought to make certain his stand was clearly understood by the Jeffersonians. The next day, he spoke again with Senator Giles, emphasizing that he disdained exchanging political support for personal advantage. Any aid he had given or might give to the administration was "governed solely by public considerations," and he particularly wished it known "that I have no personal expectations or wishes whatsoever." Giles politely replied that he had never doubted this.

When he talked with Giles, JQA had on his desk a letter full of wisdom from John Adams, who considered the situation "clear, plain, and obvious": his son simply was not designed by nature for partisan politics. "You have too honest a heart, too independent a mind, and too brilliant talents" for a political career. The father predicted that the Massachusetts legislature would not give JQA another term in the Senate, leaving him "numbered among the dead." Even so, the senior Adams urged his son to be of good cheer. "Return to your professorship," John Adams advised, and also "to your office as a lawyer. Devote yourself to your profession and to the education of your children."

JQA assured his parent that he saw his "situation" in the same light. To be dismissed "from my public station" would mean "my vanity may be affected, but in every other respect it will be a relief." Then he reminded his father of what he was stressing to everyone: he would never solicit an appointment in government service. And anyway, he added, "the prospects of the nation are such that a seat in the public councils cannot be an object of my desire." Consequently, he claimed to look eagerly toward a literary career. The practice of law, he said, was "a business for which I know myself to be indifferently qualified," and to be resumed only if necessary.

While Federalist Boston digested JQA's participation in the Republican party powwow, newspaper assaults became rougher, and he began to receive anonymous letters calling him a traitor. When even his brother Tom expressed dismay, John said he had not thought his family would suspect that he had joined the enemy to save his political skin. Could they not accept that, while he had indeed voted at the Republican caucus, he was otherwise "a mere spectator"? As for being rewarded for deserting Federalism, he explained his new prominence in Senate councils as merely reflecting his growing seniority and therefore no cause for gossip.

If he expected these explanations to satisfy persons back home, he was sorely mistaken. The uproar over his supposed collaboration increased, leaving him nothing but the limp position that the world must trust him. Simply believe in me, Adams began to beg constituents as he continued to emphasize how only the national interest guided his every move in Washington.

One of the sharpest skeptics was none other than Abigail Adams, who sent her son a vigorous rebuke for attending the caucus. His action had, she claimed, "staggered my belief," and she charged him with behavior "inconsistent with your principles."

Much offended, an exasperated John replied: "I could wish to please my country, I could wish to please my parents—but my duty I *must* do. It is a law far above my mere wishes." Privately, he said Abigail's letter had been "a test for my firmness, for my prudence, and for my filial reverence. May I be assisted to stand the test without impairing either of these duties."

Besieged by such censure, Adams finally chose to defend himself by publishing a pamphlet. Dated March 31, 1808, it took the form of a public letter to Harrison Gray Otis as representative of JQA's opposition, and had a circulation of five thousand copies. But if the aim of the essay was, as John put it, to restore unity in American politics, the result fell far short. A Federalist editor called Adams "one of those amphibious politicians who lives on both land and water, and occasionally resorts to each, but who finally settles down in the mud." Elsewhere, he was described as a "party scavenger" and as one who was busily "courting the prevailing party." One newspaper said JQA represented Napoleon Bonaparte instead of Massachusetts.

WITH INDIGNATION TOWARD HIM growing more strident in Boston, Adams set out for home on April 27, loudly insisting that he

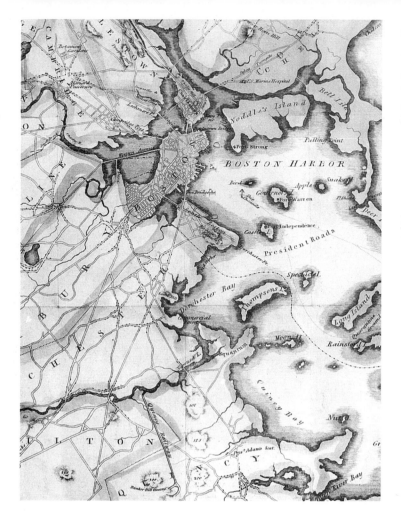

This detail from an 1830 map by Abel Bowen suggests the distance JQA had to cover when he walked from Quincy into Boston, the city where he often felt uncomfortable.

JQA was born in July 1767 in the cottage shown at left center. Over the years 1803 to 1808, U.S. Senator Adams and his family spent several summers in this typical New England dwelling, pictured here in the 1880s. The house still stands in Quincy, although all signs of its once rural surroundings have been eradicated by urban sprawl.

In 1822, JQA's cousin Eliza Susan Quincy sketched the coastal village of Quincy, which had remained part of Braintree into JQA's adult years. The cemetery in the foreground was where he went to ponder the legacy of probity and industry he inherited from forebears buried there. The church structure across the road was replaced in 1828 by a granite building that today is known as the Adams Temple.

The predominance of the Atlantic Ocean in JQA's environs is evident in Eliza Susan Quincy's 1822 water-color sketch of Mount Wollaston farm, which sat on Quincy Bay. Their forebears had acquired the spectacular location in 1637. It forever pained JQA that, although he eventually owned the farm, he never lived on it.

Abigail Adams sat for Gilbert Stuart when she was first lady, but the portrait was not delivered until 1815, a delay typical of the artist. His talented daughter Jane Stuart painted this copy, which could be said to improve upon the original.

JQA felt so much reverence and affection for his aged father that he persuaded Gilbert Stuart (the Adamses always spelled the artist's name "Stewart") to come to Quincy to paint the old president in 1823. The result is considered one of the artist's finest efforts, especially after his daughter Jane prepared this improved copy.

Quincy November 10th 1818

My ever dear, ever affectionate, ever dutiful and deserving Son.
The bitterness of Death is past. The grim Spectre
so terrible to hueman Nature has no sting left for me.

My consolations are more than I can number.
The Seperation cannot be so long as twenty Seperations
heretofore. The Pangs and the Anguish have not been
so great as when you and I embarked for France
in 1778.

The Sympathy and Benevolence of all the World has been
such as I shall not live long enough to describe
I have not strength to do justice to Individuals. Louisa Susa
Miss Harriet Welsh, have been with us constantly. The
Three Families of Greenleafs, Mrs John Greenleaf, has
been (your Mother Said it to me, in her last moments
"a Mother to me"). Mr Daniel Greenleaf has been really
the good Samaritan.

Louisa Harriet and Mrs John Greenleaf have been
above all praise, Mr and Mrs Quincy have been more
like Sons and Daughters than like Neighbours. Mr Shaw
and your Sons have been all you could desire.
Your Letter of the Second is all and no more than all
that I expected. Never was a more dutifull Son. Never a
more Affectionate Mother. Love to your Wife. May you never
experience her Loss. So prays your Aged and Afflicted
Father John Adams

J. Q. A.

The bond between father and son can be sensed in this letter John Adams sent to JQA in 1818, after the death of Abigail Adams. The old man's penmanship would soon falter from palsy, a familial disorder that eventually affected even JQA's fine script.

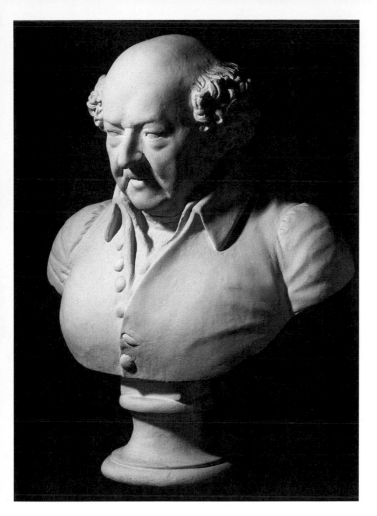

This plaster bust of John Adams, created by J. B. Binon in 1819, was considered remarkably lifelike. JQA cherished it, as did Jefferson, Lafayette, and others who owned copies.

Thomas Boylston Adams was secretary to JQA when this miniature was painted in 1795, during their stay in Holland. Tom Adams was forever marveling at the volume of writing JQA could turn out. The brothers remained on congenial terms particularly because they were careful to take their recreation separately, according to their very different tastes.

A year before his marriage in 1797, JQA sat in London for this portrait by John Singleton Copley. At that time, the young diplomat was more attentive to his romance with Louisa Johnson than to his assignment as U.S. minister in the Netherlands, a lapse for which he later scolded himself.

The date and provenance of this portrait of JQA's bride, Louisa Catherine Johnson Adams, are uncertain. It may have been painted by Mather Brown in 1797, around the time of her marriage, or perhaps by Edward Savage in 1801, after her arrival in America. Whoever the artist, the likeness seems to capture the charm that JQA found irresistible.

Located near the Tower of London, this church was known as All Hallows Barking at the time of JQA's marriage. Dating from Roman and Saxon times, and mostly destroyed by bombs during World War II, the restored building is now known as All Hallows by the Tower. Visitors are informed that the sixth president of the United States was married in the church. They also learn that the decapitated body of Archbishop William Laud is interred there.

Louisa's mother, Catherine Nuth Johnson, deftly cornered JQA into admitting his desire to marry her daughter. This was in 1796, when Mrs. Johnson's portrait may have been painted by Mather Brown. By then, her days as one of London's social leaders were numbered. Soon she would accompany her bankrupt husband in disgrace to the United States.

In 1785, Mather Brown painted this portrait of Abigail "Nabby" Adams, JQA's sister, whose parents had brought her to England hoping she would forget an engagement in Massachusetts of which they disapproved. Matters became only worse, for Nabby soon married her father's secretary, Colonel William S. Smith, a union that proved calamitous for JQA's finances.

Elizabeth Shaw Peabody, JQA's kind and thoughtful aunt, reluctantly posed for Gilbert Stuart in 1809. But unlike her sister Abigail Adams, she found Stuart very entertaining. As JQA knew so well, his aunt was of a very different disposition than his stern mother.

When Charles Robert Leslie painted Louisa Adams in London during 1816, she was enjoying the happiest period of her life. It was no wonder, then, that she cherished this portrait.

Louisa Adams insisted that this bust of JQA, created in 1818 by Pietro Cardelli, was a splendid likeness. JQA was then at the peak of his diplomatic career, serving as secretary of state in James Monroe's cabinet.

This 1823 portrait of George Washington Adams, JQA's ill-fated eldest son, was painted by Charles Bird King. The artist was encouraged to picture George Adams as his parents liked to think of him, holding a book and appearing studious. The pose was highly misleading.

John Adams II, the president's second son, sat for Charles Bird King soon after being expelled by Harvard for engaging in a riot. The young man's brief life thereafter was scarcely more successful.

Unlike his older brothers, Charles Francis Adams lived to be his parents' mainstay and joy. This portrait was painted by Charles Bird King when Charles Francis was age twenty. He was soon to marry a very wealthy woman.

This recently discovered profile shows JQA's son Charles Francis Adams as he appeared during his father's last years. His skillful management of JQA's property and early success as a businessman and political pamphleteer eased JQA's sorrow over the failed lives and early deaths of his other sons.

This daguerreotype shows the Adams mansion in Quincy as it appeared in 1848. The residence, called the Old House by the family, crowned a working farm which JQA operated at an annual financial loss. In all, four generations of Adamses would occupy the house before it was given to the American people and, soon thereafter, became a national shrine.

Only after old age made it difficult for JQA to engage in his long walks and garden work did he have the patience to linger over tea with Louisa Adams in this parlor of the mansion in Quincy. For many years, the beautifully paneled walls were painted white to allow better light as JQA read aloud to his wife.

The fireplace in JQA's bedroom in the Quincy mansion is surrounded by tiles he brought back to America from his tour through Silesia in 1800. The room also became a scene of torment for JQA and his family when granddaughter Fanny Adams died in the big bed in 1839.

After JQA's death, Charles Francis Adams built an imposing stone structure next to the Adams mansion in Quincy. It was designed to hold JQA's library, an undertaking the old man himself had planned but could find neither the money nor the energy to carry out. To the right, barely visible under the window, is the desk, once in the federal House of Representatives, at which JQA was trying to speak when he was toppled by his final stroke.

Taken by Mathew Brady at the time of the Civil War, this photo shows the F Street residence where JQA lived during many of his years in Washington. The house was once owned by James and Dolley Madison. Both the Madisons and the Adamses made the spacious quarters a gathering place for Washington society.

Louisa Adams experienced the usual delays that accompanied Gilbert Stuart's work. He undertook to paint her portrait before 1821, but did not finish it until 1826. The artist resisted the pleas of President Adams to complete the project promptly. When it was finally displayed, Louisa was one of the few persons who did not admire it.

My Son Charles Francis Adams. Boston

Washington 1. Jan 1 1848.

My dear Son.

On the commencement of a new year, my thoughts intensely turn to you, to the partner of your life, to your children, and to the giver of all good, in thanksgiving for all the Blessings which you have been and still are to me, and in fervent supplication for the favours of divine Providence upon you — one and all — Especially that you may be sustained in your incorruptible incorruptible integrity through all the trials which may be reserved for you upon earth, and that whatever may be their attendance here, of which I abate not a jot of heart and hope, you will at least be sure of the approbation of your maker.

A stout heart and a clear conscience, and never despa

your ever affectionate father

John Quincy Adams

Shortly before he died, some of JQA's strength briefly returned, enabling him once again to write in a readable hand. This letter was the last he sent to his son Charles. The old man's call for a stout heart and a clear conscience had resounded throughout a lifetime of diary- and letter-writing. Avoiding despair, however, had been difficult for JQA.

In the center of Quincy stands this church, the Adams Temple, built of granite quarried from Adams land. Completed in 1828 to replace an aged wooden structure, it shelters a mausoleum where the remains of JQA and his wife and parents repose. Before JQA's coffin was interred beneath the church portico, it rested in the Adams family vault, visible in the foreground. By JQA's time, five generations of his ancestors had been laid to rest in this burial ground.

would not speak ten words or write two lines to hold any office, including that of president. But his emphasis began to change when, after reaching Quincy on May 8, he learned that the Federalists in the Massachusetts legislature were determined to turn him out of office immediately.

At once, his pride and anger took command. Putting aside his familiar (even tedious) insistence that he was eager to leave the Senate and politics, he began to behave like any candidate eager to retain an office. This almost amusing behavior reflected the senator's wish to depart Congress with dignity and on his own terms. So, saying nothing about an eagerness for teaching and writing, JQA huddled with his political allies to seek ways of avoiding defeat. He listened attentively as cousin Billy Shaw and other associates discussed how to thwart the enemy when the legislature decided Senator Adams' future.

Throughout, John was careful to stress that, should he lack a summons from the people, he would lift nary a finger to keep his office. This was easy talk, however. Were not faithful friends surrounding him and urging that he be their man and try to remain in the Senate? Should not every individual take a civic post when the public wished it? For Adams, the answer to such questions now seemed obvious, so that he was soon participating in a monthlong struggle to save his Senate job.

He made a concerted effort to be seen around town, attending numerous dinners and parties. These, however, resulted in such severe digestive upset that he was obliged to postpone his first lecture at Harvard until May 13, when, still unsteady, he had to be accompanied to Cambridge by his physician, Thomas Welsh. Returning to Harvard and his students proved to be the best medicine available, and JQA reported that after meeting his class, he was "much relieved."

Five days later, he attended an ordination service at which he expected to greet only friends. Instead, he encountered a clergyman named Osgood, who "attacked me in a rude and indecent manner on the subject of my letter to Mr. Otis." In replying, Adams applied his cutting wit: "I told him that in consideration of his age, I should only remark that he had one lesson yet to learn of which I recommended the study as specifically necessary, and that was Christian charity."

Finally came the moment arranged by JQA's opponents: on June 2, 1808, the Massachusetts House voted on Senator Adams' future. The question was a clever one. Members were asked whether a decision to fill Adams' seat for another term should wait until the prescribed time, February 1809. A majority was expected to vote against the proposition, dooming John. The balloting took place amid an astonishing furor that produced a scene, according to JQA, "as if the salvation of the country, or what was substituted for the country was thought to depend upon getting me out."

When the smoke cleared, Adams' supporters had reduced their man's anticipated margin of defeat by mustering 213 votes against 248 for John's opponent and Harvard classmate, James Lloyd, Jr. The Senate vote the next day yielded 17 for Adams to 21 for Lloyd. While all this was going on, John passed the time ostentatiously browsing in bookshops and reading at the Athenaeum library.

Despite the defeat, he could have remained as senator until 1809, but the legislature thwarted this by adopting a resolution on June 7, directing that he vote to repeal the embargo. Faced with an instruction he could not obey, he immediately resigned, saying in a brief letter to the legislature: "I now restore to you the trust committed to my charge." He stressed that he had deemed it a duty to support the Jefferson administration in vindicating "the rights essential to the independence of our country, against the unjust pretensions and aggressions of all foreign powers." James Lloyd was elected on June 9 to fill the unexpired portion of the Adams term.

THE EMOTIONAL COST JQA paid for this public rebuke may have been enormous. Louisa believed her husband was tormented by his rebuff. If so, he masked his hurt. Virtually nothing in his voluminous papers and journal reveals any distress. While tradition claims he was ostracized after losing his Senate seat and spent the following year licking his wounds, the reverse seems more accurate.

During the ensuing months, he and Louisa kept busy as active participants in Boston social life. They mingled with friends and strangers during summer evenings spent walking along Boston's Mall. In late July they were hosts at a party for forty guests. In October, amid much bustle, they welcomed sixty friends to a ball which required that they use an empty house next door for the overflow; dancing went on until the early hours of the morning, leaving JQA so dissipated the next day that he admitted he was good for nothing but idleness.

Adams also had academic duties to engage him, as well as the details of his law practice. He kept up with newspapers, became reacquainted with books he had brought back from Europe, enjoyed the Natural Philosophy Club, and dined with friends. At the table he sometimes encountered political talk, but usually, he reported, it was good-humored. And if there were gloomy moments late at night, he comforted himself with reassurances of having done his duty at every hazard, and he rejoiced in the embrace of "a good conscience."

As for being deceased politically, Adams was still more alive than it suited him to be. Massachusetts Republicans considered him a hero and sent several delegations to urge that he run for Congress, a race it seemed quite likely he would win. He refused to do so, however, mainly because he would have been pitted against his cousin Josiah Quincy, the incumbent, whom he considered a moderate Federalist. The Republicans then sought Adams as their nominee for governor of Massachusetts. Here again, he declined with thanks, but not before conferring with his father, who gave him no encouragement, whereupon John announced: "I set my ambition aside."

He turned instead to books and writing, with each day—usually begun with the reading of four Bible chapters and a sermon by Bishop Tillotson—holding new intellectual interests. He now mainly studied Queen Anne's reign through Jonathan Swift's history of the last four years of her rule and Smollett's writings about the same period, when the Whig and Tory parties struggled. "I could not but remark how much these times here resemble those," Adams reported, adding that "the future is likely to resemble them in their worst features."

After settling into this comfortable schedule, he noticed that for once he was able "to employ all my time in a manner very agreeable to me." He read until the failure of daylight made him close his books. The greatest trial seemed to be finding patience in helping his restless son George study French. There was more success with the four students JQA accepted to read law under his direction. Their presence cheered him as an indication that his repute had, if anything, risen in some quarters. Usually he talked with these students daily between 11 a.m. and 2 p.m. except for Friday, when he walked to Cambridge and his Harvard duties.

By year's end, however, Adams' move into private life had proven not entirely comfortable. Embarrassed financially, with no relief in sight, he accepted two legal cases that necessitated his pleading before the United States Supreme Court early in 1809. It may have been more than coincidence that this schedule put him in Washington just as Madison's first presidential administration began and when many appointments to public posts would be announced.

Accordingly, when news of his travel plans circulated around Boston, Adams was more than ever the subject of gossip; one rumor contended that he would be named secretary of war. With scant success, he tried to persuade anyone who would listen that such reports had no foundation—while privately, he kept reminding himself that the possibility of an appointment required "the steady possession of myself."

Certainly, appearing in the capital at inaugural time made him seem to be joining the many federal office seekers assembling at the public trough. Even members of his family suspected he was more interested in securing an appointment than in defending his clients. After all, with a stroke of the pen, Madison could make JQA's financial worries disappear. Abigail Adams was particularly blunt in her admonishment: "I do not wish to see you under existing circumstances any other than the private citizen you now are. The period is not yet arrived when your country demands you."

Despite such pressures, Adams seemed calm enough as he presided over a large dinner Louisa and he gave just before he departed on January 26. His guests heard him repeat that he was going to Washington only as an attorney, and mainly to argue before the Supreme Court in behalf of John Peck, the defendant in what became the noteworthy case of *Fletcher v. Peck.*

TRAVELING MOSTLY BY SLEIGH, Adams reached Washington on February 2 and began visits with his political friends, even dining with President Jefferson. He found the soon-to-retire chief executive reading newspapers. Jefferson told John that it gave him great joy to think that soon he would never have to look at a newspaper again.

On February 9, JQA went before the Supreme Court, which sat in Long's Tavern on Capitol Hill. His first pleading before the Court involved a minor case, *Boardman and Pope v. Providence Insurance Company.* This went well enough, until the justices questioned him about a corporate issue on which he was unprepared.

A chastened Adams became more serious about studying every night until 2 a.m. so as to be ready when the Court called *Fletcher v. Peck* on March 1. At issue were millions of acres in land grants that the Georgia legislature had made in 1794 and then rescinded in 1796. During the interval, these grants had been taken up by speculators, who sold many of them in New England.

One of the purchasers was Adams' Boston client John Peck, a member of a Massachusetts land company. In turn, Peck sold acreage to Robert Fletcher of New Hampshire. When Georgia annulled the validity of the purchase, Fletcher and Peck entered a collusive suit concerning a breach of title. On March 2, Adams spoke in behalf of Peck before the Supreme Court from 11 a.m. until 4 p.m., but he sat down dissatisfied. Harvard's professor of rhetoric and oratory saw his presentation as lacking in clarity and organization, and being so "dull and tedious" that he was surprised the court heard him through.

Actually, the justices appeared to have been impressed by his reasoning. In their final opinion, not issued until 1810, the Court held that by canceling the grants the Georgia legislature had destroyed contracts. This could not be permitted, for, according to the Court, the federal Constitution proclaimed contracts to be inviolable. It was this finding that gave the case its timeless significance and glorified the Constitution's Article 1, Section 10.

On March 4, after finishing before the Court, Adams attended the inauguration of James Madison, who spoke too softly for his address to be heard. John also took part in the festivities and balls linked with the great occasion. Then, two days later, came the news he had awaited: While he was at breakfast, a messenger brought a note from the new president asking to see Mr. Adams that morning. When John presented himself, Madison disclosed that the emperor of Russia wished to have a representative of the United States in his court. Apologizing for the short notice, the president proposed to send Adams' name immediately to the Senate for confirmation as minister plenipotentiary. He assured John that the appointment would last several years.

Adams consented at once. Whether this particular position pleased him, he did not say—nor was there much point in commenting, since the Senate quickly declined to have any emissary in Russia at that moment, although the majority of JQA's former colleagues emphasized that there was no objection to him as nominee. Sending word of this decision to Louisa, John managed to say that it was a relief not to go abroad. "With respect to ourselves and to our children, it would have been attendant with more trouble than advantage." Louisa was surely not deceived by this bravado.

After a miserable trip with boring companions over bottomless mud, John reappeared in Boston on March 26, once more proclaiming a determination to use his leisure for literary work and to overcome his indolent nature. He would avoid those trifles "that do filch away by half hours all my time." Not that there was much leisure at hand. He had lectures to give, student declamations to judge, a legal practice to nurture, and students in his office to train. All of these, however, he now seemed to manage while at the same time reading classical authors, notably Demosthenes.

Meanwhile, he did not ignore the continuing political crisis in U.S. foreign relations. In a major statement, he attacked the position of his former Federalist associates, whom he continued to assail as selfishly regional in outlook as well as blindly pro-British in behavior. His critique—published as a review of a volume containing writings by the late Fisher Ames, a high priest of New England Federalism—proved so popular in newspaper installments that it was issued in pamphlet form.

The essay evidently did nothing to alienate Adams from much of Boston society. His fellow club members appeared delighted to meet at his house, while invitations to dinners and other convivial events took the Adamses away from home more than they preferred. There were occasions, however, when onetime friends sought openly to avoid meeting John on the street, and his inveterate foe, the aged Reverend Osgood of Medford, took the opportunity to denounce him while delivering the Election Day sermon in May; Adams was not present, but Pastor William Emerson reported that Osgood had uttered sentiments for which he "ought to be hanged."

Privately, JQA mused: "Perhaps I have too much indulged the suggestions of my own judgment, and paid too little deference to that of other men." While this statement might sound like the beginning of wisdom, events prevented him from pursuing the thought—even were he so inclined. On the evening of July 3, as he sat down to read, two boys knocked at the door and handed him a recent issue of the *National Intelligencer*. The Washington paper contained the electrifying news that on June 27, the Senate had confirmed John Quincy Adams as minister to Russia after Madison had resubmitted the question.

Next day the Fourth of July holiday began as planned, with John and his father attending a celebration put on by the Bunker Hill Association. As the program got under way, Billy Shaw rushed up with letters for JQA from Washington confirming the appointment, including a message from Secretary of State Robert Smith enclosing the commission as minister.

John had much on his mind as he tried calmly to complete the day's festivities. These included taking his family up to a neighbor's roof to watch the fireworks on the Common as he worried over the burning debris from rocket displays that dropped around them.

Throughout the Fourth, he already knew that he would accept the post in Russia, despite his father's advice against it. The main drawback, of course, was leaving the teaching post at Harvard, a strong tie that, JQA said, "I break with great reluctance." Privately, however, he was jubilant, thereby showing how much he had been yearning for an office under Madison. "I have now received an appointment of great trust and importance, totally unsolicited, and confirmed by every vote in the Senate, excepting my personal enemies, and two others, who voted not against me, but against the mission." These two dissidents had spoken of him with the "highest approbation." John acclaimed the appointment as the salvation of "my own personal reputation."

The Russian assignment also allowed him, as he put it, an honorable means of putting distance between himself and those Federalists who continued to persecute him. But this seemed to be a pro forma statement, since the diary entries surrounding it are full of his complaints that his demanding social life left him no time to think and read.

Immediately, preparations began for the long voyage and life abroad. It had to be a hurried effort, since the chances were slim that the new minister would reach St. Petersburg before the water route to the Russian capital was frozen. Advised that to do so, he must sail by the end of July, Adams decided not to await the uncertain arrival of a U.S. Navy ship. Instead, he accepted the offer of passage on a commercial vessel owned by William Gray, a good friend, prosperous Boston merchant, and lieutenant governor of Massachusetts. Gray was delighted at this opportunity to enter the lucrative Russian market. The embargo had been repealed the previous March.

Adams took as an assistant William Gray's son Francis, who would pay his own expenses in order to learn about international commerce firsthand. Other companions were John S. Smith, nephew of the secretary of state, and Alexander H. Everett, who would function as student-secretaries. These young men were welcome, but it was with great misgiving that Adams yielded to pressure from his mother and agreed to employ sister Nabby's son William Steuben Smith as his private secretary. Young Smith, known as Billy and a favorite of Abigail's, had recently returned from Venezuela after being captured as part of a group trying to incite revolution. He had narrowly escaped the hangman.

Meanwhile, Louisa had chosen as a companion her sister Kitty Johnson, whose flirtatious ways in the presence of so many young men soon made both Adamses uneasy. Two-year-old Charles Francis Adams was the only son to accompany his parents.

While putting financial matters in order and overseeing the packing, JQA received a letter signed by members of Harvard's junior and senior classes expressing regret at his departure and urging that he publish his lectures. Delighted by this, but saying it was a step "which I had not contemplated," he immediately sought approval from members of the Harvard Corporation. There being no objection, he hastily gathered the thirty-six lectures into a manuscript, which he left with Tom Adams to see through the press. "To live in the memory of mankind by College Lectures is not the aim of a very soaring ambition," JQA conceded, "but I have no reason to look for any higher glory from posterity, and with that I ought to be content."

On July 28, he gave a final lecture in Harvard's chapel, filled with students and members of the public. So moved was he by the occasion that when finished, he added what he termed "some thoughts on taking leave of the College." Calling the students his best friends, he accompanied his remarks to them with what had become a characteristic mannerism, frequently striking his hands together as he told the class that in times of adversity they must look beyond self-interest. To escape that "dissipation of the mind which is the wretchedness of prosperity," they should be diligent in the study of letters, science, and religion. By reading the words of "the mighty dead of ancient days," they would escape the "galling" dependence upon "the mighty living of the present age." In this way, when even friends might desert them and the community abandon them, Professor Adams' listeners could find refuge in "the patriotism of Cicero."

As this profoundly self-revealing commentary implied, John was deeply stirred as he put aside his professional place in the life of the mind. He assured his students, whom he called colleagues, that only an "unsolicited" summons from the nation was tearing him away from them. He consoled himself and them with the reminder that they would never be truly separated, no matter how vast the distance between them, so long as they joined with him in contemplating "the luminaries of the moral heavens."

Stepping down from the lectern and surrounded by the students, Adams was satisfied that he had thwarted those Federalist adversaries whose anger had led them—or so he believed—to try to poison his students against him. "Sophistry pimping for envy," he called their tactic.

The final lecture behind him, he now gave full attention to the voyage ahead, doing so under the poorly disguised disapproval and sorrow of his family. His mother summed up the Adamses' outlook when she told Aunt Elizabeth: "Indeed, my dear sister, a man of his worth ought not to be permitted to leave the country." But there was something more to rankle Abigail: it was not appropriate, she said, that her son should resume a public career after being so "traduced and vilified."

John ignored this as he packed boxes of books to be taken to the Athenaeum for safekeeping. He did, however, discourage a proposal by Boston's Republican citizens to honor him with a farewell banquet. He was too occupied, he assured them; and indeed, he was very busy. A new will must be prepared, innumerable callers had to be greeted, and some belatedly discovered books had to be sorted—circumstances that "occupy me almost to distraction." When Louisa and Kitty went down to Quincy for family farewells on August 3, John claimed he lacked time to go with them.

The next day, Captain Bickford, master of the *Horace*, announced that the ship would sail on August 5, a Saturday. That morning, Adams and his party arrived at Lieutenant Governor Gray's Charlestown wharf with unusual promptness. There they found a delegation of relatives and friends waiting to say farewell. The group did not include Abigail Adams, who sent a note saying that to be present would only add to her "agony." (She had already launched what would prove a successful campaign to have history believe it was chagrin and hurt that drove her son to accept a place with the detested Jeffersonians.)

The bells of Boston and Charlestown were ringing the hour of 1 p.m. when the *Horace* moved under a fresh breeze. The U.S. minister to Russia did not slink away scorned and unnoticed, despite Abigail's claim. He received salutes from the Navy Yard; Fort Independence paraded the garrison in his honor; and all the ships in Boston Harbor paid tribute, including the now legendary *Chesapeake*. At 4 p.m., Tom Adams and Dr. Thomas Welsh, who had wished to be with John to the last moment, returned to the Harbor in a cutter. By dark, the land behind the *Horace* could barely be sighted. It was the last John Quincy Adams would see of America for eight years.

WITH THE VOYAGE BEGUN, John poked around to find his books on Russia, only to discover that by mistake he had sent them to the Athenaeum. The blunder meant that he was stuck with the familiar classics and more recent literature. Deciding for the moment not to read and being in a cheerful mood, he opened a new volume of his

journal, where he inscribed a prayerful poem he had composed for the
day:

> *Oh, grant that while this feeble hand portrays*
> *The fleeting image of my earthly days,*
> *Still the firm purpose of this heart may be*
> *Good to mankind and gratitude to Thee!*

CHAPTER EIGHT

St. Petersburg

Blessed are they who can bear disappointment without losing their temper.

NO EMPEROR COULD have ruled a kingdom as firmly as John Quincy Adams did the *Horace* as the ship carried him and his party to St. Petersburg. He was determined that no impediment, be it from nature or man, should prevent his timely arrival in Russia. Not only did he consider it a duty to be prompt in his assignment, but there was also the satisfaction of distancing himself from the furor of American politics. Whatever else life in St. Petersburg might hold for him, he expected it to be an opportunity to use his talents for the United States without the carping of those whom he saw as self-seeking partisans.

The voyage soon taxed the limited patience of the Adams contingent. The crowded setting—seven adults and a child eating and sleeping in one small room—pushed John to confess: "I find the power of self-abstraction fails." Still, despite the "excessive irritation upon the nervous system" brought on by the situation, he managed to read fifteen chapters from the Bible most days, as well as a good deal of Plutarch. He wrote a few letters, made entries in his journal, played cards, and fished for cod on the Grand Banks of Newfoundland. There was also much time for reflection as he stared across the ocean, musing how "the rest of mankind, for the time being, seems to be inhabitants of another planet."

Although Massachusetts was now far away, Adams found a means of feeling close to sons George, age eight, and John, six, who had remained behind with relatives in Quincy. He gave shipboard hours to writing a long "Letter to my Children," a treatise devoted to those concerns that the father himself never allowed to stray far from his mind: morality, dutifulness, self-discipline, devotion to learning, and the value of understanding history.

The letter's spirit was captured in his charge to the youngsters: "Take it, then, as a general principle to be observed as one of the directing impulses of life, that you must have some one great purpose of existence. . . . How to employ our faculties in such a manner as to produce the greatest quantity of human happiness is a problem of no easy solution." He implored his sons to seek the way "to make your talents and your knowledge most beneficial to your country and most *useful to mankind.*" It was an admonition intended for the father himself perhaps more than for his children.

This remarkable letter was finished just as the *Horace* reached Norway on September 18, 1809. The war between England and France had made the Scandinavian region jittery whenever a strange ship appeared. The British bombardment of Copenhagen had pushed Denmark into an alliance with France, so that Adams experienced what seemed like incessant inquiries and inspections by Danish officials. The delays these caused, as well as unfavorable winds and severe storms, meant that it took almost a month for the *Horace* to pass along the Øresund, the strait between Denmark and Sweden. At one point between Copenhagen and Malmö, the passage became so narrow that navigating at night was impossible.

Often, Adams was called ashore to explain his status as an emissary on official business. On one such errand, he visited a bookshop and found a history of the reign of Peter the Great, which brought him much-needed diversion as the *Horace* continued its eastward struggle against fierce winds. Finally, in early October, the ship entered the Baltic Sea, where the autumnal gales grew even wilder.

On October 13, Captain Bickford, fearing for his ship, announced that he planned to return to Copenhagen and remain there for the winter. JQA promptly overruled him, believing it was his "duty" to do so as long as any chance remained that St. Petersburg might be sighted before the dreaded ice blocked the way to the city. Two days later, the wind veered in the *Horace*'s favor, and the ship soon reached the Gulf of Finland. On October 22, at 1 p.m., the Adamses entered the harbor of Kronstadt, from which they could be sure of reaching St. Petersburg.

Immediately, the voyage's frustrations were forgotten as a flotilla of Russian men-of-war escorted the *Horace* into Kronstadt, where JQA was welcomed by a Russian admiral. After spending the night ashore, the Adams group proceeded by government boat to St. Petersburg, a journey of three hours. "We landed on the quay of the river Neva, just opposite the magnificent equestrian statue of Peter the Great."

It was exactly eighty days since the *Horace* had sailed out of Boston. The Adamses discovered that they had arrived in the nick of time, for the Russian capital quickly became a frozen asylum. News from America would be rare until early May, when the ice broke up in Kronstadt harbor and allowed ships to enter. Meanwhile, John's insistence on reaching Russia would bring a handsome dividend for the *Horace*. While awaiting spring, Captain Bickford sold the ship's cargo for a profit of $115,000.

Adams was unprepared for the improvements he saw in the Russian capital since his stay there in 1781–82. Even more gratifying was finding that representatives of the United States were no longer ignored, as Francis Dana and Adams had been thirty years before. Quite the contrary. As a welcomed diplomat, JQA could hardly have hoped for greater success. His talent for intelligent conversation soon made him one of the most respected members of the international corps, which comprised ambassadors from France and Sweden and ministers from Prussia, Denmark, Sardinia, Saxony, Bavaria, Württemberg, Holland, Spain, Naples, Westphalia—and, of course, the United States.

None of these emissaries, however, would match Adams in attracting and retaining the friendship of Alexander I, the czar or emperor of Russia. Ten years John's junior, Alexander, at thirty-two, was already well known for his humane and enlightened ways. Adams soon found himself a favorite walking companion of the emperor, who had the startling custom of ambling along the quay without escort, courteously nodding to citizens he passed.

At first, Adams had feared that he might not be able to do the walking in St. Petersburg that he considered essential for good health. The streets were reputed to be hazardous, and using them for exercise had gone out of fashion. "The immense number of carriages constantly driving and the violence with which they drive keeps the walkers in perpetual hazard of being run over." But then he discovered the advantage of exercising along the canals and particularly the quay, which was where he often encountered the emperor.

Like John, Alexander spoke French fluently, which was fortunate, since one of the American's disappointments was having no time to learn Russian. The two always talked as they strolled, frequently discussing the latest international news as the emperor sought to be well informed on world affairs. He also peppered John with questions about the United States. Adams had arrived just at a time when Russia's problems with France and England made friendship and commerce with the young republic desirable. In addition, there were personal inquiries, evidently Alexander's way of showing kindness while he tried to learn more about this American and his nation. The emperor's curiosity ranged from Adams' exercise habits to his headgear and the fact that the American rarely wore gloves.

After Alexander quietly gave John permission to appear at court without a wig, the American grew downright fond of him. Consequently, upon hearing that the emperor had fallen from his horse, Adams hastened to the palace to inquire after his friend's condition. Word was privately conveyed to him that the czar had suffered a mashed finger, a bruised knee, and a scraped forehead. The prospects were excellent that he would soon be greeting Mr. Adams on another walk.

And so he did, the day after John had attended one of the numerous balls given at the palace. Alexander inquired as to whether the American was fatigued from the evening, to which the prudent John replied that he was not. His Majesty, however, was more willing to admit his weariness and said that the event had lasted much too long. This gave Adams courage to mention how overheated the palace rooms had been, which brought the czar to exclaim: "Mon Dieu"—how true! He pledged to consider limiting a ball to three hours. John acknowledged to himself: "I did not reply, for it might have been too uncourtly and even uncourteous to have said how much I would have been willing to abridge it."

Other diplomats were quick to see that Adams had the favor of the emperor. Though the United States paid its ministers so meagerly that John and Louisa could not compete in dress and entertainment, this handicap was not as severe as most observers had predicted. Because of the Adamses' personal relationship with the emperor and empress, they were often excused from full compliance with courtly niceties. In addition, they were sometimes invited to the palace for informal visits.

Alexander and his wife, Princess Elisabeth of Baden, were childless, so that both were fond of getting down on hands and knees to play with young Charles Francis when the Adamses brought the boy along on their quiet calls at the palace. The czar often assured John that he understood an American's need to be far more frugal than, for example, the French ambassador, whose annual budget was a million rubles—more than $300,000 then. The U.S. minister's salary was $9,000 a year.

COMPARATIVE POVERTY WAS but one domestic shortcoming of the Adamses' stay in Russia. The winters were brutally cold and interminable. Someone in the household always seemed to be ill, so that the only really warm room had to be used as a chamber for the sick. Just finding a dwelling had been difficult enough. Apartments in the capital were scarce and fearfully expensive to rent, while the cost of a house was out of reach. Consequently, the Adams party spent its first eight months in St. Petersburg crowded into rooms at the Hotel de Lourdes, which proved wretched, and then at the Ville de Bordeaux on the Moika Canal. Even these quarters might not have been found were it not for the assistance of Levett Harris, whom President Jefferson had appointed U.S. consul in St. Petersburg. Harris became John's valued friend as well as associate.

Unfortunately, there was one dismal feature of Russia that Harris could not help the Adamses elude. Soon after disembarking, the entire party, excepting the young male secretaries, was kept housebound by severe diarrhea from drinking water from the River Neva. Barely able to crawl to his first diplomatic appointment, John came away from it with some mildly comforting information, which he shared with the stricken Louisa: all newcomers to the capital must endure dysentery until their digestive tracts came to terms with the Neva. The process, he said, was called "seasoning."

Despite his discomfort, John forced himself to make the visits obligatory for new diplomats. During one of these early outings, a dinner given by the emperor's highest-ranking official, Chancellor Nikolay Rumyantsev, Adams found himself surrounded by guests who were all "covered with stars and ribbons—beyond any thing I had ever seen." The grandeur of the dinner—"magnificent in every particular"—so distracted John that he managed momentarily to forget his digestive upset and was able to take pleasure in the "many pointed and formal civilities" tendered him by Count Rumyantsev.

Slowly the family's health improved. Louisa and Kitty began attending the theater, and John sought friends in the diplomatic corps with whom he could talk about art and literature. He regretted that some ambassadors preferred "a game they call *creps*" to conversation. John learned, to his dismay, that the pastime customarily required that players ante up 25 rubles (about $8) to throw the dice. Gambling was so commonplace, he soon discovered, that even those who played whist usually risked 5 rubles on every point.

Games of chance were, along with gossip, a staple of the nighttime social gatherings that every member of the diplomatic corps felt it prudent to attend. Quite different were parties where guests spent the evening out of doors sliding down hills of ice, sitting on nothing more than their outer garments. Women were expected to wear fur habits for the occasion. Even when there was a slight thaw, the fun proceeded, no matter if participants went about with moist undersides. All these social events usually did not end until 4 a.m. or later, obliging Adams to admit that he frequently arose after 10 a.m. and often not much before noon, after which it was soon time to prepare for another evening's extravaganza.

While dinners to which he was invited sometimes allowed gentlemen to appear in frock coats, most such events required full dress. To his relatives in Quincy, he sent what he intended as a slightly tongue-in-cheek description of the grandeur of dining at the Russian chancellor's residence. Emphasizing his preference for simple ways, he reported ironically: "I went only in a chariot and four, attended by two footmen in livery, and driven by a coachman on the carriage box, and a postillion, between boy and man, on the right side horse of the leading pair." Upon arriving, as he described it, he marched past twenty footmen lining the staircase "like so many statues." Before dinner, drinks of "shalls," or cordials, were served, accompanied by cheese "and other stimulants to appetite."

A dinner usually included many courses, together with numerous wines. For dessert, Adams said, fruits and ice creams were offered, along with abundant liquors, which also meant frozen champagne. "The attention of the servants to the guests at the table is so vigilant that you scarcely ever have occasion to ask for anything," he explained to his family. "The instant you have emptied your plate, or that you lay down your knife, and fork, or spoon, your plate is taken away and a clean one is given you in its stead. . . . If you have occasion for a fresh supply of bread, the footmen perceive it at least as soon as you do yourself."

Adams marveled at how these amazing servants foresaw each wish and need of the guests. "Everything moves like a piece of clockwork." He also noted that there was little intemperance, despite the overflowing strong drink, and claimed that there would be more drunkenness at one dinner in the United States—usually followed, he recalled, "by a carousal of six hours long, swilling upon a mixture of madeira wine and brandy"—than at fifty in Russia.

Fortunately, by mid-February 1810, as the Lenten season approached, the daily routine of dinners and dissipation slowed, allowing Louisa and John to search for an apartment. Anticipating success, they snapped up a supply of furniture and china at a bargain price of less than $1,600. When an acquaintance, Count Einsiedel, vacated an apartment, the Adamses were offered a lease for it. They were delighted, since the annual rent was merely about $2,000. It had walls three feet thick and a stove in every room. Windows and doors were doubled in the winter, each window having a hinged pane that could be opened for ventilation. Thus it was possible, John assured his relatives, to hold the temperature in each room at 65 degrees Fahrenheit—with bedchambers kept much cooler, a Russian practice.

After leaving the hotel and moving into their new quarters, they had to employ fourteen live-in servants, so that household expenses soon doubled. Gradually, it dawned upon the minister why his $9,000 salary had become so inadequate. The servants were proving to be a pack of thieves as they followed the St. Petersburg custom of making a profit from the discharge of many of their duties. Not even an Adams could entirely defeat the system. "It is, I believe, the law of nature between master and servant that the servant shall spoil or plunder the master." By the end of 1810, however, the Adams household was living within its means, thanks to the dismissal of some employees and to meals being catered.

Doubtless the greatest advantage of the Adams apartment was an extra room that became John's private refuge. In the quiet of his study, JQA found more time to read—sermons, Sir Walter Scott's just published poem *The Lady of the Lake,* and treatises on national economies. With the arrival of summer, long hours of daylight allowed him to read and write even past midnight. Here he could also supervise the work of nephew Billy Smith, the legation's overweight secretary, whose penmanship was sometimes impenetrable.

During 1810, Adams mostly used his study to begin what became ten years of intermittent research and writing concerning the history of weights and measures in civilization. The project started with his attempt to understand the Russian arrangement of weights and measures, and to compare it with the English and French systems. "I find it extremely difficult," he admitted, as he "wasted" an entire day trying to achieve a precise grasp of France's units of measure. There were many moments when he wondered whether he was using the project as an excuse to postpone less intriguing tasks.

Nevertheless, he went on with it until he was interrupted on August 8, when a package arrived containing his Harvard lectures, published in two volumes as *Lectures on Rhetoric and Oratory, Delivered to the Classes of Senior and Junior Sophisters in Harvard University*. He sat down with them and, losing all awareness of time, read from 4 p.m. until 2 a.m. Astonished at how utterly absorbed he had been, Adams said: "What a portion of my life would I give if they would occasion the same accident [forgetting time] to one other human being." He was delighted by his lectures, calling them "the measure of my powers, moral and intellectual. In the composition of them I spared no labour and omitted no exertion of which I was capable." All of which meant, he said, that "I shall never, unless by some special favour of Heaven, accomplish any work of higher elevation."

Thus reassured, he became more relaxed about spending time with Louisa seeing the sights of St. Petersburg, which included exploration of the city's great buildings and museums. Particularly pleasing to both Adamses were visits to the Hermitage, whose "magnificent" collection of art John pronounced as "without end." He frequently "lagged behind and after nearly three hours of inspection, felt only the wish for three months of examination." Another favorite was the exhibit at the Imperial Academy of Sciences. So impressed was John by the edifice itself that he measured it by pacing, calculating that it was 454 by 382 feet.

It took only a little tugging on Louisa's part to lead her husband through the social whirl of the season. He took pride, despite himself, in knowing that the emperor and empress insisted on seeing at court Mrs. Adams and her sister Miss Johnson, both lovely in their republican style. Not only were both Louisa and Kitty charming and intelligent individuals who conversed easily in French, the language of diplomacy, but they were also something of a novelty, since ministers and ambassadors rarely brought their wives to St. Petersburg.

THESE FESTIVE OCCASIONS were an opportunity for John to listen as his diplomatic colleagues chatted about European affairs. After digesting their remarks, along with insights gleaned from reading newspapers and journals for two or more hours daily, he prepared letters for the secretary of state that became, in the opinion of President

Madison and his associates, invaluable explanations of European events occurring at the height of Napoleon's power.

It was not one of these official epistles, however, that proved to be his most memorable. After three months in Russia, Adams had found time on February 8 to pen a first letter to Abigail. In a tone more teasing than serious, he exclaimed how costly it was to live in St. Petersburg. Knowing that Abigail recalled the fearful expenses she and her husband had once faced in Paris and London, the son assured her that prices were far higher in Russia.

To prove it, he exaggerated by listing only the largest amounts charged for annual rents, emphasizing that an acceptable apartment required $10,000—although luck eventually brought him one for $2,000. He had found a new wardrobe to be necessary, for no garment brought from Massachusetts could be used in public—he overlooked mentioning that he had managed to do so. Three times the number of servants needed in Europe was required—another of John's tall tales. In short, all official personages lived beyond their means in St. Petersburg. It was a circumstance he would just as soon escape, he told his mother.

While his letter then proceeded to describe "the bright side of the situation," John's outlandish comments about cost were just what Abigail wanted to hear. She took him at his word and interpreted the letter as a cry from a penitent son to be recalled from St. Petersburg. Since she had always been strongly opposed to his accepting an appointment from Jefferson's faction, it was easy for her to make the story of expenses in Russia a justification for working to bring him back to America.

Abigail's first step was to send a message to President Madison exclaiming about the fearful personal sacrifice that serving in St. Petersburg was imposing upon her son. Surely the president would not wish to prolong this burden? Madison was not entirely taken in by Abigail's appeal, which he received at summer's end in 1810. "Your highly respectable mother," the president informed John, had described JQA's personal situation as "ruinous" and "insupportable." Since the minister himself had said nothing about the matter, Madison suggested that "the peculiar urgency manifested in the letter of Mrs. Adams was rather hers, than yours."

Although he told John that he would be sent the official paperwork needed to leave for America, the president urged that he not use it. Instead, he should seek to circumvent the hazards of St. Petersburg so that he would remain in a post where his talents were sorely needed. Madison also pointed out how awkward it might appear for Adams to depart after serving barely a year. "I do not disguise my wish that the continuance of your valuable services may be found not inconsistent with your other and undeniable duties."

The president knew that after receiving such a letter, Adams would stay in St. Petersburg—at least until he might be summoned home to take up new public responsibilities. That call came much sooner than anyone had anticipated. In September 1810, Associate Justice William Cushing of the U.S. Supreme Court died. Cushing, a Massachusetts citizen, had sat on the high bench for twenty-one years. To fill the vacancy, Madison's supporters in New England urged the appointment of "honest, able, independent" John Quincy Adams.

Pleased by this advice, Madison submitted Adams' name to the Senate, which promptly endorsed the nomination, whereupon John was informed that "the President has thought proper to avail the public of your services at home." With this notification came the documents needed for Adams to take leave of the emperor. It seemed like a perfect solution for all involved: a strong intellect would join the Supreme Court, much of New England sentiment would be gratified, and John could at last withdraw with dignity from the expenses of living in St. Petersburg.

But Adams had no wish to return home, particularly if it meant becoming a judge on the nation's supreme bench. He much preferred to remain abroad, even after his parents described for him their jubilant thanksgiving for "this preservation of your family from ruin." But fearing that his son's dislike of the law might cause him to hesitate to accept the post, John Adams went on to warn that if the appointment was declined, it would create "national disgust and resentment" at what might appear to be excessive ambition. Abigail sent her assurances that a seat on the Supreme Court brought more honor even than being president.

Facing this sentiment at home, it turned out that JQA could hardly be straightforward about his reasons for refusing the appointment—not even to the president. Writing to Madison on June 3, 1811, he emphasized how humble he felt at being selected and how deeply he wished it were possible for him to accept the position. But he could not. "Peculiar circumstances" in his family must detain him in Russia at least for another year. Thus did he delicately announce that Louisa was pregnant and could not undertake a sea voyage. It meant that he was bound to St. Petersburg "by ties which the affections of a husband and parent can neither dissolve nor sever."

Adams was more candid with his friend Judge John Davis than with Madison. He told Davis that even had Louisa not been with child, "my decision would probably have been the same as it was." Nothing, however, was said to Madison or even to Judge Davis about the more basic reasons hidden in John's heart: how he detested legal work, how he scorned the paltry salary paid an associate justice ($3,500, compared with the $9,000 he received in the diplomatic corps), and how he feared that, being by nature aggressive and impatient, he would have difficulty maintaining the restraint and balance that the post required. But there was yet another reason—perhaps the most important one—which he shared with Tom Adams.

His brother was probably not in the slightest surprised when he received John's confession: "I am also, and always shall be, too much of a political partisan for a judge." JQA may have felt he must save some face by adding that while, of course, he knew how and when to transcend partisanship, "I do not wish to be called so often and so completely to do it, as my own sense of duty would call me, were I seated upon the bench." And besides, as he insisted to Tom, "literature" was still his calling.

The very private acknowledgment that he tended, after all, to be a political campaigner who would be uncomfortable on the bench was a startling one for JQA. It represented one of the more successful moments in his lifelong effort to understand himself. Only in his journal— and briefly to Tom—did he confide that the nomination to the Supreme Court had brought him to understand that he was, after all, no more free of partisanship than other men. Laid aside for the moment was his customary scornful talk about factionalism.

MEANWHILE, LOUISA WAS ASTONISHED when she learned that her pregnancy was the official reason her husband gave for declining a place on the Supreme Court. She had considered him optimistic about her condition, for although she had experienced two miscarriages in Russia, this latest pregnancy was presenting little difficulty. She appeared much more vigorous during 1811 than John, with his coughs and colds. His latest complaint was of an "excessive heaviness" that inevitably came over him, especially during the long winter darkness, after dining at 4 p.m. He attributed the condition to age and declining vigor, ignoring the possibility that too few hours of rest at night, combined with a large quantity of wine with dinner, accounted for his falling asleep at his desk or over a book.

As spring finally arrived, Adams had more than Louisa's and his own physical condition to worry him. His unofficial secretaries, Gray and Everett, decided to return to America, believing that in two years they had learned all St. Petersburg had to teach. Next, John was informed that the building his family lived in had been sold, obliging them to move, regardless of their long-term lease. These disappointments produced another prolonged period of insomnia. "A disordered stomach and nervous agitations arising from many deep anxieties upon my mind" roused him usually at 2 a.m.

Within a few weeks, however, he was much restored. Partly, this was because, to his surprise, he found himself delighted with the summer residence he had been compelled to take after vacating the apartment. The Adamses had moved by boat to Apothecary's Island, about four miles from the center of the city. It was John's birthday, July 11. To his amazement, by evening he had safely put away "a trunk with my most valuable papers" and "got up our iron bedstead just in time for the night." The next morning, he discovered that they were situated close to the emperor's summer palace, where there were concerts by the royal band.

While Adams could walk into town, the new residence was "as quiet and undisturbed as if it was a hermitage a hundred miles from the city." Colleagues from the diplomatic corps came out to visit. One brought along his translation of Plutarch's treatise on the delays of divine justice and asked John to read it. None of these distractions, however, kept John's thoughts from Louisa as her pregnancy approached its term.

On their fourteenth wedding anniversary, he took the extraordinary step of devoting much of his diary entry for the day to comments on their marriage, which, he acknowledged, "has not been without its trials, nor invariably without its dissensions between us." Despite both their natures being "quick and irascible and mine being sometimes harsh," he assured his diary that Louisa had always been an affectionate and faithful wife. "My lot in marriage has been highly favoured."

Far advanced in pregnancy, Louisa continued to take long walks around the island, and even opened their summer retreat to guests for a large dinner party only a fortnight before she "confined herself to her chamber." On August 11, a nurse was summoned, and John uneasily awaited the birth as he tried to read sermons.

After twelve hours of labor, during which he joined the midwife at Louisa's bedside, a much-desired daughter was born. At once, and with great glee, JQA sent the news to Abigail Adams. "I think this will convince you that the climate of St. Petersburg is *not* too cold to produce an American." On September 9, in an Anglican service with many diplomats attending, the infant was christened with her mother's name. Emperor Alexander's offer to serve as godfather was declined, John fearing that much of the American public would misunderstand this gesture of cordiality.

Baby Louisa Catherine's life began happily for her and for her parents. Mother and child quickly recovered from the birth, while John found a pleasing new apartment in Little Officer's Street, only a five-minute walk from their previous residence. The rent, which included 110 cords of stove wood, was an amazingly reasonable $1,800 per year. By October 8, as cold weather set in, the last boatload of furnishings was hauled to town from Apothecary's Island, allowing the Adamses to be settled for winter.

With official business still scant, John undertook anew to use the long season fruitfully. A revised schedule was attempted: rising at 5 a.m., a cold bath, reading of five chapters in the German Bible, and a six-mile walk before breakfast was his idea of a satisfying start to the day. When he sought more exercise, the French ambassador recommended tennis, advice Adams spurned: "I do not understand it and think it too late to begin to learn." He resolved, however, to train himself to reduce the amount of wine he consumed at home and elsewhere.

This determination had begun one evening as he was dining at the Austrian minister's residence. The table became so noisy that he could not hear his neighbors' words. Left alone with his thoughts, he realized that usually he drank heavily because he so enjoyed the conversation going on around him that he became unaware how often he was emptying his glass. The lesson was blunted, unfortunately, when the racket at the embassy that night left him with the same headache that immoderation would have caused.

His resolve to be temperate soon weakened, along with other efforts at reformation. The cold bath was abandoned, blamed for causing his "fluttering nervous agitation." Next, getting up at an early hour was deemed unreasonable after long nights spent at parties. "I shall arise no more by candle light this winter and I consider my resolution as having in a great measure failed. . . . Whether I shall have the spirit to resume it depends upon the will of Heaven."

As it happened, during St. Petersburg's deep winter of 1811–12, Heaven was much in Adams' thoughts, a turn of mind that had begun soon after daughter Louisa was born. At that joyful event, he renewed his religious meditations with unprecedented intensity. Previously, he had often complained of letting worldly thoughts and problems distract him from attentively reading the Bible or a sermon. Nor, he conceded, had he been regular in attending church in Russia, preferring to be a spectator at services of the Greek Orthodox and Roman Catholic congregations.

But now, blessed with a baby daughter, he found himself able to read religious literature with greater concentration. He returned to studying sermons by Bishop Tillotson, adding, as well, homilies by Laurence Sterne, whose fame as the author of *Tristram Shandy* has obscured his earlier success as a country preacher. Adams particularly enjoyed Sterne's sermon on the Levite and his concubine. "I was more than once unable to refrain from laughter and from tears."

Mostly, however, these meditations meant serious business, as John pledged to open himself and his children to divine inspiration. Toward that end, he began a series of letters on reading the Bible addressed to his son George Washington Adams, about whom there was increasing parental concern. Not only did George face the expectations normally vested in firstborn sons, he also carried a sacred name. He was about to pass his eleventh birthday, the same age, as John remembered, when he himself had faced the temptations of Paris.

Although his son was living in the comparative safety of Quincy with John's frail Aunt and Uncle Cranch, the father felt he could no longer rely upon them to discipline such a difficult boy. George was variously described by relatives as hyperactive, erratic, brilliant but undisciplined, effeminate, and lazy. Even before he began the letters on Bible reading, John had sent George much advice, but hardly of a nature to calm him. A typical admonition: "I hope always to hear that among your companions the best boys are your best friends. I trust you will always be ashamed to let any of them learn faster, or by his good conduct, make himself more beloved than you."

But more was needed, Adams concluded, than merely secular advice. To help George please his parents, John began letters that stressed the importance of Bible study. He foresaw two additional merits in the project: it would enable him to bolster his own moral and spiritual faith, and it also appealed to his scholarly nature. As a result, he pursued his scriptural reading and writing in George's behalf with such zeal that the winter of 1812 brought him to a state of religious exaltation.

Inspired by reading sermons, the Bible, books of theology, and such Greek thinkers as Plato and Socrates, Adams summoned George to join with him by letter in seeking a virtuous life. He stressed chapters 25 to 30 in the Book of Exodus, which disclosed how love and adoration had entered the Judaic religion. According to John, these attributes thereby took "a stronger hold of human affections and human reason than the whole system of Greek mythology put together."

He urged his son to realize that while evil was the natural propensity of mankind, all mortals had the duty to aim for perfection with God's help. George was reminded repeatedly that "Heaven has given to every human being the *power* of controlling his passions, and if he neglects or loses it, the fault is his own, and he must be answerable for it."

If we assume that these letters did not overstate JQA's outlook, they show him fearful that both his own and his son's human weaknesses would render them vulnerable to the lures of the world. The correspondence offers one of the clearest glimpses of the tangle of insecurity that had handicapped John since youth—and that he was, sadly, successful in imparting to George.

Obedience to God's word in the Bible was the only avenue toward "the complete conquest of our own passions," the father assured the boy back in America. Adams was beseeching himself as well as George when he wrote: "Endeavor my dear son, to discipline your own heart" and to be "fruitful of good works." These words were part of the final letter of the series, dated September 14, 1813. The entire group was published thirty-five years later, soon after JQA's death.

While preparing these epistles, he filled his diary with thoughts concerning faith. "Religious sentiments become from day to day more constantly habitual to my mind. They are perhaps too often seen in this journal. God alone can make even religion a virtue, and to him I look for aid that mine may degenerate into no vicious excess."

Aside from this episode in St. Petersburg, Adams rarely moved beyond a rational approach to questions involving religious faith, although he always claimed to be a Christian and to acknowledge an afterlife. Even on this topic, however, his position reflected a deliberate rationale. "If the existence of man were limited to this life," he wrote, "it would be impossible for me to believe the universe made any moral sense." If, however, one took for granted a future state of retribution, then Adams conceded that the wicked might flourish in this life until they were called to account in the hereafter. This being so, he was content to settle back, patient with "the delays of divine justice."

While on occasion he thought carefully about whether Jesus Christ was divine, usually he preferred more manageable reflections, such as considering Christianity as a guide to morality. Here his interest could be avid, so that in reading straightforward sermons such as Laurence Sterne's homily on Herod, he would put them down with regret, wishing they were not so brief.

Of course, reading sermons and writing about the Bible to George were not the only tasks to which Adams dedicated his generous amount of leisure during the winter of 1812. Indeed, he often gave much of each day to educating Charles, his four-year-old, although at times he complained that these were hours he might otherwise have devoted to "the production of something more important than teaching a child the first elements of knowledge."

Charles was a very bright boy, so his father undertook to discover through him the conditions in which individuals learned best. The challenge of holding a youngster's attention intrigued Adams, especially because of concern over the way his own concentration was so easily distracted. At least for children, he said, "the sugar plums yet serve as a guard against the sentiment of toil, but to dispense them with efficiency is a delicate task."

Even with these goodies, however, Charles proved difficult to work with. "His eyes fly over the page, and when I am pointing to one letter, he insists upon looking at another, upon turning over the leaf, upon hunting for a picture, upon anything but naming the letter to which I point." The experience was an uncomfortable one for the parent. Watching Charles' eyes wandering from his tasks, Adams noted sadly: "I find to this day the same thing in myself, and it is the greatest, perhaps the only cause which has found the voyage of my life in the shallows." The true genius, he said, "is nothing but the power of applying the mind to its object."

It was not all study, however, when he filled the role of parent. He and Charles often walked together, and the father gallantly sought to play games with the boy as well as to read to him. Once, Adams took Charles to watch circus acts in St. Isaac's Square, where "I had anticipated the pleasure of seeing him delighted with them." But, alas, the first performance, by tightrope dancers, left Charles so frightened that "after seeing them four or five minutes, he said he wanted to come away." When John tried to coax Charles to watch another act, the boy refused. After sending him back to the apartment with a servant, Adams lingered to observe more spectacles. But "as I had been disappointed in the expectation of seeing Charles enjoy the sights, I went no farther but returned home."

UNFORTUNATELY, WHEN HE GOT THERE, he wished he had stayed away longer. Finding that letters from America had arrived by an overland carrier, he was convinced that they brought bad news, and his hands shook to the point that he could scarcely open the envelopes. Even so, he said, "My anticipation of evil was far less than the reality." The first message revealed that Louisa's mother had died on September 19, 1811, at age 54. She was the victim of a fever that carried off many persons in the Washington and Baltimore area, also including Louisa's brother-in-law, Andrew Buchanan, who had married Louisa's sister Carolina. And the packet included mail from Quincy that was equally distressing. Aunt and Uncle Cranch had died on October 15 and 16, and sister Nabby had come home to endure a mastectomy.

Not at all upsetting, however, was a letter from President Madison confirming that, having declined a Supreme Court seat, Minister Adams was to remain in St. Petersburg. Madison said nothing to enlighten John about rumors published in European papers that his next assignment would be to represent the United States in London.

With the prospect of remaining in Europe indefinitely, the Adamses sent instructions to Quincy that sons George and John should set out for Russia as soon as possible. "I can no longer reconcile either to my feelings or to my sense of duty their absence from me," said JQA. Since the deaths of Aunt and Uncle Cranch, George was at the Peabody academy and John lived with his grandparents. "I must go to them or they must come to me." The outbreak of war between the United States and Great Britain later in 1812, however, forced a deferral of the boys' travel until 1815.

Impatience to have the children under his supervision caused John's insomnia to worsen. At least that was the reason he gave for his sleeplessness, rather than blaming aftereffects from the many diplomatic dinners he continued to attend, occasions where "lessons of temperance multiply upon me." Following an especially exhilarating dinner, he acknowledged: "I did not close my eyes." Could it have been caused by "the excess or the coffee after dinner," he mused, or was it worry over the sons in America?

No DOUBT IT WAS a bit of both, but by now Adams also faced larger concerns outside the household that kept him awake in 1812. It was clear that the uneasy relationship between France and Russia would soon collapse into war. The prospect, of course, deeply troubled his friend Czar Alexander, so that the ruler's conversations with the American minister gradually lost their lighthearted touch.

Not that Alexander entirely gave up on cheerfulness, as on the day in March when he broached the subject of flannel underwear. He proudly reported to Adams that he had defied his physician's orders and removed his undergarment while it was still winter. The doctor said to do so would kill His Majesty. When the latter asked about John's habit, the American admitted he was less courageous: he was so accustomed to wearing flannel in cold weather that he said he knew he would die if he took it off. The czar further astonished John by describing how he always dressed himself before an open window.

Meeting Adams a fortnight after this enlightening exchange, Alexander was in a far different mood, exclaiming that he now believed war with France was inevitable, despite all he had done to avert it. He was correct, for three months later, Napoleon invaded Russia at the head of 500,000 troops. By then, the Russian emperor was wholly occupied with the mortal danger to his country. "The convulsive trials of the times must be continued," Adams wrote, adding that "relief from these agonizing struggles of mankind is yet remote."

As he mourned for Russia, JQA also grieved for his own country. Reports reaching St. Petersburg claimed that hostilities between the United States and Great Britain were inevitable. "To my great sorrow, I pray it may yet be avoided," he wrote at the end of July, not knowing that Madison and the Congress had formally declared war on England on June 19, 1812. Word of this action did not reach St. Petersburg until August 6. By then, however, Adams found it difficult to concentrate on his nation's peril as he watched the emperor seek to rally the Russian people to turn back the invaders.

Russia's noble families had assigned to the army one of every ten peasants for defense against Napoleon, so that on an August morning, the American minister stared in amazement as a multitude of these recruited serfs arrived in the capital from the countryside. They came mostly in one-horse wagons, bringing their families to take leave of them. The sight was awesome. If this new army could be disciplined, Adams thought, "there is little danger for the country to apprehend from the invasion under which it now suffers."

Events bore out his judgment, for on October 19 the French army was compelled by these peasant forces to begin its fabled retreat from Moscow into the grip of Russian snow and ice. Much relieved, Adams reported to Washington that never "since the creation of the world" had "a greater, more sudden and total reverse of fortune" befallen a leader. Napoleon had failed "owing to his having despised his enemy."

Russia might have been spared, but Adams could not fend off assault by an array of personal troubles in 1812. He had to reprimand his friend and associate Levett Harris, the U.S. consul, for taking advantage of his position to make large personal profits. Harris' actions might not have been legally reprehensible, but Adams saw them as morally corrupt. The confrontation between the two Americans became "loud and highly irritated on both sides." It embarrassed John to recall "the tone, with vehemence of manner and sharpness of voice," that he had used with Harris. His anger was a weakness that he admitted "too easily besets me and which I have many years struggled to subdue."

Then there were Adams' domestic distresses, which were much more exasperating than the disagreement with Harris. Misbehavior among the servants was one problem. While there had been earlier difficulties with the staff, serious trouble began only after Nelson, an aide whom the Adamses had brought from America, accepted a job in the palace, where the emperor sought to keep a retinue of black servants. Nelson was replaced as steward by a man named Waldstein, whose corruption soon became evident to Adams when he learned that the household bills were going unpaid.

The discovery of this "pillage" obliged John to give precious hours to checking supplies in the pantry and the wine cellar. To his horror, he found that 373 bottles of wine were missing, of which 272 represented "the choicest and most costly wines I had." He realized that Waldstein had been forging tradesmen's signatures on receipts, and that a great deal of coffee had vanished as well. To make matters worse, when Adams ordered Waldstein out of the house, the steward refused to leave, so that help had to be summoned to escort the culprit from the premises.

Next to be employed as steward was a black sailor, Thomas Baker, who had been abandoned by the captain of his ship. This choice proved a second disaster when Adams learned one night that Baker was in bed with a female, despite orders against bringing women into the house. "His vices are women and drinking. The natural consequence of which is stealing of every kind." What made JQA even more indignant was the discovery that Baker's room had been the scene of sexual frolic for many weeks. Baker's successor, Louis Rubin, proved to be another thief. Finally, John had the inspiration to appoint his footman Pierre as steward after realizing that he was "the best man-servant I have met with in this country."

There was one more unhappy experience with a servant. Adams said little as he paid the bail needed to release his coachman, who had been arrested for parading along the streets of St. Petersburg in a woman's dress. With that, the comic-opera aspect of John's life came for the moment to an end.

THE COACHMAN'S ESCAPADE was a trivial matter compared with the trouble brought by a relationship between Louisa's sister Kitty Johnson and John's nephew Billy Smith. The affair made John recall a warning Louisa had given him before they sailed for Russia. She had predicted that if Kitty—a vivacious spinster of twenty-four who un-abashedly sought the company of males—went with them, trouble was sure to come along.

When she arrived in St. Petersburg, Kitty was prepared to be in-terested in all the young men who were serving as Adams' secretaries and aides. Apparently Francis Gray responded with enthusiasm, creat-ing what John at the time dourly called "a situation of some delicacy." He turned to a sermon on "the character of the *woman who was a sin-ner*," a topic which he underlined heavily in his journal.

After Gray suddenly decided that it was unwise to linger in Russia, Kitty's romantic ways took her into the embrace of Billy Smith—which, in turn, inspired a reference in Adams' diary to "circumstances which I would not commit to paper." The most he allowed himself to say was that "every precaution of prudence" had been futile in keeping the couple apart. On New Year's Day 1812, Kitty confided to Louisa that she was pregnant.

Immediately, John had a "very solemn conversation" with his secretary-nephew. To the uncle's relief, Billy "professed a sincere and earnest wish to do what is just and right." Then, before going to talk with Kitty in her room, which she now refused to leave, Adams paused to pray: "God grant me in this day of trial the spirit of integrity and of fortitude which it requires." The young woman accepted Billy's proposal of marriage as conveyed by her brother-in-law, so that on February 17, 1812, Adams could record that "William Steuben Smith and Catherine Frances Johnson were married at my house."

At dates unknown, Kitty's infant was born and died in St. Petersburg, although neither event was mentioned in Adams' diary until September 10, 1817. The family manuscripts contain only hints about the birth.

The household upheaval caused by Kitty and Billy was soon replaced by an even graver worry which began for the Adamses on July 13, 1812. On that day, daughter Louisa fell victim to dysentery. At first, it was blamed on teething—she was cutting seven teeth at once. After a few weeks, the baby seemed better. Then, three days after Louisa began weaning the year-old youngster, the disorder recurred and never relented. At the recommendation of their physician, the Adamses leased a small cottage at Ochta, seven miles out of the city, where Louisa, the baby, Kitty, and Charles Francis planned to spend a month in the fresh air while John made a daily walk into the city.

The change lasted barely a week, for by September 9, tiny Louisa had grown so weak that she was brought back to town. Even his favorite sermons could not now soothe Adams' thoughts. "My mind was too much agitated and absorbed by the condition of my child to read with suitable improvement." He found indescribable "the long continued agonies of a lovely infant." Then, on September 15, the patient died amid convulsions and torment, suffering probably from total dehydration. No relief had come when the doctors caused blisters to rise on the pitiful child's shaven scalp so that, they said, bodily poisons might escape through the brain.

Two days later, after the Anglican Order for the Burial of the Dead was read, Adams attended the interment of "my darling infant" in the English cemetery "on the Wasili-Ostrof." There "I saw her deposited in her last earthly mansion, on an elevated spot of ground."

He then joined his wife in a period of paralyzing sorrow, remembering the youngster as being "as lovely and promising a child as ever was." Unable to overcome his grief, he said: "There is nothing on earth that can administer relief to my affliction." The little girl had been "our *only* daughter, and lovely as a Seraph upon earth." To his father, he wrote: "the desire of my eyes, the darling of my heart is gone." And to Abigail: "The wound of the heart still bleeds. It can never be entirely healed!" He could not sleep for having to recount through the night how baby Louisa's "every gesture was of charm," and how "every lisp" had brought him rapture.

To worsen matters, Adams believed his own health was collapsing, as he could neither rest nor read. "It is the torture of Tantalus"— "when up I cannot keep myself awake and when in bed cannot sleep." He thought he noticed a developing tremor in his hand, "a flutter of the spirits," and "a perpetual sensation of hurry." The condition was not serious enough to keep him from rising at 5 a.m. and walking six miles before breakfast. "I find it irksome to stay within doors."

The family's doctor in St. Petersburg gently besought John to relax, suggesting that he should partake of some fine wines. Adams' rejoinder was terse: "The lust of the flesh is already too prone and in which I indulge myself more than enough." He preferred his own prescription: "curb the appetites." In his study chamber, where it often was so cold he could scarcely hold his pen, he did manage at the end of 1812 to write the lines: "Why art thou cast down, oh my soul! And why art thou disquieted within me? Hope thou on God."

IN THIS CRUEL FASHION, the bitterly chill winter passed, with early spring 1813 finding both John and Louisa slowly emerging from lassitude and despair. He was able to resume his religious meditations, to read Cicero once again, to write long letters to his father, and to instruct son Charles for several hours a day. Here there were cheering prospects, as the boy showed an improved capacity to learn.

Although Charles would not be six until August, he was reading several chapters a day in the English Bible; by this tactic Adams induced his son to speak English rather than French and German, with which the child had become far more comfortable. After reading came arithmetic: Charles recited the multiplication tables in English and French and read numbers to "hundreds of millions." To John's added pleasure, the boy now sought his company, even taking long walks with him before breakfast. And, of course, Charles asked many questions. "I endeavor to amuse him and at the same time to convey instruction to his mind through the medium of everything that happens."

There was another reason why Adams emerged from his doldrums by winter's end in 1813. His work as a diplomat now seemed to have a larger consequence, where before he had often felt wasted on trivial routine. Particularly encouraging were the latest benefits from his association with Emperor Alexander. The discourse between ruler and diplomat had reached its most significant level during the French invasion. War was a subject that weighed heavily upon the emperor, whose education in Europe had given him a strongly pacifist disposition. It grieved him that the United States had been drawn into the conflict.

Alexander also recognized that Russia needed to collaborate with a rising commercial power such as the United States. Consequently, he began emphasizing to Adams in their conversations that he was now willing to support the cardinal aim of American foreign policy, freedom of the seas, the policy that governed John's tactics abroad. Seizing this advantage, Adams secured the emperor's help in arranging the release of numerous American merchant ships held captive by Denmark.

The most important moment came, however, when Alexander asked John whether his services might be welcome in mediating the war between England and the United States. Going far out on a limb, Adams replied in the affirmative, although at that point he could not know how Washington would view the offer. He had no reason to worry. When news of the czar's gesture reached Madison, who had recently been reelected, the president hailed what Adams had accomplished and promptly accepted Alexander's offer.

The delighted Madison understood the difficulties under which JQA had been obliged to operate so far from home. He offered the nation's gratitude by urging Adams to accept, once peace was secured, the highest American position abroad, that of minister to Great Britain. Until that was possible, the president had another assignment: Adams was to be a negotiator for peace. Madison named him, Senator James Bayard, and Secretary of the Treasury Albert Gallatin as the commission that would discuss with England an end to hostilities. These talks were to be under Russian auspices.

The news that he could be leaving St. Petersburg for the peace negotiations made a sheepish Adams admit that he had not been fully appreciative of the city's advantages. There were "comforts and pleasures," he acknowledged, "which while enjoyed constantly I have not estimated as they deserve." He suddenly realized how much he would miss the time for study and writing that came with life in Russia. It was an opportunity for scholarship that, of course, he insisted he had largely wasted.

NOW, AS "ENVOY EXTRAORDINARY and minister plenipotentiary," John wondered where, except from Heaven, he would find the "zeal, integrity, and discretion" his new duties required of him.

CHAPTER NINE

London

My natural disposition is of an over-anxious cast.

THE OPPORTUNITY for which John prayed was slow to arrive. James Bayard and Albert Gallatin were tardy in reaching St. Petersburg, and when the two exhausted men finally turned up, on July 21, 1813, they, along with Adams, soon learned that their coming to Russia had been unnecessary. Great Britain proved unwilling to consider peace under Alexander's auspices. If there was to be a treaty, it would not be negotiated in St. Petersburg.

For the next nine months, Adams waited in the Russian capital for word about where England might choose to discuss ending hostilities. Most of this time, he bore the considerable burden of the presence of Bayard and Gallatin. Not only did he have to struggle to keep up his own hopes that peace was possible; he also had to try to calm his new colleagues as they awaited some move by London. Bayard and Gallatin were strong personalities, and each loudly expressed opinions about what should be done. Since the two understood little of the complexities of European diplomacy, they severely taxed the patience of the veteran Adams.

Had Adams been well disposed toward his associates, the long delay might have been easier to endure. Neither man was particularly good company—at least not in John's opinion. As a senator in Washington, he had not often associated with Gallatin, then secretary of the treasury. On the other hand, Senator Bayard had been an unpleasant colleague. Although he arrived in St. Petersburg with reports that Massachusetts was eager to send Adams back to the Senate, the news

did little to help John overlook what he called Bayard's "odious" behavior due to "intemperate habits." Still, JQA managed to be civil
toward him.

The Adamses sought to be hospitable, inviting the Americans frequently to dine and showing them the sights of St. Petersburg. One
such occasion had a comic side, when John and Louisa took Gallatin
(Bayard had awakened "indisposed" that morning) to visit Count
Ozarovsky at his palace at Czersko-Telo, about seven miles from the
capital. While they were dining with the count, at a nearby inn the
Adams coachman became helplessly drunk from the wine John had
ordered with the servant's dinner. "We had some difficulty," John reported in an understatement, since it was several hours before the
Adamses succeeded in getting the coachman in condition to drive.

The most annoying side to Bayard and Gallatin's stay was that it
interrupted John's daily walks and especially his reading and writing.
With obvious relief, therefore, he recorded the Americans' departure
on January 25, 1814, for London, where they hoped at close range to
discover England's intentions.

With his guests gone, Adams tried to settle back into his former
routine, now a bit less comfortable because of "lumbago," which he
blamed on a "relaxation of the fibres." The disorder brought on "a
sort of dizziness in the head which is painful and distressing." He did
not mention that his complaint might have been due to many nights
spent peering up at the stars from a rooftop, a recent practice growing
from the study of astronomy, which he had undertaken just before
Bayard and Gallatin arrived to distract him.

Initially, he had sought to learn about astronomy as a means of
fathoming the chronology of events in the Bible. But now the subject
fascinated him on its own account. "I find it easy to engage my attention in scientific pursuits," he acknowledged. The more he pondered
astronomy, the more enthralled he became and the less he fretted
about England's delay in agreeing to discuss peace. He was struck particularly by the Copernican concept that the planets, including Earth,
revolved around the sun. Surely it was only a theory, Adams mused,
admitting that his powers of abstraction were so weak that he could
not understand "the imaginary circles with which the astronomers
have encompassed the globe to explain the revolutions of the heavenly
orbs."

He was convinced that new discoveries would someday alter
mankind's knowledge of the skies. "I am not appalled either by the distance or by the multitudes of the fixed stars," he wrote, "for space is in-

finite, and however great the multitude of worlds may be, he who created and governs can number them, though I cannot." And so he
watched as his studies "spread and widen before me." Ahead he saw
"hills peep over hills" as reading about science remained "the most delightful of occupations" and left him wishing for forty-eight-hour days.

When his eyes grew weary, Adams allowed himself to break away
to attend one or another of the numerous book auctions held around
the city. Although he reported no success on one occasion in bidding
for the volumes he wanted, "on the other hand, I purchased some
books I did not want." Writing to his father about these auctions, JQA
received a chastening reply. Himself once equally susceptible to buying books, John Adams warned: "I think neither of us can boast of
much discriminating judgment in our choice. We have many good
books, but thousands that are comparatively worth very little." It
pained the elder Adams to think of what he might have purchased
over the years, instead of so much English, German, French, and
Dutch "trash."

This observation stung the son, who indignantly assured his father
that there was nothing inferior in their libraries. The two of them simply had outgrown many volumes, but these would be of great value to
their descendants. To explain, JQA pointed out that once Tom
Thumb, Jack the Ripper, and Goody Two-Shoes had been "the most
delicious enjoyment of my life"; now he found himself too busy with
science to read simply for pleasure.

He might also have mentioned his interest in history. Studying the
past drew more than its share of his attention as he continued to wait
patiently for news. Some striking ideas emerged from his historical
reading, including his conclusion that emigration had always brought
humanity new strength. This led him to assure Benjamin Waterhouse
at Harvard that Yankee character would be improved by removal to
the "howling deserts" of interior America.

Another bit of dubious wisdom John drew from history was his
prediction that there was an encouraging aspect to the United States'
involvement in the War of 1812: "There are energies in the constitution of Man which a long protracted peace always weakens, and sometimes extinguishes altogether. Occasional war is one of the rigorous
instruments in the hands of Providence to give tone to the character of
nations." He hoped this would be true of the United States.

If only mankind could have the leadership it needed. Yet Adams
found that history showed how unlikely this was because so many
superior statesmen ultimately had been ruined by a "passion for

women." This pernicious vice, he claimed, was particularly deplorable in persons of high station, where it was often uncontrollable, leaving potentially great men with no more than "the disgrace of a goat."

AMID THESE INTRIGUING SPECULATIONS, word about peace negotiations finally arrived on March 20, 1814. The English government had informed Madison that it was willing to talk face-to-face about ending the war, and the president had named his team already in Europe—Adams, Bayard, and Gallatin—to represent the United States. They were to be joined by two others, Speaker of the House Henry Clay and Jonathan Russell, U.S. minister to Sweden. The negotiations would take place in the Swedish city of Göteborg.

Adams was elated. "This opens upon me a new prospect of futurity and a new change in the scenery of life." The opportunity to share in doing something so significant transformed him. His physical complaints began to vanish, and his outlook became downright buoyant, leading him to marvel that more writers could not see how human existence had a bright as well as a dark side. "Life in all its forms, high and low, has great, numerous, and exquisite enjoyments."

The prospect of separation from Louisa redoubled John's interest in her. His attention now became ardent, and, to Louisa's astonishment, he even shared the details of his financial holdings with her. The two enjoyed carriage rides together, and John allowed her to help in packing and in buying supplies. Their shopping was not easy, since St. Petersburg's merchants mostly closed their doors during the lengthy Easter holiday.

Adams' greatest concern was purchasing a coach for overland travel, but none could be found until a friend, Countess Columbi, proved willing to sell one. Her carriage was too heavy, he feared, but it was the best he could locate in the scramble to be off on his latest adventure. And so, in his lumbering vehicle, he started toward Sweden on April 28. "I have become once more a wayfaring man, and am separated from every part of my family."

Traveling with a Finnish servant, Axel Gahlroos, Adams did not reach Stockholm for nearly a month. Mostly, the interval was spent in Estonia, waiting in the city of Revel (modern-day Tallinn) for the ice in the Gulf of Finland to thaw enough to permit the short voyage to Sweden. The time passed agreeably, of course, thanks to music, theater, visits with acquaintances, shopping for books, and reading. One volume in particular, the memoirs of the Duc de Sully (1560–1641), caught Adams' attention. The Frenchman had been a brilliant official for Henry of Navarre, and his career showed John how "stubbornness of resolution and perseverance" were essential in truly great character.

Still reading Sully, he sailed for Stockholm on May 20. The sight of the Swedish capital again amazed him as he marveled at how such a city could have been built on a cluster of islands, "or rather upon a number of rocks." After paying the proper calls and making a start at opening the mass of letters and official papers from America that awaited him, Adams and Axel set out for Göteborg on June 2 in the bulky Russian carriage, now drawn by six Swedish horses.

The next day, a messenger met them with word from Henry Clay, who had arrived in Hamburg, that the peace conference had been moved from Göteborg to the Belgian city of Ghent. Consequently, after a few more days in Sweden, JQA put his carriage aboard the *John Adams,* a U.S. corvette that would take him to Holland. Amid much ceremony and a thirteen-gun salute honoring John Quincy Adams, the *John Adams* set sail on June 12. Five days later it reached Amsterdam, to JQA's relief. "I have seldom found myself more fatigued than on my arrival here." Even so, and despite an enervating cold, he walked about in a city that held many memories. Meeting a fellow peace commissioner, Jonathan Russell, Adams offered him a seat in his carriage, and the two began journeying to Ghent on June 22.

Along the way, they passed The Hague without time to stop. Even so, Adams was stirred: "I can scarcely account to myself for the sensations I felt on approaching The Hague where I resided at several of the most interesting periods of my life." He remembered his return there from Russia in 1783—"the precise time of my change from boy to man." Then he recalled how, fifteen years later, he had come back to The Hague from London, having fallen in love with Louisa—or, as he described it, having experienced "the social passion . . . with all its impetuosity." The city held recollections "altogether so sweet, that if I had been alone I am sure I should have melted into tears."

Thus inspired, Adams continued to Ghent. En route, he had what proved a splendid bit of luck. To replace his servant Axel, who wished to return to Scandinavia, he recruited a promising new man: Antoine Guista, a Piedmontese soldier left adrift at the close of the Napoleonic Wars. Guista proved to be a superb aide and stayed in the employ of the Adamses for fifteen years.

The hiring of Guista and other practical matters took up a generous part of John's almost daily epistles to Louisa. "It is proper you should know the exact condition of my affairs," he explained. Fortunately for his lonely wife, he also wrote of how much he loved her and of how he missed her presence and that of Charles Francis. He advised Louisa in detail about how to carry on his youngest son's education. The letters also contained interpretations of European politics and accounts of travel.

While all of this interested Louisa, what most delighted her was the way her spouse made his letters charming messages of love. Once, he requested that she kiss Charles for him and gallantly added: "As for you—as the song says, 'that fruit must be gathered from the tree'—Adieu!" Adams acknowledged that for persons "who truly love," separation brought increased fervor, which explained why he felt "an ardour beating at my heart." He prayed that he and Louisa might speedily be restored "to each other's arms" when he pledged to kiss her, promising "it will not be at your bed-*side*."

Along with such gallantries, Adams shared with Louisa his anxiety over the issues facing the negotiators at Ghent, as well as his fears concerning his ability to play his part. They were well-grounded misgivings, as it turned out, for when the British and American commissioners finally held their first meeting on August 8, it was clear the goals of the two groups were very different.

FOR THE U.S. DELEGATION, success would mean resolving such long-standing issues as impressment of American sailors, blockades, and other maritime grievances. The British wanted to establish a neutral Indian buffer zone in the Northwest and demanded major cessions of territory from Maine across to what is now western Minnesota. Equally delicate were such points as the right of Americans to fish in territorial waters off British North America and the military control of the Great Lakes.

The potential conflict between the two delegations was but one of the dangers at Ghent, as Adams assessed the situation. He realized that the American representatives, of whom he had been listed by Madison as nominal head and spokesman, were sharply divergent in individual personality and outlook. As time passed, he came to despair about amity being preserved among his colleagues as much as he feared for the prospects of achieving it between the two warring nations.

A principal cause for discouragement, as Adams was the first to recognize, arose from his own emotional makeup, particularly his tendency to be short-tempered. As he had grown older, it had become increasingly easy for him to flare into anger when matters did not go his way. More than ever, he became quickly impatient with individuals he considered fools or lazy. These traits made him—the man who was at the time America's most experienced diplomat—notorious for harshness, tactlessness, and even rudeness. Such were his handicaps in Ghent.

Little of this escaped Adams. In a letter to Louisa, he offered an astute explanation for his shortcomings of temperament. "My natural disposition," he said, "is of an over-anxious cast, and my struggles to accommodate myself to circumstances which I cannot controul have given my constitution in less than fifty years the wear and tear of seventy." No professional analyst could have offered a shrewder diagnosis.

Fear of failure and the insistent parental summons to greatness, the all-too-familiar concerns that had been instilled in him as a youth, bore down with unprecedented ferocity upon Adams in Ghent. His "over-anxious" nature responded predictably when the negotiations thrust him into a situation where he felt insecure, and he quite lost the amiability that, twenty years earlier, had made him a genial leader among the young men of Boston.

John's unpleasant side was strikingly displayed once Albert Gallatin belatedly arrived from Paris. After the group had eaten together for the first time, Adams resolved to take his meals alone, saying of his colleagues: "They sit after dinner and drink bad wine and smoke cigars." Staying with them would waste precious time. Of course his solitary meals quickly affronted the others, who saw in his demeanor a poorly masked arrogance. Happily, Henry Clay intervened, and, upon the Kentuckian's advice, Adams resumed dining with the group.

Despite this effort, he continued to be a poor companion in Ghent. He felt that he had reason to be irritated. There were many conflicts among the ill-matched American plenipotentiaries. Frequently, there were encounters where Adams admitted he was not "master of myself." He did not hide his disgust, for instance, at the racket created when, down the hall from his room, Clay's card parties broke up around 4 a.m.

Poker games and other extracurricular fun shared by his colleagues had no appeal for Adams, as he more than made clear. No matter what others might be doing, he pointedly took a daily two-hour walk, usually in the afternoon once official meetings had ended. He stuck to this routine even if his associates went to the theater.

The bulk of Adams' time was given to writing—letters, diary entries, and drafts of statements for the American delegates to present to their British counterparts. Often from 4 to 10 a.m. and again at night, he was at his writing table, drawing up the latest American response to issues facing the peace conference. His colleagues had assigned him this drudgery, insisting that he be penman since he took pride in being chief plenipotentiary; then they sat back and waited to criticize his drafts.

Since Adams' pride of authorship was painfully apparent, his associates knew that rejecting his work was a never-failing means of humbling him. Afterward, should another colleague offer a draft, the group invariably received it with respect. "If any one member objects to any thing I have written," John complained to his diary, "all the rest support him in it and I never can get it through." Then, if he raised concern over some point in a Gallatin draft, for instance, "every other member supports him and my objection is utterly unavailing." Although at first he called the "severity with which I alone am treated" a "gauntlet," eventually he was reduced to wondering whether his failures might actually be due to "the fault of my composition."

While the treatment by his associates was a bitter experience, reminding him of what he had gone through in the Senate, it did nothing to lengthen Adams' short fuse. Frequently, he entered into loud arguments with his colleagues, afterward apologizing to his diary for once again speaking in such "heat." On one occasion, he accused Clay of playing a "trick" and of being "highly improper," statements he later admitted were overdrawn.

Conflict between Clay, the worldly frontiersman, and Adams, the dour Yankee, was perhaps unavoidable. But even the debonair Gallatin bore at times the brunt of what John called "the irritability of my temper." Fortunately, as John acknowledged, Gallatin had a playfulness of disposition that usually permitted him to shrug off Adams' heat with a joke.

The drain on John's scant reserve of patience worsened as representatives from the two nations began to meet more frequently, so that he was angered many times by the "overbearing insolence and narrow understandings" of the British delegates. Ironically, pride and inflexibility were the very attributes that the American delegates saw in Adams' makeup.

In writing to Louisa, he confessed readily enough to his "dogmatical, overbearing manner," his "harshness of look and expression," and his "forgetfulness of the courtesies of society." He told her he especially envied Gallatin's talent for relaxed good humor. And now he admired even James Bayard for having "the most perfect control of his temper"—Bayard's "deliberate coolness" and "real self-command" amazed Adams.

Even as he wrote this to Louisa in mid-December, his spirits had begun to lift as the prospect for peace improved. So long as there was such a possibility, he had sought to persist at the conference table, a determination helped once it became clear that an easy English military triumph in North America was unlikely. This realization inclined the British representatives toward a negotiated peace, something their chief back in London, Lord Castlereagh, had decided was essential. He kept prodding his representatives, just as Adams pushed his own colleagues.

JQA's great achievement in Ghent was to persuade Gallatin and the others to agree to treaty terms based on the status before the war. They should do so, he insisted, even if by accepting such conditions, the delegation departed from the State Department's insistence that differences between the nations must be resolved. He assured his hesitant brethren that he would take full responsibility. "I would cheerfully give my life for a Peace on this basis," he asserted. Not that he was being purely an idealist. As he knew, returning to conditions before the war meant that Americans would continue to fish in British waters, the prize his father had sent home to New England in 1783 as part of the Treaty of Paris.

Gradually, the American plenipotentiaries overcame some of their differences, with the result that at 6:30 p.m. on Christmas Eve 1814, to the astonishment of nearly every participant, a peace treaty was signed by the United States and Great Britain that ended the War of 1812. Its terms were the best John considered possible. Such painful issues as boundaries, fisheries, and the status of the Great Lakes were left to future adjudication. The quarrel over neutral rights was pushed under the table.

This happy outcome had been well served by Adams' experience in international affairs. He had struggled over five difficult months to keep his colleagues—and himself—patient with the volatility of the English negotiators. No statement could have been more sincere, therefore, when, after the ceremonial signing, he spoke for the Americans by announcing to their English counterparts that he hoped it would be the last treaty of peace their two countries would have to sign.

The people of Ghent, who had been rooting for the United States, acclaimed the treaty as a victory for their American friends. (The Americans had judiciously endeared themselves to the citizens by such gestures as inviting 150 of them to a ball.) This favoritism had been evident a few days earlier when Adams attended a concert in the city given by the Society of St. Cecilia. He recalled with pleasure that as he entered the hall, the orchestra struck up "Hail Columbia" in his honor.

Unfortunately, an amiable mood did not linger within the American delegation, which fell again to quarreling as soon as Christmas Day had passed. The fuss, during which Adams' temper flared frequently, continued into the New Year. At issue was whether the commission's papers, books, and maps should remain with him as chief plenipotentiary, as he contended, or be sent at once to the State Department via the *Neptune,* a ship on which Clay intended returning to America. Once more, Henry Clay was pitted against John Quincy Adams over a difference that JQA complained was insignificant but that "gives me more trouble than if it was important."

Assuring himself that he was acting "with great propriety" by insisting on retaining the documents, Adams opposed Clay in several highly unpleasant exchanges. Bayard and Russell joined the Kentuckian, while Gallatin sided with Adams. When JQA found himself outvoted, he caused a new storm by requiring that Clay and his colleagues submit a formal request for the materials and give a signed receipt for all documents they took.

When Clay flew into a rage, claiming that Adams dare not insinuate that a cabal of three members had combined against him, John played a trump card. He warned that this exchange would be entered into the official record and dispatched to the State Department. At this, Clay's political shrewdness rescued him. Calming down, he acknowledged that such a report would tell all America that "we had fallen to a scramble after a few books." The fuss ended with Clay agreeing to carry the books and maps to America. A triumphant Adams retained the commission's vital papers and records.

ON JANUARY 7, Clay and Bayard departed, with Gallatin soon following. Adams remained in Ghent for twenty days, making copies of precious records. One evening he enjoyed a performance of Gluck's *Orfeo ed Euridice,* and he often went into society, admitting that he found the ladies of Ghent very agreeable. The exception was a certain Madame Graban, "who is afflicted with nervous complaints," one of which was to insist that "she had glass legs."

As he confided this report to Louisa, he also told her of his own physical worries. Thanks to the long dinners and lack of exercise during his six months in Ghent, he was putting on so much weight that she would not recognize him. His clothes no longer fit.

John had notified Louisa about the peace treaty, and shared the equally satisfying, still unofficial information that Madison had kept his word: the Adamses would remove to London in order for John to become American minister once his orders reached him in Paris. Consequently, Louisa was instructed to sell most of their possessions and ship the rest to England. Then, with Charles in tow, she was to meet her husband in Paris, "where I shall be impatiently waiting for you."

When he set out for France on January 26, Adams was still using the Russian carriage, but now drawn by four horses—earlier, six had been needed because Swedish horses were smaller than normal. After pausing for a week in Brussels, where he was royally treated and where a female billiards player easily defeated him, he continued his journey, observing that the landscape and the cheating habits of officials at post stops were little changed after thirty years. Reaching Paris on February 4, he took rooms at the Hôtel du Nord, where he promptly went to bed. He found no rest, though, since his suite faced the perpetually noisy Rue de Richelieu, where carriages rolled all night.

Once his quarters were switched to the "yard" side of the hotel, he began three months of pleasure—dinners with fine French wines, evenings at the theater, ballet, or opera, and daily visits to the museums, libraries, and bookstalls. It was no wonder that John complained—only mildly—how "the tendency to dissipation at Paris seems to be irresistible." In the presence of the great city, he admitted, "I am as ill-guarded as I was at the age of twenty." All that was needed to make his happiness complete, he acknowledged, was the presence of Louisa.

She and Charles appeared on March 23. Louisa was in remarkably good health and modest about her forty-day trek from St. Petersburg across war-ravaged Europe, a feat that profoundly impressed her husband. Only after listening to his wife's tales of narrow escapes from pillaging troops did he realize what an enormous burden he had imposed on her in summoning her to France. On the other hand, Louisa had been so eager to leave St. Petersburg, with its long and lonely winters and the tomb of her lamented daughter, that she might have been willing to walk to Paris.

Immediately, she joined her husband in sightseeing and nightly theater, although her spouse deplored the "low and vulgar" Dutch influence he saw dominating most Parisian theatrical fare. This pleasing routine went on as the Adamses awaited word that official documents commissioning him as minister to Great Britain had arrived in London. Despite an impatience to be on the job, the new emissary refused to cross the Channel until all papers were properly at hand.

And so the wait continued, eased by the discovery of new distractions around Paris. One such was the city's catacombs, said to contain two million skeletons. Soon after touring this grisly scene, Adams claimed that he himself might be near death as he fell ill for most of April. His pneumonia-like symptoms were so alarming that he finally allowed Louisa to call for a physician, who, JQA smugly reported, merely prescribed "the regimen that I have been following."

By early May, he had recovered sufficiently for the family to travel to Lagrange, General Lafayette's estate forty miles from Paris. The four days there marked the Adamses' final good time in France. They were guests in a remarkable setting: Lafayette's castle, dating to 1108–37, was surrounded by parklike grounds where a thousand merino sheep grazed, along with cattle and horses. Unfortunately, rain fell incessantly, reducing Adams and his host mostly to talking about politics and books. Lafayette persuaded John to borrow a volume by Benjamin Constant de Rebecque, whose successful career, combining literature and politics, set what JQA considered an enviable example.

THE ADAMSES RETURNED TO PARIS to find the eagerly awaited announcement from Baring Brothers, a banking firm relied upon by the U.S. in London, that John's commission as U.S. minister to Great Britain had arrived. "I determined to proceed to England with as little delay as possible," he wrote. After shipping nine trunks and boxes ahead and receiving a farewell visit from General Lafayette, the family set out for Le Havre on the French coast. There they found that reaching England would be difficult. Napoleon had recently begun his brief return to power, and a renewed war between France and Great Britain threatened.

Le Havre was in such tumult and the competition for passage across the Channel so fierce that the Adamses were compelled to remain in the port town for nearly a week. John used the time to advantage, however, shopping for "a small assortment of wines" and attending the local theater. Finally, after much haggling, a Danish captain agreed to take them as passengers when John paid an outrageous fare. They departed on May 23, just as martial law was imposed.

The twenty-four-hour crossing was so tumultuous that even John verged on seasickness—"more nearly being so than I had been for upward of twenty years." Huddled in a tiny cabin, Louisa and Charles tried to sleep in one berth, the maid in another, while John placed a mattress on the floor and made a blanket from the ship's Danish flag. In this regal fashion, the United States' "envoy extraordinary and minister plenipotentiary at the Court of Great Britain" sailed to his post.

After reaching Dover and starting for London, JQA's status served him better. When the Adamses paused at an inn in Dartford for a luncheon of sandwiches and ale, a revenue agent burst in to announce that he suspected them of smuggling silks. Calling on his vast dignity, John produced a passport signed by no less than Lord Castlereagh, which threw the instantly apologetic official into such confusion that he could scarcely find his way out of the room.

At 8 p.m. on May 25, the minister and his wife arrived at their temporary quarters in 67 Harley Street near Cavendish Square, where they found their other sons awaiting them. Not having seen them for nearly six years, John and Louisa did not recognize George. Young John they considered to be small for his age. The boys had crossed the Atlantic with two promising American scholars, Edward Everett—brother of JQA's assistant in Russia, Alexander—and George Ticknor, who brought word of recent happenings at Harvard.

Also at hand was a bundle of letters from America, which John read until well after midnight while Louisa, so overjoyed at the reunion with her family, celebrated by going to a nearby public bath for the soothing effect of a warm soak. The next morning, the couple began several weeks of visits with friends when they were not showing the boys the sights of London. They had arrived barely in time to see their old friend John Singleton Copley before his death.

While Adams promptly addressed his official duties, it was now the summer season when there were few demands on diplomats. Finding that he had inherited a competent temporary secretary at the legation, the minister turned over to him such matters as issuing passports while he concentrated on becoming reacquainted with his sons. Together, they took long walks, attended concerts and the theater, flew kites, and bore up under cold baths.

In all of this, Adams sought to evaluate his children's intellectual and moral promise; the results led him to conclude that no time must be wasted in finding a suburban residence near a good school. He was convinced that George and John, along with Charles, must have nothing to distract them from diligent study. This was also the opinion of grandmother Abigail, who had sent warning that the boys required training in "virtue and usefulness."

A special worry was George, at fourteen, a tall, awkward boy. Abigail had advised that he was inclined to be the dupe of "any artful designer"; thus Adams resolved that once the family was settled, he would keep his eldest son at his side for a time. He could not fathom where folks back in Quincy had gotten the notion that George was ready to enter Harvard. It took little time for John to conclude that his son was woefully weak in all the areas of learning needed by a Harvard freshman.

With such excellent reasons to escape the "hurly-burly" of London, the Adamses searched the suburbs for a spot where the boys might be safe. Furthermore, the residence must have a study, for John insisted: "I shall be able to bring nothing into order until we get settled in a house where I have a writing chamber." The family removed to just such a place on August 1, using two carts and a wagon to carry their "baggage, furniture, and wines" seven miles to Ealing, where they had leased a house from Colonel James Clitharow. Meanwhile, two rooms suitable for the minister's official work had been rented in central London.

The Adamses were delighted with the Ealing location (today more specifically Brentford). While not large, Little Boston House (named after a local citizen) was "neat and elegant and fitted up with all that minute attention to comfort which is characteristic of English domestic life." It had, of course, the essential writing chamber, plus an orchard of fruit trees and a beautiful garden in which John and Louisa often walked. An Anglican church pew came with the rent, so the family resumed the habit of attending public worship. In this setting, together with their boys again and with no international crisis to distract them, both Louisa and John were soon very happy.

Along with 250 other pupils, including sons of the duke of Kent, John and Charles Adams boarded at Dr. William Nicholas' academy nearby. This arrangement allowed JQA to give his undivided attention to George's improvement—a demanding task, since the young man proved unwilling to arise each morning before six to start his studies with reading and translations in the French and Latin Bibles. The assignment was only the beginning of George's day. Afterward he had Edward Gibbon's journal to translate into French, and Cicero's *Philippics* from Latin into English and vice versa. The results were carefully corrected by his father, while tutors guided George's study of Greek and Italian. Other teachers were employed to improve the young man's penmanship and to instruct him in fencing.

Just as Adams was becoming enthusiastic in the role of tutor, his son faltered before the challenge and began to talk of preferring a career in the army. George suffered "bilious attacks," sought every possible excuse to visit London alone, and begged to be allowed to tour Europe by himself. A disappointed father admitted that he had failed to "inspire the souls of my three boys with the sublime Platonic ideal of aiming at ideal excellence." All that he sought for his offspring was simply what he craved for himself: "to soar to the lofty possible instead of crawling upon the ground."

But dismay over George did not prevent Adams from remaining cheerful and relaxed in England—so much so that he put aside his demand that his sons must turn into prodigies. Not only did this suddenly genial outlook bring him to participate in the family's games, music, outings, and other fun; it also led him to send an important bulletin to his parents. He told them that he was now willing to accept his sons as they were. "We must be content to take children for children."

A remarkable turnabout had brought forward a pleasing side of John Quincy Adams that was rarely forthcoming. He found himself so comfortable being minister to England and having his family beside him that his submerged cheerfulness surfaced. The prime result was a switch to being an indulgent parent as he overcame the disappointing discovery that his sons shared a fervent desire "to escape from study."

What was important was that they were good boys, he assured himself. And so he resolved to take comfort from the "reflection that they are like other children." He wrote his father and mother that he was now content that his sons would be no different in life than "other men." Their father's transformation must have delighted the young Adamses, but it would last only until the family returned to America.

JQA's startlingly sanguine attitude strengthened as his stay in England continued to bring him the most satisfying circumstances he would ever enjoy. Not that he was entirely transformed. He still had trouble governing his temper, but he began to apologize to his diary, if not publicly, for any outburst. When a carriage maker angered him, he replied harshly, but swiftly repented. "I spoke unadvisedly with my lips," he acknowledged, and added, "it is unworthy of me for such a trifle to be put out of temper." The next day, when he caught a culprit trying to pick his pocket, Adams was able to shrug it off as "another kind of British hostility."

A shouting match with an uncooperative bank clerk reminded Adams how rarely his "reasoning" and his "style" had satisfied his associates in Ghent. He now resolved to pursue his duties in England humbly and cautiously, claiming that experiences with Clay and Gallatin had taken away his "self-sufficiency" and weakened his confidence in being able either to convince an antagonist or to satisfy "those whose cause I would support."

IN THIS UNPRECEDENTED MOOD, Adams carried forward his ministerial duties, hoping he would not be deficient in zeal. He soon got on well with the prime minister, Lord Liverpool, and became actually chummy with Lord Castlereagh, the foreign minister. He also enjoyed his chats with George Canning, whom he thought the ablest member of the British cabinet but whose motives he suspected. Meanwhile, the Lord Mayor of London, a supporter of America and other liberal causes, made a great display of patronizing Adams. In all these personal relationships, John's newfound graciousness and amiable style served him—and the United States—well.

Except for greeting visiting Americans, issuing passports, and looking after modest commercial matters, the U.S. minister had few official tasks besides attending dinners, balls, and receptions. The stylish dining time of 7 p.m., which the British upper classes recently had adopted, annoyed Adams only occasionally, just as his complaints were mild when the late hours compelled him sometimes to remain in London overnight. He seemed to delight in most of the dinners to which he, and often Louisa, were invited, and his diary regularly came alive with evaluations of the conversation, the menu, and particularly the wines that could grace an evening.

Given his pleasure in these surroundings, Adams more than once relaxed his vigilance over what he contributed to conversations. Such unguarded moments sometimes brought self-reproach. After a particularly agreeable affair at the palatial residence of Lord Holland, where John had delighted in the wines and the dessert—the Hollands were reputed to have the best confectioners in London—he became so comfortable during table talk that "I offended Count and Countess Lievensky by bluntly saying that I had never known such a thing as hot weather in Russia."

As if this were not enough to regret, he went on at the Hollands to utter "two or three silly things" to the historian Sir James McIntosh. By this, he meant that he had teased the scholar over his excessively delicate treatment of legitimacy in the story of the English royal line. At this point Adams awoke to his missteps and became "altogether still and dull beyond my usual measure." This restraint lasted until he was revived by a discussion of Methodism and the tendency of the Anglican clergy to omit the Athanasian Creed. He was astonished to hear one noble lady admit that she would attend Methodist chapel if she could be sure of not being recognized.

The conversation grew so fascinating that it was necessary for Lord Holland's servants to remind Adams that his carriage was waiting. Much abashed, he rushed off, remembering that Louisa, who had attended another event, was to have called for him at 11 p.m. He found a very sleepy spouse, who pointed out that the time was long past midnight.

Even after Parliament rose, the Adamses' nightly calendar remained overbooked. Some occasions were particularly memorable. John recorded a special commendation for the turtle and venison served by the duke of Clarence at St. James's Palace, although "the wines were merely good." The conversation was better, however, for he was seated next to the archbishop of York, who entertained him with tales of King George III, at that moment still technically on the throne after nearly sixty years. The bishop disclosed that the monarch's mental illness kept him confined, that he wore a long white beard, and that the pitiful king was nearly blind but insisted on playing a piano kept badly out of tune.

Undoubtedly, Adams' favorite events were those sponsored by Lord Mayor Wood, where the American minister was the only foreign diplomat invited. John good-humoredly described how he had gently been put in his place at one of these evenings. The occasion, honoring the heroic duke of Wellington, had begun badly for Adams when he arrived in frock coat only to find all other guests in court attire. After apologizing for "being in undress," he was taken to greet the guest of honor. Immediately, John assured the duke that they had met previously, to which the hero of Waterloo replied, "Oh! yes . . . at Paris." Always one to correct the record, John shook his head. "No. At the Prince Regent's last levee," he said, adding that the duke's brother had introduced them. "Oh! Aye! Yes!" Wellington gamely but vaguely murmured, leaving Adams to concede that the duke had "forgotten me. . . . This is one of the many incidents from which I can perceive how very small a space my person or my station occupy in the notice of these persons and at these places."

Nevertheless, when his turn came after dinner to offer a toast, Adams showed the other cheek by rising to praise the duke's kinsman Charles Bagot, who was serving at the time as England's minister to the United States. This drew a very civil mention of Adams by Wellington, whom the American minister had observed closely during the long dinner and the toasts afterward. As flattery was endlessly "spread" over the duke, John noted how the hero had met a foe perhaps more formidable than Napoleon: drowsiness. Wellington unabashedly yawned like a character John recalled from Rossini's opera *The Barber of Seville*.

The Adamses, of course, were hosts to many dinners, both in Ealing and in London. Not that John was always mindful of such obligations. During one enjoyable talk, he and Lord Castlereagh forgot the time until after 5 p.m.; when he reached home, John found ten guests assembled for dinner and awaiting him. While he did not report what Louisa said to him afterward, he did record that the two were up early the next morning to begin an all-day barge party given by the lord mayor. A group of one hundred was rowed from Westminster Bridge to Richmond, where a splendid cold dinner was served amid music "in the highest style of excellence." So many toasts were drunk that JQA seemed not to mind that he had to deliver one.

Adams could usually count on his secretary to manage the diplomatic business, making it unnecessary for him to go into London more than a few hours every other day. But after six months of this comfortable schedule, the arrangement suddenly seemed threatened when John learned, to his consternation, that Madison had approved a permanent secretary for the legation: the minister's nephew and Billy Smith's brother, John Adams Smith. He got the job thanks to the latest intervention by Abigail Adams, who ignored John's warning that he wanted nothing more to do with nepotism.

Having put up with Billy Smith in St. Petersburg, John and Louisa dreaded that the second of Nabby's sons was to join their circle in England. But as the president of the United States had approved Smith, the minister had to surrender—only to find that his good fortune stood fast. This Smith proved to be an intelligent, diligent, honest assistant who eventually went on to a successful career in the diplomatic service. His reliable work in London made JQA's days in Ealing even more relaxed during 1816.

Smith arrived in December 1815, just as Adams had recovered

from the one misfortune marring the London stay. Two months earlier, he had purchased a pair of pistols from his sons' fencing master, believing that the boys needed more experience with the manly arts than they had received in America. In undertaking to teach George and John how to load and fire the weapons, JQA made a near-fatal mistake. Failing to notice that the pistol in his hand already carried a charge of powder, he added a second. Then, with the boys standing by, he fired. The pistol erupted in flame, flew a distance of ten feet, and left John's right hand badly burned and his eyes injured.

During the ensuing weeks, he lived in misery, partly from pain, but mostly because he was unable to read or write. Eventually his eye caused so much anguish that he could not even sit quietly as Louisa read aloud. He neither slept nor ate for several days, particularly after suffering six leeches to be applied to his eyelid, where most hung on for an hour. "It seemed to me that four hooks were tearing that side of my face into four quarters," Adams wrote, but he assured his journal that he had not cried out in pain.

In desperation, he consulted London's most famous oculist, Dr. Travers, who urged him to wash the eye with rosewater and await nature's healing. It was sound, if simple, advice. Soon the damage was repaired, the pain subsided, and Adams began to enjoy Louisa's reading aloud, which was for her the pleasant moment among the otherwise grim nursing duties she had skillfully performed for her stricken husband.

She chose to comfort him by reading from Sir Walter Scott, especially his recently published *Guy Mannering* and *Waverly*. After finishing these, the Adamses took up Maria Edgeworth's *Tales from Fashionable Life*. At first, John found it "tiresome," but he soon recanted and announced: "There is no modern English novel writer whom I think comparable to Miss Edgeworth." He admired her portrait of reality and her moral lessons about rising social evils, and she endeared herself to the Adamses by praising the merit of diligence and vigorous work. What literature needed, John concluded, was "more of real life and less of romance."

As his vision gradually returned, JQA found himself once again drawn to works of religion and theology. This interest took up much of his letters home. He reminded his parents that, thanks to their pious instruction, he had never been pulled away from belief when he had faced temptations of infidelity early in life. Replying from his own position of comfort with eighteenth-century Deism, John Adams tried good-naturedly to lure his son into debating biblical fallibility but was refused. Since he had not studied Scripture thoroughly, JQA claimed, he preferred to rest on faith. "I am not called upon to be its judge."

But the senior Adams persisted. Finally, JQA conceded that he cautiously followed the doctrines of Trinitarianism and Calvinism, although, he added, "I do not approve their intolerance." He said he wanted no part of Unitarianism, whose leaders, such as Joseph Priestley, ranked Socrates with Jesus. JQA contended that this was absurd, much like equating "a farthing candle with the Sun!" He challenged his father to read Bishop Massillon's sermon on the divinity of Christ, "after which be a Socinian if you can." For himself, JQA said he would be guided by faith and quipped to his father: "I hope you will not think me in danger of perishing everlastingly, for believing too much."

These genial commentaries upon his religious faith marked the summit of John's happiness in England. Never again would he be so relaxed about himself, the world, and the hereafter. During this wonderful but all too brief time, he did not feel endangered by his own folly or by the malice of others. Sensing that he was blessed with a rare moment, he made the most of it, particularly as he began writing verse with a zeal that was astonishing, even for him.

By October 1816, Adams was giving all his time to composing poems. "Could I have chosen my own genius and condition, I should have made myself a great poet." He wrote even during sittings for the portrait painter Charles Robert Leslie, or while riding between London and Ealing two or three times a week, or while pretending to listen as an Anglican clergyman droned in the pulpit, or even during bouts of insomnia. But he feared that his attempts fell far short and that he was "spell bound in the circle of mediocrity."

This latest obsession had begun after Louisa asked her husband to compose some lines in tribute to Ellen Nicholas, one of several attractive daughters born to the master of the academy where the Adams boys were students. The Nicholas and Adams families had become very friendly, gathering almost nightly to sing together, accompanied by harp and piano, and to read poetry. When John obligingly produced the verses requested, they drew such high praise from all sides that the delighted author decided to continue writing.

"The poetic fountain spouts through all its pipes," he said as he proceeded to compose lines honoring not only individuals but also some of the virtues he revered. The closing stanza of "Justice, an Ode" is one notable example:

Yet shall not Justice always wear
The garb of punishment, or bear
The avenging sword to smite,
Nor Mercy's ever gladdening eye
Permit the Ruffian to defy
The unerring Rule of Right.

Not all of his verses were so solemn. He acknowledged that some of his compositions were "amatory" in nature, lines such as a young lover might concoct. These he was careful not to share with the young Nicholas ladies.

He kept this up until late autumn, working night and day. "This evening after retiring to bed nearly at midnight, my thoughts were involuntarily worrying for a rhyme til sleep threatened to jilt me for the night." Not until rumors about himself began to arrive from America did the poet put his pen aside, taking pride in the many lines he had written. Adams saw them as an example of what he could achieve by persevering.

LATE IN 1816, travelers reaching London from New York and Philadelphia brought news that James Monroe, newly elected president, would name John Quincy Adams to "the best office in the gift of the administration"—or so Adams called the post of secretary of state. While he acknowledged that these reports were only rumors, in his journal he sounded like a believer as he made the obligatory remarks about how he lacked the abilities and temperament needed for the job. He spoke of being disinclined to accept and of how he must give no appearance of crediting the reports until an official invitation came from Monroe, which he acknowledged he expected momentarily.

The possibility that JQA would join Monroe's cabinet dispelled the cheerful spirits in the Adams household. Although she had been the soul of health and good humor since coming to England, Louisa now became despondent and ill. If her husband reentered American politics, she was certain that the attentiveness he had been showing his family would give way to the grim self-preoccupation that had been his style as a politician.

And indeed, rumors of his cabinet appointment began pushing Adams back to his stolid and impatient ways, particularly after no word from Monroe arrived to confirm the rumors. Knowing how mortifying it would be if the report proved baseless, John was left in his first unsettled and anxious state of mind since leaving Ghent. Talk of depression was heard once again. The chance that he might be summoned to the American political scene had broken open the deep schism within him: one side detested politics while the other found it irresistible.

To make matters worse, the early spring of 1817 in London was more damp, dark, and foggy than usual, so that prudent pedestrians carried lighted candles. It was amid this gloom, while Adams' spirits were at their lowest since the death of his daughter in St. Petersburg, that his suspense ended. On April 16, a letter arrived from Monroe, "informing me that he had with the sanction of the Senate committed to me the Department of State." It was, John observed, "a trust of weight and magnitude." Knowing that he was laying aside the recent joys of reading, of writing poetry, and even of fishing in Ealing's Grand Central Canal, he quickly dispatched his letter of acceptance.

Having agreed to enter Monroe's administration, Adams put the best light possible on his decision. He assured himself that the president had acted not from political pressures but from a regard for the public's interest. The thought was essential for JQA's self-respect. Was he not reentering political life because the chief executive considered him the best person for the job? He insisted on this interpretation as reports began arriving that partisan considerations had compelled Monroe to name a New Englander as secretary of state. Such talk brought Adams once again to avow that he took a public office only when the sordid side of politics had not been involved. Despite his successes in St. Petersburg and London, he could still delude himself.

He now undertook quickly to return to the United States. After he and Louisa moved into London to prepare for sailing, he fortified himself against the political harshness ahead by spending many memorable hours with a new friend, Jeremy Bentham. One of England's leading intellectuals and social critics and the founder of Utilitarianism, Bentham styled himself as a "radical reformist." His latest statement, *Catechism of Reform*, had just been published, to Adams' great interest.

Bentham sought out John immediately after the Adamses returned to the city, invited him to dine at his home in St. James Park, engaged him in lively conversation, and persuaded him to join in three- to five-hour walks every other morning before breakfast. At first taken aback by Bentham's startling ideas about social change, which the Englishman conceded would require civil war to implement, Adams was soon captivated by the scholar's brilliant talk. The only topic on which they were reserved was religion. When John announced that he was a Christian believer, his atheistically disposed friend changed the subject.

After his long sessions with Bentham, the rush of packing and farewell courtesies left little time to record anything more than fragments of the pair's discourse. However, after they had conversed without interruption during a twelve-mile walk made on empty stomachs, Adams did take a moment to mention the vigor of this man in his seventieth year who appeared fresh while John, not yet fifty, was exhausted. The American observed that while most ardent reformers he had known "are accompanied by an equal portion of dulness," Jeremy Bentham was the exception. Sorrowfully, Adams reminded himself that no one like Bentham would be waiting to walk with him in the United States.

Nor could he expect America to match London's stunning performances of Mozart's operas then under way, which John and Louisa attended amid their packing. *Don Giovanni* pleased John, who found the music "delicious to my ear," though he predicted that the opera would soon vanish from public view. He also reserved a few hours to listen one last time to debates in Parliament, and to enjoy a long visit from George Canning. He had a farewell chat with Lord Castlereagh, who warmly congratulated him on his appointment and expressed regret that it meant he must depart England—sentiments a pleased Adams felt he must dismiss in his diary as mere form.

Looking at the stacks of books, pamphlets, and papers to be boxed, Adams was incredulous at what he had accumulated in eight years abroad. "I have had all my life a passion for collecting books, of which I now feel the vanity." The library, however, was only part of the challenge. There was also the furniture acquired in Russia and England. This must go to Washington, for he had agreed to establish his principal residence in the federal capital. The plan created "embarrassing" expenses, but Adams' only gesture toward thrift was to leave much of his wine cellar—560 bottles of claret and 298 of champagne—to be sold.

The ship chosen for the voyage to New York was the *Washington;* the Adamses had exclusive use of the entire aft cabin, which Louisa had arranged to be as comfortable as possible. The party included John, Louisa, their three sons, two maids, and their household manager, Antoine Guista. The best bargain the new secretary of state could drive with Captain Forman was 37 guineas per person, plus two pounds sterling for every ton of baggage and furniture. It was a formidable load. On one day alone, the family's carriage and thirty-one trunks, barrels, and boxes were placed aboard, leaving much more to come.

On June 10, Adams wrote: "I bid adieu to London in all probability forever." The family waited at Cowes, on the Isle of Wight, for storms to abate, sailing on June 15. Thereafter, the *Washington* seemed never to outrun foul weather. So rough were the waves that once again even JQA came close to seasickness, and his loss of sleep did not help him contain his anger when he found himself regularly beaten at chess by other passengers.

The game was the only pastime that he found kept his attention, even though he had renounced it in Europe because losing left him enraged with himself and his adversary—defeat "mortifies my pride beyond endurance." Hoping to attain some self-control, he began to study chess openings in books he found in the ship's library and was grateful to note some slight improvement in his game. Yet rage at losing continued "to a degree bordering upon madness." He feared that since chess was such a "painful test of intellect," it affected his emotions too much to be sport.

The most memorable event of the voyage occurred on July 11, one of the few calm sailing days as well as JQA's fiftieth birthday. Since his commanding presence at the dining table had made him well known to everyone aboard, a birthday celebration was called for. It brought a welcome change amid the tedium at sea. Even those traveling in steerage sent him a message of congratulation, along with stanzas composed and sung in his honor by a poet at dinner below. The crew saluted the secretary of state–designate and received a generous portion of grog in return.

None of this, however, diverted Adams from his usual birthday speculations about what should be his aims in life. The thought inspired him to exchange chess for deeper study of a book of Biblical commentary he had brought along. He began discussing religion with others on board, and when a "scoffer" became sarcastic, John promptly gave his reasons "for the faith that is within me." The scene led another passenger to share privately with him a wish to explain miracles by natural causes. The encounter set Adams to wondering why others could not accept that the entire Bible was a succession of miracles from beginning to end, "and that if any one of them is admitted, it is dealing with trifles to contend about any other."

As its occupants passed the time with the conversations, chess games, male bathing in barrels of seawater, fishing, reading, and dozing, the *Washington* slowly made its way toward North America. Finally, the Adamses disembarked in New York City on August 6, after "an absence of eight full and eventful years." They found the city suffering under overpowering heat, but the weather did not prevent them from lingering. John received many callers and attended a dinner in his honor given at Tammany Hall at which Governor DeWitt Clinton presided. His escort to the dinner was the merchant and fur trader John Jacob Astor, whose interests in the Far West made him eager to cultivate the man who would lead the State Department.

After another notable dinner, the Adamses departed for New England on August 16, although not without vexation. They had missed their first ride on a steamboat, one bound for Providence, because, as John admitted, "by some negligence of mine which I should think inexcusable in another, I mistook the hour." Instead of shepherding his family to the wharf, he had been writing in the early morning until his sons pounded on the door. The mistake meant that the family had to take an evening boat, which relied on wind rather than steam. Until sailing time, JQA played chess with his sons in order to escape "as well as I could from my reflections."

Three weeks of ceaseless socializing followed the Adamses' return to Quincy. While John was warmly welcomed, of course, by his parents and other kinfolk, it was a moment of special triumph for Louisa. Where once she had been coldly treated by a scornful Abigail Adams, now the matriarch embraced her with affection and admiration—particularly for the courage she had shown in traveling with little Charles from St. Petersburg to Paris.

For JQA, the hospitality showered upon him by the many Jeffersonian citizens of Boston demonstrated once more that he was not the political outcast he sometimes claimed to be. Amid the dinners, including a public occasion with two hundred guests and other gatherings that drew half that number, he broke away when possible to view the changes in the city. The only sight he regretted was the turning of Beacon Hill into a residential area.

He had one important duty before departing for Washington: an effort to enroll George in Harvard. But the young man was still poorly prepared. Nevertheless, with perhaps a last glimmer of the fatherly tolerance he had briefly shown in England, John tried to persuade his former faculty colleagues to admit his sixteen-year-old son to the sophomore class. When the professors pronounced George clearly unready, a disappointed JQA arranged tutoring at $2 a week while George boarded with a Cambridge academic family.

As for sons John and Charles, they would attend the Boston Latin School once their father had talked at length with headmaster Benjamin Gould about their weaknesses.

These family matters took time, as did "a continual round of dissipation by the greetings and kind reception of our friends," which left JQA little opportunity to study his property and finances. Besides the land in Quincy, there were five residential parcels in Boston. Tom Adams had charge of these investments and real estate holdings, but his records were found to be woefully incomplete.

This once uncharacteristic negligence on Tom's part stemmed from his having fallen prey to alcoholism, the disorder that had carried off brother Charles Adams in 1800. John now found in Tom the same distressing behavior he remembered from his experience with Charles: no answer to inquiries about the funds and property left in his care.

Quincy was a more somber place for John and Louisa for another reason. Nabby Smith was missing from the family's reunion. She had died of cancer in 1813, three years before the death of her husband.

On September 9, the Adamses said farewell to Quincy, stopping in Boston for one more evening of entertainment; they boarded the southbound stagecoach at noon the next day. John had taken care to bring with him a new personal seal, one he designed and had cut while in London. It depicted a lyre and an eagle surrounded by thirteen stars representing the original states. The motto, Nunc Sidem Ducit, was from Manilius' *Astronomica* and was chosen, as John translated it, to impart a sense of John's reverence for the Union:

> *Now of the starry orbs, it leads the course,*
> *Extends its charms to Heaven's remotest bound,*
> *and rolling, whirls the Universe around.*

BEFORE THE NEXT EIGHT YEARS were over, Adams as secretary of state would propel the Union westward—perhaps not across Heaven, but to the continent's farthest corner.

BOOK FOUR

Faltering Ideals

1817–1829

. . . in which despair seems never far from success.

CHAPTER TEN

Secretary

The path before me is beset with thorns.

THE WORST MOMENTS of Adams' trip from Boston to Washington were at the outset. Amid intense heat, he and Louisa started by stagecoach for Connecticut on September 11, 1817. Although the dust annoyed them, John admitted that he was "musing the greater part of the day." Would his new career in Washington allow him to be a statesman, or would he be sullied by partisanship?

During the reassuring months in London, Adams had managed to suppress the painful knowledge that he, like his father, was at heart a political fighter, one for whom partisanship was as natural as breathing. He had acknowledged this to Tom Adams when declining the Supreme Court appointment. But now, en route to Washington, he dared to hope that the lofty atmosphere of the State Department would enable him to perform wonderful deeds for the nation and the world—without having to give in to his partisan impulses.

Relief from these disturbing thoughts came when the Adamses reached New London and took their first ride on a steamboat. Fascinated by the experience, John reported in amazement that the vessel covered the fifty miles to New Haven in only eleven hours, fighting a strong tide and using five cords of wood. From there to New York City took just over nine hours. The *Indian Queen* then carried the Adamses to Philadelphia, puffing along at eight miles per hour. An awed JQA acclaimed steam-powered travel, saying that it "far surpasses my highest expectation."

Most of the journey to Washington kept him surprised at the

progress the United States had made while he was abroad. He saw at firsthand the advances his grandson, the historian Henry Adams, would describe so brilliantly seventy years later in his *History of the United States during the Administrations of Thomas Jefferson and James Madison.* In the eight years since the Adamses had left for St. Petersburg, the nation's population had risen from approximately seven million to nearly nine million. The mid-Atlantic region, which John observed closely while en route to the capital, had almost doubled its inhabitants in that time, despite the unhappy effects of the War of 1812.

An increase of national wealth was apparent in the many newly constructed roads, canals, factories, and dwellings John and Louisa saw as they noted the spread of towns and cities. Trade seemed to bustle everywhere. Exports had increased by 100 percent since the close of the war. With a surplus in the Treasury, Congress recently had debated creating federal roads, canals, and other improvements, which many politicians believed would add even more speed to prosperity. President Madison had opposed such legislation, but Adams would have no such qualms about the use of federal power.

After arriving in Washington on September 20, the Adamses settled temporarily in the Nathaniel Frye household, the hospitable Walter Hellen having died in 1810. Frye had recently married Louisa's younger sister Carolina, the widow of Andrew Buchanan. Later, John and Louisa would remove to a residence they rented in Four and a Half Street, a mile from the White House and a shorter distance from the Capitol. They remained there for three years until they purchased a house on F Street.

As soon as he had greeted the Fryes, an eager Adams rushed to call upon James Monroe. The president had just moved into the executive mansion, where the damage caused by British troops in 1814 had finally been repaired, and John found him distracted by a fear of vapors from the fresh paint. But the two were able to review important international concerns before Adams set out to find Richard Rush, who had nominal charge of the State Department. They talked until nearly midnight, when John returned to the Frye residence. So exhilarated was he that before retiring he composed verses honoring this moment in his career:

> *O God, my only trust was thou*
> *Through all life's scenes before:*
> *Lo, at thy throne again I bow,*
> *New mercies to implore.*

. . .

Extend, all-seeing God, thy hand,
In mercy still decree,
And make to bless my native land
An instrument of me.

Then came the dawn, and with it began Adams' discovery of the realities he faced in Washington. An early visit from George Boyd, husband of Louisa's sister Harriet, brought the gossip going around the capital. Boyd was a minor government functionary who took pride in knowing all the political rumors, and his account quickly deflated John's anticipation of being a divine instrument for national good. The incoming secretary of state was left worrying "that the path before me is beset with thorns."

After listening to other callers, Adams knew by day's end that although America might have improved physically while he was abroad, Washington politics promised to prove more devilish than ever. It would be a hazardous place for high-minded ideals. One of the perils Boyd had mentioned arose from a shift of power in the government. Congress was now under the leadership of strong personalities— primarily Henry Clay—who hoped to control national and international policy, a design that, in Adams' view, would upset the sacred principle of balance among the three branches of government.

Pondering such revelations, a disillusioned Adams prepared to take the oath of secretary of state. "At two distinct periods of my life heretofore," he reflected, "my position has been perilous and full of anxious forecasts, but never so critical and perilous as at this time." To prove the point, he himself got off to an uncertain start when, immediately after the swearing-in, he agreed to keep Daniel Brent on as his chief clerk. Brent had powerful friends in Washington, and the political animal in Adams realized that it would be easier to keep than release him. He did not know that Brent had a habit of often staying home, claiming illness.

No partisan reality, however, could make Adams name nephew Billy Smith to a junior clerkship. Vowing that he would not place any relation in office, he stood against not only Smith but the entire family, all of whom "were up in arms against me about it." Not even Abigail Adams could make him yield, as he pointed to Billy's miserable performance as a secretary in St. Petersburg.

Actually, assembling a staff was a comparatively modest problem. The greater nuisance was the procession of callers interrupting the new secretary's effort to refine procedures followed by the foreign service and to bring order from the chaos he inherited in the department's records and library. Visitors were always vexatious when Congress was in session: members seemed to enjoy spending their mornings at the desks of cabinet officers, where most of the government's patronage was dispensed.

To avoid wasting so much time with these loungers, Adams began appearing at the State Department around noon, after the House and Senate were in session, and he remained when the office closed at 3 p.m. to clear his desk. At 5 or 6, he took documents to the president and then went home to dine. The rest of the evening and the next morning were normally given to writing. At midday he stopped in at the White House, as Monroe had instructed him to do; as Adams' predecessor in the State Department, the president wished to keep a proprietary interest in its business.

John soon recognized that Monroe intended to treat all his cabinet members as little more than flunkies. Meeting with them frequently as a group and more often individually, the chief executive found delegation of authority tiresome and seemed set upon making all the decisions, important and otherwise. This arrangement may have been Monroe's way of compensating: since Congress was determined to push him around, he could at least be forceful within his own domain. While John learned to live with the president's methods, he could not restrain himself from an occasional wry reference to "my daily report" at the executive mansion.

Also, he grew accustomed to Monroe's annoying habit of invariably insisting on some change in the content or the style of the official letters and statements Adams would labor to perfect before submitting to him. On the whole, however, the State Department got on comfortably with Monroe, for John deferred to the president's abilities and to his office.

Congress appeared less respectful of Adams and his post. He may have held the second-highest position in the nation, but he was underpaid. When he took the job, his salary was $3,500 per year, which Congress increased to $6,000 in 1819. There would have been a raise in pay enacted a year earlier, except that—according to Louisa—two senators became so inebriated, they could not return to their seats in time to provide the votes needed to pass the salary bill. Since the family's expenses exceeded his stipend, Adams had to dig into his own pocket to meet them.

The president's style and a low salary posed far less serious problems for John than the hazards created by cabinet colleagues and by certain congressmen and senators. It was evident that many of the leading politicians in the capital were bent on succeeding Monroe in the election eight years hence. Since the Department of State had traditionally housed the person most likely to be the next chief executive—Jefferson, Madison, and Monroe all served successively in the office—Adams was the individual whom all contenders felt they had to push out of the way before 1824.

Aware that the presidential aspirants, several of whom he must meet on a daily basis, would now aim to diminish his stature, Adams admitted that this "new scene" forced him to adopt "new views of the political world." He saw at once that his most vexatious enemy was familiar to him, Kentucky's Henry Clay, Speaker of the House of Representatives. In 1815, Clay had returned to the United States from Ghent determined to become secretary of state. After his election, Monroe, who believed Adams was the appropriate choice, offered Clay the War Department. The Kentuckian declined, preferring to try to direct foreign policy from Capitol Hill. It was a tactic promising nothing but trouble for Adams.

As if Clay's opposition were not enough, John had other active adversaries. These included William H. Crawford of Georgia, secretary of the treasury; Vice President Daniel D. Tompkins of New York; and the governor of New York, DeWitt Clinton. The aspirations of the secretary of war, John C. Calhoun of South Carolina, remained unclear. At this point, there was little talk about General Andrew Jackson as president.

Efforts to undermine the secretary of state took place even during cabinet meetings. The political maneuvering there, along with opposition under Clay's direction in Congress, seemed designed—at least according to Adams—to interrupt the progress of his diplomacy or to put his efforts in a lurid light. He believed that Crawford and his allies were willing even to thwart international negotiations if that would eliminate Adams as a rival for the presidency. "Oh! the windings of the human heart," John complained as he wondered how far these politicians might go in their effort "to decry me as much as possible in the public opinion."

Noticing during cabinet meetings that Crawford often advanced preposterous proposals just to annoy the secretary of state and draw him into the discussion, Adams mused: "I ought to lay it down as a rule to myself never to oppose any opinion advanced by Crawford in the Cabinet when I know that without my opposition the President will not adopt it." Upon further reflection, he added: "Perhaps it would be well to extend the rule to what is said by any other member of the administration—to avoid every conflict of opinion when it is unnecessary to effect the result, and to leave absurdity to die a natural death."

Friends who took an interest in the 1824 election were also a nuisance, as John discovered. At the outset, he had insisted to intimates that he had no wish to be president. Some of these persons, however, were not easily put off. Adams' young friend, the rising editor Alexander H. Everett, took courage in March 1818 and asked him if "I was determined to do nothing with a view to promote my future election to the Presidency as the successor of Mr. Monroe." Everett received a stern reply. John told him that he indeed would do "absolutely nothing." His business, he proclaimed, was to serve the public in the State Department.

Those who spoke about the presidency with John must have come away bemused at the ease with which an Adams could convert naïveté into bravado. With a loftiness of tone that not even the Founding Fathers had attained, he kept assuring himself and his friends that the office of president should be "spontaneously bestowed." He admitted to no one, and rarely to himself, a hope that some public servant—and particularly the secretary of state—might so benefit the nation in a selfless manner that the electorate would demand that he become chief executive. Probably, Adams' pose covered the familiar fear of failure that always dogged him. It was a dreadful thought, indeed, to seek the presidency openly and then fall short as all the nation and his parents watched.

Of course, JQA was not as hopelessly impractical as this implies. He was willing to try to keep the public well-disposed toward him; there were, it turned out, certain wholesome steps he could take toward that end. For example, he acknowledged that he must begin a more socially active life in order "to repel a reproach which has been very assiduously spread abroad of a reserved, gloomy, unsocial temper as belonging to my character." Because he was, according to himself, "a man of reserved, cold, austere, and forbidding manners," he said it was easy for his foes to portray him as "a gloomy misanthropist" and "an unsocial savage."

These depictions of Adams, which were to be widely circulated as part of the 1824 campaign, have captured the imagination of historians at the expense of the intervals when he showed those charming qualities usually kept hidden. He was the first to agree that his demeanor was defective when it came to public life. Alas, he said, "I have not the pliability to reform it." The responsibility for his being such a "silent animal," he asserted, should be fixed on his mother, who had so strenuously insisted that "children in company should be seen and not heard" that her oldest son became confirmed in the "bad habit" of accepting conversation as a waste of time.

By "conversation" Adams meant mostly social chitchat. When something valuable might be derived from talking with another person, as with Bentham in London, he could continue the discourse endlessly. Another situation where talking usually struck John as worthwhile was when he sat, as he often did, for sculptors and artists, particularly Pietro Cardelli, Charles Bird King, and Gilbert Stuart. Many painters appeared in Washington or Boston intent on capturing the likeness of this notable American, considered likely by some to be the next president. Adams was always quite willing to converse as work in the studio went on.

In exchanges with other diplomats he was known for his eloquence and persuasiveness. Usually, he took this sort of talk for granted as part of his calling. But he was not always pleased when he allowed himself to dominate after-dinner conversation. Afterward, he would complain, as he had in England, that he had "talked too much" and regretted a great deal of what he had said. Yet, as a public figure, what alternative did he have? "In the estimation of others, I pass off on the whole better when I talk freely than when silent and reserved."

To his discomfiture, his supporters had no end of suggestions about how he ought to behave. "My friends earnestly urge me to mingle more in society and to make myself more extensively known." But to do so, he had to pay a high personal price. "I am scarcely ever satisfied with myself after going into company and always have the impression that my time at home is more usefully spent."

Adams thought wistfully of how much happier he would be as a professor, a poet, or a scientist. After a "painful" first year as secretary of state, he even doubted "whether my appointment was for my own good or for that of my country." He was convinced that life in the State Department made him more a political lightning rod than an architect of international policy. Of his summons to the office, a disgusted Adams would announce: "As yet I have far more reason to lament than to rejoice at the event." Indeed, "I wish every hour of my life he [Clay] had succeeded in keeping me from it."

FORTUNATELY, THE SECRETARY soon overcame his early disgust. By the close of Monroe's first term in 1821, Adams was taking pride in what his office had accomplished. He could see that under his leadership the United States had registered important achievements in foreign affairs. Looking back over these first four years, he admitted that the record brought him "satisfaction, solid and pure." He had managed the department well, overseeing many reforms in organization, creating a library, preparing early state papers for publication, and guiding the office's removal to a new building in the autumn of 1819.

There, he had even been prepared to be a firefighter, as on the night he was awakened by a commotion outside. When he realized that the State Department building might be ablaze, he was up, dressed, and on his way to the scene. Relieved to find that the burning structure was across the street from State, he nevertheless remained on guard in his office until 5 a.m. lest sparks be carried across to his building.

The wait provided a quiet time to think along familiar lines: how he hoped to do marvelous things for humanity and how he wished to accomplish them outside of politics. "Literature has been the charm of my life," he mused, no matter that "the operations of my mind are slow, my imagination sluggish." Would he ever produce "some great work of literature" that would permit him "to have lived in the gratitude of future ages"?

Then, with morning light and the fire across the street put out, he came back to earth. He acknowledged that for now it must be foreign affairs by which he would serve mankind—even though later that morning the State Department waiting room would be jammed with congressmen and strangers arguing in behalf of some worthy friend's appointment to a consular or secretarial post.

Despite this prospect and stimulated by a night of standing guard, Adams went home to prepare for the day ahead, determined that political intrusions should never take him "helter-skelter" through a second term in the department "and leave no permanent trace of my ever having been in it." The confidence in his outlook came from knowing that by then, late in 1820, he had made lasting achievements as secretary of state.

Mainly, the diplomatic attainments between 1817 and 1821 involved overcoming long-standing dangers in the United States' relations with its two competitors on the North American continent, England and Spain. Adams had turned first to some of the prickly questions between England and the U.S. that had been left unanswered in Ghent. With the capable assistance of Richard Rush, who had gone to London as his successor, John oversaw the negotiations leading to the Treaty of 1818. This agreement established the northwest boundary between the United States and Canada at the 49th parallel to the Rocky Mountains, and left the region beyond open to citizens of both nations.

Almost as important was the treaty's reaffirmation that Americans could fish off the coasts of Newfoundland and Labrador. It also renewed a commercial understanding between Great Britain and the United States, and agreed to leave for arbitration the claims of slave owners for property carried away by the British during the War of 1812.

The Treaty of 1818 served as prelude to Adams' even more notable accomplishment, the Transcontinental Treaty of 1819 with Spain, sometimes known as the Adams-Onis Treaty. Negotiations took place in Washington, John working directly with Luis de Onis y Gonzales, Spain's representative in the United States. The two grappled in the quiet of old-fashioned personal diplomacy, with the outcome often in doubt. Finally, however, their labor produced an agreement that pushed aside many of the barriers blocking America's march toward continental power.

One of these hindrances had been the presence of Spain in Florida. While West Florida had been owned by the United States since 1813, Spain occupied East Florida. From there, with some English aid, the Spanish seemed to be encouraging raids by the Seminole tribe into Georgia. In 1818, General Andrew Jackson led troops into Spanish Florida to seize troublesome posts and to execute two British traders said to have instigated attacks on the United States by the natives. Adams was the only cabinet member to insist that Jackson had acted properly. Despite Spain's indignation, Jackson's deed went unrebuked after Monroe realized that public opinion sided with the general.

Knowing Spain faced trouble enough in its Latin American colonies, Adams was not intimidated by its bluster. Through brilliant statesmanship in talks with Onis between February 12 and 20, 1819, he produced a treaty that the Senate praised and approved. The terms he secured included taking ownership of Florida for $5 million, to be paid to Americans who had claims against Spain. He gained a very favorable boundary between the Louisiana Purchase region and Spanish Texas, running along the Sabine, Red, and Arkansas rivers to the Continental Divide, where it turned west to the Pacific Ocean along the forty-second parallel. Spain agreed to surrender any claim to Oregon.

But then, after the Senate's unanimous endorsement, the earth seemed to collapse under the secretary of state. To Adams' everlasting mortification, Clay was the first person to discover a serious error in the treaty's Article VIII. With obvious pleasure, Clay notified Adams and Monroe that the document as written would allow two enormous Spanish grants of land recently made in Florida to be valid after the United States took possession.

John was aghast. During the negotiations with Onis, he had persuaded the Spaniard to fix the year 1802 as a deadline after which such land grants would be null and void—at least he believed that year had been agreed upon. Yet somehow a date of 1818, greatly advantageous to Spanish interests, had slipped into the document undetected by the usually eagle-eyed Adams.

The blunder made John furious with himself and pained for his country. He said the treaty was doomed to be "a magnificent abortion." While his enemies crowed and President Monroe spoke darkly of international fraud, Adams acknowledged how all along he had feared the treaty "was too great a blessing not to be followed shortly by something to alloy it." Although he claimed the sobering experience was sent to purge him of "all vanity and self-conceit," he moved at once to redeem the situation.

With the assistance of his friend Baron Jean-Guillaume Hyde de Neuville, the French ambassador, and the cooperation of Onis, the error in the treaty document eventually was corrected. Then the worry became whether the government in Madrid would agree to a modification so disadvantageous to Spain. As Adams waited uneasily for the decision, his anxiety produced one of the most amusing scenes in his tenure as secretary of state.

At 10 o'clock on an August night in 1819, Adams arrived in New York City on his way to a summer holiday in Quincy. When he learned that the helpful French ambassador was also in town, he set out to locate him, ignoring the late hour. Finding Hyde de Neuville at the French consul's residence, "I roused him from his bed and held a dialogue with him, standing at the door of his home, and he in his night cap with his head out of the chamber window."

It was like a scene from a Molière play, Adams admitted, as he explained to the sleepy baron that the untimely intrusion was only because he had to catch a steamboat for New England at dawn. After the comical conversation, however, John decided to postpone his departure, hoping for further encouraging talks with the optimistic French emissary.

Not until February 12, 1821, could the State Department breathe easily. On that day, Adams received a copy of the treaty with its vital modification intact and approved by the Spanish monarch. The Senate promptly endorsed the agreement, the two nations formally exchanged ratifications, and the United States took possession of much of the western half of the North American continent. Even so, Adams continued to smart from the experience, bitterly recalling how Henry Clay and others had "snickered" at his discomfiture.

ADAMS' CHAGRIN WAS DUE to more than the treaty episode. Throughout Monroe's first term, there had been other kinds of ill-spirited talk at the secretary's expense, spitefulness that grew from subjects not immediately involving politics and diplomacy.

Soon after settling into Washington, the Adamses discovered that intrigue percolated everywhere, which meant that social life in the capital was tainted by the partisan craftiness to which John claimed he was "utterly averse." After living abroad for eight years in two of the world's most sophisticated cities, he and Louisa had forgotten how suffocatingly provincial Washington was.

Certainly, getting around town was a shock to anyone who had been in St. Petersburg and London. In 1817 as in 1807, mud or dust in Washington's streets often made being a social animal hazardous, as much for sturdy gentlemen as for delicate ladies. Showing up at festive occasions could be a challenge, as the Adamses soon learned when their carriage tipped over in the mud's deep ruts. "It was a mercy that we all got home with whole bones," John reported.

When the same sort of accident flipped the French ambassador into the mud, his savage remarks about the misery of living in Washington were pardonable. In fact, there were many new faces in the capital each session, since congressmen and senators, along with foreign representatives, found life there so unpleasant that many refused to stay or return. Those who replaced them rarely made congenial company for the Adamses, who were accustomed to chatting with Europe's literary figures, not to mention czars, princesses, and dukes.

Given their natures and their experiences overseas, it was no surprise that John and Louisa acted as if they could live in Washington as independently as they wished. They did not appreciate how senators, congressmen, and other officials and their families valued social custom. What else was there for those who dwelt in the wretched village that was the seat of government for the United States of America?

Consequently, Washington gossips had a field day whispering about how the Adamses' time in Europe had left them haughty and proud of being different, particularly after John got out his strange Russian winter coat and hat. Such talk was used to advantage by Clay, who assured Monroe that Adams simply did not understand republican ways and that someone like Clay himself would make a better secretary of state. While Monroe was not taken in, many were so eager to proclaim the Adamses as more alien than American that even the wildest yarns about them were believed and repeated.

To John's utter astonishment, a year after he entered the cabinet, he was obliged to explain to an uneasy Monroe that there was no basis to the rumor that England's prince regent had asked him, Adams, to represent him at the christening of a baby born in Washington to the English minister Bagot and his wife.

This story had been fueled by animosity over an unpopular decision the Adamses had made barely four months after returning to the capital. They roused the indignation of the town's social elite when they decided that, regardless of what others in the cabinet might do, they would not undertake to call upon "every stranger who arrives" in Washington. This apparent snobbishness flew in the face of a custom dictating that cabinet members and their wives humble themselves by making the first visit to every member of Congress at the start of each session. For John, ignoring such a tradition promised to save time and avoid a tax on his limited fund of patience.

The decision, however, cost him far more interruption at the State Department and in his study than would have resulted from numerous perfunctory visits. The outcry over the Adamses' attitude was such that Louisa was summoned by Mrs. Monroe to explain herself. While the first lady claimed poor health as her own reason for being a recluse, she advised Louisa that previous secretaries of state and their wives had carefully initiated contact with anyone of consequence who appeared in the District. Unmoved, Louisa informed Mrs. Monroe that she would gladly return any visits paid to her, but that she would initiate calls only upon those persons she chose.

A group of hostile senators presented themselves at the Department of State to inquire sardonically whether the secretary was aware that a precious tradition was endangered. Why was he not continuing to call upon them? This encounter astounded John, just as Louisa had been surprised by Mrs. Monroe's severity. The Adamses did not appreciate that the uproar was due mostly to presidential politics until John learned that the wife of Treasury Secretary Crawford was steering her husband toward the presidency by herself being the first to call on all legislative wives who came to Washington. Mrs. Crawford knew that these women had husbands who would eventually choose the Republican party's presidential nominee in congressional caucus.

Disgusted, JQA watched as this maneuver brought the Adamses "into disgrace with all the members of congress who have wives here . . . and thus it is that this paltry passion for precedence works along." He called it the "senseless war of etiquette visiting." When the "caballing and intrigue" against him persisted, he felt obliged "in self-defense," as he put it, "to write a letter to the president and another to the vice president stating my principles, and my reasons for them."

Well before these letters were written, however, the Adamses had seized the initiative with a shrewd countermove by making their home a social center—although they were not always comfortable with certain unexpected visitors. Upon occasion, callers created mild sensations. Once, when JQA returned home after a long day at the office, he found three Osage Indians in his parlor. Since Big Bear, Big Road, and Black Spirit had come without an interpreter, they and the secretary sat solemnly looking at one another for a time, until the trio began to admire the furniture and lamps. Eventually the visitors departed, but not before they had marveled at the slender waist of one of Louisa's young nieces.

The Adamses wrested the initiative from their social critics by a single, dramatic stroke: they invited three hundred guests to a ball in late January 1818. The event, their first approach to Washington society, was a triumph. Since the capital's streets were unlighted, it was the sort of evening that made it risky for guests either to take a carriage or to walk. Nonetheless, two hundred brave persons managed to find their way through a very dark night to join in the dancing and games (though some suffered accidents en route).

Soon, John and Louisa were being applauded as hosts of some of the most successful social events in the town's memory. According to Louisa, her husband worried as much over an approaching party as he did over a treaty. The couple's victory was due mainly to Louisa's skill in planning entertainment, especially after she had shrewdly overseen the enlargement of a sizeable house Adams purchased with borrowed money in the autumn of 1820. (A portion of the building still stands at 1333–1335 F Street NW.) It proved a perfect place for large gatherings, while also containing a study for John and his books and papers.

Although the Adamses survived the storm over making social calls, John still had to contend with visitors to his office who rarely had more than their personal benefit in mind, no matter how carefully they might seek to disguise their motives. Members of Congress, callers from around the country, and even JQA's friends took up business hours with political talk. Their advice and warnings even followed the secretary home, where he glumly wished his study could afford the quiet he had enjoyed in St. Petersburg and Ealing. Interruptions and distractions were so numerous that he was sometimes left piteously calling for "more time, more time."

ADDED TO THESE OFFICIAL and social drains were new personal difficulties. Family cares in both Washington and Quincy seemed to multiply and often absorbed Adams after visitors cleared out of his office. When it came to kinfolk and money matters, he was as much a worrier as ever. Whether presiding at the State Department or working in his study at home, he rarely could banish from his mind a son's escapade, a brother's failure, a parent's infirmity, or some other personal worry. Chagrined that these troubles could weaken his official and intellectual efforts, he blamed it on "a gross and culpable want of Fortitude, for which I ask the forgiveness of Heaven, but which is its own punishment."

Once again, the conduct of his children made him anxious and irritable. He squirmed at the possibility that each son would fail the family's expectations—"May none of them ever realize my fears," he prayed. The tolerant view adopted in England was discarded, and his rigorous demands as a parent were restored. These could be distilled into a simple rhetorical question: excellence on a child's part was simply to be expected, was it not? Thus, it followed that George must prove himself worthy of Harvard, and John and Charles must meet the demanding requirements of Boston Latin.

Adams had felt personally insulted when Harvard consented to admit George only to the freshman class, steadfastly rejecting the advanced standing JQA claimed was deserved—had not he himself tutored George in England?

But, thanks to politics, there was now a deeper concern vexing Adams: he feared that laziness or imprudence by his offspring might be used to weaken his standing in public life. No wonder a skittish JQA was often impatient. When son John expressed hope that his father would forgive an occasional folly, the parent shot back: "I shall do no such thing. If my son will be rash he must take the consequences." While Adams might be eager to commend a son for achievement in learning or deportment, unfortunately he was usually so occupied by business that opportunities for praise passed unnoticed.

There was always time, however, to hand a son some favorite Adams motto, such as: "*Toil* is the price of all learning and all excellence."

In 1819, there having been no alarming filial sins, JQA allowed George and John, aged nineteen and seventeen, to come to Washington for the Christmas holidays. Twelve-year-old Charles had arrived in the capital the previous September to enroll briefly in a school operated by George E. Ironside. The three boys were shown around Washington, which included listening to debate in Congress and attending social events at the White House.

Ever watchful, the father noticed that the youths seemed timid and awkward, leading him to decide that they must be compelled to dance. They did so, at first with great reluctance, but to their parents' delight, they soon took to it with zest. JQA believed in the "usefulness, both physical and moral, of dancing." The skill was likely to produce in a young man the "easy but respectful and delicate familiarity of conversation with women."

As for himself, Adams acknowledged that he had learned to dance too late to develop that "fund of conversation" useful for talking with the ladies. As a result of this misfortune, "I have always been reserved and cold in my intercourse with them." Painfully aware of this "defect" in his own manner, he vowed that "I would fain preserve my children from it."

IF JOHN QUINCY ADAMS was as dour as he contended, we should ask what accounts for those moments when he was an attractive figure, as he had been in youth or when discussing literature with some well-informed person. Put another way, what did it take to silence Adams' numerous inhibitions and bring forth his charm?

His happier side emerged, as in London, for instance, when anxiety about himself, particularly a fear of failure, could relax temporarily. Often, this genial behavior came from the reassuring effect of alcohol. Those who remembered an ebullient Adams usually were recalling him at dinner or at a party where wine was abundant. By his own admission, he drank a great deal of wine—as did most persons in the early nineteenth century. A memorable story pictures him in high spirits, astounding other guests by unerringly identifying the sources and types of numerous wines served anonymously that evening at dinner.

But the morning after dinners and parties usually found him back to his taciturn self, whether he was in his study, at his office, or somberly walking. His was a nature ordained to be darkened by worry, over his relatives and himself. Only a rare time of family joy, an occasional professional success, or, most often, moments of bibulousness could release him temporarily from his torment.

EVENTUALLY, THE ADAMS SONS returned to New England, leaving what their father called a "void" in the household—and a redoubled concern about their supervision so far away. John and Louisa made up their minds to spend several late-summer weeks annually in Quincy and Boston so that they might see to their children's well-being. The holiday also promised them relief from the capital's political and social carping, and from the high temperatures and humidity for which the District was notorious.

With the arrival of each Washington summer, Adams would begin groaning that the heat was "insupportable." He complained of sitting of an evening on the porch "almost gasping for breath" and warring with spiders, mosquitoes, and other bugs. There was no escaping them, since the screenless windows in their residence had to be left open in the hope of air.

After two months of such misery, it was clear to him that he must flee to the sea breezes in Massachusetts. Unfortunately, these visits often meant trading the capital's humid weather for family problems—which sometimes made a return to Washington welcome.

At least he no longer had to dread the once-cruel ordeal of travel itself by stage or packet ship. Now, thanks to steam power, the trips between Washington and Boston were a comparative pleasure. Adams considered the steamboat "one of the greatest and most beneficial inventions of modern ages." Not only was its speed an advantage, but he usually met on board "a great variety of company with whom you can associate or from whom you can keep aloof at your pleasure."

He had such an encounter with Supreme Court Justice William

Johnson, a fellow passenger in October 1819. Adams began to converse with the South Carolinian, only to find him such "an anti-classical despiser of Homer and Virgil" that it seemed hopeless to talk with this "very ingenious and learned man." So, taking advantage of the mobility offered by the large vessel, Adams slipped away to more comfortable discourse with a Baptist clergyman, and the two were soon sharing their satisfaction at the absence of the gambling tables and all-night drinking bouts so familiar on earlier, wind-propelled vessels.

A kindred blessing accompanying steam travel, in John's opinion, was the religious material that he found "scattered about the cabins to attract the attention of the idle." While aboard a steamboat, it was frequently his pleasure to spot a book "which upon opening it you find to be a Bible." The one flaw to this otherwise perfect way to speed along was the noise from the engines and paddles, which Adams admitted could be alarming "to weak nerves."

But while his nerves easily withstood the racket of steam travel, they began to fray when he faced the problems awaiting him in Quincy. These difficulties were now much greater since Abigail, the matriarch of the Adams clan, had died on October 28, 1818, one year after her son's return from Europe. Death resulted from a bout with typhoid fever that began after John and Louisa returned to Washington from their 1818 summer holiday.

John had not returned to his mother's bedside, nor did he attend her funeral, which drew many of Massachusetts' leading citizens. It became Louisa's task to explain to astonished relatives that her husband had been detained by his many official burdens. She could hardly have added—if, indeed, it was accurate—that his absence was the ultimate testimony to a lifelong resentment of his mother's domineering ways.

Although Adams' diary commentary concerning Abigail's death had a perfunctory air, there was no mistaking the genuineness of his distress at her loss when he arrived in Quincy in September 1819. With her stern presence no longer a restraint upon family waywardness, it was left to her eldest son to resolve problems that were more than the frail John Adams could handle. Of these, the chief worry was Tom Adams.

Not only had his brother been a disappointment as JQA's financial agent, Tom's own affairs were now in shambles. His career in law and politics had not flourished, and his ever larger brood of children was a burden on his own financially strapped father. It was painful for the family to admit that Tom's plight arose from habitual drunkenness and gambling.

But when JQA tried to discuss these matters with him, Tom vanished for five days. After the fugitive had returned and recovered somewhat from a monumental hangover, a sleepless JQA worked out a generous arrangement for supporting Tom and his dependents, who were to reside with John Adams. Tom pledged sobriety and obedience, promises often made before. In exchange, JQA took some of Tom's debt-laden property, a selfless act, since it was understood that eventually the realty would revert to Tom's heirs.

Assuming support of his brother's family left JQA's own properties even more in debt. Since these would require careful supervision, he turned for help to Edward Cruft, who had married a second cousin of John's. Cruft was also a loyal political supporter, along with another Bostonian, Peter Paul Francis DeGrand, who counseled Adams on investments. Both advisers tried to interest him in attending political gatherings when he was in Massachusetts, but with scant success. The secretary of state preferred to shelter himself in his father's library, where tempting volumes abounded.

The "delicious" contents of his father's bookshelves were much on JQA's mind when he went to Boston on October 7 to sign a new will in the presence of witnesses who had agreed to meet him in the library room at the Athenaeum. While awaiting the group, he began looking about and, to his vast dismay, found very few of the volumes and pamphlets he had entrusted to the Athenaeum when he went abroad in 1809. It meant the very best of his collection had disappeared. The librarians were unable to explain the loss, and since he had left no listing of his books, they would be difficult to trace.

The Athenaeum discovery embarrassed JQA. Here was an ironic disclosure of his own carelessness at the very moment he was signing a will admonishing his heirs to consider the Adams library and papers as "the most precious portion" of the estate. As JQA's eldest son, George Adams stood to inherit the collection, which was thereafter to be passed down through the generations "as long as the books shall last and the succession be continued."

Although an abashed JQA would have preferred to use the rest of his holiday searching for the missing books—or at least reading in John Adams' or the Athenaeum's library—he had to yield occasionally to social and official demands. Besides the "perpetual" banquets and other gatherings the Adamses were obliged to attend in Boston and Quincy, there was always a pile of documents at hand, sent by the

State Department's chief clerk. Daniel Brent seemed merciless as he kept shipping bundles of letters to his chief, who moaned that "many of them urgently require that I should act upon them, but I find it utterly impossible." Each letter was "a summons to return to my duty at Washington."

BUT AFTER HE HAD CLOSED his summer holidays and was back in his office, Adams invariably rediscovered that he could not be diligent enough to satisfy himself. As always, the thieves of his time were more than his personal and public worries—his own makeup was involved, for even at middle age and holding the second most important office in the republic, he still lacked the power of concentration he so craved.

The persistence of his undisciplined attention could have been another aspect of Adams' sublimated rebellion against the incessant prodding to be famous that he had endured from his parents and, of course, from himself. His often erratic mental style was perhaps a more subtle assertion of independence than the avoidance of his mother's funeral.

In view of JQA's everlasting preaching to his sons about toil, application, and diligence, did his own shortcoming make him a hypocrite? Hardly, for his diary entries were filled with abject indictments of himself for being drawn from his near sacred duties. He wondered whether this susceptibility to distraction was one of the weaknesses "which Dr. Rush in his work upon the mind, describes as naturally leading to madness." He considered his condition to be an "imbecility of will." Yearning to give every moment to useful employment, he claimed it was his "nature" that led him astray.

Fretting over what he considered so much lost time in Washington, he would repeatedly try a familiar remedy: seeking to function with no more than a few hours' nightly rest. This determination rarely succeeded for long, as it had failed in Europe. Little sleep, along with a heavy dinner and much wine, inevitably brought evenings of drowsiness instead of achievement at his desk. This was one weakness Adams admitted he knew exactly how to overcome: "extreme temperance not only of eating, but of drinking." It was also a remedy he seemed incapable of applying.

Of course, his grumbling over time wasted was grossly unfair to himself. His days were packed with activity and decisions as he faced the demands that came with responsibility for America's foreign affairs. Aside from attending to official documents and correspondence, he tried to read forty newspapers each week. His position required careful reports to his diary; using his fine penmanship and an astounding memory, he recorded each day's events in great detail across many pages.

The rigor of such a schedule forgotten, Adams could rarely enjoy a pleasurable diversion without reproaching himself for time lost—only a long walk or a swim in the Potomac River was a warranted departure from his paperwork. When his ungovernable curiosity frequently detained him overlong with a book, he suffered his own rebukes. Nevertheless, when he could no longer endure documents and politics, he turned instinctively to the classics: "To live without having a Cicero and a Tacitus at hand seems to me as if it was a deprivation of my limbs." When he took up poetry by Alexander Pope, or Plato's dialogues, or essays by Francis Bacon, the hours flew by—until it was time to scold himself. In his admiration for Bacon, Adams went so far as to claim that the philosopher's astuteness about the world was excelled only by the Book of Proverbs.

When in 1820 JQA was elected president of the American Academy of Arts and Sciences, his erudition by then well known, the news was predictably bittersweet. "The arts and sciences have been the objects of my admiration through life. I would it were in my power to say they had been objects of my successful cultivation. Honours like these produce in my mind humiliation as well as pride."

Unlike his love of books, Adams' interest in theology had the advantage that one day of the week must be set aside for religious activity. He saw Sunday as a "proper time" for spending hours on this subject. Sabbath worship still occurred in the House of Representatives, although as Washington grew, sectarian congregations began to flourish. Adams attended them morning, afternoon, and evening, taking care usually to appear at a different church each time.

One reward for such devotion was his election as president of the American Bible Society. He agreed to accept this office—no matter that he was also secretary of state—because he had become alarmed by two developments in the nation's religious attitude: the contrasting appeals of Unitarianism and Evangelicalism. These schools of thought challenged the very personal spiritual views he had adopted while in Europe. Consequently, after 1817 his diary began featuring rebuttals of genial Unitarianism and of intolerant Fundamentalism, both of which he considered to be threats to republican society.

Representing these camps in Adams' view were Horace Holley

and Jedidiah Morse. A famed geographer, Morse was also a Congregational pastor in Charlestown, next to Boston. Holley was one of New England's brilliant young Unitarian ministers who is mainly remembered today for vainly striving to make Transylvania College in Lexington, Kentucky, a rival of Harvard. After Holley once preached at services in the Capitol, Adams emerged disgusted. What he had heard, he complained, was more a lecture than a sermon. When Holley proclaimed the story of Creation in Genesis to be no different than other fables of long ago, Adams reported: "I could scarcely sit and hear him with patience."

One autumn, JQA met Holley at a dinner in Boston. After the dishes were removed and the twenty-five guests had begun conversing, Adams found himself debating the minister. Their exchange, he reported, "almost became a controversy," so that "the attention of the whole table was turned to us." Since the topic was religion, Holley's training soon left the discussion "much to my disadvantage," as John admitted. He was rescued when Alexander Everett and Daniel Webster "relieved me" by asking questions of their own, although the minister remained "quite a match for us all." What particularly vexed Adams about Holley and other Unitarian spokesmen was their success in appealing to "the liberal class who consider religion as merely a system of morals." John saw a shameful example of this in Henry Clay's comment as the two walked down from Capitol Hill one Sunday after hearing a Unitarian sermon. Clay announced that he was "much pleased with this system of religion that the clergymen of Boston are now *getting up*." Adams rarely underlined words in his diary unless he was profoundly disturbed.

As distressing as he found the easygoing outlook of religious liberalism, JQA was even more offended by the intolerance he saw in the ardent Calvinism that revivalism had spread across America while he was abroad. The impact came vividly home to him when he talked with Jedidiah Morse, who had lately become a missionary to the Native Americans. Adams regretted that his guest's fine mind had become so "trammeled by a vicious religious education," but he admired Morse's "indefatigable industry." What the geographer needed was a more modest faith, by which Adams meant that Morse should join him in acknowledging that many questions of theology must remain mysteries.

In Washington as in Europe, Adams preferred to emphasize the sublime moral beauty of Christ's teachings, leaving issues of Protestant doctrine to faith. "It is enough for us to know that God hath made foolish the wisdom of this world."

THE ENTICEMENTS OF THESE RELIGIOUS diversions illustrated a weakness in himself that much distressed John: how easily he was tempted from his important official assignments. The most embarrassing of these lapses occurred when, as secretary of state during Monroe's first term, Adams prepared a report to Congress dealing with weights and measures. The task's enormous intellectual challenge should have made it highly attractive to him, yet no episode in John's life was more ironic than his dalliance in completing this project, which he knew would bring him great private satisfaction and intellectual pleasure.

He found the task awaiting him on his first day in the State Department. On his desk was a Senate resolution dated March 3, 1817 (the House would pass a similar version on December 14, 1819), directing that he report on the regulations and standards for weights and measures prevailing in the Union. He was also to study how other nations had established uniformity, and then to recommend a basis on which the United States could do the same.

A more appealing assignment for John's scholarly nature can scarcely be imagined. His study of Europe's standards for weights and measures during the long winters in St. Petersburg in fact gave him a head start in meeting Congress' directive. But there was one difficulty. The abstruse and obscure aspects of the assignment would require hours of concentration and painstaking thought by a secretary of state who, ashamed, said he found such application impossible. In those days, there were no research associates or other aides to whom he might have handed the chore.

Nevertheless, Adams made a typically energetic beginning. "I was much busied," he recorded proudly in October 1817. Within a few months, however, he was sounding the familiar refrain: "A day totally wasted." Assuredly, he was not wholly to blame for work on the project remaining unfinished until February 1821. To fulfill the assignment, he had to request that each state submit its regulations concerning weights and measures so that he could prepare an abstract to accompany his report to Congress. Unimpressed with the importance of the inquiry, many states had been slow to reply, and when they did respond, the information they sent was often incomplete, inappropriate, or inaccurate. In addition, Adams had difficulty securing the books and measurements he needed.

Even so, the work could sometimes move nicely, with JQA hugely enjoying himself as he studied or wrote for two hours by candlelight, beginning at 5 a.m. Occasionally after dinner, if drowsiness was at bay, he would get "involved in certain arithmetical calculations which absorbed the entire evening." Following such gratifying progress, he would record how "the calculations seized hold of me again this morning and consumed two or three hours of my time." The project "fascinates and absorbs me to the neglect of the most necessary business and even of my daily diary."

But then, perhaps the next day, he would begin to falter in the face of interruptions, distractions, and mysterious inertia. There would be months at a stretch with no progress, except to enlarge the accumulation of his self-rebukes. Finally, late in the spring of 1820, Adams recognized that if he did not submit his work to Congress by February 1821, Monroe's first term would expire with this major task undone. The thought of the embarrassment sure to result compelled action as nothing had before. Through the ensuing summer, autumn, and winter, he toiled mightily. He even disregarded his father's plea that he "throw the weights and measures up in the air" and come to Quincy for his annual holiday.

Instead, he remained in Washington, where, despite the ghastly heat that summer, it was quiet. His family went off to Maryland on holiday, Louisa saying of her husband: "His whole mind is so intent on weights and measures that you would suppose his very existence depended on this subject." She was scarcely exaggerating, since he had now decided the survival of his self-respect required finishing the report.

At first the task had seemed hopeless. After reading some of his earlier drafts, Adams pronounced scarcely a page acceptable. Since the writing and experiments must be done over, he resolved to save time by making only brief entries in his diary. The results of the effort were gratifying. As the summer wore on, the more intently he worked, the greater was his pleasure—"my views of the subject multiply." By then, the story of weights and measures had led him into philosophical speculations, and he wondered whether some in Congress would think these ridiculous.

He tried to write at least three report pages daily that summer, usually rising at 3 a.m. There were also experiments to carry out. One time he was seeking the exact proportion between the average weight of a kernel of wheat and the weight of a given quantity of grain, and the next he was striving to be accurate between pennyweight and troy weight. The research inspired him to pronounce a maxim good for scientists of any era: "Decisive results can only be drawn from multiplied experiments."

When New Year's Eve arrived, Adams could rightly claim that the past year had been "the most laborious" of his life. For six months, he had worked steadily on his report, though the task was yet not finished to his satisfaction. This was because he had continually been elevating his sights, even to the point of hoping that what he would present to Congress might attract public interest. Where the project had first promised to be merely a dry enumeration of tables and formulas, under JQA's powers of interpretation, it had become a vision of what government could do for public well-being.

Consequently, Louisa was a bit premature when she welcomed the arrival of 1821 by exclaiming: "Thank God we have no more of weights and measures." Not until late February was the work complete enough for John to show the manuscript to anyone. Fortunately, there was an individual in Washington whose judgment Adams trusted enough to ask for an assessment of his work. This was Secretary of War Calhoun. His evaluation proved candid and sobering, for he warned that many in Congress would consider the manuscript "too much of a Book for a mere official Report." Calhoun feared that Adams might have buried the practical importance of his findings under digressions into history and philosophy.

While John had foreseen this danger, he considered it a responsibility to disclose the profundity of the subject. He pointed out how for sixty years, with all of Europe's philosophical and mathematical learning readily available, the continent's ablest minds had sought a universal system of weights and measures. Given the limited resources he had to work with in Washington, he believed he had reached the best possible result. Indeed, hurried and imperfect though his report to Congress might be, he acknowledged that his work represented the most important "literary labour" he would ever complete.

His remarkable research had led him to exhaustive discussions on how the act of weighing and measuring had been practiced across history. At the other extreme were his soaring visions of what humanity might yet attain. Principally, however, the *Report of the Secretary of State Upon Weights and Measures* was a hymn of praise for the French metric system and the need for a universal arrangement of weights and measures, a hardly startling proposal.

The *Report* became memorable for its long philosophical and historical treatment of the subject. Adams clearly was in love with the meter, which he pointed out was a 40-millionth part of the earth's circumference. If this simple unit could become universal in use, he rhapsodized, "one language of weights and measures will be spoken from the equator to the poles." This would be a step toward "that universal peace which was the object of a Savior's mission . . . the trembling hope of the Christian."

Without hesitation, Adams claimed that if the world adopted the metric system, the upshot would bring "the foretaste here of man's eternal felicity. It would help cast down the Spirit of Evil . . . from his dominion over men." If a permanent, universal uniformity of weights and measures was ever achieved, Adams predicted that those who brought it about "would be among the greatest of benefactors of the human race."

Although it had slight impact at the time, Secretary Adams' *Report* became, for the small circle of those genuinely interested, the finest scholarly evaluation of the subject ever written. It has remained so for nearly two centuries. While the work is ponderous and complex beyond belief, and begs for the revision that its author knew was merited but had no time to give, it clearly reveals his love of learning—and possibly his pleasure in flourishing his erudition. He encouraged Congress to have many copies printed, with two hundred alone designated for use by the Department of State. The secretary wished to mail his *Report* to learned societies in Europe and America, as well as to individuals who he believed should know what he had done.

EVEN AS HE PROUDLY distributed his work, Adams was unable to put out of mind the recent debate in Congress over the admission of Missouri as a state. Though he had been confined to a spectator's role while the controversy occupied much of 1819–20, the excitement was so intense that it often kept the secretary of state from his weights and measures. At issue had been whether the Louisiana Purchase area should be opened to human bondage. How Missouri was allowed to enter the Union would decide whether slavery was to remain confined to the Old South or be unleashed in the West.

When the Southerners won the day in March 1820 through what

became known as the Missouri Compromise, Adams was mightily disgusted. He believed that the "bluster" of the "white slavocracy" had cowed the Northern representatives. Seeing the future of the Union and the dignity of humanity at issue, he yearned to enter the debate—never was there "a theme for eloquence like the free side of this question."

But, sitting in the bleachers, he had to be content with confiding to his diary the part he wished he could have played in the arguments. "Oh! if but one man could arise with a genius capable of comprehending, a heart capable of supporting, and an utterance capable of communicating those eternal truths that belong to this question." Had he the chance, he insisted that he would have frankly exposed slavery as an "outrage upon the goodness of God."

Despite his fuming, Adams felt that he had to support the Missouri Compromise, which admitted Maine as a free and Missouri as a slave state and banned bondage from the Louisiana Purchase north of the 36-degree-30-minute line. He justified acquiescence to this agreement through a belief that it might preserve the Union until the North gained the courage and strength to destroy the slave system. Meanwhile, the debate had confirmed his scorn for the slave owners and their spokesmen. He called slavery and its defenders "morally and politically vicious."

Not until the summer of 1821 was the controversy finally settled. By then, Monroe and Adams had begun second terms in their respective offices, at which point John started to think about what he would do after Monroe's administration ended. Reading, writing, teaching, and conducting scientific experiments suddenly no longer seemed occupation enough. "I shall want *an object of pursuit*," he emphasized, something "which may engage my feelings and excite constant interest, leaving as few hours as possible for listlessness, repining, or discontented broodings."

Louisa Adams agreed completely with this self-assessment, but for reasons of her own. More so than her husband, she recognized how politics had taken command of him. It was ridiculous for him even to consider becoming a private citizen, Louisa believed, knowing that he "would not live long out of an active sphere of publick life and that it is absolutely essential to his existence." Much as she wished he could retire from politics, she predicted in 1821 that during the next four years her husband would be consumed by striving for the presidency, an office Louisa knew he must pretend he was not actively seeking.

In the presidential election of 1820, Adams had received the only vote not cast for James Monroe by the electoral college. This auspicious sign redoubled the number of friends and supporters who implored him to compete actively against Crawford, Clay, and others who would seek the presidency in 1824. His associates warned him that unless he came into the open as a candidate, as John recorded, "I shall break my own neck."

To these cordial pleadings, he replied with his familiar, ponderous refrain: "My conduct is governed by a sense of duty and delicacy alone." He told his good friend Joseph Hopkinson that if the office of president became "a prize of cabal and intrigue," he wanted "no ticket in that lottery." As it turned out, this statement by no means meant that he did not wish to be president.

He began his second term as secretary of state hoping that if he continued to be successful, the American people might ask him to be their president. This outlook represented his idealism at its most extreme, for amid all his pious talk about "that consciousness of right which I never have forfeited," and about how he had pledged "never to ask the suffrage of my country, and never to shrink from its call," Adams knew well enough after four years in Washington that "the whole system of our politics is inseparably linked with the views of aspirants to the presidential succession."

And yet, degrading though the pursuit threatened to be, JQA recognized that to be president offered the means by which he might best "do good to the utmost of my power." To gain history's verdict that he had been a great benefactor of humankind was still his prime aspiration. If he could not win such repute by achievement in literature or science, then politics might have to be the means. The question in March 1821 was whether Adams would be willing openly to enter the arena where the fight to succeed Monroe had already begun.

CHAPTER ELEVEN

Summons

There is nothing so deep and nothing so shallow which political enmity will not turn to account. Let it be a warning to me to take a heed to my ways.

JOHN QUINCY ADAMS' second four years as secretary of state were given only in part to chasing the presidency. He was, after all, still a highly conscientious public official, so that when electoral agitation increased the annoying interruptions at the State Department, he decided that he must squeeze more time from each twenty-four hours. To do so, he began getting up before 3 a.m., a Draconian remedy that soon backfired.

"The greatest difficulty that I find in rising early and at a regular hour is that when I steadily pursue that intention, I awake earlier every morning than the preceding one, til I lose the due and necessary sleep of the night, the consequence of which is a most painful drowsiness the ensuing day."

When he could not locate more hours, Adams undertook to discourage those who called frivolously at his office by meeting them with "coldness and reserve." His demeanor bespoke both an impatience with the presidential scramble and a desire to concentrate on the several issues of foreign policy that remained before the State Department. One of these entailed working again with his friend Hyde de Neuville, the French ambassador, to develop a commercial convention between the United States and France. Some skillful strategy by Adams brought agreement in 1822.

Another issue involved Stratford Canning, the English minister, with whom Adams turned to consider the seemingly eternal controversies between London and Washington: maritime rights, the slave trade, and commerce. Adams was a realist, recognizing that Britannia still ruled the waves. Even so, with the aid of Richard Rush, who continued as U.S. minister in London, he reached some of his goals in this area and opened the way for later successes during his presidency.

While Russia's irksome territorial claim along the northwest coast of North America could not be ignored, the secretary's most difficult hemispheric challenge was the clamor for independence raised by Spain's colonies in South America. For Adams, this led to a "vital concern": were North and South America open to colonization from nations in Europe or Asia? He decided to make this question central to an Independence Day address he delivered before the citizens of Washington in 1821. In doing so, he chose deliberately to enter "warfare of the mind . . . in defence of the character of our country."

Insisting to his audience that he was there as a private citizen, Adams first offered obligatory praise for the righteousness of America's Revolution, after which he made the startling prediction that England would eventually be forced to give up India. After this opening, his address emphasized mainly that the United States must be prepared to recognize the independence of South American nations. While he carefully denied that his government had colonial aspirations, he also stressed that other nations were not welcome in the Western Hemisphere.

In thus speaking, Secretary Adams clearly helped himself politically. There was no safer ground for a presidential candidate than to flay Great Britain on the Fourth of July, particularly in Washington, with its memories of the recent torching of the city by English soldiers. Indeed, his remarks became downright scornful of Britain. He spoke of how in 1776 the English had begun "an unjust and cruel, and so far as there was a drop of kindred blood in their veins, an unnatural war against their countrymen in this hemisphere."

But there had been benefit from England's aggression, he emphasized. Thanks to America's own experience under colonial domination and during the American Revolution, the Western Hemisphere should never again be encroached upon by foreign powers. Coming from a secretary of state, this holiday oration was strong medicine for the rest of the world. Canning ascribed its tone and content to Adams' pursuit of the presidency, and he warned his superiors in London that an address using rancorous and vindictive language "can hardly be viewed with indifference by his Majesty's government." Adams' speech, of course, drew largely favorable attention across the United States, a response that seemed a pleasant surprise for him.

Two years later, the moment arrived toward which the oration had pointed. This was the creation of what became the Monroe Doctrine, which evolved late in 1823 as a response to reports that, with France's backing, Spain was preparing to send troops to put down rebellions in South America, a continent over most of which it had held sway for centuries. Since Great Britain saw such a move as hostile to its own global interests, it proposed that the United States join it in public opposition to this enlarged Spanish intrusion in the Western Hemisphere.

While the United States had not yet recognized the independence of the new Latin American republics, Adams, along with President Monroe and some members of Congress, was moving in that direction. Others also took an interest, including two ex-presidents. When Jefferson and Madison learned that Spain might crush freedom in South America, the two elderly statesmen urged Monroe to enter the coalition proposed by England. John C. Calhoun, the secretary of war, even expressed a willingness for the United States to join with England in a war against other European powers.

Amid this hue and cry, Adams calmly insisted that it would be wiser if the nation remained alone in warning the world that the Western Hemisphere was no longer to be intruded upon. He added that if Europe should tamper with strivings for independence in Latin America, the United States must consider such action as hostile. He proposed the same response to Russia's encroachment in the Northwest quarter.

These threats were debated during two memorable cabinet meetings, on November 7 and 21, 1823. For his part, Adams urged Monroe to seize the opportunity for the nation to stand alone in protecting the hemisphere. In what has become a famous passage in JQA's diary, he summed up the argument he had presented at these meetings: "It would be more candid, as well as more dignified, to avow our principles explicitly to Russia and France, than to come in as a cock-boat in the wake of the British man-of-war."

The secretary of state won the day, save in one respect. While he advised that this policy be announced through diplomatic channels, Monroe insisted on incorporating it in his forthcoming annual message to Congress. When it was delivered, on December 2, 1823, the world was notified that the United States would thereafter build its foreign policy upon principles that Monroe drew largely from Adams: the republic's political philosophy and institutions were different and separate from those in Europe; the Western Hemisphere was now closed to further colonization by foreign powers; the United States would keep out of purely European matters while respecting existing European dependencies in the New World; and finally, any attempt by European powers to expand their interest in the Americas would be deemed a threat to U.S. security.

This announcement by Monroe represented one of Adams' finest contributions to the emergence of the United States as a world power. Proud of his accomplishment, John nevertheless reminded himself that his record in the State Department still fell short of "my own ambition." What was his highest aspiration? To lead the civilized nations into a noble agreement that would regulate neutral and belligerent rights, an accord that he said would be "a real and solid blessing" to humanity. If he could bring the world such a treaty, he conceded that he would "die for it with joy [and] go before the throne of omnipotence with a plea for mercy and with a consciousness of not having lived in vain for the world of mankind."

Particularly at moments of such exalted sentiment, Adams was especially prone to dream that somehow he might be chosen president without being defiled by actively campaigning for the post. With such a victory, he imagined himself becoming a vigorous leader of both the United States and the world. But then reality would inevitably break in on these reflections as the undertow of partisanship pulled him along.

He spent many hours simply brooding over the cost of seeking the presidency: "Evening heavy and unremittingly idle." He often claimed that thoughts of the election left him inefficient and unable to sleep. Even the theater became an enemy. After a performance of *Macbeth*, he looked at himself and others in Washington and said he saw many Macbeths, men driven to evil deeds, yet racked by guilt.

These thoughts were also stimulated by reading Horace Walpole's *Memoirs of the Last Ten Years of the Reign of George II*, an intimate treatment of British government between 1750 and 1760. "The public history of all countries and all ages," Adams concluded, "is but a mask, richly coloured. The interior working of the machinery must be foul." The struggle for power, the treachery of associates, and the unwholesome bargains that Walpole described comprised a story that "might be told of our own times."

For relief, he briefly took up cantos from Lord Byron's *Don Juan*, just being published. He paused over cantos three to five, finding them "very licentious and very delightful." The poem's "bursts of tenderness and flights of sublimity" brought to Adams' mind memories of Wieland, the German author whose work he had admired and translated during those blessed days in Berlin when he had planned a literary career.

Then it was back to political books. This time he took up the Bishop of Winchester's biography of William Pitt, which had the benefit of reminding him that statesmen could struggle nobly. While he had Pitt on his mind, Adams had to endure impatiently a Unitarian sermon on the grace of humility. He objected to praising humility because it led to talk of sacrificing the natural propensities of the human heart. Surrounded as he was by political taunts and false charges, Adams said he would try to be humble, but only with a "firm and determined spirit which will not suffer itself to be made the sport or the instrument of others."

He was thinking, for instance, of a recent attack on him by a Philadelphia newspaper "on account of the negligence of my dress." According to the proud secretary of state, the editor had charged "that I wear neither waistcoat nor cravat, and sometimes go to church barefoot." Such assaults made Adams groan over the kind of despicable strategy that he claimed prevailed in presidential campaigns. "There is nothing so deep and nothing so shallow which political enmity will not turn to account. Let it be a warning to me to take a heed to my ways."

But what about the criticism of his dress? His mother had often complained about his unkempt appearance, and Louisa had tried to coax him into being more attentive to his person. After reading the newspaper account, he admitted that when the weather was hot, he did remove his cravat and substituted "around my neck a black silk ribband." Nevertheless, his carelessness never ceased, apparently an easy and lifelong form of rebellion against his otherwise compulsive reverence for duty.

As for this and other editorial assaults, he preferred to let them remind him of how Walpole had used a satirical style in recounting his experiences in political warfare. "And shall I too not have a tale to tell?" Adams mused. Any biographer would certainly agree.

By 1823, Adams acknowledged that even Sunday worship was leaving him "too much absorbed by the world for due devotion to the Lord's day. I carry too much of the week into the Sabbath and too little of the Sabbath into the week." A visit to a Quaker meeting confirmed this. "I found myself quite unable to reduce my mind to that musing meditation which forms the essence of this form of devotion."

His reflections were feeble at best, "rambling from this world to the next, and from the next back to this."

As the matter of presidential succession came more and more to dominate "this world," Adams used another favorite way besides sitting in church to soothe his spirit. During the humid Washington summers, he became more diligent about swimming in the Potomac. Other persons, however, were unlikely to find much fun in his approach to the sport. He undertook to compete against his own high standards by striving, day after day, to see how much farther he could swim without touching bottom. As when he persisted in taking regular walks when he was ill, he found grim satisfaction in proving his endurance through these swims.

During the summer of 1822, Adams set a new personal record by swimming for fifty minutes "without too much exhaustion." A year later he accomplished eighty minutes, at which point he admitted that this must be the limit, for Louisa and his physician were imploring him to abandon such "excess." While he agreed to get out of the river after an hour, he created a new challenge for himself by experiments involving swimming while clothed. He took care to record the results from each day's effort. At least here was one area of endeavor in which he could retain mastery over himself while outdoing others.

ADAMS CERTAINLY NEEDED this reassurance, since there was more than the scramble for the presidency to dismay him in the years preceding the election. To his disgust, he found himself the chief witness in one of the era's most fascinating court cases. The litigation involved his sometime friend Levett Harris, who had served as U.S. consul in St. Petersburg when the Adamses lived there.

In 1820 Harris brought suit before the Pennsylvania Supreme Court against John D. Lewis, who had been a merchant in St. Petersburg when Harris was consul. Lewis had discovered, as had Adams, that Harris was taking payoffs from merchants and shipowners in return for illegal favors. Believing himself a victim of Harris's, in 1819 Lewis had published a pamphlet entitled "Consular Corruption," which was distributed in Philadelphia and Washington.

Adams was convinced that politics was behind Lewis' colorful accusations, which quickly attracted public attention. As a knowledgeable party, he was required to give several depositions concerning the case, often during lengthy evening sessions in Washington. His suspicion that partisanship lurked behind the litigation was strengthened when Harris—and Lewis, for that matter—chose as counsel some of John's enemies. To Adams' dismay, among the attorneys showing up at his front door to take depositions were Henry Clay, William Lowndes, Daniel Webster, and Harrison Gray Otis. Furthermore, Treasury Secretary William H. Crawford openly supported Harris as part of his presidential campaign. Of Crawford's strategy, John told himself: "Ambition debauches memory itself."

The case moved slowly because Harris was conveniently unable to find his consular records. Unbelievably, some were later discovered in the woods near King of Prussia, Pennsylvania. Without these records, Adams had to draw heavily upon his memory and his trusty diary. The process was painful, since he was obliged to concede in sworn testimony that while minister to Russia he had known of Harris' corruption, which had included even the sale of vice-consulships.

When Adams was asked why he had not made this information public, he replied that he had wanted more proof, and that to have exposed Harris would have meant revealing dubious practices by the Russian government and by many American commercial houses. He contended that these disclosures would certainly have had a pernicious effect upon America's delicate situation in wartime Europe. Also, wishing to be totally honest, he added that Harris was always a kind friend in St. Petersburg, especially when little Louisa Catherine died. Of these good deeds Adams said, in a deposition of August 14, 1821, "I can never forget them."

Privately, JQA was stunned that Harris would go to court in a case where he knew the charges against him were entirely true. How could a talented person such as Harris have been so tempted by venality? "He made a princely fortune by selling his duty and his office at the most enormous prices," Adams assured his diary. "I was very slow and dull of sight." The whole sorry affair led the secretary of state to pray: "May the law of truth be ever upon my lips, and that of honour ever in my breast."

The case, in which Harris sought damages of $100,000, eventually came to trial in February 1827, and resulted in his being awarded $100, although several members of the jury would have preferred to make it fifty cents. Lewis' defense had been weakened by his inability to prove absolutely every contention in the accusing pamphlet. Afterward, however, Lewis enjoyed success in business and letters, while Harris sank out of sight.

Just as this imbroglio was awakening uncomfortable memories of Russia, Adams found himself literally confronted by another vexing reminder of how dishonesty had flourished there under his nose. Knocking at his door in August 1822 was his troublesome nephew Billy Smith. Smith and his wife, Kitty, had returned to Washington after a futile attempt to make a living working for the navy in Pensacola. While by no means having forgotten Smith's gambling debts and his submission of false claims for expenses as a government employee, the Adamses nevertheless made the unfortunate pair members of their household. After all, Billy was one of the few persons John could beat at chess. Already heavily in debt to his uncle, Smith soon was coaxing more loans from him. Eventually, he was taken off to debtor's prison.

It was, however, another relative, this time a cousin of Louisa's, who took the greatest advantage of JQA. In July 1823, George Johnson asked him to purchase the Columbian Mills, a local flour business Johnson owned. The proposition was made at a moment when John was in a pessimistic mood, believing it unlikely that he would be summoned to the presidency and wondering how he might find income to replace his official salary.

Taking little time to evaluate the mill and without consulting Louisa or others, he paid $32,000 for the business, deeming it a gift from Heaven that would be "useful and respectable." So inspired was he that he shrugged off his belated discovery that a bank was about to foreclose on Johnson. Nor was much thought given to the dilapidated condition of buildings and machinery, even after Adams was informed that it would cost at least $12,000 to refurbish the business.

The only precaution he took before the purchase was a hurried drive out along Rock Creek to see the site. Rather than inspect it carefully, he preferred to think of the "just and virtuous motives" that were impelling him to help both George Johnson and himself. It would be "a leap in the dark, but man must Trust." His faith wore a bit thin, however, when he faced hedging by both Johnson and the Bank of Columbia before the deal was completed on August 11, 1823.

By then, Adams was complaining that "the affair of the mills now absorbs too much of my time." Nor was he pleased on learning that Johnson and the bank had given him a faulty deed to the property. Most distressing, however, was his discovery that he had not studied his own resources sufficiently, so that he had to sell some of his government bonds and mortgage his Washington residence in order to complete the purchase.

Then came an even more costly error: he gave management of the enterprise back to Johnson, a proven incompetent. Soon, there were disheartening reports that business was not proceeding smoothly.

Grinding flour, Adams sighed, could prosper only "with the blessing of Heaven, which I implore." By November it was clear that Heaven tarried as the milling business went from bad to worse, remaining a drain on family resources for many years.

ADAMS' ORDEAL with the Columbian Mills seemed to affect his attitude toward raising his sons. It was as if the father, fearing that his own deportment and prudence were faltering, chose to increase the pressure upon his offspring to meet high expectations. While each of the sons was subjected to this form of transference, none suffered more from it than George Adams, the eldest.

George's plight had begun in August 1821, when John traveled to New England for his son's Harvard graduation ceremonies. He had arrived anticipating a splendid performance by George, who had surprised everyone a year earlier by winning Harvard's Boylston Prize in oratory. But the award was misleading, and John's pleasure in the achievement was soon forgotten when he found that George merited only a modest part in the commencement exercises and carried out even that assignment—according to the senior Adams—poorly. There was more paternal dismay upon learning that George ranked merely thirtieth in his class.

Even so, Adams footed the bill for a party given at Smith's Tavern after commencement to honor his son, and he insisted on inviting the governor of the Commonwealth, as well as Harvard's president. The occasion was much more a political event than a tribute to a graduate. Afterward, Adams departed for Quincy, his fragile hopes for George in disarray.

In Quincy, he heard news that prompted him to ride back to Cambridge the next day: fourteen-year-old Charles Francis Adams had been granted only a conditional admission to Harvard. The reason given was that he had made a poor translation from the work of the Roman historian Sallust.

Convinced that Charles' mastery of Sallust was perfectly acceptable—and not bothering to check carefully for himself—an indignant Adams reappeared at Harvard to notify President Kirkland that he suspected Charles had been "unfairly treated." His skepticism seemed confirmed when Kirkland informed him that Charles' faculty judge had been Professor Edward Tyrrel Channing, whose recent appointment to no less than the Boylston Chair had been openly opposed by

Adams on the ground that the nominee was incompetent. (In fact, Channing would go on to serve with great distinction for thirty-two years.)

Adams immediately saw Charles' failure as Channing's revenge on the parent. Consequently, Kirkland was obliged to listen as ex-Professor Adams denounced Channing as unfit generally for the Boylston Chair and particularly to sit in judgment on an Adams. After John subsided, Harvard's president defended Channing and refused to displace him as Charles' examiner. Kirkland did agree that the outraged father could be present when Channing met with Charles three weeks later.

After making this arrangement, Adams discussed the supposed victimization of Charles with a sympathetic friend, Professor Henry Ware. Talking with Ware and others, he grew even more severe in his criticism of Channing, scornfully pointing out that after two years as Boylston Professor, he had yet to deliver an inaugural lecture. As for the wretched oratorical performance by students during the recent commencement exercise, he said that Channing was clearly to blame. Adams' heated behavior was a notable indication that the rising presidential campaign, with its taunts and slander (and his reluctant participation in it), could sometimes get the best of his self-control.

Three weeks later, as John and Charles were about to set out again for Cambridge, the father finally took the time to appraise the young man's skill in Latin. The result was mortifying. Adams had to admit that Charles was indeed deficient, despite all his efforts to instruct the lad in St. Petersburg and Ealing. Had he known how poorly qualified in Latin Charles was, Adams announced, he would never have permitted him to apply for admission.

But it was now too late to retreat. The pair rode to Cambridge for Charles' second encounter with Channing. It was an uneasy trip, for Adams felt that his repute was more at stake than Charles'. A few hours later, however, he emerged from the examination vastly relieved. Charles had acquitted himself well enough to pass and be admitted unconditionally to the college.

This modest success was quickly forgotten, however, when Adams learned more about his children's performance at Harvard from its president. Weary of being vexed by the secretary of state, Kirkland decided that the senior Adams should be made aware of the weaknesses of sons George and John. JQA was informed that not only had George graduated thirtieth in his class, but John now stood forty-fifth in a class of eighty-five. Again, Adams' temper got the best of him, and he insisted that Kirkland prove Harvard was not persecuting his family. Kirkland promised to assemble the facts.

In Quincy, Adams found that George had been inexcusably careless with $35 that Louisa had asked him to give to one of her nephews. Instead, George had turned the sum over to an acquaintance, and the money had promptly vanished. Fuming from his latest meeting with President Kirkland, JQA gave way to rage and scolded George so severely that he soon repented of it. He had condemned his son for "heedlessness and want of consideration," which left the excessively sensitive George deeply "affected." Admitting to himself that he was guilty of much "unkindness" to his child, Adams could not sleep that night. As he tossed and turned, he kept thinking of "the welfare and future prospects of my children."

He also brooded over his discovery of how much time they apparently had wasted at Harvard. Familiar worries kept nagging him through the long night. "I had hoped that at least one of my sons would have been ambitious to excel," he admitted. Instead, "I find them all three coming to manhood with indolent minds. Flinching from study whenever they can." It was, he recorded, "bitter disappointment. The blast of mediocrity is the lightest of the evils which such characters portend." He did not mention, if he remembered, the conclusion he had reached in London that it was best to accept his sons as they were. But of course that was before his reentry into the strain of political life.

Deprived of sleep and with his patience exhausted, Adams returned to Cambridge the next morning, hoping to hear from Kirkland an acknowledgment that the boys had indeed been unfairly evaluated by the faculty. Instead, the president produced facts about the scholarly achievement—or lack of it—on the part of both George and John Adams. After a humiliating recitation of their absences and poor marks, JQA's assault collapsed. He feebly warned Kirkland that if the new term produced any signs of faculty prejudice, it would be "my duty" to withdraw his sons from Harvard.

The wrathful father went at once to John and Charles' room in the residence hall, where, ignoring their howls of protest, he passed sentence upon them: they would not be allowed to come to Washington for the long Christmas holiday. No dances and parties at the White House for them. Instead, they were directed to spend the time in Quincy studying under their grandfather's supervision. Furthermore, until then the two were not to leave Harvard Yard.

"I saw they were much affected," JQA noted with grim satisfaction after leaving the boys. Although both his wife and his father urged JQA to be merciful, he only grew more stern. He asked Kirkland to keep watch over John and Charles' scholarly and moral behavior and to report the smallest infractions. As for George, he must accompany his parents to Washington and begin legal studies with his father.

Though, once back in the capital, Adams found that he had little time to instruct his son, George was compelled to arise at 5:30 a.m. to begin his studies, which at first addressed the history of the Middle Ages and the works of Cicero. Soon, George managed to break an ankle while horseback-riding and to acquire other afflictions that compelled even his father to allow him to give up. Eventually, the young man was sent back to Boston for study in Daniel Webster's law office. (Paradoxically, while the Adamses profoundly distrusted Webster the politician, they were willing to have George, and later Charles, receive legal training from him and others in his office. Actually, the great Webster paid little attention to his many students. Charles Francis reported that he talked with his mentor only once, and then for all of fifteen minutes. There seemed to be little danger that a son of JQA's would be contaminated—and, after all, Webster's firm was one of the most successful in New England.)

Thus did George slip out of his father's immediate concern, to be replaced by his brother John as chief contributor to the Adamses' public and private woes. The young man infuriated his father by writing to beg for a change of mind about the Christmas holiday. Could he and his brother not come to Washington after all? The request brought an irritated response, which began with a recitation of the advantages in intellectual preparation that life had generously given the Adams boys. Next, JQA spoke of what it was like to discover that a son was wasting his potential; for him, the mortification was inexpressible. Therefore, to see such a derelict offspring in Washington would bring no satisfaction. "I would feel nothing but sorrow and shame in your presence."

Then came a paternal decree: not until young John was ranked among the ten best students at Harvard would he be allowed to visit the capital. Learning to do his duty would be the best means by which the son could demonstrate that he was worthy of his name. Indeed, JQA promised to greet John as "an affectionate and grateful child" when, and only when, his standing at Harvard equaled what JQA's had been: second in his class. That day never came. A few months later, John's career at Harvard turned catastrophic.

Having failed to impress his father, John evidently chose to become a rebel by joining a large number of his classmates in a riot. The young men were protesting the treatment of an esteemed fellow senior to whom Harvard's faculty had assigned an inferior role in the upcoming commencement exercises. In May, thirty-nine students, including John Adams, were dismissed and denied their degrees. Although his son was allied with many of his classmates, the event so crushed JQA that a month elapsed before he could bring himself to write to his disgraced offspring.

By then, the parent had calmed, and he refused to rake over the scandal with John, saying he simply could not discuss it. Instead, adopting a stoical compassion, JQA invited his son to start life in Washington by living with his parents. In the father's judgment, the worst had happened. One of his children had succeeded in ruining himself. Even so, the senior Adams urged Harvard to be generous with the dismissed students. When the college declined to reverse its action, the fight went out of him—except for ignoring an invitation from Kirkland to attend what should have been John's commencement exercises.

AMID THE DISTRESSING SUMMER of 1823, JQA also realized that his father had become very frail. "He is bowed with age and scarcely can walk across a room without assistance." The old man's condition at age eighty-eight made the prospect of his death very real to JQA for the first time, leading the son to regret any occasion during his Quincy visits that took him from John Adams' side. He summoned Gilbert Stuart to capture his venerable parent on canvas before it was too late.

As he joined his father in calling on other aged relatives and friends around Quincy, JQA found that he could forget politics while listening to the elders talk of former times. Their recollections brought out the genealogist in John and set him to studying wills and other ancient records. Once more, he was impressed by the fact that, until his father's achievements, four generations of forebears had toiled and died unsung. Of their careers John commented: "Laborious, frugal, and honest lives can be safely ascribed to them all. May nothing worse ever be said of mine or of those of my children." How would he measure up after returning to private life? He would need employment, he assured himself, that would "intensely engage my attention."

While thinking of where private life would place him, he began noticing how many of his New England friends now dwelt in mansions that were "more princely than Republican." Since his strapped finances would not allow him such elegance, he decided to make his next career an agrarian one. To learn more about farming, he visited Josiah Quincy and took a "ramble" across his cousin's fine acreage. This inspection went well enough until Josiah insisted that the secretary of state view his new "piggery." The fastidious Adams observed that, while undoubtedly profitable, pens for the swine were "not cheering either to the sight or to the scent." Raising fruit trees was more congenial, he decided, and he put pigs and plows aside.

During holidays in New England, he did enjoy driving the family chaise. When his father remained behind, JQA sometimes encouraged the horses into such speed that twice in 1823 the carriage was overset and his passengers, he admitted, "narrowly escaped getting their necks broken." One such accident occurred in front of Governor William Eustis' residence, where Adams had dined handsomely. He did not report how much of the governor's wine had been consumed, but he did speak of some unsettling political talk. When Eustis mentioned "deep intrigues in operation" against Adams, the latter resisted curiosity and "asked no questions," but suppressed dismay may have caused him to apply the whip more than was prudent.

WHILE IT MAY HAVE BEEN EASIER for JQA to appear aloof from such gossip in Boston, partisan antics were harder to ignore in Washington. The years of Monroe's second administration were among the most difficult of Adams' life. In large part, this was due to his exasperation. He knew that his dour personality and his refusal to seek the presidency openly gave rise to allegations of antidemocratic principles, and he was convinced that this gossip would keep the public from recognizing his superior qualifications for the highest office.

One thing was certain: Jackson, Clay, Calhoun, and Crawford were far from bashful about displaying their eagerness to be president and had more pleasing personalities than JQA's. Yet, as John tirelessly reminded himself and Louisa, no opponent had a record for public service that remotely approached his. Would his outstanding attainments be lost, he wondered, because he had "no powers of fascination"? For him to try to pretend otherwise, he told Louisa, would be ridiculous, since it would be "out of nature."

While Louisa herself dreaded moving into the White House, she was fiercely loyal to her husband—so much so that, on one occasion at least, she encouraged him to make an effort to appear as an agreeable fellow before the public. She did so from Philadelphia, where, always the compassionate nurse, she had gone to care for Thomas Baker Johnson, her ailing brother. Hearing complaints from leaders of the local Adams faction that their man was losing ground because his enemies were attributing his cold manner to "aristocratic hauteur, and learned arrogance," Louisa immediately urged her husband to join her in Philadelphia and show voters that he could unbend just a bit.

Her advice brought an indignant reply. Showing his frustration, Adams asked his spouse whether it actually took such behavior to become president, and if so, "what then? There are candidates enough for the Presidency without me—and my delicacy is not suited to the times. There are candidates enough who have no such delicacy. It suits my temper to be thus delicate." He cared not a bit, he assured Louisa, if others said he had an aristocratic temperament. He would not mimic his opponents' "cringing servility, nor insatiate importunity." He accused her of believing that he yearned to be president. Not true! His letter seemed to shout at Louisa as he claimed that politics caused most men to lose "the thread of [their] morals." He wanted no part of such men.

Increasingly, the partisan assaults angered Adams. To one supporter he expressed his disgust at tactics used by persons bent upon "excluding me from the field of competition." And such dirty work seemed highly successful, as he pointed to newspapers across the Union that "have teemed with slander, false and foul, upon my character." But he insisted that he would not counterattack. "If the old prudential maxim that God helps those who help themselves is morally applicable to the pursuit of public honors and trust, I shall certainly be the most helpless candidate that ever was presented to the view of the American people."

Such embattled talk found Adams taking his idealism to its usual extreme. He informed a friend that he preferred the votes of five men who chose him for his record of public service than the suffrage "of a whole Sodom of political chapmen, who would barter a Presidency for a department or an embassy." Nevertheless, despite his bravado, a subtle change became evident in his stance. Beginning in 1822, he started to remind his allies that whenever citizens might form a movement in behalf of his election, he would "leave it to take its course." Statements such as these were the closest he came to acknowledging that he was running for president.

Unconsciously, perhaps, he preferred another campaign tactic: to keep himself before the public by efforts to clear his name against slander. Defending the Adams reputation became his surrogate for overt campaigning. The prime example of this was his response when supporters of Crawford and Clay began besmirching his character and record of service, his two most sacred possessions. In Adams' mind, such attacks justified his entering the battle—with an ire that was sometimes awesome—for he could believe that he was doing so in self-defense. Assaults on his name sometimes brought rejoinders so harsh that a casual observer might be excused for seeing them as simply campaign outbursts.

It was Jonathan Russell, Adams' colleague during the negotiations at Ghent and now a Massachusetts congressman, who caused the most memorable of these angry defenses and created what his victim called "the most painful situation of my life." In 1822, Russell publicly stated that at Ghent, Adams had been so eager to secure northeastern coastal fishing rights for New England that he had been ready to sacrifice the West's future. Russell claimed that Adams would willingly have allowed England free navigation of the Mississippi River.

While the treaty signed at Ghent included no such boon for the British, Russell clearly wanted voters in Kentucky and other western states to believe that Adams had been prepared to betray them. His strategy was to publish two letters he had written to Secretary of State Monroe shortly after leaving Ghent in which Russell had expressed misgivings over Adams' indifference to the West while applauding his own and Clay's defense of the region.

JQA considered Russell's use of these letters to be part of Clay's presidential campaign, although Calhoun claimed that Crawford was "the hand behind the curtain." The "plot," as Adams called it, sought to ruin any chance he might have in the region along the Mississippi River, an area from which any New Englander had to draw support in order to win the White House. While this potential damage alarmed John, he was even more infuriated that Russell had pictured him as betraying his obligation to represent the entire American people in the negotiations at Ghent.

Fortunately for Adams' cause, Russell blundered fatally. In making a copy of one of these letters to present to Congress and voters, he added falsifications intended to enlarge the harm it would cause. After Adams discovered the hoax, it was easy for him to prove how the perfidious Russell had altered the document in order to defame him. So clearly did Adams show Russell's villainy that even Clay was obliged to repudiate his henchman. JQA's vindication was soon complete: Russell was eventually defeated for reelection and ruined.

But this victory was not enough to satisfy John. His rage and desire for vengeance were such that he could not be dissuaded from clubbing Russell long after he had been vanquished. Even Monroe, who wished that such an ugly matter would not disturb the peace of his last years in the White House, could not calm him. Instead, the president's soothing approach to the Russell case made Adams lose his temper, bringing the two into a shouting match.

Seeking more blood, Adams took the opportunity to polish his own good name before all regions of the nation. Essays he wrote on the treachery of Jonathan Russell were published in several newspapers sympathetic to the Adams cause, including the *National Intelligencer* and the *Boston Statesman*. But these brief statements could not contain all the exhaustive—and exhausting—detail that Adams believed the republic should have before he could feel wholly vindicated. Consequently, he spent the summer and early autumn of 1822 writing his second book in two years—one vastly different from the volume on weights and measures. Entitled *The Duplicate Letters . . . Documents Relating to Transactions at the Negotiations of Ghent,* the enormous "pamphlet" was filled with official papers, interspersed with Adams' "remarks." These observations mainly stressed that Russell was part of a foul scheme to inflame passions between the nation's geographic sections, whereas John insisted that he wrote for no party or political purpose. He simply wished the book to warn of the broader danger in Russell's sin: "leaguing invidious and imaginary sectional or party feelings with the purposes of the [foreign] enemy."

Those who instead saw in Adams' book a depressing example of time wasted by treading on an already fallen enemy could not appreciate what a comfort it was to one of his temperament to believe that he had faced and won "a trial for my character before my country." His severity with those who besmirched him was even more cutting in his diary, where he called Russell Clay's "jackal." He claimed that every bad passion in the human heart was arrayed against him, while his own cause was that "of truth, of honesty, and of my country." When Louisa and friends advised that he relax a bit and let the furor subside, he refused, insisting that his enemy's doctrines had not been thoroughly exposed and that Clay was "working like a mole to undermine me."

The benefit of Russell's backfired scheme was that it released Adams to campaign for himself as earnestly as any other candidate. There was a crucial difference, however. He claimed to aim not for an office but to save his reputation. Meanwhile, his camp was gleeful that their man had spoken out, but they wished that he would quit while he was ahead. Adams halted only when he was convinced that his replies to his enemies would "abide unshaken the test of human scrutiny, of talents, and of time."

EVEN SO, much as he might enjoy righteous wrath, JQA remained uncomfortable with campaign skirmishing. With less than a year remaining before the election, in speaking of the campaign's effect upon him he echoed words once uttered by Jesus of Nazareth: "Would that this cup might pass from me." So why did he stay in the race? To withdraw would have been easy, for he never became a declared candidate. And, indeed, there were many opportunities when he might have announced a desire to retire from public life. Yet the closer the election drew, the more tenaciously he held on.

He did so for reasons more complex than simple hunger for the highest office in the land, although that ambition certainly was present. His most important motive was an unalloyed desire to stand tall in history as a benefactor of the republic and of mankind in general. If the nation rejected him, Adams believed, he would be forever disgraced in history's eyes. He also wished to emulate—or surpass—his revered father's distinguished career, and thereby burnish the Adams family name. This led to a dread that he might fall short of the parental expectations that had been drummed into him as a youthful prodigy. All these pressures combined to keep JQA in politics and particularly in the race for president. While he never quite said so, by 1823 he had reached a point where being anything less than president would show his family and posterity that he was merely human after all.

Rarely could Adams speak candidly in his journal or his letters about his reasons for actively seeking an office—assuming that he fully understood them himself. It was more important that he deplore at length what his foes were compelling him to do. In 1824, the last year of the campaign, he often found it wise to ignore his diary, or to enter only sketchy and unrevealing tidbits. There was one exception, however. In a diary entry written May 8, in which he described a visit from John McLean, the postmaster general, Adams did disclose much about how the campaign affected him.

McLean conveyed good news: the Adams electoral ticket in Ohio expected victory. JQA received this hopeful sign with mixed feelings. He wondered in his journal if it was wise to become optimistic, since "whether I ought to *wish* for success is among the greatest uncertainties of the election." If only he could await the event "with philosophical indifference," but that would be, as he put it, like trying to hold fire in one's hand by thinking of frost. "To suffer without feeling is not in human nature," he acknowledged, before coming to the heart of the matter: "When I consider that to me alone, of all the candidates before the nation, failure of success would be equivalent to a vote of censure by the nation upon my past services, I cannot dissemble to myself that I have more at stake upon the result than any other individual in the Union."

But was he adequate for the work of being president? Adams' reply to this question in his diary must have been unique among candidates in American history. "He who is equal to the task of serving a nation as her chief ruler must possess resources of a power to serve her even against her own will. This is the principle that I would impress indelibly upon my own mind." He believed that a president must rely on "wisdom and strength from above," not from the electorate.

And what if he did lose the election? Facing that prospect, as he often did, he took comfort in the example of John Adams. As the campaign drew to a close, he composed lines in honor of his parent which suggested the stance the poet-candidate could take if he were turned down by the Republic.

> *By Friends deserted and beset by Foes,*
> *Thy soul clung closest to thy country's cause,*
> *Vain their foul venom to infect thy life,*
> *Thou stoodst erect, amidst a falling world.*

As the presidential election loomed, JQA speculated for the hundredth time whether a victory would have any value after the demeaning fight necessary to win the public's summons. Certainly he understood campaign tactics—at least those used by others, if not his own. He had watched his opponents closely, missing no maneuver as Crawford, Clay, Jackson, and Calhoun, along with their henchmen and newspaper editors, took presidential campaigning to what Adams saw as new depths of scheming and demagoguery.

Ironically, the sordid sight seemed to make him all the more ambitious to outdistance these paltry partisans, for as 1824 wore on with painful slowness, Adams' desire to win overcame the weakening scholarly, reclusive side of his nature. He was no longer tempted to retire to his books and verse, thereby leaving the nation whatever president the electoral canvass threw up. He first showed this new intensity about running when he himself designed an event for January 8, 1824, that many observers considered the formal opening of the Adams campaign.

Perhaps invigorated by his success in shaping the Monroe Doctrine, he had proposed to Louisa early the previous December that they give a great ball to honor General Andrew Jackson on the approaching ninth anniversary of his victory over the British at New Orleans. At first, an astounded Louisa opposed the suggestion. But then, as she reported it, Adams took her into his confidence and unfolded a strategy that convinced her to cooperate. He told her that he wanted Andrew Jackson as a running mate.

A startled Louisa listened as her husband insisted that not only would Jackson be a worthy vice president, but he could bring essential western support to the Adams ticket. Also, JQA was disturbed by reports that Jackson had rising popularity in New England. The prospect of Yankee support for someone besides himself led Adams to urge his amazed lieutenants to negotiate with the Jackson camp about backing the general for vice president. In JQA's judgment there was no other tactic available. As he observed in his journal, it was now too late to try to "controul" (JQA's word) New England opinion against the Tennessean. Instead, Jackson must be wooed.

With this reasoning in mind, Louisa obediently undertook to carry out her spouse's plan for a ball honoring the Hero of New Orleans— who, of course, could hardly refuse to accept such a tribute to his wartime victory, even if he suspected Adams' motives. While Louisa made decorations and supervised servants and the conversion of her residence into a large dance hall, John was appearing at every public occasion throughout the holiday season, events where his presence was not unusual and where he might approach individuals who could affect the election's outcome. The Adams ball soon became the most eagerly awaited of these holiday festivities.

On that night, an estimated one thousand guests somehow pushed into the Adams house to dance, drink punch, and gawk at Andrew Jackson. Celebrants had such a good time that they remained into the early hours, many to talk about the evening's high point: as Louisa was escorting Jackson through the rooms to meet the multitude, she found herself suddenly covered with oil when a lamp hanging above her spilled its contents. The accident led many in the crowd to exclaim that since their hostess had been thus anointed, it must be a favorable omen for the Adams candidacy. Louisa kept her dignity, retorting that she was certain only that her gown had been "spoilt." Later, during the midnight supper, Jackson offered such a gracious toast to his hostess that many guests departed thinking he and Adams were now closely bound.

THEY WERE MISTAKEN. Despite the great social success of the ball, Jackson left it still wishing to be nothing less than an active contender for the presidency, which meant that four competitors would go down to the wire: Jackson and Adams, along with Clay and Crawford. Early signs from Pennsylvania, where Calhoun had placed his hopes, were so discouraging that the South Carolinian had settled for being the vice presidential candidate, where he had the field largely to himself.

On February 14, all candidates except Crawford boycotted the dying device of the congressional caucus, which the Georgian won. Of the sixty-six votes cast, Crawford took sixty-two; Adams received two, Jackson and North Carolina Senator Nathaniel Macon one each. There had been a time when the caucus clarified who was likely to be the next president. In 1824, however, it only increased the confusion. Rumors and rumors of rumors sought to explain how states were leaning or which candidate might eventually align with another.

The bedlam meant that the candidates' opinions on such questions of the day as the tariff, slavery, interstate highways, and uniform bankruptcy laws were badly distorted by speculation. The electoral process became infuriatingly ambiguous, so that many of the callers Adams received in the winter and spring asked for clarification of his views. The string of inquiries was an advantage to his cause, for if he must campaign, he preferred to do so by spending most of each day talking with members of Congress and other visitors.

When evening came, he was nearly always found at the theater, again chatting with the politicians and citizens who lined up to speak with him. The theater, along with the halls of Congress, the local churches, his office, and his residence, was a setting where John knew he might plausibly converse with everyone while not being seen, at least in his eyes, as seeking votes.

Keeping track of the callers to his office, he recorded that 235 appeared during March and 264 in May. To each he gave at least thirty minutes of his attention; some especially influential persons received three hours. "The Presidential canvassing proceeds with increasing heat," he reported, although his journal included few summaries of these conversations.

One recorded exchange took place on May 1, with Congressman John Reed of Massachusetts. During this chat, Adams recalled, he informed Reed that there was only one barrier to an Adams victory by a "large majority" in the electoral college. This was the suspicion on the part of many Republicans that he was still a Federalist and thus likely as president to be overly sympathetic to the interests of New England. According to JQA, the absurdity of this prejudice ought to be recognized by anyone who remembered the abuse he had taken from Massachusetts Federalists. Obviously hoping that Reed would spread the word, Adams assured him: "If it should be the pleasure of the people of the United States that I should serve them as their President, I should be the President not of a section, nor of a faction, but of the whole Union."

During the summer, more malicious rumors kept spilling out from what Adams called the "electioneering caldroun." One of them held that John Adams had broken politically with his son. Other reports pretended to know to whom JQA had offered political appointments in exchange for support. When asked about these charges, he replied that he was "not disposed to sell the skin before the animal was taken."

He was less genial about the personal attacks he received. When Calhoun and his supporters were blamed for spreading harmful reports about Adams, JQA told one of Calhoun's allies that "my complaint was not that attempts were made to tear my reputation to pieces for the benefit of Mr. Calhoun," but that they were accompanied by "professions of great respect and esteem." He marveled at how one politician might attack another and yet do so "with no manifestations of enmity."

At least the Jackson and Crawford camps did not disguise their dislike of Adams. In August, by JQA's count, there were fifteen newspapers around the nation whose task was "to run down my reputation" and to "defame and disgrace me." It was apparent, he said, that "no falsehood is too broad and no insinuation too base for them." For him, it seemed that "every liar and calumniator in the country was at work day and night to destroy my character."

Not one word did Adams say about the brutal assaults his managers made upon his opponents, so it remains uncertain to what extent he may have known about his forces' activities or encouraged them as they gave blows as lustily as they received them. This averted gaze was perhaps a feat more amazing and absurd than his lofty insistence that he did nothing to coax the voter. As an avid reader of the national press, he had to know about the tactics of his supporters.

Perhaps he suppressed the knowledge by giving attention to his personal difficulties, which persisted even in the last months of the presidential race. He was particularly anxious about Louisa, who was suffering from erysipelas, a strep infection often called St. Anthony's Fire, which mainly entailed painful, burning facial eruptions along with fever, vomiting, and severe headache. She spent part of the hectic summer of 1824 at a spa near Bedford, Pennsylvania, trying the mineral waters "for the restoration of her health." Adams conceded that Louisa was "dejected" and that he was "deeply affected at parting with her."

Before long, he himself had had enough of Washington and the campaign and resolved to "take a month of holiday to visit my father and dismiss care." Departing the capital at the beginning of September, he predicted that "I shall probably never pass another summer in this city." In Philadelphia he met Louisa, who was much improved and willing to go to Quincy with him. Cheered by her presence, he enjoyed watching his steamboat attain the astonishing speed of ten miles per hour while racing another vessel.

Adams arrived in Quincy to find his father crippled and nearly blind. Yet "he bears his condition with fortitude" and remained eager to talk politics, JQA reported, astonished that one could suffer "the total prostration of his physical powers" and yet have his mental capacity "scarcely impaired at all."

Once the pleasantries of the reunion were finished, JQA had to face private vexations, some of which temporarily shoved the election to the back of his mind. A chief worry continued to be the behavior of son George. Charles Francis claimed that his brother had "the weakness of a child [and] is easily a dupe." Agreeing with this view, their father sought to strengthen George by talking with him during a fishing outing to Nahant, but the conversation did little to dispel his concern.

Hoping for inspiration, Adams paid another visit to Quincy's old burying ground, where he studied the granite stones marking the resting place of ancestors. "Pass another century," he reflected, "and we shall all be mouldering in the same dust or resolved into the same elements." Brooding over himself and his sons, he could only hope that their graves would speak of "blameless lives."

There were moments, of course, when the vacationing Adams could not escape politics. While he managed to discourage public dinners in his honor, close friends and partisan associates in Boston and Salem insisted that he dine with small groups. On such occasions, he unbuttoned enough before these supporters to concede that Jackson was now likely to win the largest number of electoral votes. Consequently, Adams advised his supporters not to make Jackson their second electoral choice (each elector cast two votes); doing so might assure the general's election as president and Calhoun's as vice president.

Despite his many pledges to avoid appealing to sectional prejudices, Adams could not resist reminding his Massachusetts friends that a victory for Jackson and Calhoun would mean "absolute proscription of New England" and an exclusion of Massachusetts' interests in the next administration. Since he believed both the region's and the nation's progress called for using federal powers to build interstate highways and to encourage manufacturing, he pictured Jackson and Calhoun as foes of genuine progress.

IT WAS A DISHEARTENED secretary of state who set out for Washington "to finish my term of service and to meet the fate to which I am destined." On the way he was detained in Philadelphia, first by legal matters, and then by insistence that he remain to participate in a festive welcome for General Lafayette, who had begun a triumphant tour as a guest of the United States. There were also delays in Baltimore, where JQA was trapped into another round of salutations for Lafayette. Consequently, it wasn't until the second week of October that Adams was back in his office, and by then the outcome of the campaign was clear: no aspirant would take a majority of either electoral or popular votes.

At that point in American politics, general elections for president and vice president had not been invented. Instead, on varying days voters in each state chose from among persons or slates pledged to support one or another candidate for president in the electoral college. In six states the legislatures rather than the public named the electors. If no person received a majority in the electoral college, the Constitution decreed that a choice among the three candidates receiving the most electoral votes would devolve upon the House of Representatives; each state delegation would cast one vote. A winner needed a majority of the states voting. The rules did not require that these delegations support the favorite of their state's voters.

The national results were at last complete in early December, but they only confirmed what everyone knew. John Quincy Adams was the victor in New England and partially in New York, which gave him 84 electoral votes and a popular vote of 114,023. The plurality, however, went to Andrew Jackson, who received 99 electoral votes and a popular count of 152,901; he carried much of the South, along with some Middle States. The third-ranking candidate was William H. Crawford, with 41 electoral and 46,979 popular votes, taken mostly in Virginia and Georgia.

Running fourth in the electoral college—and thus dropped from the House balloting—was Henry Clay, who had 37 electoral votes from Ohio, Missouri, and Kentucky, and a few more popular votes than Crawford, 47,217. John C. Calhoun easily won a majority of votes for vice president in the electoral college; had he not, the winner of that office would have been named by the Senate.

Between late December and February 9, 1825, when the House was scheduled to choose the president, Adams joined the rest of Washington and most of the nation in speculating over the outcome. It remained much in doubt until the very last, which convinced him that if he won, his administration would function at a great disadvantage. The possibility that Jackson, who had received more popular support than any other candidate, might not win in the House had begun to spread indignation in parts of the nation. There was even talk of civil war from a few hotheads.

As he continued wooing any undecided House member, Adams did so with a heavy heart. This was not the sort of summons from the Republic he had hoped for. On the flyleaf of the diary volume containing his entries for January 1825, he wrote: "In vain from care woulds't thou be freed." Curiously, the diary did not mention that on New Year's Day, Congressman Robert P. Letcher from Clay's home state had brought news that two-thirds of Kentucky's congressional delegation planned to vote for Adams.

The report should not have been surprising, even though Kentucky voters had ignored Adams in their balloting. The determination of these congressmen simply reflected Clay's power over his fellow Kentucky representatives. Letcher's report was Adams' first sign that his victory in the House of Representatives was now possible. Six years later, he recorded that Letcher had visited him "a week before I had any conversation with Clay upon the subject"—which was JQA's way of emphasizing that he had not bargained to influence the Kentucky delegation's vote.

Not until January 9 did Clay tell him of his decision to throw

Adams the support of his three states. Clay believed Adams to be the least evil of the choices before the House, mainly because the two agreed that the Union must be strengthened by higher tariffs and federal support for roads, canals, and manufacturing.

With three additional delegations now on his side, Adams allowed himself a cautious observation: "Until recently I had not expected it would be necessary for me to anticipate the event of my election as one for which it would be proper for me even to be prepared." Yet his improved prospects left him in a grim mood. He confided to his old friend Rufus King, now retiring as senator from New York, that while "the present state and aspect of things . . . are flattering for the immediate issue," he admitted he dreaded becoming a minority president. Equivocal success "would open [me] to a far severer trial than defeat [would have brought]."

Five days before the House voted, Adams took another look at what winning or losing would mean. "To me the alternatives are both distressing in prospect, and the most formidable is that of success. All the danger is on the pinnacle. The humiliation of failure will be so much more than compensated by the safety in which it will leave me that I ought to regard it as a consummation devoutly to be wished, and hope to find consolation in it." Even as victory seemed near, in the quiet of his study, the familiar ambivalence was awakened, stronger than ever.

Nevertheless, until the last moment he continued to reassure and cajole countless callers. The business of the State Department was largely forgotten in the face of rumors that the Jackson and Crawford camps might yet unite. Adams had good reason to be uneasy. Ever since Clay's support was announced, he had listened to demands that the Kentuckian be richly rewarded for his help.

At the other extreme, he heard threats, particularly from the Jackson and Crawford backers, that if Clay received a high post as his payoff, the Adams administration would be wrecked by public anger. According to the Jackson camp, the citizenry would see Clay's appointment as proof of a corrupt bargain to deprive Andrew Jackson, the voters' favorite, of his rightful place as chief executive. All that Adams said in responding to those who asked about any plans for Clay was that if support from the West should bring him into the presidency, then he naturally would wish to involve western leaders in his cabinet. "The object nearest to my heart [is] to bring the whole people of the Union to harmonize together."

On the day before the House voted, forty callers besieged Adams in the morning alone. "The city swarms with strangers," he noted, and it seemed as if all of them wanted to give him advice. Then time for speculation came to an end. Early on Wednesday, February 9, he wrote, "May the blessing of God rest upon the event of this day." Taking care to proceed as usual, he walked to the State Department at his customary time, there to occupy himself while, in the Capitol, the House of Representatives chose a president.

It was assumed that a decision would be several days away. No candidate was expected to receive a majority of states immediately. But soon Alexander Everett burst into the secretary's office with the astonishing bulletin that the House had required only one ballot to elect the next president. Adams had received the vote of thirteen state delegations to Jackson's seven and Crawford's four. Clay had succeeded in delivering Kentucky, Missouri, and Ohio to Adams. The victor also had taken Louisiana, Illinois, and Maryland from the Jackson camp and, of course, he carried the six New England states.

The decisive vote was New York's, whose delegation had been divided all along. One of the state's leaders for Crawford, Martin Van Buren, later explained how Adams won there. The story centered on General Stephen Van Rensselaer, a wavering member of the New York delegation who had been a Federalist and was related by marriage to Alexander Hamilton. JQA had once carefully assured the general that an Adams administration would hold no grudge against veteran Federalists, but Van Rensselaer was still wary as he took his seat for the House vote.

While his New York colleagues waited for him to put a ballot into the delegation's box, the venerable congressman bowed his head to pray for divine guidance. When he opened his eyes, he saw an Adams ballot at his feet. Rejoicing in this sign from "on high," Van Rensselaer picked up the paper and deposited it with those of the other New Yorkers. It proved to be the one vote needed to bring the state into the Adams camp and make Adams president. The story became one of the legends of American elections.

Upon learning of his victory, the president-elect first scribbled a brief note to his father informing him of "the event of this day" and adding, "I can only offer you my congratulations and ask your blessings and prayers." He went home to receive the embrace of his family. Louisa reported in her diary that she kept her foreboding to herself.

The Adamses then attended a public reception at the White House long scheduled for that date. The rooms were so crowded that some people could not enter. JQA's congratulations included a hand-shake from Jackson, whom Adams described as "altogether placid and courteous." When John and Louisa returned home, he carried a hopeful heart, a mood lifted even more when a band of musicians ser-enaded him until after midnight. He closed the day of his victory as it began, "with supplications to the Father of mercies" that his election would "redound to His glory and to the welfare of my country."

CHAPTER TWELVE

Gall

A base and formidable conspiracy.

IT MAY CONFOUND some readers that a biography of any American president should devote only a single chapter to his administration. Nevertheless, such brevity seems appropriate for John Quincy Adams. His four years in the White House were misery for him and for his wife. All that he hoped to accomplish was thwarted by a hostile Congress. His opponents continually assailed him with what he claimed was the foulest slander. Consequently, while Adams sought reelection in 1828, he did so mostly from stubborn pride, and he actually looked impatiently toward his certain defeat by Andrew Jackson. For the remaining twenty years of his life, he reflected on his presidency with distaste, convinced that he had been the victim of evildoers. His administration was a hapless failure and best forgotten, save for the personal anguish it cost him.

UPON LEARNING that a second Adams would be president, old John sent word that "the multitude of my thoughts and the intensity of my feelings are too much for a mind like mine in its ninetieth year." He was able to invoke "the blessing of God Almighty" upon his son, who, he said, had already received it "in so remarkable a manner from your cradle!"

Certainly, this heavenly bounty had included much talent, but JQA's abilities would prove largely useless to his presidency. Just before the election, the astute Albert Gallatin, who remembered Adams well from their days in Ghent, had pictured him as "a virtuous man, whose temper, which is not the best, might be overlooked; he has a great and miscellaneous knowledge, and he is with his pen a powerful debater; but he wants to a deplorable degree that most essential quality, a sound and correct judgment." The president-elect wasted no time in demonstrating the validity of Gallatin's judgment.

The day after he was named chief executive, Adams welcomed a House committee led by Daniel Webster, who called to give formal notification of the election result. Choosing to emulate Thomas Jefferson, who had also been selected by the House but under very different circumstances, Adams read a statement to the delegation in which he noted that he was the first president to enter office lacking a majority of electoral votes. He spoke of wishing he could refuse the office and enable the American people to make a new decision. But since the Constitution did not allow a second election, "I shall therefore repair to the post assigned me by the call of my country . . . oppressed with the magnitude of the task before me."

All that sustained him, he explained to the delegation, was the certainty—unwarranted, as it turned out—that as president he would have the "generous support" of the American people, the same citizens who had stood with him "in the vicissitudes of a life devoted to their service." After hearing this prophecy, the committee departed, and Adams turned to the first task of a new administration, which was to staff the federal government. Once more, idealism led him away from reality.

He was determined to choose persons for their talent, not party loyalty. "Pernicious" was how he described the spoils system, whereby jobs on the public payroll were given to partisan favorites. He claimed that the practice infested the republic with "a perpetual and unintermitting scramble for office." To set a different example, he vowed that no public functionary should be displaced except for cause, and he sought to retain every member of Monroe's cabinet. He urged Crawford to remain as treasury secretary, and he tried to make Jackson secretary of war. Both of them refused to accept.

It was, however, in selecting his own successor at the State Department that Adams undid his strategy for nonpartisanship and national unity. He asked Henry Clay, to whom he owed his election, to serve as secretary of state. The offer was extended after the House had elected Adams—not before, as is often alleged. The president-elect claimed that there were many reasons why Clay was the best choice. As a western leader, he would assure a national perspective in the administration. He was a person of experience in foreign affairs. He was a man of undoubted ability. He and Adams had long agreed that a strong and united nation could come about only through more aggressive federal legislation. As for Clay, he was eager for a job that Adams' success once again had proved to be the path to the presidency.

Nevertheless, despite Clay's merits, giving the Kentuckian the second most important office in the national government showed JQA's political ineptness. Since the new president had a long record of doing what he thought was right in the face of warnings, his action was not surprising. What *was* surprising was that Clay, normally so shrewd, accepted the position. For the rest of his life, he readily admitted that joining the Adams administration was the stupidest act of his career.

At the time, however, the stouthearted and optimistic Clay had convinced himself, as he also tried to assure Adams, that his nomination would receive only "trifling" opposition in the Senate, despite the rising indignation at his appointment. Finally, on March 7, 1825, shortly before adjourning, the Senate confirmed Clay as secretary of state, but not by the wide margin so glibly predicted by the Kentuckian. While all the other nominations were approved unanimously, Clay entered office by the embarrassing tally of 27 to 14. It was, said a startled Adams, the opposition's first act in carrying "the banners of General Jackson."

A few days earlier, Adams had finished writing his inaugural address, although a severe cold and sleeplessness made the work difficult. After bidding farewell to his staff in the State Department, he spent inaugural eve quietly at dinner with two old friends and then received Clay for a chat. The next morning, March 4, found the public in Washington choosing between two entertainments: the swearing-in of a president and a visiting circus. Many seemed to prefer the political show, for when Adams' official procession started at 11:30 a.m., a "cavalcade" of citizens escorted it to the Capitol, along with the usual companies of militia. The president-elect rode in one carriage with the secretary of the navy and the attorney general. President Monroe followed in a second vehicle.

A "crowded auditory," as Adams put it, pushed into the chamber of the House of Representatives to watch Chief Justice John Marshall, "holding a volume of the laws," administer the oath of office, and then to hear the new president address the nation. His remarks included an obvious attempt to squelch rumors about his anti-democratic outlook. "Our political creed is, without a dissenting voice that can be heard, that the will of the people is the source and the happiness of the people the end of all legitimate government upon earth."

Then came conventional statements about the history and present prosperity of the republic. Adams praised his predecessor, condemned "the collisions of party spirit," and urged that only persons of "talents and virtue" be installed in public office. The ardent hope of the new administration was stated late in the address when Adams reminded his audience that "the magnificence and splendor" of public works had been "the imperishable glories of the ancient republics." Just so would "unborn millions of our posterity" give thanks for the "roads and aqueducts" that the American republic must now create—or so Adams clearly intended.

A sympathetic listener noted that the president was "at first a little agitated—but soon recovered his self possession, and spoke with great clearness, force, and animation." It produced, said Congressman William Plumer, Jr., "one of the most august and interesting spectacles I ever witnessed." It was also one of the lengthiest, for Adams had not spared his audience.

After the ceremony, he shook hands with Monroe and many in the chamber. The same procession then escorted the two presidents to their homes, which for the moment still meant the White House for Monroe and, nearby, the Adams residence on F Street. There they greeted throngs of friends and the merely curious. The new first lady arose from her sickbed to join her husband in welcoming visitors. He then went alone on a rainy evening to the inaugural ball, where he remained until after midnight.

It took six weeks for the Adamses to settle into the White House. The place had been left in such disarray by the Monroes that Louisa shrewdly invited members of the public to view the untidiness and the battered furniture passed along to her family. Adding some of their own possessions to household equipment they purchased through a small congressional appropriation, they had the White House in decent enough shape by April 5 to permit some of the family to sleep there.

Two days later, they dined in the mansion, although Adams continued somewhat longer to use his F Street residence for executive business. By the close of April, having sold the rest of their furniture at auction, John and Louisa were finally established. Their son John, whom Harvard had expelled, would serve as the president's private secretary—JQA's fervent opposition to nepotism having been waived in this urgent case. Louisa had the company of two nieces. One was Mary Hellen, orphaned daughter of Walter Hellen and Louisa's sister Nancy. Mary had become engaged to her cousin George Adams. The other niece was Lizzie Adams, second child of JQA's brother Tom. There were nineteen servants, led by the indefatigable Antoine Guista.

A tourist transported back to 1825 from the late twentieth century would scarcely recognize the Executive Mansion, sitting as it did on an often muddy road only two blocks from open country. The present-day office wings did not exist, and the grounds were given over mainly to a huge garden and an area where the household's cows, horses, and sheep grazed. The structure itself could seem almost barnlike when the wind clattered through it. Neither plumbing nor running water was available for the first family. The president's office was on the second floor.

It seemed that any citizen had ready access to the White House, except for the frustrating evening when Adams himself had difficulty gaining entrance. Returning home from his third church service of that Sunday, he found the doors locked and the porter gone off with the key.

Upon moving into the White House, Adams had anticipated a regular routine, thinking this was possible because the bothersome Congress was in recess. He had no such luck. Although the legislators had left the capital, many of them continued to befoul the name of the new administration from home. The uproar took Adams' attention from his work as adversaries everywhere, it seemed, denounced his "corrupt bargain" with Henry Clay. JQA also heard himself called an elitist who cared so little for the voice of the common man and so much for becoming president that he had schemed to get the office.

"Corruption and Bargain" became a national chant, particularly in Tennessee, where plans began at once to avenge the perceived mistreatment of the state's favorite son. In October 1825, the legislature nominated Andrew Jackson to run for president in 1828. Jackson promptly resigned his seat in the U.S. Senate to devote himself to the campaign, a move that Adams soon was calling "a base and formidable conspiracy." He became fond of the word *conspiracy*, which was natural enough for one who had read and reread Tacitus' tales of how courageous statesmen of antiquity had stood for good against the evil of conspirators.

The first victims of the rising opposition were Adams' intentions for improving the republic. These plans never moved much beyond the paper on which he had stated them. The few proposals that did reach Congress later in 1825 were either defeated or stymied. Such, for example, was the fate of Adams' belief that the United States should participate in the first hemispheric move toward a pan-American union, which Simon Bolívar had initiated. To do so meant sending delegates to a congress in Panama in 1826, a step that Senator Martin Van Buren and other Jackson spokesmen skillfully opposed.

Adams' adversaries so artfully delayed and denounced the Panama-mission proposal that when delegates were grudgingly approved, it was too late for them to attend the conference. In the debate, the president was accused of willingness to abridge U.S. independence and sovereignty, and of intending to take the nation into South American and European conflicts. It was during these discussions that Senator John Randolph of Virginia memorably denounced the "corrupt bargain" between Adams and Clay, saying their administration combined "the puritan with the black-leg." To Adams' mortification, Clay challenged Randolph to a duel, from which the combatants emerged unscathed in all but dignity.

Early in the Panama furor, Adams made a mistake of extreme proportions when his first annual message gave his opponents a broader basis on which to rally. In late autumn 1825, as he wrote the address and with "conspiracy" flourishing all around him, he decided to shape his remarks more for future effect than for the moment. Rather than pound on a national mind that he believed had been closed by his critics, he decided to seek a place in the esteem of future generations.

What made the message both memorable and vulnerable to scoffers was its proclamation that the federal government bore responsibility for mankind's cultural, scientific, and general welfare. For instance, Adams called on the nation's leaders to promote knowledge. He made the startling claim that Congress had a duty to advance science, an obligation he insisted was more important even than the building of roads and canals. Here, according to the president, were the noblest of the republic's tasks, including geographical exploration and the creation of a national university. Improved patent laws and a system for uniform weights and measures must also be enacted without delay.

Finally, Adams offered the proposal that drew him the greatest ridicule. He urged the establishment of a national astronomical observatory, where a professional staff would be "in constant attendance of observation upon the phenomena of the heavens." Using words that came back to haunt him, the president spoke of the nation's disgrace in having no observatories while Europe had 130 of "these light-houses of the skies."

Not even his cabinet could support these pioneering policies. After taking ninety minutes on November 23 to read a draft of the message to his department heads, Adams received much cautionary advice from these astonished and alarmed gentlemen. Several expressed their misgivings, mainly over his call for extraordinary federal legislation, and claimed that neither Congress nor the public would be likely to see such proposals as either wise or constitutional.

Even Henry Clay, ardent nationalist though he was, said that some of the recommendations were "entirely hopeless." William Wirt, the attorney general and Adams' good friend, called the message "excessively bold" and a "spirited thing," the effect of which he "dreaded." The cabinet predicted that when the address was published, numerous citizens would believe Patrick Henry's prophecy "that we wanted a great magnificent government" had been realized.

Listening to these concerns, Adams wondered whether it was "fitting" that he be "intimidated" by criticism. He sought to assure his associates that his message looked beyond a single session of Congress. "The plant may come later, though the seed should be sown early." In private, he reminded himself that "the perilous experiment must be made. Let me make it in full deliberation and be prepared for the consequences."

Thus it was that Adams' first annual message, with its advanced ideas largely unaltered, arrived at the Capitol—in those days presidents did not deliver their views orally—at noon on December 6. Its ideas were doomed, for the cabinet members proved to be good prophets.

His message's reception was devastating to Adams. No one appeared to share his vision for America, one he had hoped would bring him enduring fame as a benefactor of humanity. Instead, his views drew jeers from many members of Congress and newspaper editors, while angry taunts were aimed at some of his speech's rhetorical challenges, such as: "While foreign nations less blessed with that freedom which is power than ourselves are advancing with giant strides in the career of public improvement, were we to slumber in indolence or fold up our arms and proclaim to the world that we are palsied by the will of our constituents, would it not be to cast away the bounties of Providence and doom ourselves to perpetual inferiority?"

Since this tangled language sounded like a presidential rebuke of the American people, Adams' words were used by the "conspirators" to remind the nation that this was the chief executive who had bargained to override the public's will in choosing a president. It was with great understatement, therefore, that JQA mentioned receiving "much criticism upon the Message." Newspaper attacks ranged from "bitter invective" to solemn warnings that the president intended to desecrate the Constitution through his "latitudinarian" schemes. Rumor had it that the revered Jefferson found the message full of heretical ideas.

The barrage left Adams hurt and angry, particularly after he learned that some critics were saying "that I have taken Caesar as my model." Pretending to fear the administration's talk of exercising federal strength, a few senators went so far as to introduce a resolution to indict the president for usurpation of power. At this, JQA blew up, telling one supporter that senators now sought "to accuse, try, and convict me in secret inquisition, without hearing me in my defense; without even letting me know there was a charge against me."

Proposing to let the Senate do its worst, he announced that he would stand before the country on what he believed was solid ground. But instead, the political earth crumbled beneath him, for whether Congress was in session or out, the abusive criticism from the swelling band of "conspirators" went on during the rest of his hugely unsuccessful administration. Thanks to a fragile alliance of Jackson, Crawford, and Calhoun forces, not even Adams' foreign policy was safe. Besides torpedoing the pan-American conference, the opposition hindered or blocked such seemingly uncontroversial endeavors as negotiating boundaries, improving the West Indies trade, and recovering losses from France suffered by Americans during the Napoleonic era.

Domestic undertakings were even less successful. All of Adams' scientific and educational proposals were defeated, as were his efforts to enlarge the road and canal systems. A design to strengthen the Bank of the United States as a centralized credit authority and a plan to refinance the public debt were lost. His campaign for a national bankruptcy act was blocked, as were efforts to increase revenue from the sale of public lands. In short, a vengeful opposition was delighted to kick around almost every legislative proposal that hinted at Adams' determination to pursue national development through federal means. Usually, his supporters in Congress could not muster enough votes for a successful defense.

Learning from their futile effort to avert disaster for Adams' first annual message, when the time came for cabinet members to face the second message, they requested a draft to discuss in private. Although he reluctantly agreed, the president doubted that this was "a safe precedent to follow," fearing it might encourage the cabinet to seek control of the message. He need not have worried. The members merely recognized that the more their chief was assailed by his enemies, the more stubborn he might become. Trying to help him, the department heads thought they could be more effective if they prepared their advice outside JQA's forbidding presence.

Clay and the others were correct. President Adams became more determined to remain his own man—and, as he thought, the people's man. He must do this, as JQA put it, despite "the protracted agony of character and reputation which it is the will of Superior Power that I should pass through." Nevertheless, he adopted many of the cabinet's suggestions for making his remaining annual messages somewhat more realistic.

Such help availed little, however, as the administration's woes steadily deepened. Mid-term elections in 1826 returned an opposition majority to Congress, leaving Adams to sigh that "the days of trial are coming again." He quietly acknowledged the success of those forces combining against him. From every corner he heard of "meetings and counter meetings, committees of correspondence, delegations and addresses against and for the Administration, and thousands of persons occupied with little else than to work up the passions of the people."

The exasperating legislative branch soon was taking so much attention that Adams was obliged to forsake the sacred task of making daily diary entries. "I shall lose irretrievably the Chain of Events," he complained. His ordeal was "inexpressibly distressing," depriving him "of leisure for reflection." By most evenings, the president admitted, "my strength and spirits are both exhausted." Of such days, he wondered, "how many more?" He no longer dared to hope that the public would suddenly recognize that their president's "character and reputation [are] assailed by a base and formidable conspiracy."

Perceiving that his chance at national leadership had slipped away, a grievously disappointed Adams grew moody, haggard, and, at times, perhaps clinically depressed. Much of his physical and emotional decline stemmed, of course, from the humiliation of being victimized by Andrew Jackson and his followers. Adams now openly despised Old Hickory, whom he called illiterate and governed by passion—although as recently as 1824, he had spoken approvingly of the general's abilities and of wishing to have him as a running mate.

It galled the president that someone like himself, who had earned the respect of czars, prime ministers, and distinguished men of science and letters, must receive the abuse of unschooled and self-centered partisans. There was no escape, he said, but to "await my allotted time. My own career is closed."

Dogged by such thoughts, he moped in the White House while Louisa watched him with sympathy and alarm. There was no particular health complaint to note, she explained to son George, except for "almost total loss of appetite and a general weakness and languor." JQA had dropped so much weight that his clothes hung loosely on him.

THE SUCCESS OF HIS ENEMIES was but one reason why Adams became so despondent. Had the presidency offered benefits for mind and soul, he might have mustered more resilience against the anger of the conspirators. Instead, his bleak outlook made him exaggerate the tedium that came with holding the highest office. But, of course, an Adams could see no choice except to carry out his "wearisome official duties."

Before facing these daily chores, he normally was up by 5 a.m. and reading several Bible chapters, keeping handy a volume of commentary. Then he thumbed through a number of newspapers before taking a vigorous walk or swim. He ate breakfast at 9 a.m. and was in his office until late afternoon. This schedule shifted the White House dinner hour from 4 p.m. to 5 p.m. or beyond, since visitors often kept the president from punctually beginning his second walk of the day.

When dinner was finished, he sometimes chatted with Louisa or played billiards with relatives. Usually, however, he worked in his study until 11 p.m. There he finally had time for such chores as signing land grants and patents or for reading lengthy documents stemming from courts-martial. Such a schedule meant that the first family usually attended social events without the president. Even Christmas brought no exception to this routine. If there were extra moments, Adams spent them in making diary entries.

The president felt guilty about his recent inattentiveness to his diary. Since the start of 1795, he recalled, he had kept a daily journal without interruption, usually with time to record thoughts on many subjects. What was the cost of thus being a faithful "journalizer"? he wondered. "Had I spent upon any work of Science or Literature the time employed upon this diary, it might perhaps have been permanently useful to my children and my country."

Now, however, the diary was being marred by gaps and brevity. At best, the harassed chief executive kept two journals, one with the barest record of a day, the other with fuller accounts. It was this latter volume that suffered most because of his office routine. As he endured the ordeal of being president, he chuckled grimly whenever he heard that someone considered his chair to be "a bed of roses."

The most irritating thorns were, as before at the State Department, the now innumerable visitors who lined up outside his office, most of them either "in search of place" or "solicitors for donations." Some callers were prompted merely by curiosity. Any citizen could take a place on the stairs leading to the executive chamber, there to wait a turn to see the president. More impatient individuals often simply barged into the office.

While cabinet meetings were normally uninterrupted, Adams could not otherwise be certain of quiet when conferring with such lieutenants as his staunch ally John W. Taylor of New York, briefly Speaker of the House. Because of the lack of privacy in the daytime, these loyal followers often found it prudent to meet with their chief after dinner in his residential quarters.

Not even George P. Todson—a physician who had been dismissed from the army, was angered by Adams' refusal to overrule the sentence, and had publicly threatened to assassinate him—was denied access. Advised to omit his daily walks while Todson was in town, the president proceeded as usual. Finally, the outraged physician appeared at the White House on December 16, 1826, only to have the courageous—or foolhardy—Adams face him down with a stern defense of the army's action.

Although Todson withdrew, he stayed around the capital to try a new strategy. He renounced any intent to murder the president and over several months appeared frequently to demand either reappointment or money. Each time, he was refused. "This incident," Adams wrote, "forcibly brings to my consciousness the frail tenure upon which human life is held." He prayed that "the Spirit of God [would] sustain me and preserve me from any weakness unworthy of my station."

The episode was the most alarming event in JQA's administrative routine. Fortunately, there were more welcome exceptions to the usually dreary sort of caller. Such a diversion accompanied Bishop John England of Charleston, who brought along a French citizen who was willing to sell to the United States a secret means of "conveying correspondence beyond the sea without danger of its being intercepted."

While the Frenchman keenly interested the president, he was even more intrigued later when "a wretched looking man" barged in to announce himself as both Saint Peter and the Messiah. With remarkable patience, Adams listened to the man's "wild incoherent strain" of talk, and then asked him who he had been before he became Saint Peter. The reply was "Peter McDermot, an Irishman," which so amused John that after the caller departed, he left his desk to go outside and inspect the silkworms he was cultivating. To his delight, he found that one had, by presidential count, laid 238 eggs.

Rarely, however, could even these worms afford escape from the "worrisome detail" that overcame Adams, including, for instance, confidential sessions with the superintendent of the Military Academy at West Point concerning immorality said to be rampant among cadets. According to the superintendent, the young men had become clever about smuggling liquor onto the premises for drinking bouts where faces were averted so cadets could not testify against one another. He also brought to the president's attention the plea of a candidate for admission who asked not to be required to remove his clothing for a physical examination.

At other times, Adams' encounters with military matters meant listening to aged veterans who called to explain why the government should relieve their destitution. Particularly moving to the president was the case of Joseph Wheaton, a person of failing memory, who described what it was like to be compelled to live with his daughter and her "worthless husband."

Occasionally, a guest could be useful. Eleazar Parraly, a traveler who simply wanted to see a president while passing through Washington in November 1826, strode into the executive office unannounced, interrupting a conversation between the president and the secretary of state. On discovering that his visitor was a dentist, Adams was so delighted that he excused Clay and "took the opportunity to have a decayed tooth drawn." This done, Parraly "scaled off the tarter which has been for years collecting upon my lower front teeth." (JQA had been remiss about seeing his Boston dentist, and at that time Washington was still too much a village to support the practice of dentistry.) When the dentist detected another bad tooth, Adams asked him to return the next day and extract it. Parraly did so, and then refused to accept the payment the president pressed upon him, taking only "a recommendation."

Save for the occasional exceptions, the weeks and months of sitting in the presidential office left the bookish and easily bored Adams lamenting the waste of hours. "There is no time so ill-employed," he wrote, "as that of listening to the self-eulogium and importunities of these petitioners for petty offices." He was careful to maintain "a chilling frigidity" in their presence, since his callers' eagerness for even a promise led them "to construe every kind word into one."

By 1827, this numbing routine, combined with the barrage of partisan criticism, was causing Adams both physical and emotional distress. With loss of sleep, indigestion, and lassitude as his main bodily complaints, he said the thought of continuing in public life left "a chill of indifference creeping upon me from day to day." To improve his health, he began regularly taking an ounce of castor oil, although he admitted that his condition was "complicated with internal piles." What else could he say but that life "now bears heavily on my nerves and spirits. Patience!"

He sought this virtue in three services of worship on Sunday and then in writing critiques of the sermons. The president now divided his time among the Unitarian, Presbyterian, and Episcopal denominations, giving each sect its turn, either morning, afternoon, or evening.

Unfortunately, the homiletical powers of Washington's clergy were not of the highest order, challenging Adams to be a tolerant worshipper. This was not always possible, as when a guest speaker at the Presbyterian Church warned of sudden destruction certain to come upon his auditors because they did not believe "that we preach Christ crucified." When the same minister led the congregation in a closing hymn by Isaac Watts, which claimed that men "were more base and brutish than the beasts," Adams could only shake his head and imagine that if this was said to a church member on any day but Sunday, the pastor would likely be knocked down.

The president wished that ministers could be content simply to speak of the Bible's "sublime morals, its unparalleled conceptions of the nature of God, and its irresistible power over the heart." He also urged more emphasis on the life and death of Jesus, without its supernatural aspects. One clergyman especially pleased him with a sermon drawn on a text from Ecclesiastes, chapter twelve, beginning: "Remember now thy Creator in the days of thy youth," and concluding: "Vanity of vanities, saith the preacher; all is vanity." The message sent Adams back to the White House praising this "overpowering exhortation" and claiming that there was nothing so sublime even in Homer, whom John believed to be a contemporary of the Biblical author.

Appearing as widely and as regularly as he did in the churches,

President Adams was frequently visited by congregational representatives asking for donations and especially for sizable loans. After lending to several religious projects, he grew more prudent. When Charles Bulfinch, the architect, interceded in behalf of the Unitarian association's needs, Adams replied "that my experience of lending money to religious societies was not encouraging." Pointing to amounts on which not even interest had been forthcoming, he said that churches "seem to consider the payment of their debts as not among the obligations of Christianity."

Very rarely did the president venture out to hear secular lecturers. He did go to hear Robert Dale Owen expound communitarian ideas, which left Adams unimpressed. He found much more fascinating a series of talks by a phrenologist. When the expert paused one evening to urge that ladies not attend his next address, the president made certain to be present, although the night was very humid. The topic proved to be "the organ of amativeness," and he came away from the lecture—which he found "more indelicate than philosophical"—disgusted and convinced that he had heard enough about "either phrenology or craniology."

On the other hand, he seemed unable to do enough walking or swimming. He sought a minimum daily distance of four miles for his walks. A favorite route was from the White House to the Capitol, where he strode around the square and then returned home, clocking himself usually at one hour and twenty minutes. Another route, taking ten minutes fewer, went to Georgetown and back. This was not exercise of a relaxing nature, since the president usually competed against himself, trying to better his time.

Because he was out walking long before dawn, Adams rarely had a companion on his excursions except, as usual, for Chief Justice Marshall, who may have been the only other early riser in the capital. The advantage to the president of relying on walking for respite and health was that no one pestered him with warnings against the habit. This was not the case when hot weather arrived and he switched to swimming in the treacherous Potomac. Louisa was indignant that he should take such a risk, and friends and strangers also urged him to desist. After one narrow escape, even the newspapers voiced concern.

In what was to be the most notorious swim by any president, JQA, his son John, and Antoine Guista went to the river early on June 13, 1825. They found an ancient boat tied at the bank, and Adams proposed crossing the river in it in order to swim back. After inspecting the old skiff, young John refused to have anything to do with the scheme and returned to the White House. Guista had no choice, of course, but to go along and row.

Halfway across the river, the boat filled with water, and the men jumped overboard. Antoine was naked, and quite easily made it to the far shore, but the president, who had not yet removed his long-sleeved shirt and pantaloons, found himself in serious trouble. "While struggling for life and gasping for breath, [I] had ample leisure to reflect upon my own discretion." Somehow, he managed to reach land, after which he admitted that only "by the blessing of Heaven our lives were spared." John vowed on the spot that never again would swimming be used "to show what I can do. . . . I must strictly confine myself to the purposes of health, exercise, and salutary labour."

Meanwhile, when the boat capsized, he and Guista had lost their clothing and shoes. The shirt and pantaloons that had nearly pulled the president under were wrung out and donned by Guista so that he could search for a vehicle to carry them back to the Executive Mansion. Now entirely unclad, Adams stayed behind to sit on a rock and ponder his folly. By then, a passerby who witnessed some of the excitement had taken a garbled report into town, starting a rumor that journalists picked up, to the effect that the chief executive had drowned.

Guista had difficulty getting help, so five hours elapsed before the president sheepishly reappeared at the White House. "The affair is altogether ridiculous," Louisa snapped. He could only reply: "I thought the boat safe enough." Seeking an ally, Louisa urged the family physician to counsel Adams against swimming, particularly in fresh water. While the doctor gave the advice, he did not persuade his patient that swimming harmed the liver. "He attempted some demonstration about the absorption of vital air in the water upon the viscera, which I neither understood nor believed."

The swims continued, although often shortened or even skipped once the president discovered another form of relaxation: working in the White House gardens. Here his rising enthusiasm sometimes kept him overlong, so that a grimy chief executive had to be summoned to face a line of impatient callers. There was also pleasure in searching for acorns in the woods around Washington, for Adams envisioned beautifying the capital with many fine oaks. This hobby he called his best means to "chase Anguish and doubt, and fear, and sorrow, and pain." As he planted row upon row of tree seeds, he acknowledged how the attractions of gardening made his other forms of exercise "tedious and irksome."

Adams often took delight in being on his knees at dawn, weeding and talking with Ouseley, who oversaw the White House grounds. This "excellent and scientific gardener" tended the thousand varieties of flowers, shrubs, herbs, trees, and vegetables that the president calculated grew on two acres of White House ground. "I ask the name of every plant I see," and Ouseley supplied most of them. But there were so many that it was "confounding to the judgment." The challenge made Adams limit his swims to ten or fifteen minutes, so as not to shorten his hours in the garden.

The president's delight in the world of plants had its limits, however. An agricultural society invited him to appear at a meeting in Baltimore and show his support for the farmers of America. Adams declined the opportunity: "It is apparent that the Society wish to make the President of the United States part of their exhibition," he complained. "To gratify this wish I must give four days of my time, no trifle of expense, and set a precedent for being claimed as an article of exhibition at all the cattle shows throughout the Union."

He foresaw demands for his appearance multiplying "from week to week," pressing his ingenuity in devising "numerous excuses and apologies." But the chief justification he saw for the decision to avoid such appearances, which he dreaded anyway, was that "this is no part of my duties, and some duty must be neglected to attend to it. Seest thou a man diligent in his business?" This profoundly Adamesque outlook, of course, often led him to reproach himself for spending so much time in his own garden and away from his office. Following him everywhere was the specter of duty at the unhappy presidential desk.

EACH SUMMER BROUGHT what JQA anticipated as the ultimate escape from the woes of Washington: a visit to Quincy. And, as usual, New England provided domestic troubles to replace the political ones left behind. The worst of these were the gambling and drinking debts run up by George Adams in Boston, whose engagement to cousin Mary Hellen in Washington was in trouble. The parent paid these by various subterfuges, such as buying the books in George's library but allowing him to keep them. Meanwhile, JQA resorted to verse in exhorting his son—one line beginning "Rule thy Soul" and another, "*Spurn* the deadly draught of pleasure."

As long as John Adams was alive, JQA had dared to hope that the old man would manage some miracle in George's character and behavior. But John Adams died on July 4, 1826, leaving not only George but a host of new problems for the president to face in Massachusetts. After letters from home had advised him that his father's condition was dire, JQA left for Quincy on July 9, only to learn upon reaching Baltimore that John Adams had died on the Fourth, as had Thomas Jefferson.

The nation was much stirred by the news that the two principal authors of the Declaration of Independence should be recalled by God on the nation's fiftieth birthday. JQA beheld "visible and palpable marks of divine favour" in the coincidence. When he arrived in Quincy, he listened with amazement as family members described his father's last moments. At the instant the old man expired, he was told, "a clap of thunder shook the house" and "a splendid rainbow arched immediately over the heavens." Inspired by these accounts, JQA attended numerous services and orations memorializing his father, including even two sermons preached by Harvard's troublesome President Kirkland.

Eventually, the mourning subsided enough that JQA could examine John Adams' will, for which he and cousin Josiah Quincy would be executors. (In 1822, the elder Adams had provided financial assistance for construction of a new church building in Quincy and for support of a Latin academy.) Reading the document, he found that as principal legatee, his personal burdens were greatly increased. His father's hope had been that the decrepit family mansion and surrounding farm would not be sold. While the will urged JQA to take ownership, if he did so he must establish a $12,000 trust for brother Tom, still alcohol-dependent. This step would represent Tom's half-share in the property.

There were a dozen other beneficiaries, including the town of Quincy and its parish church, all of whose benefits John Adams intended must come through John Quincy Adams as trustee for the estate. To fund such payments, the remainder of old John's land, along with the contents of the mansion, were to be sold at auction.

So far, so good. But instead of conducting the sale to raise money as his father had intended, JQA used it to acquire nearly all of his parent's property, a decision that brought an appalling financial load. After all, the president's resources were already depleted by the profitless Columbian Mills, and the earlier purchase of the Mount Wollaston and Penn's Hill farms in Quincy, acquired when he saved John Adams from bankruptcy.

To take ownership of his father's residence and farm and the other parcels of land seemed highly imprudent to all but JQA. Louisa, distressed, spoke bluntly in describing to her husband the folly of "a large, unprofitable landed estate which has nearly ruined its last possessor." According to her, even an angel would find this *"utterly and decidedly impossible."* Despite Louisa's advice, John took over the family mansion (now the centerpiece of the Adams National Historic Site) and borrowed money to set up a trust for the Thomas Adams family. He announced that after his presidency, he would live in the old house.

After this step, JQA secured a second large loan in order to buy the balance of his father's estate. At this imprudence, Louisa became so indignant that she refused to remain in Quincy. For the balance of the summer she stayed in Boston, while her husband worked with a team of men to make an inventory of all John Adams' possessions and to survey and appraise many woodlots, salt marshes, and other parcels of realty.

Unlike his paperwork in Washington, the president faced these chores in good spirits. With the surveyors, he sloshed for many hours through mud and water, the season having turned unusually rainy. Describing one day's labor, he reported spending "upwards of five hours traversing the woods, climbing rocks, wading through swamps, and breaking through the brakes. It was literally a tangled forest." Large snakes were killed, and the mosquitoes were "appalling," said to be the worst in memory.

Despite such rigors, Adams believed that George—as eldest son, someday the likely owner of this property—should know everything about the land. Consequently, he insisted that the young man accompany the survey team. George soon crumpled under the task and took to hiding in his room, claiming to be ill. These latest signs of his son's neurotic condition were more distressing to the president than the prospect of his own enlarged indebtedness.

Finally, on September 19, the auction of John Adams' woodland and salt marsh was held at French's Tavern in Quincy. Among those present were proprietors of a newfangled device called a railroad, intended to afford access to the town's granite quarries, who planned to compete with the president in bidding on the property. Consequently, Deacon Josiah Adams, a cousin, was selected to act as JQA's agent at the auction and instructed to bid one dollar more than whatever the railroad spokesmen should offer. The deacon succeeded, spending $9,255.55 in behalf of JQA.

Eventually, the president, to his delight, found that he had bought over 80 percent of his father's land. "I have prepared in great measure

for myself a place of retirement from March 1829 for the remainder of
my days." After leaving "the vain pomp and tumult of the world," he
wished in Quincy to employ his time "in a manner worthy of that
which has engaged my youth and mature years."

In early October, the estate chores were finished, and JQA notified
the heirs that, after the sale, the total value of John Adams' legacy was
$44,709.47. After deducting debt payment and funeral expenses, a
balance of $42,000 remained for distribution among fourteen heirs,
each portion amounting to $3,000. These payments would have to
come from JQA's pocket, since he had purchased nearly all of his
father's assets. The mansion house and its 95-acre farm alone had cost
him $22,000. With the farm tenant paying a yearly rent of $450, John
figured the property would yield about 3 percent annually, less than
the interest on the debt.

Before concluding these worldly matters, the president made a
point of sitting in his father's pew in the old parish meeting house—
where he could not help but think of another burden. After the new
church was finished, built with support from John Adams' estate, and
which would come to be known as the Adams Temple, JQA would
have to see to the construction of a burial vault beneath the church.
The crypt was to contain the remains of John and Abigail Adams,
moved from the cemetery across the street.

The moment also seemed appropriate for the president to become
a member of the congregation to which most of his ancestors had belonged for "little less than two hundred years." So, on October 1, 1826,
John entered into communion with the Quincy church, a step he conceded he should have taken thirty years before. During the service, in
which he made a public confession of faith in Christianity—"very
short and in general terms"—he listened to an appropriate sermon
drawn from Ephesians 4:1, which urged: "Walk worthy of the vocation
wherewith you are called."

THEN IT WAS BACK to Washington, where the president arrived in
time to hear William Wirt deliver an oration of two and one-half hours
honoring John Adams. JQA resumed his "wearisome official duties"
while suffering severe head pain, mostly from exhaustion. Believing
that he now faced a "crisis of my earthly destiny," his thoughts veered
between a beleaguered administration and the manifold weaknesses of
George Adams, which had become so evident during the summer.

His prime fatherly duty, the president believed, must be to place

George's feet on the path toward righteousness. Many admonitions were sent to his son. Only the parent's side of the correspondence survives. The letters included scoldings over George's failure to send reports about his father's business affairs. In others, Adams shared what were his own sources of strength in times of trial, particularly listening to music. An oratorio did more to sustain him, he told George, than the delights of the Worcester Cattle Show.

Mainly, however, he showed how he feared that his son would go down the path of intemperance that had taken John's brothers to destruction. "I have been *horror struck* at your *danger*," he said, adding that "it was a *danger* that distresses me even to agony." The parent pleaded that George avoid alcohol, tobacco, and other vices, and stop sending merely "promises upon promises" of improved behavior. "Above all and embracing all, methodise your *mind*." When there was no response to these urgings, the distraught father had to live with "troubled thoughts, the most oppressive of which regard my son George."

In a few months, the bitter disappointments and frustrations of both his presidency and his fatherhood had brought Adams near to mental and physical collapse. "My health has been languishing, without sickness," he reported in a diary entry of unusual length. Ordinarily, he took only four to five hours of sleep, although "not of good repose." He was continuously vexed by abdominal distress and loss of appetite. More alarming, however, was the mood he described: an "uncontrollable dejection of spirits." He asserted that the depression was now so severe that he had begun to experience "a sluggish carelessness of life, an imaginary wish that it were terminated."

Finally, his physician sternly intervened. According to the president, Dr. Huntt insisted that he "doff the world aside and bid it pass; to cast off as much as possible all cares, public and private, and vegetate myself into a healthier condition." This required another stay in Quincy during August and September 1827.

Once at home, he began to sleep better and to swim regularly. He rarely saw or spoke of George during this holiday, his diary being an account mostly of his fishing outings, his pleasing toil with garden and young trees, and his negotiations with the railroad for rights to cross his land. He told of becoming better acquainted with Peter Chardon Brooks, the richest man in Boston, to whose daughter his son Charles was now betrothed. And, of course, he described his excursions with friends. Thirty of them joined him on a fishing expedition, where the president caught nothing and became severely sunburned.

When the largely happy holiday closed in early October, Adams resumed complaining that he was still depressed, that his health continued to "droop," that his character was being assailed, and that George's behavior was unimproved. He was pleasantly distracted, however, when supporters along the way to Washington wished to fete him, particularly in Philadelphia, where the public's welcome was astonishing.

When the boat arrived, citizens at the wharf set up three cheers for the president. Later, when he prepared to depart, "several thousand persons" had assembled to see him off. With shouts of support, many of them pressed onto the boat and "thronged the deck till it became almost impassible." Suddenly appearing remarkably presidential, Adams shook hands with several hundred Philadelphians until the boat signaled departure. More "hearty" cheers from the "multitude," which he returned "with a bow, waving the hand, and saying 'God bless you all!'"

This extraordinary experience left JQA deeply touched. He was naturally relieved that there had been "not the slightest disorder" during his appearance, and he also characteristically cautioned himself against being carried off by "vain or unworthy sentiments of exaltation." He preferred that the crowd's shouts should excite "solemn reflections . . . in my mind." These were chased away, however, in Baltimore, where another welcoming throng could not drown out the drunken racket raised by friends of Jackson's. Eventually, Adams backers themselves became a problem by refusing to leave the front of the president's hotel until he came down to shake a few more hands.

These testimonials did not shake John's certainty that he would be defeated for reelection. Nor did he retain the improved health and more cheerful outlook gained in Quincy. A niece reported being shocked at his haggard appearance once he was back in Washington. President Adams, she said, seemed "a man harassed to death with care."

Unfortunately, Adams found little at his desk to soothe him. Of the accumulation of letters, he grumbled there was "nothing in them worth the time consumed in the perusal of them. . . . Of the immense multitude of letters that I have received and been doomed to read since I have held my present office, one small file would embrace all that are worth preserving." Nor was there comfort in his callers. "The perpetual succession of visitors from breakfast to dinner crazes me."

The president retained courtesy enough to comply when a group of strangers wished to tour the White House—he showed off all but "the bedchambers." That was also the unfortunate day when son John came to ask permission to wed cousin Mary Hellen, who had broken her engagement with George Adams. JQA was opposed, and he and Louisa disagreed angrily on the subject, until finally he capitulated. John Adams II married Mary Hellen on February 25, 1828.

WITH THE PRESIDENTIAL ELECTION just months away and with this upheaval in the family quarters, Adams' outlook was not improved when members of his cabinet brought new evidence that John McLean, the postmaster general, was ardently working to elect Andrew Jackson. While there was "no doubt upon my mind McLean is a double dealer," Adams wrote, he shrank from firing him, calling the experience a prelude to even worse trials as he faced enemies "of the most abandoned immorality . . . having neither reputation to lose nor principle to restrain them." Such, he said, was Andrew Stevenson of Virginia, Speaker of the House of Representatives, who Adams claimed had risen to power "on the ruins of honor and virtue."

Meanwhile, the president's own morality was being challenged in newspaper stories. He especially resented one claiming that in St. Petersburg the Adamses had offered up Louisa's maid as a sacrifice to the sexual desires of Emperor Alexander. By the spring of 1828, such assaults made the road ahead seem so foreboding that JQA wished he might "be spared the agony of witnessing the futurity before me."

Every member of the cabinet, except the traitorous McLean, was the target of Jackson journalists. A badly wounded and ailing Clay sought to leave the administration, foreseeing only more insult and, ultimately, defeat. He, as well as the other cabinet members, received warm sympathy from the president. "As the rage of the tempest increases and the chances grow desperate," he said, "each one will take care of himself." He wanted to find any way possible to rescue his friends from his own "political downfall."

Adams persuaded Clay not to retire to Kentucky "to die," but to take a medical leave. The secretary of state's physician had assured the president that emotional distress ("decay of the vital powers") was Clay's affliction. Adams urged Clay to visit Philadelphia, which was then the nation's medical center, while promising that he personally would handle the State Department's work. Clay consented to take leave, weeping at the president's words of encouragement. Of course, Adams had been moved by more than charity. Were the secretary to resign at the campaign's height, JQA knew it would be "a disastrous occurrence," joining others "of deep humiliations which are thickening about me."

By this time, the future seemed so gloomy that the president could hardly help being relieved when a caller introduced himself as a messenger "from God Almighty." A long conversation ensued, for Adams decided that "there seemed to be some method in this madness." He was impressed particularly when the visitor, whose name was Forman, announced in God's behalf that it was time for the United States "to enter the wilderness for renewed nourishment." Upon hearing this, Adams opened a Bible "which I keep habitually on my writing table" and joined delightedly with Forman in sharing interpretations of the Book of Revelation.

At length, when the clamor of other visitors outside the president's office could no longer be ignored, Adams reluctantly informed Forman that for the moment he could not "receive more of his communication," but urged him to return. God's messenger departed rejoicing, promising another visit—of which no record survives. Instead, a bearer of more earthly tidings appeared in the doorway, Treasury Secretary Richard Rush, who brought news that during the Adams administration the public debt of over $16 million had been reduced to just under $5 million.

Rush's report came too late to share with Congress, which had adjourned to campaign against the president. Adams saw them depart with relief, for he himself was looking eagerly toward his last vacation in office. This had to wait, however, until he had done a bit of his own electioneering. On a fearfully hot Independence Day, he traveled a few miles outside Washington to speak at the groundbreaking for the Chesapeake and Ohio Canal. The project was dear to those who, like Adams, favored internal improvements. He even believed the ceremony should take on "a religious character."

It turned out otherwise. After being handed a spade, Adams addressed the assembly of two thousand persons until, at the appropriate moment in his remarks, he tried to thrust his shovel into the earth. Instead, it hit a solid object. The president and his spade persisted without success. Finally, "I threw off my coat, and resuming the spade, raised a shovelful of the earth, at which a general shout burst forth from the surrounding multitude."

Astonished by the event, the president pondered what it implied. He realized that by removing his coat he had "struck the eye and fancy of the spectators more than all the flowers of rhetoric in my speech and diverted their attention from the stammering and hesitation of a deficient memory." Despite the success, there was cause for a man of Adams' dignity to worry. He feared that foreign representatives would think it "a strange part for a President of the United States to perform."

Even so, he seemed to display other common touches during that election summer. Washington citizens encountered him on horseback, a substitute for his walks that he hoped would better stir his sluggish digestion. The inspiration came when James Barbour, who had left the cabinet to become U.S. minister to Great Britain, gave his horse to the president. After saying he must pay for the animal, Adams took up riding with his usual zest, claiming that outings of twenty miles were his goal.

When he insisted that son John accompany him, the younger man lasted only a few days before giving up. "I have already broken down him and two horses," the father reported with some satisfaction. Meanwhile, Barbour's horse proved excellent in all respects but one. He had a weakness in the left hind ankle "which is dangerous," the president admitted.

By early August, when he set out for Quincy, the president was confident he could ride horseback to Baltimore. He stopped overnight and reached the city twenty-four hours after leaving Washington, a distance of 36 miles. The effort left him rain-soaked, very sore, and willing to admit that he was still "disused" to such a long journey on his horse. Fortunately, at this point he chose to ship the mount on to New England while he boarded a steamboat for Philadelphia and points north.

Back in Washington on September 13, Adams found the last days of the bitter presidential campaign under way. By now, his scorn for Jackson was unrestrained. He said the general was "incompetent both by his ignorance and by the fury of his passions." Then the president began to wonder what the campaign might do to harm his own character. "In the excitement of contested elections and of party spirit," he acknowledged, "judgment becomes the slave of the will. Men of intelligence, talents, and even of integrity upon other occasions, surrender themselves up to their passions."

Mortifying as he found it to ask for votes, Adams spent many hours conferring with persons who were daily striving for his reelection. These were lieutenants who held comfortable federal jobs, thanks to the president. Besides Tench Ringgold, marshal of the District of Columbia, Adams' chief campaigners included such clerks as Daniel Brent, Philip R. Fendall, Tobias Watkins, and William Lee.

At times, these strategists must have found their man exasperating, hindered as Adams was by a deeply divided mind. At one moment, he heartily wished himself rid of office. Then the side of him that was proud, sensitive, and ambitious would take over, causing him to hanker for a fight. His ambivalence left Adams hoping that he could win while averting his gaze from the partisan sins committed in his name. He continued to read the papers, however, which brought him to remark: "A stranger would think that the people of the United States have no other occupation than electioneering."

It was not always easy to avoid knowing what his supporters were doing in his behalf. There was the day, for instance, when Senator Samuel Bell of New Hampshire called to urge the president to contribute money through an Adams son for establishing a German newspaper in Pennsylvania that would support the administration. In declining, JQA informed Bell that he left to others how to use money in his behalf. He told him he wanted nothing to do with campaigning, even though he had been urged to pay for "agent-emissaries" and "itinerant preachers."

The presidential campaign of 1828 amply deserves its reputation for vicious partisan exchanges. Adams' side gave as good as it took. Indeed, the most memorable slander came when his forces circulated the story that Andrew Jackson and Rachel, his much-loved wife, had an adulterous relationship before Mrs. Jackson was divorced from her first husband. This alleged sin was denounced loudly and described luridly by the Adams faction, which never paused to explain that when Andrew and Rachel were married, they were not aware that her divorce proceedings were incomplete.

Jackson never forgave Adams for this defamation, blaming him personally for it, and thus for the death of Rachel, which the general ascribed to a heart broken by the campaign. Meanwhile, Adams continued to profess ignorance of sins committed in his name. He preferred to speak of "the skunks of party slander" and their capacity for "falsehood and misrepresentation" as if these culprits and he lived in different times and places.

Nothing that Adams said before the election implied a secret belief that he might win. On the other hand, there was no indication that he knew how badly he would be trounced by Jackson, whose backers had the best organization and propaganda. They skillfully reminded voters of the "corrupt bargain" that had made Adams president in 1825. JQA's supporters never could tarnish the image of Jackson as a heroic general-of-the-people who was fighting a Yankee aristocrat attired in elegant clothes (what an exaggeration that was!), who had acquired European manners and a "foreign" wife, and who had bought a billiard table for his pleasure in the White House. Nor could the Adams partisans make their candidate's belief in protective tariffs and a national system of roads and canals seem anything but dangerous to most of the public.

By 1828, the national citizen vote for president was pushing the electoral college into the background. Out of nearly 1.2 million ballots cast, Andrew Jackson's majority was 56 percent, while his electoral edge was a convincing 178 to Adams' 83. New England's states and Delaware went for the president, who also shared the electoral votes of New York and Maryland with Jackson. There was unexpectedly bad news from Pennsylvania, where Adams had been accustomed to being a welcome visitor. His friends there could muster only a third of the popular vote for him.

On December 3, when the news of his defeat was confirmed, the president consoled himself by riding his horse for ninety minutes before he received many callers who "unseated my tranquility of mind." Most of them were persons who had gone down to defeat with him. "The sun of my political life sets in the deepest gloom," he acknowledged, having in mind less his loss than the "mortification" felt by those associates who suffered because of him.

PERHAPS LOSING SO CONVINCINGLY made it easier for the president to accept defeat. Within days, he seemed a new man. Even Louisa conceded that good spirits now prevailed around her, and that her husband was rapidly regaining his lost weight. This brightened outlook was somewhat misleading, for actually the president was buoyed by the belief that he would soon be free to avenge himself. When urged to be cordial to the president-elect, he retorted that while he would respect Jackson's office, he would "make no advance to conciliation with him." Claiming that he had never "wronged" the general, JQA insisted that "much the reverse" had prevailed—"he had slandered me."

Adams harbored deep resentment at those who had defamed him and driven him from the presidency. He felt that he was being hounded into "an old age of retirement, though certainly not of repose," by "a combination of parties and public men against my character and reputation such as I believe never before was exhibited against any man since the Union existed." The record must be corrected lest posterity be deceived by those who now were "exulting in triumph over me." It tortured Adams to think that generations to come might be unaware of how he had devoted "my life, and all of the faculties of my soul to the Union, and the improvement, physical, moral, and intellectual, of my country."

This anger notwithstanding, the White House continued to become a happier place. One of Washington's leading socialites, Margaret Bayard Smith, no friend, claimed that the Adamses' cheerfulness was feigned—"this assumed gaiety," she called it. Attending a party given at the Executive Mansion on December 28, she watched mistrustingly as both John and Louisa displayed "social, gay, frank, cordial manners," and she wondered what had happened to the familiar "haughty reserve." Instead, the Adamses had hired a band and thrown open the official reception room for dancing.

Despite Margaret Smith's suspicions and his own plans for vengeance, Adams' good humor appears to have been genuine. One of the clearest glimpses of his restored comfort was his delight after the election when he heard one of Washington's finest female voices sing the hymn "Angels ever bright and fair," accompanied by an organ. The beauty of the performance, said Adams, "lap'd me in Elysium." In mid-January, when good friends called to chat, the president could report that "we had much convivial conversation. . . . I was overtalkative and in a flow of spirits."

By early February, however, as the Adamses prepared to leave, taking up rented quarters until they would depart for Quincy in the spring, John returned to a nagging concern. In private life, would he find the initiative to undertake significant intellectual endeavor with the self-discipline needed to complete his projects? Or would he suffer from boredom and lassitude as a result of withdrawing from politics? "I can yet scarcely realize my situation. . . . I cannot yet settle my mind to a regular course of future employment."

Under such apprehension, all he could do, he told himself, was to pray that he might "habituate myself to interesting occupation. Could I be sure of retaining the . . . 'engagedness'. . . so essential to comfortable existence, I should endure my fate with composure perfectly philosophical." He talked of plans "to bury myself in complete retirement, as much so as a nun taking the veil." Doubtless these were sentiments sincerely meant at the time—until his thoughts were spurred by that sharp, desperate need to prevent history from distorting his name.

Consequently, the defeated president was already hinting of reappearing in the public arena. He told one close friend that while his objective was "absolute and total retirement," should the public summon him again to its service, he would not decline, "except for reasonable cause." His confidant, Congressman Charles Miner of Pennsylvania, was urged to share with no one what he had said, "for I wish not even to give a hint to the public that I am yet eligible to their service."

Amid his inner turmoil of pious resolve and prodding anger, Adams did not await a return to Quincy and the healing balm of time before he set out to let the future know the truth about himself. Even as he was explaining that he would now retire into a deep seclusion, he had begun plans to justify himself before history, although he preferred to speak of it as an obligation to work for "the cause of the Union and of improvement."

BOOK FIVE

Astonishing Results

1829–1848

. . . in which a tumultuous old age becomes the best of times.

CHAPTER THIRTEEN

Grief

I am sick at heart.

ON MARCH 4, 1829, Andrew Jackson's inaugural day, the sun bathed Washington in springlike warmth as the public flocked to observe the ceremony. Among the few who stayed behind was John Quincy Adams, who remains, with his father, one of only two retiring presidents not to have appeared at their successor's swearing-in. But then Jackson had not paid the customary courtesy call on the outgoing president, either. Actually, all but one member of JQA's cabinet had advised him not to attend the inauguration. So bitter was the antagonism left by the election that conventional gestures would have appeared ridiculous.

So, late on March 3, Adams rode away from the White House to join Louisa and the family, which now included a granddaughter, at their temporary residence two miles from the Capitol. Called "Meridian Hill" because it stood on the original center line of the District of Columbia, the house belonged to a friend, the widow of Commodore David Porter, and so pleased the Adamses that John offered Mrs. Porter $14,000 for it, a sum she declined.

While Washington marked the start of a new administration with the memorable invasion of the White House by a crowd of Jackson admirers, muddy boots and all, Adams was occupied in finishing a lengthy document defending his name and record. It seemed a satisfying way to spend his first weeks as a private citizen.

The project had begun in the final months of the 1828 presidential campaign. It was inspired when his old adversaries, the New England Federalists, published faded gossip about Senator Adams' alleged sellout to the Jeffersonians during 1807–1808. These partisans still believed that he had betrayed his native region by putting national interests uppermost, and they hoped for revenge by contributing to his defeat by Jackson.

Although some victims of such slander would have seen how easily they might have minimized the attack by ignoring it, not so President Adams. Angered by what he fancied was danger to his honor, late in the 1828 campaign he issued a reply to the gossip, using the columns of the *National Intelligencer*. He reminded the public that his assailants were the same Federalists who were inclined to dissolve the American Union at the Hartford Convention of 1814–1815 when delegates from the New England states, led by Massachusetts, had met in secrecy in opposition to the War of 1812. He also added the more sensational charge that as early as 1803, many of these same Federalists had been advocating a separate New England confederation.

This presidential counterattack brought a public demand from thirteen indignant Yankees that Adams name those persons he had accused of conspiracy to set up a Northern Confederacy. When he changed his tone and responded mildly, saying that it would be in the best interest of the Hartford Conventioneers to let matters rest, his offended opponents refused the offer and, instead, issued an appeal to the nation, claiming that President Adams had brought them and Massachusetts into disrepute. They demanded a full hearing.

Actually, these New Englanders did Adams a favor in the last weeks of his losing campaign for reelection—they distracted him with a call to a battle in which he was confident that right was entirely on his side. When he lost at the polls, this new fight cheered him, and he devoted his last three months in the White House to gathering evidence to demonstrate that conspiracy had indeed abounded in New England. As it happened, the leaders of the alleged plot had always been enemies of the Adamses.

When friends dropped by the White House in the weeks before March 4 to inquire about JQA's plans for retirement, he gleefully predicted that he must devote the remainder of his life "to defend and vindicate my own reputation." Those who dared to suggest that he adopt a calmer approach to the challenge were ignored. "I was born for a controversial world and cannot escape my destiny," he assured his son Charles. "I shall be hunted down in privacy as I have been in public," he claimed. "My life must be militant to its close."

Once he moved out of the Executive Mansion, John's delight in the fight increased. His New England adversaries, he said, "pounce upon me like so many king birds upon an eagle." With great satisfaction, he quoted Shakespeare's line "Sweep on, you fat and greasy citizens—." Visitors were obliged to listen as he read aloud from the lengthening draft of his reply to the Federalists, and when his more courageous auditors suggested that what he had written was "too bold and passionate," he was crestfallen.

How was it possible, Adams wondered, "to write upon such subjects without indulgence of feelings"? The more he studied the Senate journals from 1807 and 1808, the larger grew his confidence in his cause. "I find little to censure in what I did; nothing in what I intended." Thus assured, he insisted to everyone that he must "write with the boldness of truth." He did so with "intenseness of application" until the "justification" was completed in late April.

Just as the writing was finished, news came that his son George had died. The calamity so curbed Adams' zest for battle that he chose not to publish what he had written. The huge manuscript was left to posterity. It was a document that his son Charles said "told the truth far too violently to be useful." Finally, in 1877 the work was edited by Charles' son Henry Adams and published as *Documents Relating to New-England Federalism, 1800–1815*.

THE DEATH OF George Washington Adams occurred soon after he was summoned to the capital to assist his parents in traveling to Quincy for the summer. He was also advised that in the months ahead he would live in close association with his father. The prospect of having JQA over his shoulder may have been too much for George, who was increasingly disposed to gamble, drink, and shirk hard work. Also, he had recently made pregnant a young employee of the Welsh family, Adams kinfolk, in whose home George was a boarder.

Apparently terrified by the thought of how his stern father would take this latest indiscretion, George left notes hinting at suicide when he departed for Washington at the end of April. Witnesses who had been on the steamboat with him recalled that he spoke wildly, as if in a paranoid state. Before dawn on April 30, he vanished, presumably overboard. Only his cloak and hat remained. A month passed before the corpse was recovered from Long Island Sound.

After learning of his son's probable fate, JQA was devastated and remained nearly helpless with grief for a fortnight. He was filled with contrition, fearing that he had pushed his son harder than the weak young man could sustain. "Blessed God!" he prayed. "Forgive the wanderings of my own mind under its excruciating torture!" Imploring divine mercy on his son's pathetic soul and thinking of his own disappointments, he could not put out of his mind the usual question: "My God, my God, why hast thou forsaken me?" With a "broken and contrite spirit," he claimed his final hopes for earth were now destroyed, and that "I have nothing left to rely on but the mercy of God."

Adams tried to distract himself and Louisa by reading Horace Walpole's writings aloud. This and the passing of time seemed to help, so that by the close of May, he was writing again, beginning a history of parties in the United States. But his heart clearly was not in the task, and on June 11, accompanied by his son John, he set out for Quincy, where he anticipated living in seclusion year-round. For the moment, Louisa remained behind. "The parting from my wife was distressing to her and to me. The afflictions with which we have been visited . . . have so weakened us in body and mind that our dejection of spirit seems irrecoverable."

There was balm of sorts for him in New York City, where he learned that George's body had washed ashore on City Island. He lingered long enough to inspect the coffin, but had not the "nerve" to lift its lid. Deciding to await cold weather before moving the body to Quincy, the grieving father took George's recovered personal possessions back to Massachusetts. The firstborn son's tragic story ended in the chill of November, when his remains arrived for interment in the family vault. Watching the quiet event, Adams reflected: "May I cherish the hope that this afflictive dispensation comes not as the first stroke of the destroying Angel, but as the discipline of a chastising hand."

Even before the burial service, however, George had caused renewed heartache. Tales concerning his illegitimate child and other mischief led some persons in Boston to attempt to blackmail JQA. Suffering this indignity in silence, Adams left Charles to repulse the schemers. After much mortifying notoriety, the scandal slipped from public attention, along with George's child and its mother, Eliza Dolph. Neither of them apparently drew any compassion from the Adamses.

Mostly, JQA spent the summer and autumn of 1829 trying to absorb the punishment of losing both a son and the presidency. Much of the time he spent alone in the old Adams mansion, which he now owned, brother Tom and his family having removed to another part of the village. Son John returned to Washington in July, and Louisa finally chose not to make the trip to Quincy.

In the ensuing solitude, Adams rushed from one project to another, leaving each barely begun. "Charles says I have too many irons in the fire," he reported as he began digging through his father's papers with an eye to writing a "biographical memoir" that might eloquently defend his parent against enemies, many of whom conveniently had become JQA's as well.

This obligation kept his attention only briefly, however, before he was lured away, first by genealogical investigation—"the annals of the family are short and simple"—and then by the books in the Adams library. Always there was the daily arrival of numerous guests to occupy him, including cousin Josiah Quincy, now president of Harvard, who brought the latest gossip from the college. At other moments, JQA went into his garden or wandered restlessly over his land, while his diary talked of a "great waste of time" and "deficiency of energy." Would he ever learn to persevere? he wondered.

In fact, the summer of 1829 involved several worthwhile enterprises. First among them was unpacking the thirty-eight boxes and six trunks of books he had shipped from Washington. Many of these containers had remained unopened since the contents were purchased in London. The work set him to recollecting his earliest reading habits, in particular, how at age ten he had set out by himself to appreciate John Milton's works, having listened while his parents lauded the poet as first in their esteem.

But for him to grasp *Paradise Lost* at that time, JQA admitted, "I might as well have attempted to read Homer before I had learnt the Greek alphabet." He recalled how the experience had left him weeping in frustration, not merely because he had failed to see what his father and mother so admired in Milton, but because "I was ashamed to ask them [for] an explanation." He did not enjoy Milton until he was thirty.

Quite different thoughts came when he opened a box containing his set of Voltaire's writings. After taking time out from unpacking to read some of the published letters, Adams turned away in disgust, declaring them "grossly and shamelessly indecent." The letters led him to think of Voltaire's burlesque on Joan of Arc, *La Pucelle*, which he called "fit only to be read in a brothel." It was a work of the "grossest and basest immorality," which he contended arose from Voltaire's "rancour against Christianity." To Adams, the martyred Joan of Arc deserved "not ridicule, but reverence."

Frequently that summer, he was called from his library work for other worthwhile tasks, including serving as an executor of his cousin Ward Nicholas Boylston's will. Furthermore, he saw to establishing a Latin academy in Quincy in compliance with John Adams' will. He composed the words for a memorial tablet to be affixed at the front of the Quincy church in honor of his parents, and he resumed surveying the numerous woodlots purchased from his father's estate.

Then there was his trip to the town of Medford, beyond Cambridge, where on September 3, Charles Francis Adams was married to Abigail Brown Brooks. This brought an alliance of sorts between the Adamses and the Everetts. Edward Everett had married Abby Brooks' older sister Charlotte. Everett was well launched by then on a career variously as legislator, governor, Harvard president, and orator. In time, however, he would prove to be too much a compromiser to suit the Adamses.

Surprised by how busy the summer had kept him, Adams finally left for Washington after Thanksgiving, traveling much of the way in the company of Daniel Webster, whom he found "averse to conversation." He was relieved when the coach from Baltimore dropped him at the door of his son John's new residence, which stood across the square from the White House. Here the senior Adamses proposed to spend the winter. Money inherited by their daughter-in-law from her father had been used to build the house.

BACK IN WASHINGTON, Adams' diary became a record of the Jackson administration's problems. The entries relied heavily on reports brought by each day's callers, and although he usually dismissed gossip, he relished hearing about his successor's difficulties. When asked his opinion of Jackson's annual message to Congress, Adams replied: "I had not laughed so heartily at reading any thing since my first acquaintance with the expedition of Humphry Clinker"—a reference to Tobias Smollett's 1771 comic novel.

The schedule John followed that winter was a familiar one. Each morning, in rain or shine, in sickness or health, he walked up to and around Capitol Square, a journey in which Chief Justice Marshall continued to be a frequent companion. Then, after reading his beloved Cicero, he took up his pen, this time to write a long essay treating the recently concluded Russo-Turkish War.

This commentary—"the first attempt I have made at regular historical composition"—would be published in the *American Annual Regis-*

ter. Deploring his "incompetency to write worthily of the subject," he occupied himself with the essay until April 1830, when he was able to send the editor a completed manuscript much longer than the prescribed forty pages. The essay roamed far beyond its subject because he admitted that his goal was to influence the mind of Europe by emphasizing the value of negotiation.

After concluding such a lofty enterprise, Adams was predictably glum without another worthwhile endeavor. "I am suffering distress of mind," he conceded, "longing for the capacity to give some value to the remnant of my life, and conscious that those aspirations must be vain." He could not forget that he once had a chance to elevate mankind through politics, but it had slipped away. Each day seemed darker, until he blurted out that never had he done anything useful, a realization, he said, that left him "little composure of mind and no energy for action."

Carrying this bleak mood, Adams set out in June for another New England holiday, this time with Louisa, daughter-in-law Mary, and granddaughter Mary Louisa. Son John remained in Washington to try, without the requisite talent and vigor, to grind some profit from the Columbian Mills. The travelers reached home sick and exhausted. "Every step I take is with fear and trembling. I cannot express what I feel," Adams admitted, acknowledging that much of his mental state was worry over John, who now seemed another victim of the family's scourge, alcohol.

Not even reading Cicero brought comfort in the summer, nor was there pleasure in puttering with infant trees and looking after real estate. JQA did nothing but listen as Charles urged him to make a serious effort at writing about John Adams. Charles was worried about his father, in whom he saw "a manifest change. A kind of want of purpose which alarms me." When pressed to begin research in John Adams' papers, JQA resisted, claiming he was overpowered by the magnitude of the task. Instead, he usually took a two-hour nap each day and then complained: "Shall I never do better?" Meanwhile, the weather in July grew so hot that when he went for a daily swim, he wore a white nightcap to protect his bald head.

Adams' moroseness became strikingly apparent when Harvard's Professor Nathaniel Bowditch could not stir him with an invitation that ordinarily he would have seized. When Bowditch asked Adams to deliver the annual lecture before Boston's Mechanics Institute later in the summer, the prospect roused no enthusiasm. After politely agreeing to think it over for a month, JQA eventually declined.

By mid-August, he had become seriously depressed. The only consolation he now claimed to find in life was the planting of trees, and this he did on the recommendation of Cicero and other classical authors. Here, at least, was a deed, simple enough, that served generations to come. His life would soon end, he predicted as he pondered Cicero's remarks concerning death, and it was well he should now prepare for his own demise, since "I have no plausible motive for wishing to live." He asserted that his uselessness "makes death desirable." He was sinking, Adams admitted late in August, "into dejection, despondency, and idleness."

Then, just in time, September brought cheer. First, it was after a physician failed to appear, leaving Louisa to oversee Mary's safe delivery of a second granddaughter, whom the family chose to call Fanny. This happiness made Adams willing to attend the bicentennial commemoration of Boston's founding on September 17. As he joined the dignitaries gathering at the State House for the procession to the Old South Church, some of his enemies offered to shake hands. This pleased him, as did his discovery that in his honor, two marshals had been named to escort the former president to the crowded meeting house.

The only flaw in the celebration occurred while Josiah Quincy was delivering the day's oration. As he closed his remarks, a bench upstairs broke with a noise that terrified many in the audience, who, believing the gallery was about to fall, rushed out of the building. Calm was restored, however, and the ceremony ended with the singing of Handel's "Hallelujah Chorus" and a display of fireworks on the Common.

Then came an event intended to close the day. It was one Adams had somewhat dreaded: a party at the residence of Lieutenant Governor Thomas L. Winthrop, where Adams expected the guests would include mostly his adversaries. But he soon spotted such friends as the Everett brothers and Charles Bulfinch, as well as a scattering of Coolidges, Crowninshields, and Silsbees. Most important, as it turned out, was the presence of two of his longtime supporters, Boston *Patriot* editor John B. Davis and the Quincy district's congressman, the Reverend Joseph Richardson of Hingham.

The pair requested permission to call on Adams the next day, barely hinting at the purpose of the visit, except that it stemmed from the wishes of Richardson's Unitarian parish that he retire from politics. Watching the trio in conversation, Edward Everett assumed that they were discussing whether Adams would run for Congress. As soon as he could take the former president aside, Everett eagerly asked him what he had said concerning the opportunity. The reply: "I had nothing to say about it."

On the way back to Quincy, however, Adams recalled how, ten days before, the editor of the Boston *Courier* had urged the citizens of the Plymouth District to send the former president to Congress. At the time, he had dismissed the editorial, since the paper had never been friendly. It turned out that his hunch was only partly correct. As a Clay supporter, the *Courier*'s aim was to ensure that Adams would not get in the Kentuckian's way by himself running for president in 1832. The best means was to have Adams enter the House of Representatives.

The morning after the Boston festivities, there was an early frost on the ground. Richardson and Davis arrived promptly and, indeed, with an eloquent plea that Adams accept an invitation to stand for Congress. After emphasizing how he would be assured of victory, the guests shrewdly observed that it would ennoble the House to have him take a seat. Replying at once that the picture of a former president sitting even as a town selectman had inspiring aspects, Adams then donned his familiar cloak of coyness by speaking of "age and infirmity," and of "not the slightest desire to be elected." He did take care to add, however, that while he would not seek the office, if the people should call upon him, he "might deem it my duty to serve."

This was the signal his callers were awaiting, and, needing no more encouragement, they departed to begin the campaign. Although the election was set for November 1830, the victor would not take office until the Twenty-second Congress was convened a year later.

THE PROSPECT of a seat in the House had such portent that Adams chose for the moment not to discuss it even in his diary. He kept mostly quiet on the matter until after he won the election. He may also have remained silent because he was distressed by an angry commotion his running for Congress had caused at home. Louisa even vowed that if her husband returned to politics, she would not accompany him to Washington.

Nor did it help when Charles asked what had happened to his father's pledges about a life of scholarship. The son insisted that taking a seat in Congress would bring loss of dignity, set an unfortunate precedent, and draw new assaults from enemies. Privately, Charles complained that his parent "is not proof against the temporary seductions of popular distinction, to resist which is the most solid evidence of greatness."

In the weeks preceding the election on November 6, Adams moved ever so carefully toward active candidacy. He informed inquirers that he was indeed a qualified citizen of the Plymouth District and that he wished only to see the public act spontaneously. He worried over reports that the Jackson Democrats would fiercely oppose his election, particularly after his formal nomination by the national Republican party occurred in mid-October, at which time Adams finally assured his backers that he would accept the will of the people. To himself, he fretted a bit: "I am launched again upon the faithless wave of politics."

On November 7, Adams was announced the winner. He had received 1,817 votes against 373 for the Democratic candidate and 279 for the nominee of the old Federalist party. The lopsided victory elated him, as he called his election an answer to prayer. He claimed that it brought a place of dignity from which he could strive anew to serve mankind. Also, the post would carry duties that would inspire diligence in one who lacked self-discipline, or so he hoped. The election's highest importance, however, was that he could believe he had been vindicated. Had not citizens now freely given him their confidence?

His first election to Congress produced one of the most passionate and revealing expressions to be found in JQA's journal. "No one knows, and few conceive, the agony of mind that I have suffered from the time that I was made by circumstances, and not by my volition, a candidate for the Presidency till I was dismissed from that station by the failure of my election." He had hidden his feelings at that defeat, he acknowledged. Then had come George's death and the attack by his New England enemies. In the face of these griefs, plus his recent failure to be reelected president of the American Academy of Arts and Sciences, Adams admitted that it seemed he was "deserted by all mankind." His only solace had been to repeat the song of Blondel the minstrel to the imprisoned Richard the Lionhearted:

> "O, Richard! O, mon Roi!
> L'univers t'abandonne."

But now all this sorrow could be set aside. Adams asserted that the spontaneous call sending him to Congress was more gratifying than being chosen president. "No election or appointment conferred upon me ever gave me so much pleasure." It troubled him, of course, that "the dearest of my friends [Louisa and his sons] have no sympathy with my sensations."

Whatever may have been said to coax Louisa is unrecorded, but she eventually relented and set off for Washington, going on ahead of her husband while he waited until December 8 to depart on the heels of a violent snowstorm. He caught up with her in Philadelphia, where they lingered so that he could confer with his literary and political friends. He found them evenly split on the wisdom of his taking a seat in Congress.

The more notable feature of the journey to Washington, however, took place on December 17, during the stretch from Baltimore to the capital. A railroad had recently been built between the cities, and the proprietor implored the Adamses so ardently to take their first ride by rail with his company that they consented; as a prominent advocate of internal improvements and as a new member of Congress, JQA could hardly refuse. But he soon wished he had, for the train had difficulty keeping on its single track in heavy rain, making endless delays inevitable. Although Louisa lost patience and switched to a carriage, her husband made a rare attempt at being politic by remaining in his seat and eventually beating Louisa home by an hour. His companions in the train car had been "dull beyond ordinary stage fare, and we were a coach full of mutes."

His renewed spirit soon displayed itself in the capital. Now his complaints were confined mostly to inflamed eyes and a worsening cough, conditions probably due to irritation caused by smoke from coal burning in the fireplaces. He and Louisa greeted three hundred callers on New Year's Day 1831, after which he began talking informally with congressional members who shared his outlook. He even spoke frequently with Vice President Calhoun, who wanted Adams' aid in his own opposition to President Jackson. Here JQA proceeded cautiously. "Mr Calhoun's friendships and enmities are regulated exclusively by his interests. His opinions are the sport of every popular blast."

By the end of January, Adams found himself so cheerful that he said "my own condition is now of unparalleled comfort and enjoyment." In addition to politics, he threw himself into literary work, including an examination of the recently published letters and memoirs of Thomas Jefferson. He relished pointing out the errors and sins of the Virginian. "He tells nothing but what redounds to his own credit," Adams scoffed, claiming that throughout his career, Jefferson had shown perfidy "worthy of Tiberius Caesar."

From Jefferson, he turned to begin what became a memorable literary enterprise: a lengthy poem about King Henry II's conquest of

Ireland. The feat resulted from what John called "one of these rhyming fits" which until that point had made him, as he put it, merely "one of the smallest poets of my country." Now, whether he was lying in bed, taking a walk, or simply sitting, he said, his mind could not escape "the melancholy madness of poetry."

At the outset, Adams had intended composing a comic poem, but the subject and "my natural sliding into gravity" meant that "all my attempts at humor evaporated in the first canto." By April 16, he had completed two thousand lines, which, he said, gave him "the measure of my own poetical power. Beyond this I shall never attain." Even so, though the result fell far short of his aspiration, he took heart that he still possessed "an insatiate thirst for undertaking again higher and better things." This thought accompanied the poet when he and Louisa departed for another summer in Quincy.

After pausing in New York City to call at the bedside of the dying James Monroe, Adams overruled Louisa and, in the face of a rising northeaster, insisted that they take a boat through Long Island Sound to Providence. The trip became a harrowing experience even for Adams, who had boasted of being fearless in dangerous weather. "With every thump of the sea upon the bow of the boat, I had full leisure to reflect upon my own obstinacy in resisting good advice."

Once Quincy was safely reached, the summer of 1831 passed quickly, for Congressman Adams had much to occupy him besides the usual concerns over property, trees, and the ever-weakening Tom Adams. A political step became necessary when neighbors in his Plymouth District were drawn to the sentiment rising in America against Freemasonry. Since it seemed prudent not to oppose this social and political movement and since he was against secret societies in principle, Adams enlisted as an Anti-Mason and watched closely as the party grew stronger and proclaimed itself against Andrew Jackson, who was a high-ranking Mason. When, that September, the Anti-Masonic party sponsored America's first nominating convention, Adams did not step aside when the gathering considered his name as a candidate for president. He was apparently relieved, however, when his friend and ally William Wirt became the nominee.

The Anti-Masonry movement gave JQA a welcome excuse that summer. He could conveniently blame involvement in it for his latest reluctance to work on a memoir of John Adams, even though a disgusted Charles Adams claimed the literary project was far more valuable "than participation in an excitement like this of Masonry." For JQA, however, drudging through his father's papers lacked thrills and would not produce immediate public results. Consequently, when he was not consorting with Anti-Masonic leaders, he preferred to give the balance of his time to enterprises more quickly completed and pertinent to the moment than writing a biography of his father.

When he was invited to deliver the Fourth of July address in Quincy, Adams' creative impulse responded. Not that the task was easy. He wished to rebuke South Carolina's inflamed talk of defying federal legislation through the doctrine of Nullification. This theory, springing mainly from the mind of Vice President Calhoun, held that a state had the power to declare a federal law null and void within its borders. This states' rights principle reflected a deepening unease in the South, particularly South Carolina, over such perceived federal threats as a protective tariff and restraint on slavery's expansion. Always a stout-hearted Union man, Adams was angered by the notion that a state could defy the will of a national majority. To refute this idea, Adams grumbled that he needed much imagination, memory, and judgment, all powers he said were in him now decayed with age.

These doubts about his capacity disturbed him so much that they delayed work on the oration. Suddenly despondent, JQA tried to console himself by remembering that his failing strength was "the course of nature and the will of Heaven. Why should I complain?" This acute awareness of growing old also led him to renewed brooding over his career. Here he was, aged and able to see "nothing I have done for mankind." But since his infirmities had not stifled "the insatiable longing to do something," he said glumly that he must live with "the conscious shame that it will never be done."

Not until July 3 were these distressing thoughts overcome, allowing Adams to finish the oration—and to his satisfaction. "How severe a censor it behooves me to be upon myself!" The struggle was worth it, for on the Fourth his contribution was a huge success, despite a temperature well above 90 degrees and an "overflowing" audience. Mercifully, he omitted a third of the manuscript, so that it took a mere hour and a half to deliver the remarks. In them, he called the claim of sovereign statehood an "hallucination," warning that it could lead a state or states to war against the federal government. He closed with the ringing phrase "Independence and Union forever."

Although prayers, anthems, soloists, and poems had graced the program, the perspiring audience somehow survived to interrupt Adams frequently with cheers and applause. This helped him out of any lingering moodiness, as did the news that the printer had soon distributed four thousand copies of the oration, with orders pouring in for more. Praise for the address had arrived in Quincy from other parts of the nation—a source of enormous satisfaction for the speaker.

Barely rested from his labors, Adams learned that James Monroe had died on the Fourth, just as John Adams and Thomas Jefferson had in 1826, and that the Boston Common Council invited JQA to deliver a tribute to the departed Virginian. The task occupied most of his time until the day he gave the speech, August 25. Once more, anxiety prevailed, making him claim that anything he said about Monroe would play into the hands of "a combination of parties against me." He professed his certainty that he would be "an ignominious failure."

Instead, the oration was his second triumph of the season. Part of the success could have come from the audience's relief when he spoke with comparative brevity, omitting well over half of his prepared remarks, which later ran to ninety-six printed pages. Earlier, the crowd had not had an easy time of it, having walked or ridden to the Old South Church in "a pouring rain," and then facing "wrangling and fighting to get in," only to wait in suffocating heat through prayer and music before Adams could try to make his shrill voice heard above the "trucks, wagons, and carriages rolling over the pavement in the streets adjoining the church."

The address wisely emphasized Monroe's role in the founding of the republic—talk of the nation's Fathers invariably pleased any crowd in New England, even the much-put-upon members of JQA's audience. Under the circumstances, not everyone in the church may have caught a bit of irony tucked into Adams' florid prose. After praising Monroe for urging Congress to establish a system of internal improvements (an idea Monroe would not have endorsed but for JQA's prodding), he gently poked fun at Congress for having insisted "that a power competent to the annexation of Louisiana to this Union was incompetent to the construction of a post-road, to the opening of a canal, or to . . . the institution of seminaries of learning."

After the audience clapped long and loudly, a sweating and hoarse Adams returned to Quincy in a happy frame of mind, which he retained during his remaining two months in Massachusetts. Aside from the usual devotion to long walks, trees, neighbors, and Holy Scripture, these weeks went mostly to revising the Monroe oration for what proved a very popular publication, and to writing a long essay on the current state of affairs in England for the *American Annual Register*.

By late October, these achievements gave him the unusual pleasure of being able to look back over a summer without shaming himself for wasting time. His two orations would, he contended, endure "as long as any work of mine." Furthermore, they were sure to bring "respect for my character." What had all this cost him? He admitted that he had "totally suspended the biography of my father."

UNFORTUNATELY, these gratifying reflections had to be abandoned once he returned to Washington on November 13 to begin his first term in the House of Representatives. His life soon was dominated by the Twenty-second Congress, which ran from December 5, 1831, to mid-July 1832, and from December 1832 to March 1833. Even on days of foul weather or sickness, he usually was faithfully present in committee meetings or in his seat, seeking to master every detail that came before the House—and to have a word to say on most topics.

The main issues facing Congress were a move to lower tariff rates and whether to keep the national bank alive. Both inevitably involved Adams because, to his dismay, he found himself appointed chairman of the Committee on Manufacturing. Though he would have preferred attending to foreign relations or the congressional library, he gave himself unreservedly to creating a tariff that would spur economic growth and that appeared less threatening to the plantation states than earlier revenue bills had seemed. The "Adams Tariff" did not calm South Carolina, however, to JQA's disgust. He also battled in behalf of the Bank of the United States, another institution that, like a protective tariff, he insisted was important for a powerful America.

Although he quickly became a fierce combatant in House debates, warning particularly against the danger in talk of Nullification and Southern rights, congressional service soon began to discourage Adams. He had hoped to accomplish so much, but the issues were complicated and worldly, offering him little chance to fight for moral ideals—the sort of campaign he had claimed as his calling since youth. Losing the presidency had left him more zealous than ever to represent virtue. "It is my wish," he said in December, "to fill every moment of my time with some action of the mind which may contribute to the pleasure or the improvement of my fellow creatures." But instead, Southern threats to the Union seemed to make service in the House as frustrating for Adams as he had found the presidency.

Not only did the House disappoint him, matters at home also tended to push Adams back into a dispirited mood. Chief among these domestic concerns was the now-undeniable fact that his son John was dependent on alcohol. The sight brought anxiety "more than I can endure and reduces me to the weakness of a child," said the father, adding that the only release would be by his own death, which he claimed to welcome. Life had become akin to "Indian torture, roasting to death by a slow fire."

The son's decline became doubly distressing after word arrived that JQA's brother Tom had died on March 12. The sad event was no surprise, since it had become clear that Tom would pay the same price for abusing alcohol that had been charged to other family members. Even so, Adams found Tom's loss a "deep affliction" as he recalled "how dear and how affectionate he has been to me through a long life." Tom's widow, Nancy, and some of their children were now largely dependent on JQA, who feared he would soon be unable to pay these impecunious relatives their due from John Adams' will.

After returning to Quincy in time for his birthday in July, the dejected congressman saw nothing to encourage him. "I commence the sixty-sixth year of my life in great distress of mind." His only relief, he said, "is *occupation*. To keep the mind as constantly as possible employed. All before me is dreary." And so it remained, unrelieved even by news that his long poem *Dermot MacMorrogh or the Conquest of Ireland*, written the previous year, would be published as a book in an edition of one thousand copies. Although the volume quickly went into a second edition, much corrected by the author, its sufferings at the hands of political critics led Adams to growl: "I lament its publication."

After the disappointing holiday of 1832, Adams carried a somber spirit back to Washington. He drew no pleasure from another session of Congress, particularly after Jackson had been reelected president. Victory for his archenemy made him even more combative and irritable in debates, bringing Charles Adams to lament that his father's "temperament as well as his situation very much unfit him for that body." But not even Charles could appreciate that while the congressman might seem lively in defending such causes as the national bank during the day, in his few hours of sleep the old man dreamed the dreams of one for whom "life becomes a burden."

Consequently, when back in Quincy in the spring of 1833, Adams was so filled with despair that nothing helped him avert a depressed state as serious as the one he had suffered as a youth in Newburyport. The strain he had endured during and since his presidency could no longer be denied its price. This emotional descent was slowed only briefly by an invitation from Dr. George Parkman to dine with the actress and author Fanny Kemble, who was touring the United States with her father, the famed actor Charles Kemble. Miss Kemble—a niece of the recently deceased Mrs. Sarah Siddons, who was Adams' favorite actress—had asked for an introduction to the former president.

Momentarily, Adams' spirits revived, and he accepted the opportunity eagerly. His admirer might be female, but he saw her as a child of whom any parent, particularly one of his own unhappy experience, might be proud. "Withal, a most affectionate and profitable daughter," he observed of Miss Kemble, who, through her success on the stage and in publishing, had rescued her father from debt. He added the inspiring facts that she was "perfectly unexceptionable in her deportment and regular in attendance upon religious duties."

He prepared for his meeting with Miss Kemble by reviewing her writing. "As a sort of personage myself of the last century, I was flattered by the wish of this blossom of the next age to bestow some of her fresh fragrance upon the antiquities of the past." The dinner at Parkman's residence in Boston took place on May 11, giving Adams the rare delight of discussing subjects like Shakespeare with persons as knowledgeable as he.

Unfortunately, the enlivening effect of the evening soon vanished with the news that President Jackson was coming to Boston to receive an honorary degree from Harvard. Jackson was "in every way unworthy of it," rumbled Adams, who told cousin Josiah Quincy, the university's president, that "I *could not* be present to see my Darling Harvard disgrace herself by conferring a Doctor's degree upon a barbarian and savage who could scarcely spell his own name." He predicted that it would be long before Harvard could "wash out" this stain caused when it "bowed the knee to Baal." Was it possible, he reflected, that "time-serving and sycophancy are qualities of all learned and scientific institutions"? Consequently, he made a great point of remaining in Quincy and working among his seedling trees when Jackson appeared at Harvard.

Adams took satisfaction in talk of Jackson's bouts of fatigue and illness during his stay in New England, which caused many official events to be canceled. The ceremonies at Harvard had to be postponed, as was the great public greeting for Jackson at Bunker Hill, where orator Edward Everett made "a fulsome address" and presented the president with "two cannon-balls"—all to JQA's disgust.

Adams was certain that Jackson had toyed with the good people of Massachusetts. "He is one of our tribe of great men who turn disease to commodity, like John Randolph, who for forty years was always dying." According to Adams, Jackson was "so ravenous of notoriety that he craves the sympathy for sickness as a portion of his glory," willing even to allow talk of his "chronic diarrhoea." He predicted that the president would "crawl" back to Washington, disappear briefly into the White House, and then emerge, "never in better health and spirits."

ALAS, THERE WAS no such invigoration for JQA. He found scant pleasure in his latest projects: a history of the Jewish people and further assaults on the Masons. By the Fourth of July, an alarming state of melancholy had begun. "It has been no festival for me," he admitted. "A day of gloomy thoughts, desponding anticipations, and self-reproach for useless waste of time." A week later, he reported an "irresistable lassitude" as he spent hours in bed "and brooded over the infirmities and miseries of my condition to no purpose." He could not, he said, be roused from "mental torpidity."

By the close of July, he was talking of death's approach and praying "for an easy passage." At this point, Louisa, much alarmed, sent for a physician. He was no help, however, and the patient was all the more convinced that "my only effectual remedies are Patience and Resignation, and above all preparation for my last change." Although he mustered the strength to teach a granddaughter the alphabet, his grim view remained unaltered. "I belong to the age that has passed, and can look forward with rational hope or wishes only for an euthanasia."

A month later, Adams' depressed state had become so severe that he no longer was able to sleep. Louisa and Charles proposed a desperate remedy: they insisted he make a tour of New Hampshire's White Mountains and other points in New England, accompanied by the family's good friends Mr. and Mrs. Isaac P. Davis. The trio left on August 28 for a fortnight of travel, which JQA noted with satisfaction cost him merely $50.

The excursion brought the patient only temporary improvement. Soon, Adams was again in his "old languor." It took an obvious effort for him to find even broken sentences to describe his plight: "a dejection of mind which almost makes life a burthen"—"the imbecility which disqualifies for action"—"to lie down and die is a privilege denied." What he feared most was "a lingering death, tortured with disappointments." No appetite, no sleep, no energy—these losses, along with his woeful thoughts, left him emotionally drained.

In autumn, two events occurred that steadied his spirits and relieved his despair. The Anti-Masonic party nominated him for governor of Massachusetts, some "unwelcome" recognition he nonetheless accepted—much pleased by the gesture, even if he had trouble admitting it. (Adams ran third and then withdrew his name so that the legislature might more easily elect his friend John D. Davis.)

More heartening, however, was news that Charles' wife had given birth to JQA's first grandson, a blessing, Adams wrote, "I had for some time not dared to anticipate." He was so grateful to see tiny John Quincy Adams II that he could not "order my speech aright." Nor could he escape being deeply moved when the text for his grandson's baptismal service proved to be "God hath chosen the foolish things of this world to confound the wise, and God hath chosen the weak things of the world to confound the things that are mighty." The passage brought more comfort, the grandfather acknowledged, "than I have had for some years."

Then, in early November, after playing host to Henry Clay, who was touring New England "peddling for popularity," Adams started for Washington. The journey was hardly one to sustain his better mood, for he narrowly missed death when the railroad car in which he was riding derailed in New Jersey. "The scene of sufferance was excruciating," he reported. "Men, women, and a child scattered along the road bleeding, mangled, groaning, writhing in torture, and dying." He called it "a trial of feeling to which I had never before been called."

Grateful for his escape, he began another winter season surrounded by Washington's distractions. Looking back over the summer's deep "melancholy," he could now at least rebuke himself for having failed to maintain a "becoming spirit." A Christian, he asserted, should endure with fortitude all the ills of life, never losing trust in Providence. With this statement he began a significant shift in outlook. When he reflected once again on his career, this time he gave himself credit for his achievements before he became president.

From that point forward, he made a point of stressing that it was, after all, not before but after he entered the White House that he began his decline. Much had been achieved before 1824, and he would keep this thought uppermost, even if every exertion he had made since then "has recoiled upon me." And indeed, he asked, why should he fret that he might never "recover the good will of my countrymen"? He must forget public applause, he announced, and forge ahead.

This outlook sustained Adams in politics and in private during the next fifteen years. He talked of ignoring defeats, and he could merely shrug when friends seemed to desert him. Putting his new philosophy succinctly, he vowed now to rely upon "an overwhelming consciousness of rectitude. To withstand multitudes is the only unerring test of decisive character."

Spurred by this abrupt switch to a militant self-righteousness, Adams' behavior during the new session of Congress became nothing less than pugnacious. He suddenly seemed to enjoy the attacks and taunts of enemies incurred as the House debated national banking, the tariff, and the behavior of the executive branch. To his surprise, the two houses of Congress responded by inviting him to deliver a memorial address on the death of Lafayette during the next session.

He took the assignment with him when he returned to Quincy in mid-July 1834, leaving Washington with some regret. "Public affairs, inauspicious as their movements are, afford me rather relief and relaxation from these heavier domestic and personal afflictions." By this he meant the continued decline of his son John. It was excruciating for the Adamses to face the loss of a second son to alcohol. The young man had refused to travel to New England with his parents, rejecting an offer to superintend the family's property along the South Shore. The proposal had been made in the hope of coaxing him away from Washington to live in new surroundings where unwholesome habits might be overcome.

John's physical condition was never clearly stated—"bilious fevers," heart palpitations, a slovenly and obese appearance—for his anxious parents could bring themselves to speak only in delicate terms about him. His brother Charles, however, did not hesitate to record his thoughts on the tragedy. That "the scourge of intemperance" had plagued the forebears of Abigail Smith Adams for generations, Charles said, illustrated how "vices are hereditary in families." So "severely scourged" had the family been by alcoholism "that every member of it is constantly on trial."

Thoughts about his son's deterioration kept JQA from completing his discourse on Lafayette. "I cannot sit ten minutes together quiet at my writing table." When Louisa became ill, he was so upset that he had to rush out of the house for a six-mile walk, trying to control his feelings. He began to suffer from "cramps," for which Dr. Holbrook, the family physician in Quincy, prescribed "flower of sulphur."

The painful suspense ended in mid-October with word that John was critically ill. At once JQA hastened to Washington, leaving Louisa, who was too sick to make the trip. When he reached the capital on October 22, he found his son fallen into a coma. John died early the next morning without recognizing his father. He was thirty-one.

After assuring John's widow, Mary, that she and her two daughters would always have a home with the Adamses, JQA submitted to
an overpowering grief. He sat beside his son's corpse, kissing "his life-
less brow" and observing gratefully that John's placid countenance
bore no mark of agony. Once the young man's remains were temporarily interred pending removal to Quincy, Adams faced more than
sorrow, for John had left debts of $15,000 to be added to the father's
own obligations.

The prospect made him feel virtually helpless, leaving him no re-
course but to call upon his last remaining son for assistance. JQA asked
Charles to accompany Louisa to Washington and remain long enough
to help locate money to get the family through the winter. "You must
understand that there is *now* here little else than debts," he confessed,
urging that every effort be made in Boston to raise cash. Given the crisis, Adams went so far as to promise that he and Louisa would reduce
their lavish style of living, which had never diminished since the days
spent abroad or in the White House.

He did not realize it, but when JQA acknowledged that he now
must depend upon Charles, he took another big step away from despair. Until his wife and son arrived in mid-November, though, he remained distraught, even panicky, over his financial crisis. His daily
walks around the Capitol were now mainly "to divert my thoughts
from the bitterness of my misfortunes." He felt "a dark and gloomy
terror." He brooded over what he might do "to be saved from ruin"
and spoke fearfully of losing his trust in God. Nor were his spirits lifted
by stern letters Charles sent in advance of his travel to Washington.

Although Charles had become a successful attorney, estate trustee,
and budding pamphleteer, he had a chilling manner. This he employed to prepare his father for the only way out of crushing debt: ex-
penditure must be curtailed and portions of the precious ancestral land
around Quincy would have to be sold. Sensing that Charles doubted
his parent would have the needed self-discipline to follow this advice,
JQA replied indignantly that indeed he was prepared to surrender servants, carriages, wines, and magazines. "I shall walk to and from the
Capitol as long as my legs will carry me."

During the four days that Charles was in Washington, he hoped to
hear more than solemn vows from his father, whom he called "a singular instance of a man to whom prudence never was natural." Instead, JQA took a worried, sensitive, defensive position and gave a
cool, even impatient reception to Charles' strategy for financial recov-

ery. The senior Adams emphasized—even to the point of shouting—
that he would not part with family land, a step that Charles deemed a
necessary sacrifice.

Concluding that his father wished to treat him as a "menial,"
Charles decided that he was unwelcome and that his parents could not
be helped. But when he prepared to return to Boston, Adams abruptly
regained his self-control and agreed that Charles should manage the
family's resources as he deemed best. Further, he pledged to follow the
son's urgings that he stop fretting about fiscal matters. Charles emphasized to his father how he wished "that your mind should be put at
ease at once from the anxiety which *I know* has been preying upon it
for years."

Thereafter, as he watched Charles succeed in removing many of
the causes for worry, Adams concluded that he had been wise to place
his trust in his last son. "All my hopes of futurity in this world are now
centered upon him and upon his employment of his time," the father
wrote. Immediately, it was as if a great load was lifted from his shoul-
ders, as indeed it was.

Now refreshed from putting aside the needs he had long nurtured
for public acclaim and money, Adams could turn at last to the memorial discourse on Lafayette. Delivered over two hours and fifty minutes
before a joint session of Congress on December 31, 1834, the oration
was verbose and stylized in language and sentiment—a typical
sentence described Lafayette as "the personified image of self-circum-
scribed liberty." It was a mediocre effort, and Adams recognized it
as such. Nevertheless, his emotions were now so stable that he remained calm about the speech's shortcomings.

Restored self-confidence led him to take new interest in the business before the House of Representatives. While he served again as
chairman of the Committee on Manufacturing, he had ample time to
oppose patronage policies and to defend the doctrine of separation of
powers, a stand made necessary when Congress sought to handicap
President Jackson's attempts to find a peaceable solution to a quarrel
with France.

This issue pitted Adams in the House against Daniel Webster and
John C. Calhoun (who had resigned as vice president) in the Senate.
"Calhoun's tone is so self-sufficient and overbearing, and Webster's
reasoning so utterly ignorant or unprincipled," he said, "that they pro-
voked my temper and I answer them with cutting sarcasm. The use of
this weapon is seldom politic." The debate was touched by irony, for

Adams' ardent campaign to keep the powers of the executive and the legislature separate put him on the side of Andrew Jackson.

Description of these legislative battles now began to dominate JQA's letters to Charles, which Adams knew his son would circulate among interested persons in Boston. A sure sign of his heightened respect for his son, the letters were also evidence of Adams' continued revival. Knowing that her husband was once again writing in a lively vein pleased Louisa, despite her disgust with politics. She told Charles: "Your father is a sturdy white oak and not to be crushed by the reptiles who envy his talents and would destroy him if they could."

Indeed, he was not to be felled. In a letter to Charles written after the House had finally adjourned in March 1835, JQA reviewed the furor of the session, a turmoil from which, he admitted, "my reason bids me withdraw." Then the old man abruptly became candid about why he would not retire. "A sense of duty; perhaps a lingering tenacity for existence as a public man controuling my better judgment, keeps me yet in the field of politics." He could not commit "desertion." "I must stay," he announced.

The renewal of Adams' vigor took him beyond the floor of the House of Representatives in the spring of 1835. It was evident in his diary entries as, after Congress wound up its work, he once more took up commenting on sermons. Even here, however, his increased combativeness sometimes overcame him. Once, he spoke disgustedly of a sermon by Boston's famed Unitarian William Ellery Channing, who was visiting Washington. Adams said it was filled with "common-place declamation" against war, and he charged Channing with being a servile politician in the pulpit, "a chaplain-general of blue light federalism" (an anti-Adams faction). War, said JQA, was a fine subject for the "rancorous benevolence of politician priestcraft to harp upon."

A more gentle result of his restoration was his performance as surrogate father for the two daughters left by his son John. He became their teacher. He saw to their attendance at worship services. He even took them to useful entertainments, such as the display "of wild beasts" that arrived in Washington at the end of March 1835. If the little girls had as good a time at the circus as their grandfather evidently had, the outing was a rousing success. In his diary, JQA carefully listed all the animals and their sizes, as well as the skill of the trainer, who had the lion behave like a lapdog. He noticed, however, that the trainer "did not see fit to associate with the white bear" or "the Tyger."

Once again, gossip interested him. He took special delight in a report about a beggar who slipped into the White House one night in April and found his way upstairs to President Jackson's bedroom. There, at 2 a.m., the intruder began pounding on the locked door, shouting that he was hungry. Although the fellow was taken off and locked in the presidential stable to await arraignment in the morning, he managed to escape—leaving only a colorful glimpse of what passed for White House security during 1835.

In his own residence, JQA's revival inspired him to tidy his writing chamber, which he admitted had become a fire hazard because of accumulated newspapers and magazines. He oversaw the disposition of "waggon loads" of pamphlets and old papers, all of which were piled in such "incredible" amounts that they "choak up the house." To his amazement, he found that he had been keeping a file of one hundred newspapers and perhaps that same number of journals and reviews. His copies of eulogies, orations, and sermons rose in great mounds; he deemed only a tenth fit to be kept. Trying to retain the best was "an excruciating task."

While he managed to complete such chores, he was less successful in tackling the problem of the Columbian Mills, which had been left in a calamitous state at the time of son John's death. JQA found the employees "doing nothing, having done nothing or next to nothing the whole winter . . . and likely to do nothing in the future." It proved an apt prophecy.

Disgruntled but not depressed, Adams set out for another summer holiday in Quincy in mid-May. There he announced: "I came home with a resolution to make an effort to employ my time more usefully this summer than I have heretofore done." He even spoke of resuming work on the biography of his father, but the weeds and mice in his garden of young trees quickly claimed his attention. His determination to succeed in growing trees from seed was another display of his fighting spirit. Other farmers and landowners in the Quincy area laughingly told Adams that he was foolish to cultivate seedlings in the face of New England's rigorous winters. It left him as a minority of one seeking to prove the universe wrong—a position JQA found very comfortable.

Although he kept scolding himself for wasting precious time—talk that now sounded like an automatic response—Adams cheerfully squandered much of the 1835 holiday on larks. One highlight was a fishing excursion sponsored by the Atlas Insurance Company. By midmorning, the party, which included Edward Everett and other notables whose favor the company was seeking, had anchored below the

Boston lighthouse not far out from Cohasset, and in two hours fifty fish were caught, "three fine cod" by Adams.

The Atlas hosts took pains to assure that the anglers did not go hungry or thirsty. Cold beef, Madeira, sherry, champagne, and wines were provided. For JQA, however, the day's greatest success was the "lemonade" he was served, and he carefully recorded the recipe for this remarkable version of an otherwise healthful beverage: add to a gallon of water a bottle of Jamaica rum, a bottle of cognac, a bottle of champagne, and a pound of sugar. As a minor detail, the recipe suggested including a pint of lemon juice.

An amusing coincidence occurred soon after the excursion. Adams was visited by Mrs. Philadelphia Cook, an ardent apostle of temperance, who the uneasy host said had a "face and form . . . well suited to perform the part of one of the weird sisters of Shakespeare." Trapped and too polite to stir, he submitted to an hour's reading by Mrs. Cook from literature recounting the evils of alcohol. When the visitor finally came to the point and pressed Adams to make confession, he admitted he often took two glasses of wine with dinner.

Hearing what was assuredly a conservative estimate, Mrs. Cook peered closely at her victim's face and announced that he "did not look well." This diagnosis was followed by a lengthy lecture on the evil of wine, which was proclaimed to be a "poison—it was fire." When Adams had the courage to inquire why wine was served at Christ's first miracle, Mrs. Cook replied that there was no evidence that Jesus drank any of it, and, besides, this particular wine surely must have been "pure."

After imploring him not to "pour poison down the throat," Mrs. Cook urged him to abstain from strong drink for a month as a trial. After the exhausted host feebly said that he would think about her plea, she finally departed. Despite alcoholism's destruction of two of his brothers and two of his sons, JQA never seemed to take seriously the possibility that he himself might be vulnerable to the disorder. Instead, the era's temperance movement left him alternately amused and annoyed—both responses perhaps forms of denial.

The formidable Mrs. Cook's advice was put aside a few days later when Adams set out with Charles and other men on a September tour of Nantucket Island, taking the steamer from New Bedford. Again, there was much fishing, food, and drink, but possibly the most pleasing feature of the outing was the flattering courtesy shown to Congressman Adams as crowds of residents and tourists gathered simply to stare at him. The attention troubled Charles, who considered his often cold and irascible father to have "an entire unfitness for public exhibition."

Nothing about the experience seemed to harm Adams, who in fact returned to Quincy resolved to extend his early morning walks beyond six miles. During these outings, he now had the companionship of a distant cousin, E. Price Greenleaf, whose willingness to talk about literature almost matched his own. JQA also displayed a new determination to walk more often into Boston, an undertaking of nearly three hours.

Unfortunately, all this revived vigor and cheerfulness was not quite enough to fend off his chagrin that he was failing to make a signal contribution to humanity. "I have done nothing. I have no ability to do anything that will live in the memory of mankind," he complained. Why had God rejected his prayers to be enabled to do "something beneficial to my own species?" Was it time, he mused, "for me to abandon all such imaginations and to close my accounts with this world"?

Of course, he knew it was not the moment to give up. Instead, he seized a chance to benefit Harvard, now that he had been named an overseer. Drawing upon his new aggressiveness, Adams converted what should have been a modest campaign into a crusade after he attended a program of student orations. He expressed horror at the deterioration he thought he saw in student performance. "How flat, stale, and unprofitable now!" he complained, a gripe hardly softened when the college served "a temperance dinner" to the overseers.

Proceeding as if Harvard's decline were an international crisis, Adams sought to get Lieutenant Governor Samuel T. Armstrong, also an overseer, to join in a formal expression of concern at the disgraceful exhibition. "The speaking was universally bad," he assured Armstrong. More shameful yet, half the performances were translations of English into Latin. Even the best oration was worse than mediocre. What the university needed, JQA contended, "was an electric shock to restore it from a paralytic state and I will make an effort to apply it." Armstrong, however, seemed much less alarmed, and the Adams campaign died.

NEVERTHELESS, the episode helped prepare JQA to be more zealous in combat when Congress reassembled. He announced himself ready to fight for virtue, and alone, if need be. What he needed, he said, was a cause indisputable in its purity, in whose behalf he could contend against all the forces of evil. He prayed that "a ray of light might flash upon my eyes" and show him such an ennobling cause. If he found it, he pledged to face "the fury of the storm" and to throw his enemies "into convulsions." Traveling to Washington in early November 1835, he wondered whether the light he craved might also bring him strength to cleanse the federal temple of evildoers.

To sharpen himself for battle, Adams enumerated "the devices of rivals to ruin me" that he had experienced over the course of his life. He made a listing of persons who he believed had sought to undo him, including such prominent names as Otis, Parsons, Pickering, Bayard, Clay, Russell, Crawford, Calhoun, Jackson, and Webster. These men, as well as others, "have used up their faculties in base and dirty tricks to thwart my progress in life and destroy my character." And what had he done in exchange? "I have returned good for evil. I have never wronged any one of them." His mistake, Adams insisted to his diary, was that he had neglected to fight back.

As he entered the new Congress, powered by self-righteousness, he resumed his seat eager for revenge. In a short time, he found the cause he sought, and into battle he went, hoping to benefit humanity while settling a few old scores.

CHAPTER FOURTEEN

Battle

To redeem my good name.

ACTUALLY, the light he had craved led John Quincy Adams toward not one but two causes. Both would benefit the American republic, as well as humanity at large. The first was a defense of the right of petition. The other was to create a federal institution devoted to scholarship. These stands were often so unpopular in Congress that Adams had the pleasure of thinking he stood alone against all the malevolence in the universe.

The fight that brought luster to Adams' congressional career began during the winter of 1836. While his eventual aim was to corral slavery, at first he struggled only in behalf of a citizen's right to petition the government. The right prevailed, he said, even if a petitioner should be addressing slavery, a subject taboo to many Americans. His argument drew fierce opposition from the southern slavocracy and the northern followers of Andrew Jackson. The result made him the most famous—or notorious—combatant on the floor of Congress during the next decade.

Ironically, Adams' seemingly brilliant decision to make the right of petition his cause involved mostly luck. While his defense of petitioners soon earned him worldwide repute as a bitter enemy of slavery, he had not selected the issue because of its link to human bondage. Previously he had displayed little concern about the enslaved African-American. Shortly after leaving the White House, he assured his diary that there was "misapprehension and much prejudice" about the treatment of bondsmen; perhaps a few cases of "extreme oppression and cruelty" did exist on southern plantations, he conceded, but "I believe them to be very rare, and that the general treatment of slaves is mild and moderate."

By 1836, however, he recognized that bondage appeared likely to be a permanent painful presence in the republic. What vexed him about this development was less that human beings were being degraded than that the nation must listen to southern politicians spout a "torrent of moral depravity" in justifying slavery. Adams remembered, of course, that many of these southerners had smeared his name and helped defeat him in 1828. In short, the Southern politicos had been and remained scoundrels as far as he was concerned.

He believed that owning slaves was only one of the sins committed by this group, among whom he saw a general depravity in behavior that produced men like Jefferson, Jackson, Crawford, Calhoun, and others whom Adams scorned or despised. Consequently, when he began militantly to oppose the South, it was mainly because he believed the region's representatives were unprincipled, and thus a threat to the health of the country.

While he ultimately enlisted in the crusade against slavery, Adams never supported the abolitionists. Indeed, for a time some of them were among his bitter critics after he announced that Congress had no power to emancipate slaves in the District of Columbia. He charged that radicals such as William Lloyd Garrison would willingly dissolve the Union to satisfy their ends, and disunion, he argued, would be a disaster for civilization's experiment with democracy. To avert such a catastrophe, he was content to tolerate slavery where it existed while insisting that the nation must guarantee the right of petition, even for petitions that urged slavery's abolition.

Consequently, Adams was outraged when, after sharp debate, the House of Representatives adopted a new parliamentary procedure in May 1836 that became known as the gag rule. He had done what he could to oppose approving the rule, which decreed that all petitions or memorials touching in any way on slavery would be laid on the table without being printed, discussed, or referred to committee. Southern congressmen had demanded the rule after the anti-slavery movement began flooding Congress with petitions calling particularly for the ending of slavery and the slave trade in the District of Columbia. Adams had found his mail bulging with them.

He had made a sensation of himself during the House discussion over adopting the gag rule. His search for just the right cause was ended as he began to deride and denounce the enemies of petition.

While his voice might be shrilled by age and his language often extreme and outrageous, he now felt justified in using every mental and emotional strength—and weakness—in fighting to have petitions properly received by the House.

In doing so, he rejoiced that he could oppose those persons, particularly the Jackson Democrats of the North, who believed with Martin Van Buren that being silent about slavery was a small price to pay for party unity and electoral victory. By accepting the gag rule, these Yankees gave Adams a hefty weapon with which to avenge himself against many longtime adversaries. He argued impressively that a citizen's right to have a petition received and heard was so essential for free government that it took on religious sanctity.

As the kind of cause Adams had prayed for, opposing the gag rule allowed him to defend high principle while at the same time exposing his opponents as evildoers. His assault on the slaveholders' congressional bloc soon became a lively topic in America's public discourse. What drew attention was the emergence of a new John Quincy Adams. His adopted cause transformed him into a debater so impassioned, so mischievous, so stubborn, and so radical that his foes and even some friends wondered at times if he had lost his sanity.

While others might try to cheer him on or shout him down, his wife and son watched this new Adams with a mingling of sorrow and sympathy. After forty years of marriage, Louisa could appreciate what motivated her spouse. Among her journal jottings during the congressional uproar in 1836 was an expression of hope that his aspiration would be realized—"that he may leave a fame to posterity and awaken the justice of this nation to record his name as one of the fairest midst the race of man." Adams himself could not have stated his yearning more succinctly.

At other moments, however, Louisa fretted at the personal cost her husband was beginning to pay as a zealot in Congress. "Could he only bring his mind to the calm of retirement," she wrote, knowing that it meant he must put aside "mortified vanity" and "disappointed ambition." But invariably, she was compelled to admit that if he did step down, it would destroy him. The situation left Louisa with a revealing regret: yielding to no one in her admiration for her husband's strengths, she believed that by fighting in Congress, he was wasting "all the energies of his fine mind upon a people who do not either understand or appreciate his talents."

Charles Francis Adams, an astute observer of his father, took a more down-to-earth view. "My own opinion is and has been for many years that his whole system of life is very wrong—that he sleeps by far too little, that he eats and drinks too irregularly, and that he has habituated his mind to a state of morbid activity which makes life in its common forms very tedious." Yet to try calming his father was hopeless, Charles conceded. Even when the admired Boston physician Dr. Jacob Bigelow gave JQA written instructions to seek a quiet existence, the aging warrior disregarded the advice.

After all, he was riding with more than one crusade. A second cause had been handed to him just as the fight over petition rights was looming. On December 21, 1835, a message arrived in the House from President Jackson that few members bothered to heed. Not so Adams. Although he misunderstood the president to say that an Englishman named "Simonson" had bequeathed money to the United States for establishing a learned institution, he recognized at once the message's portent. It was, he assured himself, "the finger of Providence, compassing great events by incomprehensible means."

Seeing in the bequest the wherewithal for the republic to support scholarship, as he had long urged, Adams offered a motion that the Englishman's gift be referred to a committee; according to House custom, he was automatically appointed its chairman. Soon enough, he knew all about James Smithson—that this generous individual was the illegitimate son of the first Duke of Northumberland, and that he had left his entire estate, amounting to somewhat more than $500,000 in gold, to enable the United States of America to increase knowledge among its citizens.

Alongside his fight against the gag rule, Adams now battled to keep the Smithson bequest from being "wasted upon hungry and worthless political jackals." It was a close call, but he would live to see his often lonely struggle come to a gratifying victory. Smithson's vision for America and mankind ultimately prevailed because Adams had been loudly indignant at every sly attempt by others to divert the funds for personal projects, such as using part of Smithson's money to purchase bonds issued by the youthful states of Arkansas and Michigan. Admittedly, Adams did have his own pet idea about properly spending the bequest. If he had had his way, Smithson's wealth would have created a national astronomical observatory. Here, however, JQA was haunted by the much-jeered words in his 1825 message to Congress about observatories being lighthouses of the skies.

. . .

As CONGRESS LABORED through a lengthy and acrimonious session in 1836, Adams spoke of struggling against "hireling snakes of all parties." Only a painful and seriously infected bruise on his leg, "festering and inflaming," kept him away from the Capitol during part of April. When his physician allowed him to return, he was incautious, had a relapse, and was forced again to stay at home with his limb elevated.

As the grumbling congressman sat "pining" for action, he read some English history, tried to compose poetry, and meditated "upon the decays of my own faculties of body and mind." He did seem momentarily to forget the warfare on Capitol Hill when he took up a book about Queen Mary of Scotland. Her career, and especially her sexual misconduct and her beheading, led John to ponder how, particularly in monarchical systems, the force of passion could affect public affairs. He disapproved when historians dealt tenderly with Mary's story. "She was no doubt beautiful and susceptible of warm affections," but her desperate behavior could be "palliated" only by ascribing it to "weakness in the understanding."

He found a more edifying way of spending his convalescence when a New Hampshire citizen asked that he write verses "in honour of our common country." The result was a poem appropriately entitled "Our Country," in whose closing lines Adams drew, no doubt unconsciously, a portrait of what he himself wished to become:

> *The man tenacious of his trust,*
> *True to his purpose fair and just,*
> *With equal scorn defies*
> *The rabble's rage, the tyrant's frown.*

Such a hero would receive "martyrdom's unfading crown," for

> *Undaunted, he would meet the shock,*
> *And spotless, fearless fall.*

With the heroic in mind, Adams finally was able to limp back to the House in time to enter the heated debate over whether the new slaveholding Republic of Texas should join the Union. He stoutly opposed the idea, but found it difficult to gain the floor. Repeatedly, but with rare success, he sought to speak or vote amid the shouts against him by defenders of slavery, who demanded "order, order." In reply, he taunted them by yelling, "Am I gagged, am I gagged?" The acrimony became so bitter that he confided to his diary: "I shall henceforth speak in the House of Representatives at the hazard of my life."

Eventually, most members of Congress needed a respite from the struggle as much as Adams did. After a final all-night session ending at noon on July 4, he wasted no time in departing for Quincy. Borrowing $3,000 to pay household bills and for travel expenses, he led the family and servants—eight persons in all—to New England. He was amazed when a new railroad locomotive covered one fourteen-mile stretch between Providence and Boston in thirty-five minutes. Almost as speedily, his plan for a quiet summer was overrun. The Boston city fathers immediately handed him a nerve-racking chore by inviting him to deliver a eulogy of James Madison, who had died on June 28, 1836.

The date announced for the memorial was September 27, a deadline Adams barely met—as usual. He had allowed himself to be bogged down by too grand a design for the oration, in which he proposed to picture the Union's growth from the Continental Congress to the adoption of the Constitution. His intent was, of course, to antagonize the South, with its ideas about Nullification.

Another hindrance had been the necessity of dealing with "circumstances in the life of Mr. Madison of which I cannot speak with praise." Could he pass over them in silence? Should he give offense to many of Madison's admirers? Would he "suppress the truth"? Mainly, Adams was concerned about how candid he must be in picturing Madison's ally, Jefferson. Privately, he claimed that careful research put Jefferson's "craft and duplicity in very glaring colors," and that Jefferson's treatment of John Adams was definitely "double-dealing, treacherous, and false beyond all toleration."

Despite Adams' worries about the oration's content and his failing memory, the address was a sensation, even though it took nearly two and a half hours to deliver before a large crowd on a day so dark that he could scarcely read his manuscript.

For a few days thereafter, he granted himself "a holiday for idleness." Mostly, this meant allowing time "for desultory reading, a few pages in one book, and a few pages in another." He broke away to dine with Governor Edward Everett. The "sumptuous" meal was cooked by a person who insisted that her mother had prepared the wedding feast in London for Louisa and John. As if this disclosure were not pleasing enough, Governor Everett delighted JQA by requesting a list of his publications. Although he hastened to begin the list, the congressman wondered whether what he had written was "worth the trouble."

Like most projects, this one was soon put aside. Adams now found he could not resist following new avenues of family genealogy, particularly those branches illumined by the recently discovered diary of Samuel Sewall. The old journal (1674–1729) often mentioned his early Quincy family forebears, but not in quite enough detail, apparently, for Adams was left to complain how genealogical inquiries so often led into a labyrinth where much time was lost "for more useful purposes."

By "useful," he had in mind not only the list for Governor Everett, but also another duty he had promised to undertake that summer: to train his granddaughters to plant and care for seedling trees. "They take a fancy to this themselves," he wrote, "and I wish to encourage them in it." He also happily set out four walnut trees, one at each corner of the nearby lot where Charles was building a summer home. While the son was not pleased by this intrusion on his own landscaping plans, he conceded: "Who can resist so innocent a hobby in a father?"

In this way, the summer and early autumn of 1836 passed quickly. At the close of the holiday, Adams received a strong endorsement when he ran for another term in Congress. The Anti-Masonic convention in his district had urged his reelection not because of partisan interests, but, as he recorded the thrilling words, "because of confidence in my judgment and integrity."

His gratification was only mildly diminished by the news of a Democratic victory by Martin Van Buren in the presidential election. JQA had nothing good to say about the candidates, all of whom struck him as pathetically mediocre. Van Buren, William Henry Harrison, and Hugh Lawson White were "the golden calves of the people, and their dull sayings are repeated for wit, and their grave inanity is passed off for wisdom."

In Washington, Adams dealt with the discovery of more debts left by his deceased son John by turning them over to Charles for disposition. Then he began the enjoyable task of mailing copies of his printed Madison eulogy to the many people from around the country who requested one. There was also time before Congress reopened for him to work at assembling his published writings. Governor Everett's interest in them prompted the author to have as many of his occasional pieces as possible bound and presented to his grandchildren. What better way, he thought, to ensure that future generations of the family would remember some of his ideas?

This project was put aside on December 5, when the House assembled for business. Indeed, congressional warfare soon so absorbed Adams that he even ceased writing in his diary from January through

March of 1837. For two months, he sent no letters to Charles. Consequently, one of the most significant intervals in JQA's public life remains largely blank in his private commentary.

These gaps meant that he left no account of many uproarious scenes in the House. For instance, on February 6, he outraged southern members by a clever maneuver that circumvented the gag rule and allowed him time on the House floor to upbraid those who defended slavery. As he spoke, his opponents were reduced to shouting for his punishment and censure. "Expel him! Expel him!" was heard. Undeterred, he exploited every opportunity to introduce the forbidden subject, glorying in his skill at taunting and outfoxing his enemies.

There was a personal cost for these thrills, for he admitted that attending the House of Representatives had become like entering a "fiery furnace." The impressive national response against the gag rule meant that Adams was swamped by several hundred anti-slavery petitions. The heat in the House arose from his devious ways of placing the petitions before the unwilling chamber. He was kept so busy that it was late March, three weeks after Congress adjourned and President Van Buren was inaugurated, before he could resume his "journalizing."

By then, it was time once again to issue pleas that Charles send the cash needed to bring the family to Quincy. Despite the son's valiant efforts to help, there still was barely enough money for household expenses. Income from Adams' salary as a congressman and from rents of his Washington realty brought only $2,000 annually, much of which was drained away by his albatross, the Columbian Mills. The financial crash of 1837 made matters worse: "My only relief is to avert my thoughts."

FORTUNATELY, Adams had many ways to redirect his mind before leaving for New England. The main diversion was the preparation of a long letter to his constituents, to be published in the Quincy *Patriot*, in which he sought to explain the recent congressional furor. He worked at this task while also posing, as Hiram Powers shaped a bust of him from clay dug around Washington, which Powers claimed was the finest in the world. JQA recalled that over his lifetime, his likeness had been taken by sixteen painters, five sculptors, and one medalist. "My face has been copied in my sixteenth and my seventieth year. They show what I am and what I was."

Posing for Powers also allowed him a few moments to think of rhymes, for he was often asked to write lines in the albums of ladies, young and otherwise. He also began to read the poems and letters of Thomas Gray. "There is no lyric poet of ancient or modern times who so deeply affects my feelings as Gray." Each of Gray's odes he deemed "an inestimable jewel."

By contrast, reading a recent biography of Jefferson brought less profound thoughts, especially after Adams noticed that the book did not include the well-known story of the Virginian's alleged attempt to "debauch" the wife of John Walker, Jefferson's neighbor and friend. The omission, he gleefully pointed out, was like writing a life of the Biblical King David without mentioning the Hittite's wife after whom he had lusted. He was sure that party loyalty would cause many historians to avoid evidence "disgraceful to the memory of Mr. Jefferson."

Dividing his mind between Gray's eerily beautiful elegies and worldly politics, Adams set out for New England in early May, carrying his usual complaints: old age, an agitated mind, and much anxiety. The congressional recess would last less than three months before a special session was called to deal with a crisis in the nation's finances. During the holiday, JQA passed two of life's important milestones. On July 11, he celebrated his seventieth birthday, and on July 26, he and Louisa observed the fortieth anniversary of their marriage.

The two occasions prompted very different thoughts. On his birthday, Adams sternly pointed out to himself that now he had "lived the life of man," so that any additional years must be dedicated to "purposes of usefulness." But how could he be effective, he wondered, when "the infirmities of age are thickening upon me"? A few days later, however, he was in much better spirits, congratulating himself on his good fortune in marriage as he and Louisa attended a party in their honor. Among the many guests was Grace Foster, whom he had admired before he went abroad and met Louisa. He talked at length with Grace about "those days," and about how they both had passed through much sadness since then—Grace had lost many children to consumption. "Her fate has been as checkered as mine."

Another worthwhile event of the summer was Adams' delivery of a Fourth of July address in Newburyport. His remarks pleased even himself, for in a mere ninety minutes he managed to explain how the Declaration of Independence marked a new era in the career of mankind that was second in significance only to the coming of Christ. Even more gratifying, however, was his pleasure in visiting Newburyport, where he had suffered as a wretched law student after graduating from

Harvard in 1787. Now, fifty years later, his visit caused local citizens to turn out in great numbers. Some wished only for a chance to glimpse the famous John Quincy Adams, while others were willing to stand in line to shake his hand during a town hall reception held on the evening of the Fourth.

Charles Adams, watching with amazement and a touch of chagrin as his parent responded to the crowd's attention, observed how the scholarly, haughty, and reclusive aspects of JQA's personality seemed to vanish under the gaze of the many citizens who simply "gathered to look at the lion." It was a heady experience for Adams, knowing that hundreds were unable to find even standing room to hear his oration. Seeing how his father warmed to this adulation, Charles wondered whether "a consciousness of power over the minds of men" had prompted JQA to fill the day's oration with optimism concerning the future of humanity—a prospect John usually derided.

Newburyport's triumph was followed by another success, although at first Adams feared failure. Among his many callers were the formidable Grimké sisters from South Carolina, Angelina and Sarah, who wished to have "much argumentative conversation with me upon slavery and abolition." Knowing that others also wanted him to be more extreme in opposing slavery, he was uneasy in mid-August as delegates from throughout his congressional district assembled in Quincy to discuss whether Texas should join the Union as a slave state. When participants quickly passed resolutions endorsing his opposition to annexation, an elated Adams addressed the crowd for ninety minutes. "I was frequently interrupted by cheering applause."

After the convention, the summer holiday ended, and on August 29, Adams set out for Washington and the special session of Congress. The trip left him more than ever thrilled by railroad travel, in spite of a nasty exchange he had with a "grossly uncivil" ticket agent in New York, who insisted on giving the former president a poor seat in the worst car. Fortunately, a conductor moved him to a place in the best car, where he sat with the "invalids."

Safely home and exclaiming that "the Railway is a stupendous work," Adams was again reminded of dangers on the streets of Washington. One morning, he was so concerned over "a pinching pair of shoes" that he was delayed in leaving to walk as usual to the Capitol. To make up the time, he ordered his coachman to be in front of the residence ready to drive him. Just before Adams appeared at the door, the horses ran away, frightened by the sound of a whip cracking. They dashed several blocks before overturning the carriage, purchased only the previous year, and breaking it "all to pieces."

Leaving his house, JQA was unaware of what had just happened. Assuming that the carriage was delayed, he set out on foot, "limping along to the Capitol" and "thinking of my pinched corns." He kept looking over his shoulder, hoping his coachman would catch up with him. Not until that night at dinner did a thunderstruck Adams learn about the accident. Pondering what injury might have befallen him had he been on time to enter the carriage, he retired to his study after dinner and opened his Bible to Psalm 20, whose seventh verse urges humanity not to trust chariots and horses.

After this excitement, he gave himself and his diary entirely to the business of Congress, observing with amusement that for the moment "the House has not yet got out of humour with me." In the calm before the storm, enemies referred to him as "the *venerable* gentleman from Massachusetts." Within a few days, however, the papers carried accounts of his renewed confrontations with such adversaries as South Carolina's Robert Barnwell Rhett, whose speaking style Adams preferred to call "howling." Louisa, who had remained in Quincy for a few more weeks, wrote: "I see by the papers that you are popping up as usual."

The floor of the House was not always the scene of titanic conflict. Perhaps more typical was the day when Adams privately complained that much less than a quorum was present, "and of them about half were slumbering in their seats, and the other half yawning over newspapers." A very few walked about "to keep up the circulation of the blood," while each "settee" held a distinguished member "stretched out [and] sound asleep." What Adams preferred to describe were the days when pandemonium ruled as members, mostly from the South, tried to subdue the person whom some of them called "the Madman from Massachusetts."

He could be fiendishly clever in presenting petitions from abolitionists and from Peace Society members. Although it was slow going, Adams' strategy began to succeed. He encouraged his northern colleagues to insist that petitions from citizens who were against Texas' entering the Union should be received, even if they bore on the unmentionable issue of Negro bondage. Once northern Democrats were enticed from their southern colleagues by this issue, Adams foresaw that there would soon be votes sufficient to overturn the gag rule.

His parliamentary tactics were unmatched by any House colleague. On June 16, 1838, through skillful maneuvering, he was able to have the floor for his own purposes during the "morning hour" before topics scheduled for the day were called up. He used the time for a speech that consumed parts of fifteen days. His subject was "Freedom of Speech," a topic broad enough to allow him to flay the slaveowners. Claiming that slavery was "a sin before the sight of God," he asserted that to bring Texas into the Union would only enlarge the evil.

HE STILL HAD THE FLOOR on July 9, when the House at last adjourned until December. The long stay in Washington that session had included a few notable moments away from Capitol Hill. Louisa reported to Charles how pleased she and John were that "his old friends of the Corps Diplomatique whom he knew in Europe treat him as Sons who respect their Father." Other pleasures came when the capital had a particularly good season for one of Adams' favorite entertainments, opera. He lauded a production of Rossini's *The Barber of Seville* and hailed as "delicious" a performance of *La sonnambula* by Bellini. President Van Buren and his cabinet were also present to applaud Bellini's music.

As usual, the hours at home were often disturbed by callers, not all of them unwelcome. The couple was delighted by a reunion with Dolley Madison, the former president's widow, who had recently removed from Virginia to occupy a residence next door to the Adamses. JQA had last seen Dolley in 1809, and by now her charm was legendary. "The depredations of time are not so perceptible in her personal appearance as might be expected," he announced, explaining this by adding: "She is a woman of placid, equable temperament."

Another pleasing visitor was Simon Willard, the renowned clockmaker, who at eighty-five was still an active craftsman. He and Adams recalled how the first clock built by Willard was purchased by John Adams in 1774 and now stood in the entry hall of the mansion at Quincy. Willard was assured that the clock was wound faithfully each Sunday morning when JQA was in Massachusetts. It was in perfect condition except for needing new suspensions for the weights, which Willard promised to install.

The next guest was Thomas Munroe, long postmaster of Washington until removed by Andrew Jackson. He wished to have Adams' advice on how to overcome spells of depression—the "blue devils." Admitting to extensive personal experience with Munroe's affliction,

Adams advised "intense occupation" as a never-failing remedy. He also reminded Munroe to be thankful he did not suffer delusions, as did poor John Herbert, a congressman from Maryland, who believed himself desperately poor and, according to JQA, had recently taken to running about naked in the woods around the capital.

Before leaving town, Adams lingered to prepare his sensational congressional speech for publication. The task overwhelmed him, for he had spoken extemporaneously, leaving him dependent on memory and his notes, as well as those of House reporters. When the address was published and widely circulated, it did much to rouse public opinion in the North against annexing Texas, so that by the time Congress reconvened, a frightened Van Buren administration had shied away from annexation, much to JQA's grim satisfaction.

Finally en route to Quincy in mid-July, Adams found himself so tense from the long session and the hurried preparation of his speech for the printer that digestive problems roused him around midnight during the two nights he was on the road, leaving him unable to recapture sleep. It was like entering paradise, he said, to arrive in Quincy. He remained in a weakened state for several days, barely able to creep out to his garden—and then wished he had not done so, for he found his young trees in wretched condition. "I have nothing to show for all my toil and care and anxiety."

Soon, however, he recovered and began a summer of good health. The only serious lapse occurred in early September and was entirely his fault. The family doctor had suggested that JQA's digestion would improve if he took three drops of sulfuric acid daily, after thoroughly dissolving them in water. Believing that more was usually better, Adams decided to consume not three but five drops. No one but he was surprised when he developed serious blisters on his tongue and a sore throat. He also had "a coppery taste as of arsenic" and could not relish anything he ate or drank.

Otherwise, domestic affairs were comfortable for the rejuvenated congressman. No youngsters had a more thoughtful grandpa than John. Under his supervision, granddaughters Mary Louisa and Fanny, now aged ten and eight, read the Bible in French and English. He had them do so, "suppressing nothing, passing over nothing, having no fear that their delicacy will suffer by any thing they read in that book." He also coached them in mathematics, astronomy, and gardening, and on occasion he could report: "I played Lotto with them, and sang French songs to them."

Nothing delighted him more than when the children displayed an interest in raising trees. Working to stimulate their enthusiasm helped dispel his own discouragement with gardening and returned him to digging and planting. At the close of the summer, he was clearly pleased that not only had the granddaughters toiled sturdily beside him in their own seedling patches, but that, bad luck notwithstanding, "I have several hundreds of trees, fruit and forest, from 11 to 1 year old." The older he became, the more certain was JQA that his only assured way of benefiting future generations was by planting trees.

Unfortunately, his public life kept calling him from the garden. His mail was a particular burden. Like other members of Congress in those days, Adams had no secretarial assistance, and so the demands of his constituents, made in person or in writing, piled up. Because his courage in congressional battles had made him a celebrity, he found that the recipients of many of his letters passed them on to newspapers. "This practice renders my correspondence irksome," he grumbled. "I never can be sure that what I write will not be published, and, of course, I should be cautious to write nothing unfit for publication," though to do so would give "an air of constraint to my style." Nevertheless, he carried on, using his congressional frank as he generously circulated his opinions.

Then, of course, there were matters of national consequence that followed him to Quincy. No holiday mood let him put off worrying about what harm his shortsighted colleagues in Congress might do to the Smithson bequest. More than ever, he feared that "this excellent donation will be degraded into a pack of electioneering jobs." The thought vexed him so that he welcomed aid out of an unexpected quarter. It was from George Bancroft, the rising Boston historian, who, as a Jackson partisan, had been rewarded with a federal job. Bancroft's sycophantic manner had disgusted Adams, but when the young man now promised to fight for honorable use of the Smithson money, the congressman was all forgiveness. Thereafter, he gladly loaned documents from John Adams' papers that might be useful as Bancroft worked on his *History of the United States*.

Another literary name rising in New England did not fare so well in Adams' judgment during 1838. That was the summer Ralph Waldo Emerson delivered before the graduating class of Harvard's Divinity School an address that became seminal in the development of the doctrine of Transcendentalism. Although Adams made no comment in public about Emerson's message, he was merciless in his diary, where he said that the "crazy address and oration" showed that the speaker was "ambitious of becoming the founder of a sect, and thinks there is an urgent necessity for a new revelation." As JQA observed later, it was "the doom of the Christian church to be always distracted with controversy."

As this severe criticism suggested, Adams was by nature conservative. While those who heard him call for public support of the arts and sciences might think him a path-breaker, in matters of custom and religion he was highly conventional. This extended to his feeling obliged to snuff out the rumor that he sympathized with the growing support of women's rights. For this story Adams had himself to blame, since in his remarks during the recent session of Congress he had commended the way women were speaking through petitions to the House of Representatives.

He tried to clarify his position in a reply to a letter from his feminist cousin Anna Quincy Thaxter, who had praised his "just, generous, and Christian defence" of female claims. In four pages, he carefully reminded Miss Thaxter of the "imperfections" and "frailties" peculiar to women. In the course of these ungallant and rambling remarks, he also asserted that males must make every effort not to engage a woman's "affections" other than to promote her happiness. "I look to the women of the present age with the feelings of a father," he informed his cousin.

Adams' old-fashioned outlook was also apparent in his opposition to the rising clamor for office-seekers to campaign by traveling around in order to speak at gatherings of voters. Facing reelection himself and encountering the shifty tactics of his Democratic opponents, he nevertheless refused to enter the fray by openly taking the stump. To do so, he warned, would encourage in New England "the eloquence of the Southern and Western states which would be a very pernicious alteration for this part of the country."

Of course, there was nothing deplorable about public appearances not overtly political, and Adams entered into these as if he were a veteran campaigner. After a futile fishing outing in early August, he found himself escorted to Hingham, where five hundred women gathered for a "pic-nic tea party." Finding that he was expected to speak, he first had to listen while the master of ceremonies introduced him by reading a written statement "loaded with the most fulsome adulation." After admitting that "I had the utmost difficulty to refrain from bursting into a fit of laughter," John kept his demeanor and gave what he called "a helter-skelter" address. Upon finishing, he was detained from the tables loaded with inviting cakes and coffee while the assembled females sang a "sickening" song in his honor, composed by a local clergyman.

There was better luck a month later when he attended a convention of educators in Plymouth County, hoping not to speak. When he was called on anyway, he delighted himself with a conclusion using three couplets he composed just before taking the podium. Drawn from Plutarch, this happy device produced a "thundering clap of hands." Even more gratifying was that Daniel Webster, who sat beside him, was favorably impressed, saying, "Well, you have turned Plutarch to good account."

Sweet indeed was praise such as this from a representative of those whom Adams considered to be his enemies in Boston. Instead of the old Federalists, these latest adversaries were their descendants. They were both Democrats and Whigs whose self-interest made them wish that no one, particularly Adams, would stir up anger in the cotton-growing South, thereby threatening the agricultural and commercial links that, for these New Englanders, were the essence of the Union.

But this sentiment was now being smothered by others in the region who admired JQA's fight for petition rights. It was difficult for Adams, who needed to be in battle, to lose some of his local enemies. Having fought so long for causes unpopular in the minds of many Bostonians, he disliked admitting that the city's view toward him might be changing. The citizens' "anxious desire to see and hear me," he claimed, was like "the passion of a crowd to see an execution." He seemed to take a perverse pleasure in insisting that "there is no good will to me in any part of Boston," and that "to the last gasp of my life [I] am doomed to hold my course in opposition to them all."

Before the summer was out, however, he discovered how ridiculous this attitude was. Bostonians arranged so many invitations and occasions in his behalf that he had to admit his good name was at last being redeemed in the city. The usually stuffy Massachusetts Historical Society insisted that he take the chair at a meeting. He was invited to attend a gathering of the Wednesday Evening Club, of which he had been a member as early as 1790. Next, the city fathers persuaded him to sit for a portrait by William Page, so that a likeness of the former president could be secured for display in Faneuil Hall. Ironically, Page was an enthusiastic convert to Emerson's Transcendentalism. While the painter worked, friends dropped by to chat with JQA, and when one shared a bit of humor, he recorded it. It seems that all of Harvard was chuckling about a pompous faculty member who had recently married a certain Widow Clark. On the morning after her wedding, she came down to breakfast dressed as if in deep bereavement. When her new professor-husband asked for whom she mourned, she replied: "For Mr. Clark."

Adams also prized a conversation with William Ellery Channing, Wendell Phillips, and other fierce foes of bondage who gathered around him to discuss making slavery a political issue. He came away believing that he had made progress in encouraging these men to value the Union and to see the absurdity of pressing for the abolition of bondage in the District of Columbia. But, while Channing would die in 1842, Phillips became, if that was possible, an even more ardent abolitionist until the Civil War.

By this time, Adams was admitting that if Boston could be gracious toward him, his reputation must surely be on the rise elsewhere. The city's cordiality so pleased him that as he packed for a return to Washington, he found himself for the first time in recent memory reluctant to leave New England. He called his stay "this delightful dream" and acknowledged that "this life is too delicious." Sensing this, Louisa urged her husband to linger while she went ahead to the capital.

Without her husband underfoot, Louisa oversaw the family's removal from her daughter-in-law's residence in Washington to the large house on F Street where the Adamses had lived while John was secretary of state. All was in order when her husband reappeared at the end of November, rejoicing in another reelection. Seeing what Louisa had done, he announced that he was pleased to be living once more in the residence of his most successful period of public service. Could it be an omen, he wondered, signifying that his battles in Congress were not necessarily doomed?

BEFORE CONGRESS RESUMED on December 3, Adams thought he sensed a growing friendliness toward him in the capital. When he made a perfunctory call at the White House, President Van Buren carefully reassured him that the Smithson bequest would be used honorably. Then came an invitation to dine at the home of Treasury Secretary Levi Woodbury. Upon arriving, Adams discovered that the other guests included the president and members of the cabinet, as well as an assortment of foreign ministers. Mrs. Woodbury and her daughter being the only women present, JQA was asked to escort Miss Woodbury to the table while Van Buren took in the lady of the house.

The meal then proceeded, with Adams and the president seated at the places of honor beside their hostess. JQA noted with satisfaction that most other guests "might have disputed my seat, with me a simple member of the House, but no pretensions were made."

When the House began business, there were also touches of civility displayed toward him by many of the 210 members. "Mutual greetings," Adams sourly noted, adding, "cordial on the lips." True enough. It was the calm before a storm that lasted through the three months of the session. Much of the tumult was caused by JQA, whose aggressiveness had not been softened by any courtesies shown him in Washington *or* Boston. But no matter how he fought, the gag rule was reimposed.

During the battle, however, a further change had come over the member from Quincy as he sat amid the "yells" and "agonized lungs" of his Southern opponents. Although he spoke of how he "dissected and pulverized" the arguments of his enemies, Adams now seemed bored and impatient with the petition battle. With relief, he accepted an invitation from the New-York Historical Society to deliver the principal address when on April 30, 1839, the society celebrated the fiftieth anniversary of George Washington's inauguration as president.

Pleased though he was by the task, he made little progress until Congress adjourned on March 4, and then he had to pause for his usual misgivings: "The subject is rugged with insurmountable difficulties. My reputation, my age, my decaying faculties, have all warned me to decline the task." To do justice to the celebrated day "would require a younger hand and a brighter mind." But having said this, he proceeded to write three pages a day, all the time wondering why the assignment worried him. "Such is my nature, and I shall have no quiet of mind till it is over."

Once again, he fretted needlessly. The great moment arrived, and Adams found himself surrounded by admiring New Yorkers. He admitted that the oration, which lasted two hours, was "well received" before a packed house. Afterward he was the honored guest at a dinner where three hundred persons assembled.

The speech, which proved to be one of Adams' best, emphasized that America's historic moment of greatness came with the decision at the Constitutional Convention to put aside "the irresponsible despotism of state sovereignty" and create a Union based on the self-evident truths espoused by the Declaration of Independence. In this manner, he introduced the inflammatory issue of universal human rights, which he had been extolling in Congress. By creating a Union pledged to uphold human dignity, he said, the American people had "achieved the most transcendent act of power that social man in his mental condition can perform." Such a Union, he contended, was indissoluble, since it rested "not in the sight, but in the heart." It lifted the word "*Union!*" into what he called "the simultaneous cry throughout the land." Thus did he warn the South that the federal Union was no casual agreement to be easily put aside.

The oration was immediately published as "Jubilee of the Constitution." In a few weeks, eight thousand copies had been sold by the society, and demand was rising. It was an unprecedented success, the New Yorkers assured Adams, who had himself done much to spread the fame of his remarks. Among JQA's surviving papers are carefully prepared pages of names of the individuals, famous and unsung, to whom he presented a personal copy of the speech. Not even his nieces and nephews were overlooked.

Thrilled by this enthusiasm, Adams said that "in this dark and declining stage of my existence," the address marked an accomplishment for which he "could never be sufficiently grateful to God." To dampen any excessive delight, he predicted that it would receive a few "puffs" of attention and then "it is forgotten." He was quite wrong. The public's favorable response made "Jubilee of the Constitution" one of the most influential statements concerning the nature of the federal Union. It would continue to be quoted on the eve of the Civil War and afterward.

FOLLOWING HIS NEW YORK APPEARANCE, Adams went on to Boston for another summer's stay. He was met by obligations he preferred to forget. One was his heavy financial indebtedness. Weighed down by his responsibility for the heirs of John Adams' will, he had no choice but to agree that Charles should sell whatever amount of land was needed to discharge this obligation. Then came word from Washington that the Columbian Mills needed $3,000 in repairs if there was to be any hope of grinding a profit. It was, Adams lamented, "a grievous burden which I cannot shake from my shoulders." He sent word that $600 was the most he could spend on repairs.

But instead of sinking into depression over these woes, he soon waved them aside and took up his favorite summer pastimes. He began to clock his pace during long walks—a mile in seventeen minutes or 1,060 paces. If the route was hilly or he picked up gravel in his shoe, it took 1,120 paces. There were, of course, the usual fishing excursions; during one he learned how to unhook catfish, which he was told had "the power to bite off a finger." He even began to translate Ovid's epistles between Paris and Helen, a project he had been intending to enter on for years. This, however, proved disappointing. The letters were so "scandalous," he said, that he decided to have nothing to do with them.

For more edifying reading, he took up the recently published *History of the Reign of Ferdinand and Isabella the Catholic* by William Hickling Prescott, which he said possessed "all the interest of a romance." He called Queen Isabella "that incomparable woman," and deplored how the "bigotry" so rampant in her era could have corrupted even her "pure and exalted" spirit.

Adams' comfortable mood did not remain undisturbed, however. On his birthday, the family chose to remind him that the memoir of his father he had long pledged to write was no nearer completion. It had remained untouched despite much futile encouragement by friends who, like George Bancroft, from time to time had urged him to accept secretarial help, which was available for fifty cents a day.

Finally, Louisa wearied of her husband's excuses and, for a change, put her indignation in a letter, which began by asking, What had he done to repay his parents "for their inappreciable blessings?" With all his talent, why had he not kept his vow to parents, wife, and son to prepare a biography of John Adams? Sternly, Louisa waved aside as "nothingness" all his promises to do so, for everyone could see how he was "frittering away" his precious time. She went on relentlessly. "Let me implore you to commune with your own heart, and do justice to yourself as well as to them and to redeem the past in exertion for the future." According to Louisa, writing the biography was a duty "too sacred to be trifled with under any pretensions whatever."

On the back of this remarkable statement Adams inscribed: "Good advice." Then, speaking of drawing resolve from this "letter of expostulation and exhortation from my wife," he set out to work at least an hour a day on the John Adams project. He began with an attempt to "decypher" local history and genealogy, a project that, as usual, quickly sidetracked him. He lost himself in tracing how, in the early days, such names as Quincy and Braintree had been spelled "Quinsie" and "Brayntry."

Then he drifted off to study the 1682 wedding of his great-great-grandparents Daniel "Quincey" and Anna Shepard. The ceremony had been under way in the residence of the bride's uncle, Thomas Brattle, when Aunt Brattle dropped dead. "Her corpse was laid out in the bridal chamber," during what Adams called "one of the most signal instances of joy turned into mourning that real life ever witnessed."

Soon there were other appealing distractions, so that, despite Louisa's renewed despair, her husband wandered even further away from his father's memoirs. One of these diversions was a time-consuming exchange of letters with the actor James H. Hackett concerning the character of Hamlet. Their correspondence was widely circulated in England and America, and when it was eventually published in 1844, Adams said it was "more tickling to my vanity than it was to be elected President of the United States."

What emerged from the exchange was a clear statement of JQA's reverence for Shakespeare and his belief that *Hamlet* amounted virtually to "the masterpiece of the human mind." He contended that the character drawn of Hamlet represented "the heart and soul of man, in all their perfection and all their frailty."

He again displayed his own peculiar frailty when he avoided the John Adams project by preparing another speech—that blessed vehicle by which he might quickly elevate public opinion. This time the subject was education, designed for an October audience in Braintree. He was correct in foreseeing that the address would mean another publication, not to mention a high social occasion. He spoke following a splendid meal of roast turkey, goose, and duck, along with baked ham, cranberry sauce, many vegetables, squash pie, and fine apples. But since simple lemonade was the beverage, Adams called it a "temperate" dinner.

The subject of education had roused his enthusiasm and led him to remind a large crowd that for the founders of New England, the "overriding principle . . . was Conscience." Because only learning would nurture conscience, education was vital. "Our religion is the religion of a book . . . man must be educated upon earth for heaven."

Soon after he delivered his eulogy on education, Adams found more excuses not to work on his father's biography. He began writing two lectures to expose the threatened betrayal of James Smithson's bequest, which he delivered before the Quincy Lyceum and the Mechanic Apprentices' Library Association of Boston. In them, he unfolded the story of the gift and the devious ways in which its proper use was being menaced. In doing so, he reached a new level of self-righteousness as he pictured himself to his listeners as standing against "the perversions of mankind" and battling "mountebank projectors and shallow and worthless pretenders to Science."

Nor was Adams content to confine his scorn to those who would trifle with the Smithson bequest. He somehow rambled off to denounce proponents of slavery, various banking schemes, and even the "dereliction of the fisheries." The gladiator in him was never more evident than when he closed his second lecture by pledging that his constituents would find him "assiduously at my post, agitated by many fears, and cheered by few hopes, and anxious only to discharge my duty to my country." This sacred task meant that he must enter "the sharp and angry controversies of your National Councils."

When the Boston papers praised his Smithsonian lectures, Adams reminded himself that "I ought to humble myself before God," but he delayed this rite in order to prepare the lectures for publication. They had an enduring impact and were reprinted again and again, the latest edition by the Smithsonian Institution in 1965.

ON NOVEMBER 20, 1839, just before he was to repeat his second Smithsonian lecture for a Boston audience, his granddaughter Fanny Adams died of diphtheria in the same bed in which she had been born nine years before. Adams, crushed, gave the girl "a last agonizing kiss" on her still warm cheek and went off to weep. The small coffin was carried to the Quincy burying ground and installed atop her father's casket in the Adams vault. The funeral sermon was preached by the Reverend William P. Lunt, whom JQA much admired and whom he then asked to deliver the remaining Smithsonian lecture on his behalf.

After returning to the capital in time for the House's convening on December 2, he began to hope that he and his family might learn to live within their means. To Louisa's dismay, he took the drastic precaution, if briefly, of giving up horses and a carriage and started walking to the Capitol regardless of the weather. Watching her husband trudge off into a heavy snowfall, Louisa complained to Charles: "The terrible idea of the quarter of a dollar for a Hack induces him to risk his bones and no persuasion can induce him to spare himself."

Nevertheless, there was no harm until Adams had an accident on May 18, 1840, not on the street but in the Capitol. He tripped over a roll of matting on the House floor and fell, dislocating his right shoulder. Several helpful colleagues tried to set the bone, but with no success. Finally, a physician restored the shoulder and put the arm in a sling, whereupon the victim behaved as if nothing had happened—

until he decided to attend the House without the discomfort of a coat and waistcoat. Since in those days this was tantamount to appearing in public naked, Louisa would not abide this example of her husband's sartorial indifference and ordered him to remain indoors. For a change, he obeyed.

Family members wrote for the invalid and pulled down from shelves the huge books he needed. Through it all, he remained remarkably patient, displaying what Louisa admitted was "heroic fortitude." Finally, after two weeks, he resumed his seat in the Capitol, still largely helpless and with pain that deprived him of sleep.

This experience was far more damaging to Adams than were the verbal scuffles he reentered after returning to the House. He often reported that "much vituperation, and much equally unacceptable compliment [were] lavished personally upon me." Occasionally, he acknowledged that his remarks had become "overheated" as his favorite topics, petitions and the Smithson bequest, were debated. He rather happily put up with all-night sittings of the House, and was said to have been "as merry and jocund as the youngest." By now, for Adams, nearly seventy-three, the challenge of standing guard over virtue in the House was more sustaining than even his food and drink.

When Congressman Adams went to the Treasury building after the session adjourned to collect his remuneration for his service as a member and the allowance for his travel mileage, the total amounted to a much-needed $2,241. This so relieved him that he marked his departure for Quincy by pledging that he would cling to public life "till the last of my political friends shall cast me off."

Back in New England, he eagerly awaited what promised to be a Whig victory in the 1840 presidential campaign. This new party included many of Adams' supporters from the National Republican faction of the 1820s. The Whig candidate was William Henry Harrison, whom JQA supported mainly because he was not one of the Democratic "executive jackals." This rising Whig tide brought many requests during the summer and autumn for Adams to make public appearances and addresses. Even so, he managed to find some of the "repose and meditation" he sought.

On September 1, he took a nineteen-day tour of Canada's northeastern provinces, mostly in Nova Scotia and New Brunswick. The trip was a gift of his now prosperous son Charles. The pair traveled for the first time on one of the new transatlantic steamers, which was bound for Liverpool after depositing them in Halifax. Adams was amazed at the vessel's comfort, exquisite food and spirits, and employ-

ment of a "*stewardess*" for bedchamber service—a feature he emphasized.

Once ashore, he received "overflowing civilities" from dignitaries
along the route. Since the Adamses found that they could not make
good connections to reach Quebec, they spent time in Fredericton,
New Brunswick, where JQA sat back to watch as guests waltzed at a
dinner in his honor. Eventually, father and son crossed into Maine by
stagecoach (riding with a woman "weighing at least two hundred lb
avoirdupois, and with a face for one of Macbeth's witches").

Back in the United States, Adams received many invitations to address citizens, but although he shook hands everywhere, he declined to
speak until he reached Bangor. There, after shaking several hundred
hands, he discovered that a multitude still clamored to greet him. To
please the crowd, he consented to stand on a sofa and, as he reported
it, speak briefly. On this occasion, his idea of brevity was a talk of
ninety minutes.

Warmed by his reception as a tourist, he was back in Quincy on
September 19 craving a fight—any sort of fight, apparently. He decided to go before the public as an opponent of Ralph Waldo Emerson
and his allies, calling them enemies of meaningful religion in America.
To make his case, he chose to rebut the radical social and theological
writings of the Transcendentalist spokesman Orestes Augustus Brownson, a Boston author and editor.

In Adams' opinion, Brownson had an added shortcoming: he was
a Van Buren appointee in the Boston Customs House, which led JQA
to claim that taxpayer money paid to Brownson was actually being
used to "undermine the foundations of civil society." Brownson advo-
cated what, according to Adams, was "self-delusive atheism," as well
as class warfare of the French Revolution variety, which would lead to
"indiscriminate butchery." JQA contended that Emerson also sought
to inflame men's passions against one another. Calling the Brownson-
Emerson viewpoint "odious" and the two individuals themselves
"vipers," Adams said it was "every man's duty [to] take the field"
against these enemies of public virtue.

To do his part, he began writing a lecture entitled "Faith," which
took all of his attention that autumn. Fearing that in preparing a treatise on religious belief he was "wading beyond my depth," he confined
his effort to showing that both religious and moral faith arose from the
same principle, and that faith depended upon will. By mid-October,
he was ready for Louisa and the family to listen as he read the seventy-
minute statement. He intended to present "Faith" at least to the

Quincy Lyceum, a plan his relatives approved. Fearing for his health, however, Louisa and Charles urged that he accept no other bids to speak, even though citizens were now impatient to hear him.

Brushing aside this advice, an excited Adams seized many of these invitations to speak, supplementing "Faith" with other orations as the demand grew. Among these additional topics was a revision of an earlier essay, "Society and Civilization," along with two new ones on the Massachusetts constitution and, surprisingly, the relationship between England and China. Midway in preparing these addresses, he paused to ask rhetorically if, by accepting so many engagements, he was acting less from a "desire to do good" than from "egregious *vanity* and a passion for applause."

Adams began lecturing in the Boston area by delivering his "Faith" remarks to the Warren Street Association; as usual, those attending were mostly women, in this case four of them to every male. The next night, he repeated the lecture in Quincy. He then went on to present "Faith" and the other orations to many audiences until he left New England on November 16, after his reelection to Congress.

His journey to Washington had the trappings of a royal progress as he was greeted with enthusiasm all along the way. He gave his "Faith" address once in Hartford and twice in New York City, where an astounding number, four thousand persons, gathered to listen. In Philadelphia, he was urged to accept pay for his lecture, which he politely refused. These triumphs left him in such good spirits when he arrived in the capital that he was far from weary of public speaking. Indeed, having skipped Baltimore on his lecture circuit, he returned there a week later to read "Society and Civilization."

These appearances, along with the flattering attention they brought, nourished Adams' appetite for public approval and his desire to benefit humanity. He began to relax his self-scolding—the talk of being "a common-place personage . . . about to disappear from the stage leaving nothing behind me worthy of being remembered in after ages." To reassure himself, he could now point not only to his acclaimed orations, but to yet another enduring achievement: several of his verse compositions, mostly adaptations from the Psalms, had recently been published in a hymnal, whose editor informed him that he found "exquisite comfort" from some of Adams' lines. "May I be forgiven for the joy which this saying gave me" was JQA's response.

When Congress reassembled on December 7 amid an "unparalleled" snowstorm, the spirits of Adams and his allies were high as they looked toward the inauguration of a Whig president. Word circulated in the capital that President-elect William Henry Harrison greatly admired former President John Quincy Adams. This flattery was at its loudest when Adams made the rounds of Christmas parties, where he found the "potations of egg-nog" memorable. So often did he celebrate that by the conclusion of the New Year's Day festivities, he conceded that he and other legislators had behaved more like "school-boys in the holidays" than like "gray-bearded statesmen."

FROM THE START OF 1841, Adams used every available moment to prepare for his first appearance before the United States Supreme Court since 1809. At the urging of Lewis Tappan, one of the founders of the American Anti-Slavery Society and a world leader in the movement, and other leading opponents of human bondage, he had agreed to join the distinguished attorney Roger S. Baldwin as counsel in defending thirty-nine Africans, whose story, along with John Quincy Adams' part in it, became a powerful weapon for the anti-slavery cause in America.

The Africans had been captives on the Spanish slave ship *Amistad* until they seized the vessel as it was sailing along the coast of Cuba in July 1839. The whites on board, however, gave the mutineers misleading navigational advice, which led the ship not back to Africa, as the blacks wished, but toward Long Island, New York. There the U.S. Navy discovered the vessel in late August. The Africans were taken to New Haven, Connecticut, where they were lodged in jail while their fate became an international issue.

In 1840, federal judges at both district and circuit levels had no difficulty deciding that the *Amistad* prisoners were not property but human beings, unlawfully seized in Africa and hauled off by their captors to be sold into Cuban slavery. What brought Adams into the controversy was his indignation over the appeal of these lower-court decisions to the Supreme Court by the Van Buren administration, whose lofty talk of treaty rights and the law of the seas masked its reluctance to free the captives and thereby anger southerners in an election year. The Supreme Court case was scheduled to open on February 22, 1841.

Some days before the hearing, a very nervous Adams made a serious mistake. He became so anxious over his role in the case that he lost control of his temper in the House and created what was, even for him, a mortifying scene. It arose out of his outrage at the domineering style of Congressman Henry A. Wise of Virginia, whose parliamentary maneuvers brought Adams to make an hour's speech in which, as he himself described the episode, he "arraigned . . . before the world the principles avowed by Henry A. Wise, and his three-colored standard, of overseer, black, duelling, blood-red, and dirty, cadaverous nullification white."

Afterward, Adams was appalled by his extreme language, even if it was aimed at a despised southerner. He feared that his allies might well think him the victim of an "eccentric, wild, extravagant" fit of "passion." And indeed, *insane* was an adjective some House members applied to him, leaving him yearning for "firmness to rule my own spirit." A still-shaken Adams carried the distressing memory of the Wise encounter into the Supreme Court's presence.

In the Court's room beneath the Senate chamber, he heard Roger Baldwin make the defense's opening arguments in the *Amistad* case. A day later, with fears that he would be a miserable failure, Adams rose to present the closing statement. Faltering at first, he was soon strengthened by confidence in his cause and by the presence of a large audience. His voice held out, and his thoughts became more orderly in an argument described by Justice Joseph Story as an astonishing blend of power, "bitter sarcasm," and topics "far beyond the record and points of discussion."

By this, Story was referring mostly to Adams' detours to denounce the Van Buren administration's effort to whisk the blacks out of the country and back to slavery. JQA also gave much time to exulting in the highest moral and judicial precepts, with the result that, even after speaking beyond four hours, he had not finished when the Court adjourned.

Later that day, Justice Philip Barbour died, so that pleadings did not resume until March 1, when a rested Adams took another four hours to complete his remarks. For him, the *Amistad* case was quite simple. Uniting with the abolitionists and less radical opponents of slavery, he pushed aside maritime law and property rights in order to exalt human liberty under natural law. It was much the same position taken by the lower courts.

Concluding with one of his most eloquent public statements, Adams talked of the noble service rendered by many justices now deceased—which led him to pray that each jurist sitting before him might go "to his final account with as little of earthly frailty to answer for as those illustrious dead." The judges on the bench may well have wondered whether the former president was issuing a gentle warning in expressing the hope that they might someday enter the heavenly gates to hear, "Well done, thou good and faithful servant."

Five days later the majority decision, in which Chief Justice Roger Taney concurred, was read by Justice Story. With only one dissent, the Court found for Adams' side. The Africans were declared free men, and eventually they returned to their homeland. JQA's performance in their behalf lifted him even higher in the esteem of the American public north of the Mason-Dixon Line. The praise led him to concede that, "although I fell immeasurably short of my wishes in that case, I did not utterly disappoint the public expectation."

Encouraged by his *Amistad* triumph, as well as by the inauguration of Harrison as president on March 4, Adams paid no heed to suggestions that he retire from office amid the glow of personal and party victory. On the contrary, he was eager to remain in Washington. And, indeed, why not? The president informed all within earshot that he considered Adams an old friend, indeed almost a brother. At White House dinners, Harrison customarily slapped him on the back and invited him to make the first toast.

But the sweetest moment came when Harrison asserted that Adams was the chief executive who "had been so unjustly put out." Afterward, a glowing JQA admitted that redeeming his name had been costly, for politics was now for him "as much a necessary of life as atmospheric air." Calling this addiction a weakness he could not control, he predicted that "the world will retire from me before I shall retire from the world."

CHAPTER FIFTEEN

Victory

Huzzas of the multitudes.

JOHN QUINCY ADAMS' HOPE for a strengthened republic expired
with President Harrison's death, a scant month after his inauguration.
Until that lamentable event, on April 4, 1841, life had seemed to be
beckoning to Adams. At the end of March, his good spirits carried him
across the Potomac to lecture in Virginia. He was anticipating a happy
springtime, in which the Adamses would receive quiet visits from the
president. There would be soothing dinners at the White House,
where John expected to be the center of attention.

Instead, the Adamses went to the Executive Mansion to pay their
respects at the bier of the president, dead from a bronchial disorder.
They found the coffin unattended in a hall, no bells tolling, no cannon
firing. It was a grim omen.

On April 6, in unprecedented circumstances, Adams' cousin
William Cranch, chief judge of the District of Columbia, administered
the oath of presidential office to John Tyler, the vice president. Tyler
at once claimed to be president in fact and title. This questionable constitutional interpretation, for so it was at the time, left Adams outraged
and warning that "a worthless and profligate faction" had taken command of the nation. He believed that Tyler had brashly seized the title
and was therefore a violator of the Constitution, as well as "a nullifier"
and a man without ideas. In short, Tyler was someone for whom he
had "utter distrust."

A loyal Virginian, the new president soon backed policies so
friendly to the South that Adams assigned him a place among the

worst of the "slave breeders." Despite cordial overtures by Tyler, JQA ignored the president even in casual encounters, including so intimate a setting as Washington's daguerreotype studio. The distance between the two men had ample time to widen, since, except for a brief respite in the spring, a special session of Congress involving mostly money and banking issues kept Adams in the capital until September 21.

Finally, he was off to Massachusetts for what proved one of his most enjoyable autumn holidays. He was attentive to Harvard's affairs, particularly in the campaign to establish an alumni association. He presided at the first meeting of the group, which promised to be a source of contributions for creating an astronomical observatory for Harvard, now his heart's desire. He also followed the construction of a new college library building, designed with shelf space for 150,000 volumes—plenty of room for growth, Adams believed, since in 1841 Harvard's collection amounted to 40,000. He frequently discussed these topics while dining with cousin Josiah Quincy, Harvard's president, after which their conversations usually turned to genealogy.

Being entertained in the homes of relatives, friends, and admirers gratified Adams as much as ever. He was delighted to sit at table conversing, often for five hours. The men present usually included many who could talk politics nearly as earnestly as he. His most frequent dinner companions included a mixture of friend and foe. They gathered at feasts that Adams sometimes described as "sumptuous." He mentioned one at which he was "served by negroes wearing white gloves." He even dined at archenemy Harry Otis' house in October and was urged to come again for the Thanksgiving meal. Observing that these invitations "are tenders of reconciliation which I am bound to meet in the same spirit," Adams declared the quarrel over New England disunion buried "many fathoms deep."

Another pleasing moment was a meeting with his old Wednesday Evening Club, where the conversation was literary or scientific rather than political. A report on "ancient ruins" in the interior of America so inspired him that he began again to assemble copies of all his published orations and writings, claiming that many of them were "documents long forgotten." Soon, he estimated that he had a supply sufficient to fill nearly one hundred bound sets of four volumes each. To this collection he added his latest published poem, "The Wants of Man," as well as more hymns that were paraphrases of Psalms.

His major lecture appearance during the holiday was on November 22, 1841, when he put his ideas about Anglo-Chinese relations be-

fore members of the Massachusetts Historical Society. Britain had occupied Hong Kong the previous January and was then in a trade war
with China. Charles Adams considered his father's address an "extraordinary triumph," which he attributed to New England's "devotion
to great talent." The praise left the congressman warning himself to be
on guard against such accolades. "I am so tickled with profusions of
veneration that I believe them all sincere," he said.

Fearing that praise would make him forget his duty, he reminded
himself of a visit to the British Museum in 1783 when he had viewed
the parchment of the Magna Carta, which bore the signature and seal
of his forebear Saer de Quincy. "I said to myself there is blood of that
man and there is blood of John Adams flowing in my veins." Such
blood could never "compromise" with evil, a thought that he said had
been uppermost when he defended the *Amistad* blacks.

Pledging to keep the old parchment always in mind, he began
packing for Washington at the close of November despite much discomfort from an attack of boils, which covered his scalp and his loins.
Naturally, he compared these eruptions to those afflicting Job: "the
crown of my head is hideous to behold." Nevertheless, he kept his final
Boston engagements for dinners and lectures, sometimes wearing a
white turban and on other occasions a silk cap with a tassel to cover his
diseased scalp. According to Charles, with whom he was staying, his
father's appearance created a sensation everywhere. As for JQA's tire-
less scampering around Boston, the son observed: "It is singular that a
man should find some sort of external excitement so essential to his
health."

Waiting to welcome him in Washington, Louisa was not amused
by reports of her husband's extravagant behavior and sent word that
"I wish you would do as other people do." Yet even while admonishing him, Louisa, nearing seventy, retained the capacity to charm him.
Insisting that she had become "a quiet, prisy old woman," she reminded him of how "time flies" and of her yearning for his "speedy
return to be scolded by your wife."

Dolley Madison and Louisa now reigned as the leading ladies of
Washington, setting the social tone, rather than rebelling against it, as
Louisa had in 1817. In her private moments, Louisa was much like her
husband, for she wrote poems, plays, brief essays, and a highly astute
journal filled with commentary on public and private topics. She
would deserve her reputation, bestowed by one writer after the Civil
War, as America's most literary first lady.

Once he had joined his wife, Adams showed no sign of being chastened. Instead, he announced that he would "die upon the breach" as the fight against slavery resumed, a pledge that made him resolve to develop a spirit "unconquerable by man, woman, or fiend." He was successful, for his behavior on the floor of Congress became even more strident.

When the House convened, he had the satisfaction of being named chairman of two committees concerned with his pet interests: foreign relations and the Smithson bequest. If his colleagues anticipated that this tribute would divert Congressman Adams from making a commotion over the gag rule or from seizing any opportunity to attack slavery, they were badly mistaken. By the close of January, a movement was under way in the House to censure him. Led by southerners, the effort was nothing less, Adams claimed, than "a conspiracy in and out of Congress to crush the liberties of the free people of the Union." The exhilaration of battle led him to elevate the struggle to sublime heights when he asserted that the slavocracy, which meant about one hundred members of the House, "would crucify me if their vote could erect the cross."

THE FUROR ERUPTED on January 21, 1842, during Adams' annual campaign to restore free speech by repealing the gag rule. This time his strategy was to present a petition from citizens of Georgia urging that he be removed as chairman of the Foreign Relations Committee—which obliged the House to allow him to retain the floor on a point of personal privilege. Under the circumstances, a speaker would use the time to defend himself, but instead of doing so Adams flayed the "Southern slave traders" for seeking to get him out of the way of their plot to bring slaveholding Texas into the Union.

The indignation of southern members at Adams' stratagem astonished even seasoned onlookers in the House gallery. A typical shout to the Speaker was "I demand that you shut the mouth of that old harlequin." Undismayed, Adams brought forward an even more electrifying petition. From citizens of Haverhill, Massachusetts, the plea urged Congress to dissolve the Union, claiming that because so much federal money was spent supporting southern institutions, the Union had become an unrewarding burden on free states. Although he slyly said that the time was not yet at hand for disunion, his adversaries insisted that, at last, he had gone too far by introducing such an inflammatory idea.

At first, the anti-Adams spokesmen proposed merely that he be reprimanded for mentioning the subject of disunion. But after a Kentuckian offered a resolution that accused him of "the crime of high treason," most southern representatives succumbed to blind anger and agreed to try to censure Adams, claiming that he had "disgraced his country" and merited the "severest" punishment. But the resolution of censure proved to be a fatal mistake. Adams immediately claimed the right, which belonged to any citizen, of defending himself against charges of treason. Thus, the debate over censure became a judicial proceeding, wherein the masterly JQA converted his defense into an offense. It allowed him to describe his situation with a grand flourish: he faced, he said, "a trial [in] which the liberties of my country are enduring in my person."

When moderate southerners and their northern allies saw the tactical mistake made by hotheaded colleagues, they tried to shelve the attempt to censure. But Adams arranged for the motion to table the resolution to be defeated so that he might continue what seemed an interminable scourging of southerners, whom he pictured as befoulers of the nation's sacred freedoms. As a result, it soon was no longer Adams but southerners who stood trial. As his "defense" stretched across two weeks, he took time to make personal indictments of individuals he despised. He shouted that one member who was recently in a duel had "his hands and face dripping with the blood of murder."

Throughout his "trial," Adams was in his glory. He knew that the resolution indicting him would probably fail, and if it passed, he would resign, convinced that his constituents would immediately vote to return him to his seat. While he recognized that his struggle against "persecution" had earned him cheers from the free states, his main delight was in knowing that southerners would forever see him as "the acutest, the astutest, the archest enemy of Southern slavery that ever existed," in the words of Virginia's Henry A. Wise.

Eventually, even Adams saw that the fracas ought to end and allowed the censure motion to come to a vote. It was defeated 106 to 93 on February 4. Most opponents of slavery claimed Adams' acquittal as their first victory over the South, bringing hope that soon the slavocracy would no longer rule the government of the United States.

For days afterward, Adams was busy preparing a copy of his defense for the press, all the while hearing "triumph singing in my ear." Although the writing became a tiresome chore, there was time for enjoyments quieter than scourging the slaveholders. One of these was a lengthy talk with Alexander Baring, Lord Ashburton, sent to Washington in the spring of 1842 to negotiate the boundary disputes still unresolved between England and the United States. He saw much of Ashburton, who was present when the Adamses were hosts to a hundred guests who danced until nearly midnight. The distinguished English diplomat even visited the House of Representatives, taking a seat next to Adams on the chamber floor.

Meanwhile, another luminary from Great Britain, Charles Dickens, in Washington during his celebrated tour of America, came with his wife to the Adams house for luncheon and two hours of literary talk. To JQA's enormous satisfaction, Dickens asked for his autograph, and a few days later made a great point of appearing on the House floor to bid farewell to him. Adams asserted that Dickens was "more universally read perhaps than any other writer who ever put pen to paper . . . and his reception has transcended that of Lafayette in 1824."

Dickens, Ashburton, and others who could converse about literature or foreign affairs saw the gracious side of Adams, which many of his angry congressional opponents could not have imagined existed. But not even Dickens was in a position to glimpse the loving and humble nature JQA often disclosed at home in his last tumultuous years. To Louisa, these moments brought to mind the happy days in London and Ealing. This gentle side was readily evoked by his grandchildren, of whom there were eventually eight. Toward these youngsters—John's daughter Mary Louisa and the seven children born to Charles and Abby—he was generous with his time and money, buying them books, Bibles, and toys.

Mary Louisa Adams left a childhood diary that recounted how her grandfather spent his early mornings helping her learn mathematics and languages. When he grew too palsied to make entries in his diary, she became his principal amanuensis. Another of the old man's favorites was Charles Francis Adams II, who was frequently assigned to help his grandfather. "Charley," as JQA called the future historian, eventually published his memoirs posthumously, with a recollection describing JQA as "kind and considerate" and relating how Adams liked to have the youngsters join him in his library, "walled in with over-loaded bookshelves."

Writing fifty years later, Charles said, "I can see him now, seated at his table . . . a very old-looking gentleman, with a bald head and white fringe of hair . . . [and] . . . a perpetual inkstain on the forefinger and thumb of the right hand." The grandson recalled, however, that JQA did not have "a holiday temperament"; when he was not working in his library or pruning trees or "nodding in his chair," he took "grave, sedate walks . . . absorbed in meditation."

An even more charming recollection of JQA is found in *The Education of Henry Adams*. By the time he wrote, grandson Henry—also a historian—could not remember the date of the episode, but his grandfather fortunately had recorded in his diary on June 27, 1843, that "I walked this morning with my son's third son Henry Brooks [Adams] to his school." As Henry described the event in his memoirs, it began with his "standing at the house door one summer morning in a passionate outburst of rebellion against going to school." Hearing the commotion, Grandfather Adams came down from his study and, "putting on his hat, took the boy's hand without a word, and walked with him, paralyzed by awe, up the road to the town . . . until he [Henry] found himself seated inside the school. . . . Not till then did the President release his hand and depart."

Illustrations abound in JQA's journal and letters of how he rejoiced over the grandchildren's achievements; worried if they were ill, as when Henry came near death late in 1841; and grieved for them, as he did when grandson Arthur Adams died in 1846. He was delighted when Mary Louisa was chosen queen of Washington's May Ball in 1842, and he grumbled only mildly when President Tyler turned up among the two thousand persons attending the event.

After the May Ball, it required three months of angry exchange before an exhausted House adjourned on August 31. Adams may have been the only representative who was sorry to quit. Even though it would allow him to enjoy time with his grandchildren in Boston, having to leave the legislative wars made this prospect less compelling. He admitted that he would miss the daily battles in the House against "the most depraved" men in America. A halt in fighting, he complained, left his mind "in the condition of a ship at sea in a hurricane, suspended by an instantaneous calm."

Starting for Quincy in early September, he went much of the way by steamboat, where many of the 350 passengers gathered around to shake his hand or to remind him of an earlier meeting. It was further evidence that his public repute was becoming that of a hero. "Can flattery sooth the dull, cold ear of death?" he asked himself anxiously, for his thoughts had now shifted from the excitement of the House floor to infirmity and an opening tomb. These visions persisted when he finally had time to visit his Boston dentist, who removed the tartar on his famous patient's few remaining teeth and tied together "two of the loose ones with a thread." The ordeal required well over an hour, bringing Adams to consider the hopeless state of his teeth yet another warning "to make ready for my final dissolution."

Settling in at Quincy, he tried to find comfort in the familiar routine, but with little reward. Still taut from Washington's excitement, he could only look glumly at his precious seedling trees, nearly all of which had perished. "Never was my mind in a state of deeper agitation than at this time," he admitted on September 14. He got little sleep at night, which led to naps of several hours in the afternoon. The "heavy gloom" that lingered was probably due as much to sleep deprivation as to boredom.

In a matter of days, however, he had shaken off the mood, began to rest better, and could trade his thoughts of death for the stimulation of writing another series of lectures. The demand for him to speak was louder than ever. Not surprisingly, some of these addresses proved to be thinly disguised political exhortations. Although he spoke of disliking the work of preparing his remarks and feared that he would appear as a feeble old man with poor voice and even weaker memory, once the initial speech was behind him, he relished the prospect of making others.

It being a congressional-election year, his first address was to a gathering of his constituents. Having finally outgrown his misgivings about seeming to seek office, he talked brilliantly for three hours to a cheering crowd. Meanwhile, other speakers on the platform commended him so highly that they "put me to the blush . . . in fulsome praise I can take no pleasure, and it always covers me with humiliation." But apparently he had no difficulty listening as the audience sang an ode composed in his honor, using the melody of "God Save the King," and closing with what he called a "monitorial" stanza:

> *But time shall touch the page*
> *That tells how Quincy's sage*
> *Has dared to live.*

Then the audience broke into "huzzas," and the hero's enfeeblement fell away, so that he enjoyed himself hugely at the home of a distant cousin, where he found "good company, tea, coffee, and other delicate refreshments."

From then on, the autumn of 1842 became a series of invigorating public appearances, including his annual fishing outing at Cohasset, where a leaky boat did not diminish his pleasure—nor his appetite for the excellent chowder served afterward. He was quietly pleased when, during the feasting, a schoolmaster arrived to present thirty of his scholars who wished to have the honor of seeing John Quincy Adams.

In all of this, the only occasion to make him complain was when he addressed the Norfolk County Temperance Society. While the crowd was gratifyingly large, the refreshment served was "a profusion of pitchers full of cold water." More to his liking were his appearances before lyceums in Boston, Salem, Lowell, Lynn, and Brookline. One of these occasions included a supreme moment that moved him deeply. As he was escorted into the Boston hall by the businessman Abbott Lawrence and the historian George Bancroft, the enormous crowd rose in tribute. To one who for years had felt vilified by much of Boston, this gesture and the cheering that followed were more than gratifying.

So much national attention was Adams receiving in late 1842 that people traveled to Quincy in order to converse with him as he took his daily walk. Sometimes on these outings, groups of adults and children would gather around him, urging him to enlighten them about issues such as slavery and Texas. This meant that he had to spend more time reminding himself to beware of flattery and the temptation of thinking that he had become popular.

Frequently, his lecture schedule took him far enough away that he sometimes remained overnight in the locale. He found the experience particularly rewarding in Lowell, where he delighted "a crowded auditory" with one of his favorite topics, "Democracy." That evening he was the guest of another member of the Lawrence family, a pioneering clan of New England industrialists. This was Samuel Lawrence, in whose comfortable residence he slept until 4:30 the next morning. Ready for the day, he arose but found no lamp, ink, or fire in his room, obliging the impatient visitor to lie abed for two hours until the household stirred.

It was worth the wait, however, for Adams came downstairs to find the Lawrences gathered for daily prayer. He said he was "much edified" by these devotionals. Later, as he was escorted around Lowell, he was further inspired by the sight of four thousand young ladies who worked twelve hours daily in the cloth factories for which the area had become famous. They were "all of unexceptionable morals," JQA assured his diary.

After November 11, he was in Boston and staying with Charles, who had closely watched his father's pilgrimage through the surrounding towns. "He appears to take pleasure in this itinerating way of life," Charles said, adding: "I cannot readily imagine it to be his most useful or dignified way of passing his time. He is in my opinion sacrificing the future to the present." Charles overlooked the fact that recent congressional redistricting had greatly altered his father's constituency by creating an Eighth Congressional District in which JQA lost a significant section near Quincy. The lecture swing had taken him through parts of the new area nearer Boston where Adams feared he had little support as a Whig.

Indeed, Congressman Adams claimed that it was inevitable he would lose his bid for reelection that month. "Nothing is more certain," he insisted. "May I be prepared." While it rained on November 14, the weather did not keep him from voting. As was his custom, he struck out his name on the ballot, after which he went to the nearby town of Milton to deliver another lecture. By the next day, it became clear that he had narrowly won. The Whig party fared poorly against the resurgent Democrats, whose candidate, Ezra Wilkinson, had beaten JQA in the Quincy polling by four votes.

The result promised new combat for Adams. He put himself in the mood for battle as he prepared to return to Washington, where he vowed once again "to contend against the misrule of a triumphant, fraudulent, and reckless democracy" (meaning the Democratic party). He made his usual claims that his struggle was hopeless, even though it was "the cause of my country and of human liberty." He must battle, he said, to bring about a day prophesied "when slavery and war shall be banished from the face of the earth." Frequently, he talked as if he were the only hope that freedom might survive in the United States. It was the sort of universal role he had always hoped to fill.

Craving another long fight, he seemed somewhat disappointed when Congress' behavior proved less than tumultuous during the early months of 1843. Even so, he tried his best to be "obnoxious" to the slave faction, admitting: "From an impulse that I cannot resist, I plunge into new controversies with which I ought not to meddle." Now, however, sickness due to little sleep and his "racking catarrhal cough" frequently kept him on the sidelines. He also continued to eat and drink imprudently—"I was none the better this morning for the supper last night" was a typical complaint. He suffered most during March, admitting he was to blame for having struggled up Capitol Hill on foot in a heavy, wet snow, coughing with every step.

When stuck at home, Adams fretted that his absence from the House gave free rein to those bent on war with Mexico and the annexation of Texas. He believed this to be the scheme of colleagues whom he termed "hollow-hearted and treacherous." Mainly in his mind were men like Michigan Senator Lewis Cass and Daniel Webster, whom Adams called "adventurers" willing to make "a lottery prize of their

country." Only two years before, JQA remembered, he had enjoyed
the optimism brought by Harrison's election. For a brief moment, it
had seemed as if the people were becoming "sober and rational and
benevolent." Now the public's relapse left him heartsick. His distress
filled his annual report to his constituents, which depicted the waywardness of America's government—a statement that received national circulation.

THAT SUMMER, back in Quincy, Adams immediately began working
on an address to be given when the Massachusetts Historical Society
celebrated the bicentennial of the New England Confederation. It was
a subject about which he conceded he knew little. What was worse, he
had no idea how he might weave into his remarks the crisis currently
caused by the South's wish to expand into Texas and Mexico.

Since he would appear before the society at the end of May, there
was barely time to finish the research and writing, to say nothing of devising a moral. He complained that the task merited six months of
work, not three weeks, particularly when he had to tear himself away
from delicious distractions unearthed by his research, including Cotton Mather's *Magnalia Christi Americana,* an ecclesiastical history of New
England which sought to show how God had directly revealed His
power in the colonies. "This book deserves great consideration," he
concluded, after he discovered that Mather had quoted from *Paradise
Lost.*

Adams also fell to thinking about Roger Williams, exiled from
Massachusetts Bay in 1635 for his irregular religious views, and concluded that he could not side with historians like Bancroft who "puff
him [Williams] up not only to a Saint and Hero, but to a transcendent
genius." To Adams, Williams was "a polemical porcupine from Oxford, an extreme Puritan quilled with all the quarrelsome and meta-
physical divinity of the age." Putting Williams aside, JQA completed
an address in which he emphasized that, while parties to the New England Confederation of 1643 had been homogeneous, the Union begun
in 1774 had been heterogeneous, made up of "hostile elements" and
"poisoned" by slavery.

Having thus given his remarks the all-important political flavor, a
satisfied Adams went to town on the morning of May 29 for his speech.
What followed was one of the hilarious moments of his life. Arriving in
Boston, the carriage dropped him off, not at the rooms of the Historical Society, but by mistake at the parsonage of his good friend the Rev-

erend Nathaniel Frothingham. There Adams joined a sizeable company in the pastor's study. For a few moments, he thought the group was the Historical Society, "although I could not conceive how they got there." The meeting proceeded until he finally realized, in great consternation, that he was seated with the Massachusetts Congregational Charitable Society.

Someone was found who could rush Adams to the Historical Society, where he was impatiently awaited. The group then marched to the First Church in Chauncey Place, where the celebration opened with prayer and the singing of a psalm. Beginning his address at 11:20 a.m., Adams took pity on his crowded audience, who he was pleased to note had stayed mostly awake, and ended his remarks at 1:05, having omitted a generous portion. Once more he had shown why he deserved the nickname that northern newspapers had recently given him, "Old Man Eloquent," drawn from Milton's tenth sonnet. Charles Adams, who was in the audience, observed that his father was most persuasive when he strayed from his subject. After the ceremonies, he found JQA so improved in spirits and vigor that it was difficult convincing him that he would be much the better for skipping the ensuing party and returning to Quincy.

A few days after that triumph, Adams' cheerfulness turned to indignation when he learned that two public figures he particularly loathed, John Tyler and Daniel Webster, would be in Boston for events marking completion of the monument on Bunker Hill. In JQA's opinion, to commemorate the battle of June 17, 1775, was to honor one of the great events "in the annals of mankind." It was a disgrace to have Webster speak, he fumed, but the presence of Tyler "and his Cabinet of slavedrivers" made it a "burlesque." Adams announced that he would not be present for such desecration.

He might have been absent in body, but his thoughts were at the great occasion. He visualized the banquet afterward at Faneuil Hall, intended to honor the president whom all those present "hated and despised." Wickedly, he saw Tyler's prominent nose casting a shadow "outstretching that of the monumental column," and he imagined with disgust Webster "spouting" while others "swill like swine and grunt about the rights of man." He was glad to be absent, he insisted, lest by attending he should fall into "an unbecoming burst of indignation or of laughter."

The old man did, however, climb to a hilltop in Quincy from which he could see the tip of the Bunker Hill monument and watch the smoke rise from cannon fired during the ceremonies. The sight brought forcibly to his mind that day in 1775 when he had listened to the actual sounds of the great battle.

Fortunately, another event soon took place that he could enjoy. This was Boston's annual Fourth of July oration, which his son Charles had been invited to deliver in Faneuil Hall, a fact making the occasion "of the most intense interest to me." It was the first time since 1809 that Adams had observed the Fourth in Boston. "No language can express the agitation of my feelings," he wrote, as he watched his son make a successful appearance in the venerable hall, which was crowded to capacity.

Afterward, he prepared for what became a monthlong tour of upper New York state, which kept him occupied between July 6 and August 5. The trip began as a sightseeing excursion and became a continuous "ovation" by the public. Besides Adams, the expedition comprised his daughter-in-law Abby and one of her sons, as well as Abby's father, Peter Chardon Brooks, who paid the bills. He had urged JQA to come along in order to see Niagara Falls.

The party first paused for several days to enjoy the baths at Lebanon Springs, then proceeded to the falls. Along the way, Adams was besieged for autographs or for conversation. Crowds of strangers always upset him, he complained—not very convincingly. He insisted that he lacked the "presence of mind" to cope with a multitude. Nevertheless, the pressure on him grew as news spread that the former president was coming. Towns and villages made ready to greet him. Those along Lake Champlain saluted him with cannonades as his boat passed. If the vessel paused, citizens scrambled aboard to clasp his hand. At Niagara Falls, it was clear even to him that people were as interested in viewing him as they were the cataract. Distinguished New York citizens such as General Peter B. Porter and Governor William H. Seward insisted that JQA be their guest while he was in the neighborhood.

Soon, delegations of men and boys were escorting the party from town to town, while at night there were torchlight processions. And everywhere was the sound of cheering, "the huzzas of the multitudes," which at first startled and then immensely pleased Adams. He kept a careful count, recording that he received public receptions and parades at fourteen communities, "which I pray God may not have turned my head." While that did not occur, the noise and press of crowds proved too much for Peter Brooks. He returned home at the end of July, taking his grandson with him while Abby sought refuge with relatives in Utica. Of the party, only JQA remained as he went on alone to view social progress in New York. He especially admired a girls' academy and a penitentiary—in both he found "cleanliness and order." All in all, the trip was such a success that it left his mind "a buzzing tintinnabulation" and his thoughts in a "whirlwind."

Returning to Quincy on August 5, he expected to calm himself in the village's quiet. Instead, exciting word awaited him. He had been paid high tribute by the great Anti-Slave Convention, which had been meeting in London. This recognition, along with that shown him in New York, was, he said, "too great for frail human nature to resist, or to bear with impunity." It placed the past month "among the most memorable periods of my life." But there was even greater public admiration ahead, for to his delight, he received an invitation from the Cincinnati Astronomical Society to deliver an oration at the laying of the cornerstone in November for the city's observatory.

He said he found the request "so flattering that I scarcely dare to think of it with composure." The drawback was the necessity of leaving Quincy in late October for a journey to Ohio which promised to take a month. It was a high price to pay to face more cheering crowds, and he acknowledged that he was fearful about the venture, which his family universally opposed. Louisa and others could readily see that Adams was, at seventy-six, increasingly frail. He himself admitted that he was reduced almost "to the nervous affections of second childhood."

Even so, he made ready for Cincinnati while hoping that he would take no pleasure in "human applause"; let the days to come bring only "lessons of humility." It troubled him that he might have accepted the invitation from motives of "vanity and self-glorification." Certainly, there was nothing modest about his aspiration for the oration. Planning to speak for three hours, he intended to compress the history of astronomy and to make this science "into a permanent and persevering national pursuit."

On October 20, with a fifty-four-page address completed, he furtively slipped away from Boston, taking with him a servant, Benjamin Andrews. Help was necessary, for Adams was nearly exhausted. Not only had he slept little for several nights, but on the day before his departure he delivered a nearly three-hour speech in Dedham. It was no wonder, as he admitted to himself, that he began the journey "so worn down with weariness . . . and anxiety, that my faculties seemed benumbed."

Travel brought no relief. The warm public greetings he received along the route could not compensate for the physical and emotional tribulations of the trip. As he headed southwest from Buffalo, plying Lake Erie by steamer, an early winter storm brought gale and blinding snow, with the atmosphere "cold as Nova Zembia," or so a miserable Adams put it. When the steamer finally reached Erie, he found a large crowd waiting to greet him and expecting him to make a speech. He was advised that smaller towns ahead had similar anticipations.

Suffering from a sore throat and spasms of coughing, he declined making as many of these talks as possible. He had to give in by the time he reached Cleveland, where "multitudes of the citizens of all classes" surrounded him and even followed him into his hotel room. Under the circumstances, there was no gracious way for him to avoid speaking later when he attended a huge reception in his honor.

He then boarded a packet boat on the Ohio Canal headed for Columbus, 232 miles away. Choosing not to travel by land in the hope of escaping some of the fanfare proved a regrettable decision. The boat was a miserable place. "So much humanity crowded into such a compass was a trial such as I had never before experienced, and my heart sank within me." Unable to sleep, he soon suffered from "a head-ache, feverish chills, hoarseness, and a sore throat," to say nothing of his fierce cough which he called his "tussis senilis."

Some recovery was possible during a stop in Akron, where there was a reception at which he spoke and shook hands. When "a very pretty" woman kissed him on the cheek, "I returned the salute on the lips, and kissed every woman that followed, at which some made faces, but none refused." He survived many such pauses for greetings and speeches as the canal boat passed through more than two hundred locks, each requiring "a heavy thump," while the vessel "staggers along like a stumbling nag." Hebron, Ohio, was reached on November 4, and there Adams resumed his journey by land.

Later that day, he was met by escorts, who brought a more comfortable stagecoach for the short ride into Columbus. There it seemed the entire community, including the governor, was at hand to salute him. After forty-eight hours, Adams set out for Dayton, guarded by two military companies, but before arriving, he was met by a cavalcade with "an elegant open barouche in which I took a seat and thus in triumphal procession we entered the city." There a "vast multitude" had assembled at a stage constructed in front of the hotel. More speech making was required, but no hand shaking because of "the dense mass of population" on all sides.

"I cannot realize that these demonstrations are made for me," he said, rejoicing that "they are intended to manifest respect, and not hatred." The same experience continued along the route toward Cincinnati. In every hamlet he was welcomed by speeches of loud praise while his escort grew into a procession of most of Ohio's notable citizens. On November 8, the parade arrived in Cincinnati, where Adams was hailed by "deafening shouts of applause" and so many persons eager to speak with him that he barely had time for dinner and tea.

Weary to the core and coughing, he said he was ashamed at the ineptness of his various replies to the groups around him. He deplored his words as "flat, stale, and unprofitable, without a spark of eloquence or a spark of oratory." Yet while he appeared "confused, incoherent, muddy," it astonished him that whatever he managed to say invariably earned "new shouts of welcome."

The next day was flooded by rain, so that after Adams presided at the laying of the cornerstone before "an auditory of umbrellas instead of faces," the officials decided that his oration would best be postponed one day and then moved inside. Having thus been granted a little rest, he made the long-anticipated address, delivering half of his manuscript in two hours. He read those parts where he emphasized that nothing was better suited to the nature of man than the assiduous cultivation of the arts and sciences. Afterward, and considerably restored, he enjoyed the subsequent parties, the music, and "the banquet, sumptuous and temperate."

The oration seemed to encourage Cincinnatians to hover around Adams on the following days, including a committee representing the city's "colored people," to whom he replied in another spontaneous address. After visits across the Ohio River in Kentucky and more festivity, he finally started back toward Washington on November 14, going up the Ohio River by steamer, all the while receiving salutations from crowds along the route and by vessels heading downstream.

Adams was in Pittsburgh on November 16, one day ahead of the time scheduled for a "magnificent reception." These ceremonies were to include a duplication of the Cincinnati cornerstone laying, an act intended to "promote the cause of science" among the citizens of western Pennsylvania. Although he happily praised this theme in one address, he could not resist using another occasion to give "my opinions without reserve on all the slavery questions now in agitation." He stoutly maintained that he had otherwise refrained "from discoursing upon topics of deep party feeling."

At last, after three festive days in Pittsburgh, Adams admitted that the journey was becoming "inexpressibly irksome." While he acknowledged that citizens everywhere had given him a "tumultuary, honorary" experience, he insisted that finding himself "held up as a show" and listening as "the most fulsome adulation is addressed to me face to face in the presence of thousands" ran much against his nature. And yet, even having survived Pittsburgh's affection, Adams realized with dismay that more ordeal was at hand.

Going east across Pennsylvania once again required stops at towns and villages, where he heard his praises sung before crowds, which then invariably fell silent to await words from the honored guest. His stamina sinking, he began calculating the cost to his health of the trip to Ohio. And what did he have to show for it? "Momentary joy at the experience of kind treatment from my fellow-men." He had derived from all of it "no new or useful truth"; it had merely reinforced his belief in the folly of vanity and his realization that the wise life was one guided by "humble submission to Divine Providence."

Pushing through Pennsylvania, Adams contended with "mud ankle-deep," cavalcade escorts, military bands, endless welcoming addresses, and temperate dinners until he reached Cumberland. From there, he proceeded more speedily by train, although by then he was so groggy that he could not recognize several congressional colleagues traveling in the car with him.

Once he had entered his home on F Street on November 23, he collapsed. "My strength is prostrated beyond anything that I ever experienced before, even to total impotence." Two days later, he was nearly helpless, and his usual resilience seemed lost. For a time he could do little but lie on a sofa. He slept a great deal and tried to overcome his "grave yard cough." The physicians recommended "a variety of slops and drops, pills and pastes, lotions and potions." Louisa preferred to have him take a concoction made by boiling snakeroot. He even accepted some horehound candy, but none of these remedies brought much relief, particularly to a developing nervousness and agitation that made his memory erratic. He complained that almost any event "scatters my thoughts into a cloud of confusion and I cannot retain the memory of any thing from day to day."

Yet, as an uneasy Louisa reported to Charles, despite these warning signs, "he will do nothing and take no care of himself, but lives in a state of perpetual excitement." Perhaps for that reason the old man gradually found strength, and the cough subsided enough by January 1844 for him to resume his seat in the House, where he was appointed chairman of a committee to revise the rules for the Twenty-eighth Congress.

During the next two months, Adams used this role to try building support to eliminate the rule gagging slavery petitions. Cleverly, he played the "cat-and-mouse game" by which southerners sought to avoid voting on the rules. But once again he failed. The motion to drop the gag rule was defeated in early March by a close margin. Adams laid the blame on certain northern legislators who collaborated with the South in exchange for a free hand in distributing federal spoils. He claimed that these Yankees forsook the cause of liberty just "as the Dutch traders to Japan purchased the privilege of dealing for spices by trampling on the Cross."

Into his diary Adams wrote scathing evaluations of colleagues who sold themselves to the South. Such a luckless one was Illinois' Stephen A. Douglas, who had spoken passionately in behalf of the slavocracy. According to JQA: "His face was convulsed, his gesticulation frantic, and he lashed himself into such a heat that if his body had been made of combustible matter it would have burnt out." Forgetting his own reputation for casual appearance, he scoffed at Douglas, who, "to save himself from choking," had removed his cravat and unbuttoned his waistcoat like "a half-naked pugilist."

With men like Douglas gaining strength in the Senate, Adams was amazed when his own allies temporarily defeated a treaty annexing Texas. "Moloch and Mammon have sunk into momentary slumber." According to Adams, had the South succeeded and Texas been annexed, "the skeleton forms of war and slavery [would] stalk unbridled over the land. Blessed God, deliver us from this fate!"

The congressional ordeal kept him "much debilitated and prostrated in physical strength" into the spring. He managed, however, to assist Louisa in maintaining their reputation among Washington's finest hosts. One evening was especially memorable. The Mexican minister arrived to present his sister, a Madame Quesada, who announced that only two objects in the United States interested her: Niagara Falls and John Quincy Adams. Noting that this excellent lady was of mixed blood, Spanish and Mexican, JQA carefully recorded that she was "almost white."

When there was no company at home, the Adamses still attended concerts and theater. Once again, the congressman was pleased with the operatic music of Bellini, particularly performances of *Norma* and, naturally enough, *I puritani*—"Momento!" was his comment. The couple also attended a concert by "the great fiddler Ole Bull," who had come from Norway to tour the United States.

It was, however, no musical excursion that Adams enjoyed with fellow House members on February 20, when they set out to inspect the U.S.S. *Princeton,* a new frigate with a celebrated long-range gun of wrought iron called "Peacemaker." Grumbling that the expedition was meant to pressure him into "a patriotic ardor for a naval war," he nevertheless managed to partake of "a plentiful cold collation" that the Navy had thoughtfully served.

Such a treat could not induce him a few days later to join President Tyler and others on a cruise down the Potomac to observe "Peacemaker" being fired. The event brought tragedy, for the great gun burst on discharge, killing several persons, including two members of Tyler's cabinet, and wounding many others. Shaken, Adams could only murmur, "Dies irae."

A few months later, Washington was abuzz with news that President Tyler, a widower of fifty-four, had been married in New York to twenty-two-year-old Julia Gardiner, the beautiful, orphaned daughter of Colonel David Gardiner of Long Island, one of those killed in the explosion. Adams claimed that Tyler and his bride had become the "laughing stock of the city," enacting a scene "of revolting indecency" as the world watched a president of the United States "performing with a young girl from New York the old fable of January and May."

Not that Adams himself had taken up acting his age. He tried to walk vigorously and to swim, but now he seemed prone to fall. En route to Quincy in early July, he left the train during a stop in Jersey City and tumbled four feet from an unrailed platform. Although he landed on his hip, he was not seriously hurt, suffering only a crimson bruise on his thigh "as large as a common dinner-table plate." He could limp enough during the next day to look up his anti-slavery associates in New York City. In Quincy, he suffered another fall when he lost his balance on some steps, "a repetition of the Jersey City disaster," he called it.

These accidents left him nearly immobilized for the summer, particularly after a wounded leg began to fester. There were no reappearances of the old depression, however. "My time is never tedious when I have my books around me." He said there were so many of these and upon subjects so different that they were "like baits upon a bundle of fish hooks." He especially enjoyed returning to the works of Francis Bacon, whose "gigantic intellect" he admired as much as he bemoaned the Englishman's "moral obliquity."

The quiet of the library restored Adams sufficiently that he joined a September fishing expedition, another of many arranged by his good friends the Loring family of Hingham. Fishing proved poor, and the "temperance" chowder dinner afterwards was no better, Adams sighing that there was "coffee for claret and lemonade for Madeira." Later, at an evening party given by the Lorings, John found it featured "conversation chiefly with me." Here he enjoyed himself so much that he was startled when the church bell tolled 9 p.m., the hour when the Adamses usually retired in Quincy.

With a return to Washington approaching, Congressman Adams had recovered strength enough to fight another election. He made a great commotion, locally and nationally, with his charge that a plot had been hatched by the Tyler men to haul Texas and its slaves into the Union. During October and early November, he discussed this explosive topic frequently in the Boston area, although he realized that he was likely to lose his self-control. "Oh! for a curb upon my temper!" he groaned, wondering for the hundredth time if he could ever reply to his enemies "with calmness and composure."

He exhibited neither attribute in his most important statement of the autumn, a speech on October 7 to the Young Men's Whig Club of Boston, in which he issued more warnings about schemes to grab Texas. He had become particularly sensitive because supporters of annexation were now charging that when he negotiated the Florida Treaty with Spain back in 1819, he had snubbed an opportunity to extend the nation's boundaries to embrace the Texas region.

Consequently, when an angry Adams read an early draft of the address to his family, they urged him to soften the "violence" it contained, but he contended that he was helpless to do so. It was like old times as he thundered about fighting "a conspiracy against my good name." How could he keep his "self-command" against a plot "so crafty and so base"? Still in an aggressive mood, he arrived at Boston's Tremont Temple to face a sympathetic crowd.

After a "shout of welcome shook the house," the young Whigs listened closely as Adams assailed "the conspiracy" afoot for "the robbery of Texas from Mexico." There was much enthusiasm when he warned of a great trial facing the nation. He became a prophet at this point, claiming that freedom and slavery were headed toward a "deadly conflict of arms." To annex Texas, he warned, would bring "the blast of the trumpet" for a civil and servile war. He summoned the young men of Boston to "burnish your armor, prepare for the conflict."

Most of the speech was reprinted across the nation, and used as ammunition by anti-Texas forces in the presidential campaign just closing. Meanwhile, for Adams the success of the speech made the occasion "one of the epochal days of my life." Immediately, he began receiving so many invitations to repeat his warnings that there was no time even to acknowledge many of them.

He gave his attention instead to preparing his annual interpretation of congressional events for his constituents, although once again he was convinced that he faced defeat for reelection. He was particularly concerned because the rising Liberty Party had reluctantly opposed him for his claim that the federal government was powerless to emancipate slaves in the District of Columbia and the Territories—an action that Adams contended, with regret, could not be supported by the Constitution.

Nevertheless, Massachusetts' Eighth Congressional District gave him more than 8,000 votes to the combined total of slightly above 6,000 for his opponents. "I dare not attempt to express my feelings," Adams said as he returned to Washington in late November to face the triumphant Democrats. While Adams had successfully bucked an anti-Whig trend, many of his associates had lost. James K. Polk, the Jacksonian candidate for president, had been elected over Henry Clay. The defeat left Adams convinced that the Democrats would now be able to force the slave kingdom of Texas on the Union. "I mused over the prospects before me, with the impression that they portend trials more severe than I yet have passed through."

Before resuming his agitator's role in the House, JQA "took the cars" to Baltimore, where he presided at the National Lord's Day Convention. There he found delegates from across America assembled in the First Baptist Church to debate resolutions for steps by which the nation might "remember the Sabbath and keep it holy." The atmosphere proved surprisingly similar to that of the Congress, obliging Adams to try keeping order amid "snarling debate" among presumably devout speakers who were sometimes "loudly hissed."

After favorable votes had been secured on such proposals as closing saloons, preventing military personnel from working, and forbidding Congress from meeting on the Sabbath, Adams decided that he had served long enough. Near the close of the second day of the convention he surrendered the chair, excused himself from a dinner commitment, and caught the 5 p.m. train to Washington.

Five days later, on December 3, he had reason to utter a fervent prayer of thanks to the Lord of the Sabbath. "Blessed, forever blessed, be the name of God!" he intoned, for the victory he had prayed for was won. By 108 to 80, a gratifying margin, the House had voted to approve Adams' resolution rescinding the hated gag rule. Thereafter, petitioners who urged the abolition of slavery and the slave trade would be freely heard. But it seemed an anticlimax, given the far graver challenge of Texas.

The old warrior, wrathful as ever, fumed at his ebbing strength. Was he not "the head of the anti-slavery movement in this country"? With so many battles to lead, he knew he was faltering. It was clear that the Tyler-Calhoun faction would seek "the subjugation of the Union" by annexing Texas before Polk assumed the presidency in March. Facing this act, Adams pitted his limited strength against "a league of villainy and power."

He did what he could during January and February 1845 to thwart those bent upon bringing Texas into the Union. "I can think of nothing else," he acknowledged. If Texas were admitted by a joint resolution of Congress, it would leave the Constitution "a monstrous rag." His speech of warning took up January 24 and 25, but to no avail. Texas was annexed by a majority resolution, which, according to Adams, meant "apoplexy of the Constitution."

With the "slave mongers" in control, JQA retreated to New England after the House adjourned. Loath now to travel by himself, he made the trip with his servant Ben Andrews and went first to the comfort of Charles' Boston home in Mount Vernon Street. Charles was pleasantly surprised to see his father looking as well as he did. Heading off to Harvard to attend student debates and orations, the former professor again condemned the results as mediocre—"nothing sparkled . . . no passion." Harvard did now boast of one attainment that Adams could applaud: its pledge to build an astronomical observatory, a decision that JQA said "has given me a pleasure all my own; for no other person will understand or sympathize with it."

News concerning the observatory calmed him for several weeks until June 18, when he learned that Andrew Jackson was dead. Adams' epitaph for his old enemy was blunt: "Jackson was a hero, a murderer, an adulterer . . . who in his last days of his life belied and slandered me before the world and died." When he learned that Boston's city council had appropriated $1,000 for a memorial ceremony, JQA's indignation was boundless. As for reports that Jackson had died prayerfully, Adams suggested that this was "a display of Calvinistic piety worthy of Molière's Tartuffe."

JQA seemed to grow physically weaker as the summer wore on, meanwhile saying, "I have nothing left but to lie down in silent and submissive resignation." At the end of August, he managed to attend commencement festivities at Harvard, which took him back fifty-eight years to his own graduation, when he had entered upon life "full of timid hope and awful fear." The recollections left him in a trance. "All these retrospections crowding at once upon my memory, shake my shattered nerves and confuse my mind, til my whole past life flashes before me like a luminous dream."

He came away from Cambridge convinced that he must tarry no longer in gathering his publications. "Smitten in conscience," he managed finally to assemble enough copies for binding into five volumes. He anticipated making one hundred sets, calling the five volumes "the most complete daguerreotype reflection of my mind for more than half a century that ever has been, or ever will be made." But to what purpose, he wondered, as he observed that Daniel Webster, Edward Everett, and Henry Clay already had volumes of their works actually published by reputable presses. His own writings and utterances had never "taken hold of the public mind." Was it not further proof, he mourned, that nothing would "prolong my existence in memory"?

The thought, however, brought no lasting melancholy. He spent three hours at a dinner given by Abbott Lawrence, where "the time had passed imperceptibly away, I believe, by the fascinating charm to myself of my own conversation. I blush in recording my own shame." Then he began to sit for George Peter Alexander Healy, for a portrait commissioned by King Louis-Philippe of France. Adams did this hesitantly, for he invariably fell asleep soon after a painter began work. He also was reluctant because he feared that "my countenance does injustice in my old age to my heart." His brow was now furrowed and his face so "distorted" that "my naturally tender heart has almost become a petrifaction." Nevertheless, Louisa and others strongly praised Healy's work as perhaps the best likeness ever painted of him, and the Reverend Frothingham claimed it captured his "tiger"-like nature.

Healy was barely in time, for as the portrait was finished, Adams experienced a "paralytic disorder," probably a mild stroke that made it difficult to continue his daily journal. He began dictating entries to family members while he sought to "abide with resignation to the will of my maker, his final dispensation of my existence upon earth." The family physicians advised medication, particularly "two blue pills on going to bed" and in the morning "a dose of magnesium with sulphate of potash." He tried the prescription for several days, but with "no relief." By October 10, he reported that "I find myself very feeble."

The entries dictated in his journal now became a series of outcries against "this premature impotence," this "last stage of decay." Conceding that his emotional distress only worsened his bodily condition, Adams tried to soothe himself through spiritual and religious meditation, all the time wondering "how far my own sins have to answer before Heaven" for bringing about his "involuntary shaking." He reread the Seventy-first Psalm's eighteenth verse:

> *Now also when I am old and grayheaded,*
> *O God, forsake me not;*
> *until I have shewed thy strength*
> *unto this generation,*
> *and thy power to everyone that is to come.*

Then he made his pious confession: "For I believe there is a god who heareth prayer, and that honest prayers to him will not be in vain."

He did not, however, test the Almighty's generosity by asking for the strength to comply with the invitations to speak that continued to pour in. Instead, he expended what strength he had by making a few social calls and appearing at some dinners in Boston before returning to Washington in late November to begin the most grievous twelve months in his often anguished life.

Unable to write more than a few (nearly undecipherable) lines at a time, and frail in manner and appearance, Adams was now a pathetic figure. On Capitol Hill, his colleagues recognized this. When names of House members were drawn for priority in choosing seats for the new session—and Adams ranked 155th—all those representatives ahead of him showed their deference. One after the other, they left unfilled the well-situated desk that he had occupied in the last session.

This was the only happy feature of the new Congress, as a horrified Adams watched the Polk administration undertake war against Mexico. The old man spoke as much as he could, and sought to rally younger members to oppose hostilities. Fewer than a dozen colleagues were willing to join him in voting against the war. It was easy for all but Adams to feel intimidated as the House majority shouted "traitor" against those who condemned "this most unrighteous war." Hostilities were approved on May 11, 1846, by 176 House members, who overwhelmed Adams and his ten associates.

The decision to go to war was, in his view, the gravest sin yet committed by the slavemongers as they sought to enlarge their domain. It infuriated him that the House Speaker found so many ways to ignore him when he sought the floor. Physical enfeeblement had not weakened his capacity for anger, however. Privately, he dismissed those who differed with him by choice descriptions such as "beef-witted blunderhead."

Given his frustrations, it was not surprising that Louisa reported to Charles how his father lived in "extreme nervous irritability." What was unexpected was that he still enjoyed society. He took pleasure in being host, with Louisa, to a winter party at which three hundred guests danced until after 2 a.m. When the residence was quiet, he resumed his pastime of composing verse for the albums of young ladies, the nature of universal love being a favorite theme. For himself, the aged poet laboriously penned lines that mostly spoke of a need for patience and mercy. One poem implored:

> *From the recesses of my heart*
> *Resentment's bitter stings expel,*
> *Bid all the fiends of hate depart*
> *And love alone my bosom swell.*

The war with Mexico did not blind Adams to certain more fruitful features of the congressional session. He was mightily pleased when a portion of the Oregon country was acquired through an agreement with Great Britain. He rejoiced over progress toward the creation of a Smithsonian Institution. His cheerful and thankful mood led him, two days after his seventy-ninth birthday, by "an irresistible impulse," to walk to the Potomac for a swim. After repeating the experience, the effort took its toll. "I feel as if all my bones were extracted from my body." It left him impatient for the House to adjourn on August 10 so that he might renew his strength in New England.

As JOHN QUINCY ADAMS stepped out of the railcar at the Quincy depot, a shout went up with three cheers from "a considerable assemblage of persons" who had gathered to welcome him. Touched, he could only apologize that the "extinction" of his voice made a proper reply impossible. The experience sent him home saddened as he thought about how his life's close was "near at hand," but once more he revived. His penmanship improved enough to permit brief diary entries. He was able to walk nearly two miles daily and to take the train into Boston for a shave or to visit friends. He went to Cambridge for Harvard business, and on another occasion escorted three grand-children to a circus.

Amid this relaxation, politics did not leave his mind. Thoughts of the nation's "dastardly servility to the slave mongrel oligarchy" led him to preside over "a great crowd of people . . . filling every nook and corner" of Faneuil Hall on September 24. The audience assembled to hear details of how a fugitive slave from New Orleans had been appre-hended in Boston and shipped back to Louisiana. The occasion left Adams subdued and inclined to spend more time with his Bible.

He began again to study two chapters each morning, a custom he had put aside soon after entering Congress. "I have daily and nightly warning to be prepared for a sudden summons to meet my maker," he observed. "My hope is of mercy."

Inevitably, his scriptural meditation brought him to an element of Christian doctrine that always upset him: was Christ sent by God to atone for humanity's sins? "I cannot believe it," he said of atonement. "It is not true. It is hateful. But how shall I contradict St. Paul?" He wished the Calvinist ministers would leave him in peace. In his last years, he was even more impatient with those clergymen who habitu-ally declared their congregants to be standing on the brink of Hell. He could not conceive of how persons of decent character would gather each Sunday in church to be treated like the vilest malefactors. "It seems to me as if the preacher considered himself as a chaplain to a penitentiary, discoursing to the convicts."

Would that the clergy could stress the moral teachings of the New Testament, for Adams said here was where he had come to build his faith—which he now summarized with remarkable succinctness: "I reverence God as my creator. As creator of the world. I reverence him with holy fear. I venerate Jesus Christ as my redeemer; and, as far as I can understand, the redeemer of the world. But this belief is dark and dubious."

He wrote this, he said, as he sensed death approaching, for he felt the "power of vital agency [is] extinct." He portrayed himself as "a plant withered at the root, a tree dying downward from the top." The thought of "helpless impotence" even sent him to church on what was, for him, a most extraordinary errand: to try "divesting myself of every sentiment of animosity, anger, and resentment against any and every fellow creature of the human family."

Then, with very little use of his right hand remaining, Adams tried

to write about what he called his life of failure—failure because God
had not granted him "the conceptive power of mind," and because "I
have not improved the scanty portion of his gifts as I might and ought
to have done." Had he been awarded what he had yearned to have,
the talent of a Cicero or a Shakespeare, he believed that "my diary
would have been, next to the Holy Scriptures, the most precious and
valuable book ever written by human hands, and I should have been
one of the greatest benefactors of my country and of mankind."

What wonders he would have accomplished had God bestowed
upon him "the irresistible power of genius and the irrepressible energy
of will." With such gifts, he seemed convinced, he would "have banished war and slavery from the face of the earth forever." Lacking
these endowments, he sternly reminded himself that in frail old age he
must strive for a grateful heart, and not repine at what God had denied
him. Rather, he should "implore His forgiveness for all the errors and
delinquencies of my life!"

During November 1846, his health continued to decline. He suffered from a "throat grippe." A tingling had begun along his legs,
which then became swollen, and he agreed to have his limbs rubbed
with New England rum and water. This remedy seemed less helpful
than news of his reelection, this time by a landslide. The victory encouraged him sufficiently that he decided to remain for a time in
Charles' Boston home after Louisa and the family had departed for
Washington. He moved into the city on November 17.

The change brought none of its customary invigoration. He tried
without success to make entries in his diary. An exception came when
he was stirred by a verse from his beloved book of Ecclesiastes. He was
able to copy the few words almost legibly: "Be not hasty in thy tongue,
and in thy deeds slack and remiss." The entry would serve as an appropriate farewell to his diary.

The next morning, November 20, brought a devastating event.
His friend of long standing, Dr. George Parkman, arrived to escort
him on an inspection of new facilities for Harvard's medical school. As
they reached the Common, Adams was suddenly unable to walk.
Somehow, Parkman managed to assist the victim back up the hill to
Charles' house, where he was put to bed.

For several days his right side was nearly paralyzed, he could
scarcely speak, and his mind was confused. Louisa hastened from
Washington to find her husband under the care of Dr. Jacob Bigelow
and Mrs. Fader, a nurse who JQA insisted should care for his intimate
needs. She slept in his room, either on the floor or in a trundle bed.

Meanwhile, news of the former president's "sudden and extraordinary seizure" was widely announced in newspapers around the nation.

Although medical opinion was at first discouraging, Adams surprised everyone by soon showing small but steady improvement. His mind began to clear. His power of speech returned, at first slurred, but soon normal. At this point, he prepared a will to replace one written twelve years earlier. This done, he disregarded orders and tried to get out of bed alone, only to fall and cut his head. The blow caused his memory to trick him for a time, but by November's close, he was able to receive a few callers. Dr. Bigelow announced that the patient had gained in nine days what most victims of stroke required nine weeks to accomplish.

Taking heart, Adams began assuring friends that he had experienced merely an attack of vertigo, but he gave up this explanation once he made an attempt to walk. He could not support himself, and his right leg dragged. "It was a sad and painful discovery" for her stubborn husband, Louisa recorded. "If we preserve him at all, we must think ourselves blest." But improvement continued, and by Christmas JQA was clamoring for his seat in Congress, to Louisa's distress.

She knew that his memory remained faulty, for when she read aloud to him—French poetry was a favorite—he sometimes could not remember what passages she had just finished. He now wept at the slightest provocation and "drewls like a baby," leaving Louisa convinced that he would disgrace himself if he returned to the House to face his enemies.

Quite the opposite happened, however, thanks to Adams' powerful determination. On New Year's Day, he was able to ride in a carriage, which became a daily practice. By late January, he was taking strolls out of doors. At the start of February, he succeeded in walking to church, and on the eighth of that month he set out for Washington, accompanied by his nurse, his wife, and his son. Making the journey in slow stages, the party arrived on February 12. Adams brought with him what Louisa called the "wilfulness of his character," for hardly were they inside the residence on F Street when he announced that he would attend the House on the following morning.

True to his word and accompanied by Charles, Adams returned to his seat. As he entered the chamber, friend and foe alike rose to applaud the old warrior. Thereafter, he managed to attend every day until the House adjourned on March 3.

The extraordinary extent of his recovery did not deceive him. Summoning his strength, he was able to write in his own palsied hand the announcement that from the moment he had been stricken, "I date my decease, and consider myself, for every useful purpose to myself or to my fellow-creatures, dead; and hence I shall call this and what I may write hereafter a posthumous memoir."

HE WAS, Adams said, "one of the relics of the past."

Relic

DURING THE MONTHS remaining to him, John Quincy Adams enjoyed brief intervals of physical and emotional strength. Generally, however, he grew weaker, although his cantankerous nature rarely subsided. Since he no longer had the stamina for long walks, he took carriage rides and gave more attention to reading and to the improvement of the government's new observatory in Washington.

While his handwriting improved slightly, he dictated most entries in his diary to his granddaughter and his wife. The inner Adams was best glimpsed through the few legible comments he made in his "Rubbish" notes. But these, he stoutly maintained, were inconsequential as he emphasized that his monumental diary had closed on November 20, 1846, the day of his first serious stroke.

There was no letup in his fierce concern for national affairs. One day he would rally his strength and keep visitors enthralled with brilliant conversation. The next day, as Louisa put it, "he can barely crawl." His physicians, however, advised her against trying to restrain him. Rather, they said, let him "do as he pleases as his inclination must not be thwarted." An anxious Louisa wished somehow he would "struggle against the worldly passions which war with his soul." His only chance for a final moment of happiness, according to Louisa, was if he retired from Congress, and she knew this was unlikely.

Consequently, she and the family were grateful when he agreed in early June 1847 to another summer holiday in New England. It began with a bit of bravado as he insisted on walking from the depot in Quincy to his home—and promptly paid the penalty for the overexertion by becoming highly "agitated." When Charles greeted his father, he was shocked by what he saw. "He is now a feeble old man." There

was "nothing left in him of the vigor which was once his characteristic.
. . . I feel sad when I look at him."

Nevertheless, Adams still managed to trudge up the path to
Charles' hilltop summer residence in Quincy to time the sun's rise—a
lifelong habit, since he had never seemed able to trust the sun to be
punctual.

After a month of rest, he was more than ready to enjoy a pair of
celebrations. First, the entire neighborhood joined the family in observing his eightieth birthday. A fortnight later Louisa and he were
guests at a large gathering of their Quincy friends, arranged to honor
their golden wedding anniversary. JQA was not so feeble that he neglected to provide a gift worthy of the day, presenting Louisa with a
beautiful bracelet.

Later in the summer, the family doctor asked him to try a "galvanic device," hoping that shock treatments might reduce his palsy.
Instead, the patient complained that the experiment left him even
weaker. In one of the rare deeply personal disclosures he was able to
write during his enfeeblement, he conceded: "I still struggle against my
fate and force my hand to write when it has been from the 20th of last
November disabled by an almighty hand forever."

At least he could read, summoning Milton, Herodotus, and the
contemporary English poet Samuel Rogers as his favorite authors for
the summer. Rogers' work particularly pleased Adams, who called *The
Pleasures of Memory* (1792) the finest poem of the century. Within a few
years of its publication, 23,000 copies had been sold. Why was it, he
mused, that Rogers was "almost totally forgotten"? What, indeed, was
fame?

On November 1, the family took him back to Washington. "It
seemed to me on leaving home as if it were upon my last great journey," the elderly traveler said. He was exhausted when he reached the
capital, although every effort had been made to provide rest and comfort along the route. "My disability, mental and bodily," Adams conceded, "surpasses my power of expression."

Yet once again he rallied enough to walk modest distances. He
continued to enter brief notations in his "Rubbish" book, which he
now called "minutes of my last days." In one of these, written November 26, he thanked God "for existence yet prolonged," even though he
was so "dilapidated," and said that he clung to the hope "of another
and improved state of existence."

Then came the convening of the House on December 6, an event that stimulated Adams more than might have any galvanic shock. Thereafter, no matter how poorly he felt, he insisted on taking his seat in Congress. "The House is his only remedy," Louisa acknowledged, as her husband even tried occasionally to walk at least part of the distance home from Capitol Hill.

In the House, he was treated kindly. He was not asked to shoulder committee burdens, although he insisted on joining the congressional library committee. Too weak to speak often or to be heard, he no longer troubled his old enemies. As Louisa reported, "the world seems to idolize him." He sought to sketch a daily account of congressional doings for his diary, but gave it up on Christmas Eve.

The next day, Louisa notified Charles that his father once again was deteriorating—not in mind, but physically into a "feeble and broken state." Nevertheless, his dictated entries on public business still reflected his familiar spark, until the last of these was made on January 4, 1848. Soon afterward, according to Louisa, her husband could scarcely muster the strength to attend Congress, and yet when she implored him to remain at home, "he answered as usual that if he *did* he should *die!*"

On February 5, Adams announced that death was at hand, but when Louisa took him at his word and ordered him to stay in bed while she summoned Charles from Boston, the old man quickly changed his mind and claimed to be "much *stronger*." And, for a time, he was. He attended two worship services on February 20 and was unusually lively that evening, even managing to compose a stanza of poetry at a friend's request:

> *Fair Lady, thou of human life*
> *Hast yet but little seen.*
> *Thy days of strife are few and far between.*

Before retiring that evening, he asked Louisa to read aloud one of William Wilberforce's sermons. The next morning, he arose early and appeared remarkably cheerful. Louisa spoke later of "an elasticity in his steps and movements" that she had not seen for a long time. At the accustomed hour, the carriage was brought around to take him to the Capitol, where his coachman watched with amazement at the vigor with which Adams climbed the steps.

But then, an hour later, his long career closed in a fashion that might have given him satisfaction. As House business got under way,

Adams responded one last time. Still opposed to the ongoing Mexican War, he voted "No" in a voice scarcely muffled by age when his name was called on a measure that would have commended veterans of recent battles. Then, as the clerk proceeded to read a tribute to these soldiers, Adams tried to rise and address the speaker.

Although he got partway to his feet, he could make no sound. Instead, as a deep flush suffused his temples, he clutched at his desk and began to topple. Members of the House shouted a warning, and a colleague caught him before he struck the floor. It was half past one in the afternoon of Monday, February 21, 1848.

Barely conscious, he was carried first to a sofa and then to the Speaker's private chamber. There he lingered for two days. In one of his few alert moments, it was Henry Clay he asked to greet. The old Kentuckian arrived in time to bid his friend a tearful farewell. Louisa was less fortunate, for her husband did not recognize her when she was brought to the Capitol to see him. He died at 7:15 p.m. on February 23.

Word of his death was sent immediately to admirers in such distant places as Ohio and Maine, thanks to recently strung telegraph lines. These bulletins featured the fallen hero's last words, for at the moment of his death, those gathered at his side heard him mutter a sentence. Some claimed he murmured: "This is the end of earth, but I am content." To others he seemed to say: "This is the last of earth—I am composed."

Both dying assertions were widely repeated, although the second seems more likely correct. In all his life, Adams was never content. It was a word he rarely used, for he was one of the least easily satisfied men in history. On the other hand, he always sought—and often failed—to find self-control. Death should have brought the moment when he would most wish to account himself composed.

ADAMS' COMPOSURE might have been slightly shaken had he been able to observe the eulogies and ceremonies with which America marked his dying. Impressed by the public grief extending from East to West, Josiah Quincy predicted that such an outpouring of sentiment meant that for Adams "the gate of fear and envy was now shut; that of honor and fame opened."

The official tribute began in the Capitol. According to Charles, the ceremonies of national mourning in the building marked the start of "as great a pageant as was ever conducted in the United States." The widespread sentiment was only fitting, he conceded, for it displayed "the homage of people for a truly worthy public servant." And, indeed, the citizenry responded. For two days, the remains of the sixth president of the United States reposed in state while something unprecedented took place: thousands, it was reported, filed through the Capitol to view the bier.

Members of the House and Senate immediately began to have their say, with many of Adams' southern adversaries turning chivalrous by insisting that when a patriarch fell, the people must weep. Most of the tributes rejoiced in the deceased's more than sixty years of service to the nation, and all, of course, exulted in speaking of the former president's wisdom, integrity, and Christian virtue. One congressional eulogist announced that the "crowning glory" of Adams' character "was his devotion to the cause of his Redeemer," a claim that might have brought JQA mixed feelings.

At noon on Saturday, February 25, funeral ceremonies began in the chamber of the House, the setting where Adams' battles had finally brought him the fame as well as the enemies he had so ardently desired. In an ironic touch, it was Daniel Webster, he of the "rotten heart" so often rebuked by Adams, who had been asked to prepare the inscription placed on the coffin, which stood in front of the Speaker's rostrum.

After the House chaplain had preached from an appropriate verse in the Book of Job, beginning "And thine age shall be clearer than the noonday; thou shalt shine forth, thou shalt be as the morning," and a choir had sung, the body was escorted by a parade of public personages, military units, and private citizens to the Congressional Cemetery.

There the coffin remained in a temporary vault for several days until thirty members of Congress, one from each state, were ready to accompany it on the 500-mile railway journey to Boston. The funeral train, its principal car draped in black, traveled for five days through signs of universal grief. The caravan stopped often to permit local ceremonies, and citizens stood silently in tribute along the route. The war with Mexico had become distasteful to many Americans, and to know that its most ardent opponent had fallen made their sorrow all the more poignant.

Boston, the city where once Adams had felt himself despised, now greeted his remains by exhibiting everywhere the insignia of mourning. Unfortunately, when the train arrived on March 10, a steady rain forced cancellation of elaborate ceremonies planned for outdoors. In Faneuil Hall, a memorial tribute went on without the Adams family, who had proceeded to Quincy to await the coffin's arrival.

Early on the afternoon of March 11, a bemused Charles Francis Adams noted that every prominent political figure in Massachusetts had scrambled to join in escorting his father's casket to Quincy. In the First Parish Church, where Adamses had worshipped since before 1640, JQA's friend and pastor, William P. Lunt, delivered a sermon inspired by a most touching text: "Be thou faithful unto death, and I will give thee a crown of life."

After that stirring message, there were many observances during the following weeks, including the splendid memorial tribute delivered on April 15 by Edward Everett. Now president of Harvard, Everett eulogized Adams for more than two hours in the presence of the Massachusetts legislature, which had assembled in Faneuil Hall along with a vast crowd. But nothing he said matched Lunt's moving sermon.

Temporarily, Adams' coffin was placed in the family vault he had built in the Quincy cemetery across the road from the church. It stayed there with the remains of sister Nabby, sons George and John, and other kinfolk until Louisa died in Washington four years later, also from the effects of a stroke. She had grown increasingly frail after her husband's death, claiming exhaustion from fifty years of living with him. Upon hearing of her death, both houses of Congress adjourned, an unprecedented mark of respect for an American woman.

To the close of her life, Louisa had remained outwardly a charming, delicate woman. But there was much more to the nation's sixth first lady. She was as complex and impressive a human being as her husband. Her achievement went beyond the feat of living with John Quincy Adams for half a century, enduring with him the terrible griefs and notable achievements life brought them. While this might seem triumph enough for any mortal, it leaves out of account Louisa's considerable intellectual strength.

Had she received a college education, Louisa Catherine Johnson might easily have become the scholarly superior of her spouse. Tucked away in her papers is the evidence of her keen interest in literature, medicine, and music. Where he was often disorganized and superficial, she was disciplined and rigorous.

While usually strong during family crises, Louisa crumpled at other moments, just as JQA sank into periods of depression. Her sort of collapse, however, was physical, and explainable mainly as a form of rebellion (or perhaps an unconscious attention-getting device) against being subject to an ungovernable and often aloof husband whom, as she once put it, she could neither live with nor live without.

Although Louisa was no feminist in the usual sense of the term, she stoutly denounced the shameful way men tended to treat women. But she believed it was no antidote to alter the traditional role and behavior of females; such a step would be more dangerous than the problem at hand. Let women be glorified in their accustomed roles, Louisa said, with men accepting them as full equals.

Perhaps her supreme achievement as a woman was that ultimately she won the ungrudging admiration and affection of Abigail Adams. In knowing very well how difficult her son was to live with, Abigail could only salute the woman who had brought him into domestic subjugation—or a state approximating that.

At her death, Louisa was reunited not only with JQA, but also with Abigail and John Adams. It had been arranged for her corpse to lie beside her husband's in an enlarged crypt beneath the Quincy church where the coffins of his parents had been placed in 1828.

And so on the morning of December 15, 1852, JQA's casket, draped with velvet, was brought into the church as Louisa's was delivered from the railway depot, where it had arrived from Washington. The two coffins were then carried down the stairs from the vestibule to the crypt, there to be installed in granite sarcophagi next to those of John's parents.

At this point the solemn proceedings went awry. While Louisa's modest coffin was placed easily into its enclosure, the magnificent casket that Congress had provided for John was too big to fit. The ceremony had to be suspended and Quincy stonemasons summoned to enlarge the former president's sarcophagus.

As the work progressed, JQA's grandson Charley, age seventeen, was designated by the family to keep watch. The young man could not resist the impulse to see how his grandfather's corpse had fared. When the coffin was opened, the remains were found protected by a glass shield, which quickly clouded. There was a moment, however, for young Charles and the crowd of onlookers to see "the sunken face of a very old man, on which a short stubbly beard had grown after death."

Eventually, the masons finished and John's coffin was installed in its monumental enclosure. There he would lie between the two women who had struggled in their different ways to shape his personality and his life. Abigail Adams was at his right side and Louisa to his left.

Without fanfare, the iron door to the crypt was closed and locked, remaining so until 1891, when it was first opened to admit visitors. Thereafter, it became and has remained a national shrine—certainly unique, since it marks the graves of two presidents of the United States and two first ladies.

AT DEATH, JQA knew that he had failed in his yearning to make a contribution to literature, philosophy, or science worthy of the world's admiration and gratitude. His verses were only briefly remembered. Many were gathered in a volume entitled *Poems of Religion and Society,* which appeared later in 1848, edited by Senator Thomas Hart Benton of Missouri and Senator John Davis of Massachusetts. The book was memorable mostly for the two senators' ringing announcement that the noble career of John Quincy Adams was to be a model, private and public, for all future American generations.

Also in 1848, there was public interest in JQA's religious instruction of his son George, published as *Letters of John Quincy Adams, To His Son, On The Bible and Its Teachings.* Because of the attention received by the book, its numerous errors were corrected in an appendix to the fourth edition of Charles Francis Adams' volume of Abigail Adams' letters. It, too, appeared in 1848.

After these publications, John's literary work slipped from view, except for one ironic reappearance in 1880. At that time, Ralph Waldo Emerson, a person JQA had never admired, published personal favorites from among the world's great poems in a volume he entitled *Parnassus.* This collection, which Emerson said contained only "gems of pure lustre," included Adams' August 1841 poem "The Wants of Man." These lines spoke of desiring a wife "of temper sweet, of yielding will" (surely no description of the independent-spirited Louisa), and of yearning to use "the seals of power and place" in order "to rule my native land, Her cup of bliss to fill." Finally, the last great want was the "mercy of God."

Forgotten, like his poetry, is how Adams awakened America to the beauty of German literature, while his orations and his two volumes of lectures as Harvard's first Boylston Professor of Rhetoric and Oratory are rarely read.

Still, there are admirers who have done Adams justice. They acclaim him with so much enthusiasm as an irrepressible battler for liberty in America that the congressional phase of his career has come to overshadow even his achievements as a diplomat and as secretary of state. His presidency, far-sighted despite its political ineptness, is rarely recalled.

Today, the bittersweet truth remains that while John Quincy Adams finally enjoys some of the fame for which he hungered, the renown arises from his all-consuming desire for political vengeance. His reputation has been firmly established not on attainments in literature, science, or statecraft but on what a bruised ego and thwarted ambition drove him to do. Adams' stubborn courage in denouncing slavery and censorship has drawn the gratitude and admiration of his country.

It was not poetry or science but the gag rule and the *Amistad* case that brought the aged Adams what he had so desperately yearned to have, "the People's unbought grace."

Acknowledgments

During many years of writing about members of the Adams family, I have run up a sizeable debt to helpful individuals. These obligations I sought to acknowledge in earlier volumes. Now it is time to speak gratefully of the encouragement I received in preparing this biography of John Quincy Adams.

Along with many others, I am once again greatly obliged to three institutions that serve as meccas for Adams scholarship. These are the Massachusetts Historical Society, The Adams Papers editorial project, and the Adams National Historic Site. I wish to thank the individuals who make these three organizations so invaluable. At the Massachusetts Historical Society, I think especially of Louis Leonard Tucker, director; Peter Drummey, librarian; and Conrad Wright, editor. At The Adams Papers, I am particularly grateful to Richard Ryerson, editor in chief, and to Celeste Walker, associate editor, who has a special concern for John Quincy Adams. At the Adams National Historic Site, Marianne Peak, superintendent, has become a worthy successor to the legendary Wilhelmina Harris.

Among present-day members of the Adams family, I owe much to Tom and Ramelle Adams (Mr. and Mrs. Thomas Boylston Adams). Not only did Tom suggest that I write about JQA, but he and Ramelle have provided my wife, Joan, and me with memorable hospitality. To my great regret, another family member, John Adams Abbott, M.D., did not live to read this book. I shall always remember his friendship and the many kindnesses he and his wife, Diana Abbott, showed the Nagels.

Beyond New England, there are several academic contributions I am delighted to acknowledge. I thank members of the history department and the staff of the campus library at Duke University for aiding me in many ways during the year I spent in Durham as a visiting scholar. A special word of thanks goes to Professor Richard Watson. Since our return to Minnesota, I have been helped greatly by the history department and the Wilson Library at the University of Minnesota. Regents Professor Paul Murphy, my friend of many years, has been notably thoughtful, while Sue Haskins, who manages the department, has been kindness itself. At Carleton College, Dean Elizabeth McKinsey and Professor Kirk Jeffrey have provided many courtesies.

The illustrations for this book would not have been possible without the permission of several persons and organizations: the National Park Service, the Mead Art Museum of Amherst College, the White House, the Massachusetts Historical Society, the Library of Congress, Mrs. Waldo C. M. Johnston, and the University Art Collection at Arizona State University.

Several big-hearted and talented friends have been at hand with encouragement and advice. Byron Hollinshead, chairman of American History Publications, was unfailing with his wisdom. James Anderson Thomson, M.D., psychiatrist and historian, responded nobly to my need for aid in understanding JQA's emotional makeup; no doubt I have not followed Andy's guidance far enough. Two other physician chums have been generous in helping me appreciate JQA's physical history: Lauren Woods, M.D., of the Medical College of Virginia and Robert "Rob" Sullivan, M.D., of Duke University.

I am beholden to many persons at Alfred A. Knopf, Inc., my publisher, and especially to Ashbel Green, my editor. To him, to his colleague Jennifer Bernstein, and to their associates I offer gratitude. My friend and counselor Samuel S. Vaughan of Random House has aided me in countless ways, as he has so many fortunate authors. His careful treatment of my writing has been invaluable. I owe Sam a lot.

Anyone who has followed my work over the years can sense how precious for me has been the presence and manifold aid of Joan Peterson Nagel. Her resourcefulness as editor, librarian, genealogist, and critic almost matches her success in the difficult task of being my wife. Dear Jo—how very little can I do except for her!

Sources

The prospect before anyone who writes about John Quincy Adams is both cheering and intimidating. JQA's diary, letters, and other manuscripts so essential to the biographer's art are readily at hand, available in many libraries, some in splendidly edited books and the entirety on microfilm. Thus a researcher need not endure the familiar ordeal of traveling great distances and camping in hotels in order to find and read manuscripts.

The intimidation lies in the staggering amounts of available documentation. The mileage of microfilm is daunting, for it takes 340 reels to contain the journals and letters pertaining to JQA. In addition, all these sources are, of course, in handwritten form and sometimes so faded or scribbled as to be nearly indecipherable.

With the very slightest exceptions, the significant source materials needed for a biography of John Quincy Adams are contained in a vast collection known as The Adams Papers. For decades, these manuscripts were held in trust by the family, with a tendency severely to restrict access to them. Then, on April 4, 1956, the Adams Trust gave this historical treasure to the world of scholarship via the Massachusetts Historical Society.

The Adams manuscripts soon were made widely available by a microfilming project that produced 608 reels. A letterpress edition, of which the first volumes appeared in 1961, is emerging from a collaboration between the Massachusetts Historical Society and Harvard University Press. While many volumes have been published, they have yet covered only a fragment of the sources for a JQA biography.

Consequently, it has been necessary for me to rely almost entirely upon the unedited manuscripts as they appear on microfilm, so I thank The Adams Papers' editors and the Massachusetts Historical Society for permission to quote from these manuscripts. Their quantity—and quality—is enormous, leaving no doubt as to why JQA's grandchildren remembered him as always busy at his writing table and with a perpetually ink-stained forefinger and thumb. For instance, his famous diary, with the related materials he called "Rubbish" and "Almanac," stretches from Reel 4 to Reel 52 of the Adams Papers Microfilms.

But reading these diary materials is only the first assignment for a biographer. JQA kept copies of much of his outgoing correspondence in letter-books, which are found on Reels 125–155. The reels containing the "Private" volumes were the most useful for my purposes. The original copies of letters he sent, as well as those he received, are found scattered amid the Adams family correspondence, which, for the period of Adams' lifetime, fills Reels 343–537. Of special importance here for my project were the letters he exchanged with his parents, his wife, and his children.

Finally, JQA's biographer has a seemingly endless supply of "Miscellany" to draw from. This material, found on Reels 199–263, includes financial and household records, as well as commonplace books, poetry, translations, weather records, and the like. For example, JQA's working materials and final draft for his book on weights and measures are found on Reels 234–236. Transcripts of his letters to son George concerning the Bible are on Reel 233.

In addition to the manuscripts arising directly from JQA, the Adams Papers Microfilms edition has, of course, much relevant material originating with his kinfolk. Reels 264–280 contain Louisa Catherine Johnson Adams' diary, autobiography, and literary sketches. Thomas Boylston Adams has a miscellany of useful sources on Reels 281–283, while an assortment of writing by George Washington Adams is on Reels 287–295. Of great importance is the diary of Charles Francis Adams, whose entries for the years of JQA's lifetime are on Reels 53–69. Charles' letter-books for the same period are found on Reels 156–159, and his miscellany, which includes financial records from the time he undertook to direct his father's affairs, is on Reels 297–300.

The letterpress version of the manuscripts, ably prepared by the Adams Papers editorial office and published by Harvard University Press, thus far includes two volumes of JQA's diary covering the period from November 1779 to December 1788. Two more that are forthcoming, take the diary through 1799. Fortunately, the letterpress edition of Charles Francis Adams' diary extends through February 1840. The Adams family correspondence through 1785 has been edited and published, and soon two more volumes will go to the end of 1790. Other publications by the Adams Papers editors include the diary and autobiography of John Adams, the legal papers of John Adams, and the early official papers of John Adams.

Since The Adams Papers range from 1639 to 1889, it is understandable that the publication of this treasury of sources may not be completed until the end of the next century—particularly if the project adheres to its present standards. The enterprise has benefited from the work of superb editor-scholars, whose leaders over the years have been successively Lyman H. Butterfield, Robert J. Taylor, and the present editor in chief, Richard A. Ryerson. They have been joined by such excellent associates as Marc Friedlaender, Celeste Walker, Gregg Lint, and Joanna Revelas.

Earlier editions of John Quincy Adams' writings exist, although they are incomplete and imperfect. Prime among those still useful is Charles Francis Adams' twelve-volume edition of JQA's diary, *Memoirs of John Quincy Adams* (Philadelphia, 1874–1877). My impression is that Charles included about half of the total diary, choosing to emphasize those portions dealing with his father's public career. The edition begins the diary in 1794 and closes it in 1848.

Charles Francis Adams' son and namesake, whom JQA called Charley, wished that his father had not published the JQA diary out of concern that offense might have been given to persons still living. But, the damage done, CFA2—a historian—anonymously published as *Life in a New England Town* (Boston, 1903) bits of the diary selected from a section omitted from the *Memoirs*. These excerpts contain entries made during 1787 and 1788 when JQA was in Newburyport, and are accompanied by CFA2's thoughtful and often delightful notes.

An excellent single-volume condensation of Adams' diary, drawn from the edition of 1874–1877, is Allan Nevins' *The Diary of John Quincy Adams 1794–1845* (New York, 1951). Going beyond the diary, Worthington C. Ford edited a seven-volume selection of JQA's letters and other works through 1823, *The Writings of John Quincy Adams* (New York, 1913–1917).

Other manuscript collections that hold glimpses of JQA are the papers of the Shaw and Cranch families, both in the Library of Congress, and a rich trove of letters between Abigail Adams and Mary Cranch that is housed at the American Antiquarian Society in Worcester, Massachusetts. I'm grateful to these institutions for the privilege of reading and quoting from these documents. A special word of thanks is due to my friend Timothy Forbes, who made it possible for me to see the manuscript collection of his late father, Malcolm Forbes. It includes several valuable items concerning John Quincy Adams.

As to JQA's own publications, the Massachusetts Historical Society has a fine assortment of these important sources, including numerous bound volumes of his pamphlets, essays, orations, and other occasional pieces, most of which will not be found in the microfilm edition of The Adams Papers. JQA himself saw to the binding of several sets, while his grandson Henry Adams prepared others.

Among the most interesting of these writings is JQA's essay "The Character of Hamlet" and another on "The Character of Desdemona." His "Misconceptions of Shakespeare Upon the Stage" appeared in *The New England Magazine* for December 1835. The Massachusetts Historical Society has a copy of one of the best examples of the lengths to which he could go in righteous indignation. See his 256-page volume *The Duplicate Letters . . . Documents Relating to Transactions at the Negotiations of Ghent* (Washington, D.C., 1822).

Aside from its peerless holdings of Adams' many publications, the Massachusetts Historical Society has a wealth of sources that offer another perspective on him. Notable among these is the diary of Thomas W. Ward, a contemporary who was treasurer of Harvard and an agent for Baring Brothers, the London banking house. Ward was no admirer of JQA's, and his observations upon the death of the congressman serve as an equipoise to the mass of eulogy that poured forth on the occasion.

Scoffing at the talk of Adams as "a great man and a good Christian, and almost without fault," Ward in his diary set forth his own appraisal of the deceased: "selfish, bad-tempered, envious, uncertain in his conduct, public and private,—not a good judge of men's character, unsocial. . . ." Ward was particularly struck by how JQA's last twenty years had been dominated by hatred and perpetual quarreling. Stoutly biased though it may be, the Ward diary is a manuscript every student of Adams should read.

There is, of course, much secondary material dealing with Adams. I list here only those volumes or articles that seem to me especially illuminating. In *Portraits of John Quincy Adams and His Wife* (Cambridge, 1970), Andrew Oliver presents the many likenesses of JQA and Louisa in an instructive way. Of broader value than its title implies is *A Catalogue of the Books of John Quincy Adams Deposited in the Boston Athenaeum* (Boston, 1938). This material was assembled by Henry Adams, son of the second Charles Francis Adams, and by Worthington C. Ford. Not only do the contents address the JQA collection; the book also includes information on Adams bookplates and seals and a commentary by Henry Adams II on his great-grandfather's library.

JQA's public career has been well served by biographers over the past fifty years. Three studies in particular have been of great help. The two-volume work by Samuel Flagg Bemis is often ranked among this century's best biographies and received a much deserved Pulitzer Prize. The volume titles are *John Quincy Adams and the Foundations of American Foreign Policy* (New York, 1949) and *John Quincy Adams and the Union*

(New York, 1956). It was when he closed his second volume, knowing that his work had emphasized JQA's public career, that Bemis issued his call for some future biographer to explore the man's inner life.

Mary W. M. Hargreaves published an excellent and much-needed scholarly treatment of JQA's unhappy presidential years, *The Presidency of John Quincy Adams* (Lawrence, Kans., 1985). Not only was this volume very useful to me, but its scope consoled me when I devoted only one chapter to JQA's presidency.

The third biographical treatise of high merit is Leonard L. Richards' *The Life and Times of Congressman John Quincy Adams* (New York, 1986). Broadly gauged though his work is, Professor Richards joined Professor Bemis in acknowledging that the key to an understanding of JQA's personality had not yet been found. Because, as I hope, I have discovered that key, my treatment of JQA's career in Congress is somewhat different from Richards'.

Other helpful biographies are Marie B. Hecht's *John Quincy Adams: A Personal History of an Independent Man* (New York, 1972) and Robert A. East's *John Quincy Adams: The Crucial Years 1785–1794* (New York, 1964). Two political figures of our century have written biographical notices of JQA: Bennett Champ Clark, the statesman from Missouri, published *John Quincy Adams* (Boston, 1932), and a generation later, John Fitzgerald Kennedy put JQA first in his volume *Profiles in Courage* (New York, 1956).

While William Earl Weeks' *John Quincy Adams and American Global Empire* (Lexington, Ky., 1992) is centered on the 1819 Transcontinental Treaty, it has thoughtful comments about JQA's nature and career. An important pathbreaking monograph is David F. Musto, "The Youth of John Quincy Adams," *Proceedings of the American Philosophical Society* 113 (August 1969):269–82. George A. Lipsky's *John Quincy Adams: His Theories and Ideas* (New York, 1950) struggles with a difficult subject. Valuable material is found in Lynn Hudson Parsons, " 'This Splendid Pageant': Observations on the Death of John Quincy Adams," *New England Quarterly* 53 (December 1980):464–82. Howard Jones' *Mutiny on the Amistad* (New York, 1987) follows JQA through one of his finest hours.

Several important studies were published after I completed my writing. William Lee Miller's *Arguing About Slavery* (New York, 1996) elaborately reconstructs the gag-rule controversy around JQA's heroic part in it. Greg Russell's *John Quincy Adams and the Public Virtues of Democracy* (Columbia, Mo., 1995) discusses the moral and philosophical grounding of JQA's career as a diplomat and statesman. See also Russell's "John Quincy Adams: Virtue and the Tragedy of the Statesman," *New England Quarterly* 69 (March 1996):56–74. Noble E. Cunningham, Jr.'s *The Presidency of James Monroe* (Lawrence, Kans., 1996) succinctly sets forth the administrative background when JQA was secretary of state.

Readers who may be interested in tracing the development of my view of JQA or who may wish to know more about JQA's kinfolk should read my books *Descent from Glory: Four Generations of the John Adams Family* (New York, 1983) and *The Adams Women: Abigail and Louisa Adams, Their Sisters and Daughters* (New York, 1987).

Index

A NOTE ABOUT THE AUTHOR

During the first half of his career, Paul Nagel wrote about American national ideology in essays and in two books, *One Nation Indivisible* (1964) and *This Sacred Trust* (1971). He was also variously a professor of history, a college dean, and a university vice president. Since 1975, he has devoted himself to writing, the most notable result of which is his books about the John Adams family, *Descent from Glory* (1983) and *The Adams Women* (1987), and another about the family of Richard Henry Lee and Robert E. Lee, *The Lees of Virginia* (1990). He portrayed his native state in *Missouri* (1977), and he recounted the career of Missouri's great painter in *George Caleb Bingham* (1990).

Nagel has been president of the Southern Historical Association and a trustee of the Colonial Williamsburg Foundation. He is a corresponding member of the Massachusetts Historical Society, a fellow of the Pilgrim Society and of the Society of American Historians, a cultural laureate of Virginia, and a contributing editor of *American Heritage*. With his wife, Joan Peterson Nagel, he lives in Minneapolis. They have three sons, one granddaughter, and numerous grandcats.

A NOTE ON THE TYPE

This book was set in a version of Monotype Baskerville, the antecedent of which was a typeface designed by John Baskerville (1706–1775). Baskerville's types, which are distinctive and elegant in design, were a forerunner of what we know today as the "modern" group of typefaces.

Composed by Crane Typesetting Service, Inc., Charlotte Harbor, Florida
Printed and bound by Quebecor Printing, Martinsburg, West Virginia
Designed by Robert C. Olsson

FEB '98

92
ADA   Nagel, Paul C.

        John Quincy Adams

DUE DATE
